PELICAN LATIN AM

General Editor: Richard

Fidel Castro Speaks

Martin Kenner has worked as an economist at the
United Nations and has taught economics at
the graduate faculty of the New School in New York City.
He writes frequently for the underground press
and is active in the Movement.

James Petras was educated at the University of
California at Berkeley where he received his Ph.D.
and worked in the Center for International Affairs.
He has travelled widely in Latin America and
written extensively on Latin American affairs for
political journals. He has also published a study
entitled *Politics and Social Forces in Chilean
Development* and edited a collection of writings
with Professor Maurice Zeitlin, entitled *Latin
America: Reform or Revolution?* He is now a
Professor of Political Science at Pennsylvania
State University.

Fidel Castro Speaks

Edited by Martin Kenner and
James Petras

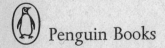 Penguin Books

Penguin Books Ltd, Harmondsworth,
Middlesex, England
Penguin Books Australia Ltd, Ringwood,
Victoria, Australia

First published in the U.S.A. 1969
First published in Great Britain by
Allen Lane The Penguin Press 1970
Published in Pelican Books 1972

Made and printed in Great Britain
by Hazell Watson & Viney Ltd
Aylesbury, Bucks
Set in Linotype Juliana

This book is dedicated to the Cuban
and the Vietnamese
people who have given North Americans
the possibility of making a revolution
and
to the young North Americans who have
taken advantage of that possibility

Contents

Preface

It is amazing that no collection of Fidel Castro's speeches has appeared in the United States until this, the second decade of the Cuban Revolution. This Revolution played an important part in defining the New Left in the early 1960s. Coming after the silent fifties, students in the early sixties reacted to two major events: the sit-ins in the American South and the Revolution in Cuba. The role of noted liberals like John F. Kennedy, Adlai Stevenson, and Arthur Schlesinger, Jr, in the United States' attempts to crush the Revolution, pushed more and more students out of the liberal wing of Democratic politics into protest politics, and finally to the point where they saw the American government as the principal enemy of the majority of the people of the world. Kennedy's hard line on Cuba, Stevenson's denial of US involvement and his subsequent role in defending those policies in the United Nations, and Professor Schlesinger's mendacious propaganda for the State Department in justifying American armed intervention in Cuba, must be credited, in part, for the radicalism of the student movement and its profound disillusionment with established institutions in this country.

As the confrontation between the United States and Cuba continued, increasing numbers of young people sensed a strong identification with the Cuban Revolution. The policies of the New Frontier made many sceptical of our own country's intentions in the world, and Fidel Castro's dramatic reforms – including the illiteracy campaign which saw thousands of city youths going to live with the poor in the countryside to teach them to read and write – made many see revolutionary Cuba as an alternative to either American or Eastern European visions of a future society.

In the early years of the Cuban Revolution, the Fair Play for Cuba Committee printed and distributed materials on the Revolution, including Fidel's speeches. By 1963, the Committee was, for all intents and purposes, dead, and the US blockade made travel and communication with Cuba difficult. Here and there, individuals or groups went to that island. But by and large, one had to depend on the American mass media for information. Clearly, this was not very satisfactory. In 1966, the Cuban government began printing a weekly review in English, *Granma*, yet it was difficult to obtain in the United States.

James Petras and I were both active in Fair Play in the early sixties. We knew how important Cuba had been for our own education and were horrified at how difficult it was to get first-hand information about the Revolution. In the winter of 1967–8 we began reading all the speeches of Fidel that we could find. It quickly became apparent that their value to the United States was greater than ever. It also became apparent that the job of selecting appropriate speeches would be agonizingly difficult. We decided, therefore, that an inexpensive, one-volume collection could not contain a representative sampling of his speeches over nearly two decades without severe editing. We did not want to cut Fidel's speeches to too great an extent, for then they would really no longer be his speeches. And we did not believe that a volume showing the development of Fidel's thought – how it changed and where it changed on important subjects – was as important to American youth as were his comments on the issues most critical to youth here today. We concentrated, therefore, on Fidel's later speeches – principally those after 1966 – which deal with armed struggle and revolution, and the vision of a communist society organized without the need for money.

Many comrades have agreed on the urgency of getting before the American Movement a collection of Fidel's speeches. Jerry Rubin and Mark Rudd spent time with us discussing the influence of their trips to Cuba on their outlook and work. At a later date, Mike Locker of NACLA and Julie Michemin of the Venceremos Brigade also spent time discussing the influence of Cuba on the New Left. Sue Parmacak, Arlo Jacobs, Sylvia Warren, and Steve Tappis helped in the various tasks of putting this collection together. And Ros Baxandall, John Jacobs, Warren Bishop, and Betty Petras continually reminded us of the value of Fidel's speeches to the Movement during the difficult period between getting the idea of such a collection and actually seeing it off to the printer. Jesus Jiminez, formerly of the Cuban Mission to the United Nations, loaned us his collection of Fidel's speeches at an early point in the project.

Finally, Martin Glass, who meticulously went over every official Cuban translation and reworked those whose English needed to be improved so as to reflect more accurately Fidel's Spanish, must be thanked. Without his assistance, this book would never have been finished.

A short bibliography suggests a number of good studies of Cuba for further reading. Also, *Granma* is available in English for those wishing to keep up with current events in the Revolution. We hope all those who read this collection will find Fidel's speeches as important and useful as we have.

Power to the people.

New York City
1 May 1969

Introduction

This collection presents for the first time in the United States the ideas of Fidel Castro in the words he uses to address the Cuban people.

No revolution in history has depended on radio and television to explain its action and programme to the extent that the Cuban Revolution has. This is not simply the result of Fidel's personal affinity for speech-making instead of lengthy written treatises. But, rather, was made absolutely necessary by the fact that so much happened so fast in the Cuban Revolution that the most effective and speedy means of communications and education (i.e., speeches) had to be utilized by Fidel. The actual period of insurrection was so brief that there was little time for ideological education of the Cuban people during the process of armed struggle; thus, most of this education had to take place after the seizure of power in January 1959. Fighting in the Sierra Maestra and in the cities lasted for only two years, concluding on the night of 31 December 1958, when Batista fled Havana. Furthermore, few revolutions have moved with such lightning speed from anti-communist, nationalist struggle to militant communist internationalism, actively promoting armed revolution in Latin America and the rest of the world. When Fidel came to Havana in early January 1959, he was viewed by the Cuban masses and the American people as a reformer, whose plans were to eliminate the political terror and corruption of the Batista régime and to confront the basic economic and social problems of the country. After little more than two years, in April 1961, the Cuban Revolution proclaimed itself socialist and gave American imperialism its first military defeat when a force of CIA-sponsored mercenaries was crushed at Playa Girón.

Edward Boorstein, James O'Connor and Maurice Zeitlin, and Robert Scheer have written interesting, readable, and informed studies on the reasons for this swift transformation. Because of the insight it gives into Third World liberation struggles and American imperialism, it is an important subject to understand, since it shows that in the Third World, national independence necessarily means independence *from* the United States. Fidel explains this very compellingly. The first section of this book contains selections from Fidel's early speeches, given in these years in which he devoted a great deal of time to explaining why the Cuban Revolution had continually to radicalize itself. This section also serves as an introduction to the main body of the book.

The guiding principle in selecting particular speeches from the innumerable ones Fidel has delivered has been to choose those which are most relevant to a North American audience. Two themes, therefore, seemed most appropriate, and both, in fact, have dominated Fidel's speeches since 1966. These themes are: (1) the necessity for revolutionaries to create the conditions for struggle themselves and not to wait for the material conditions to sweep them into power, and (2) a vision of communist society and the new 'socialist man'. Those particular aspects of the Cuban struggle, and Fidel's articulation of them, are of most interest to the youth of this country – blacks, GIs, and students – who are themselves in struggle.

The theme of struggle, of determination in the face of seemingly insurmountable odds, runs all through Fidel's works. In his trial for the abortive attack on the Moncada barracks, he turned his own defence into an attack on the legitimacy of the Batista régime and those who supported it. It ends by Fidel saying 'History will absolve me.' The armed struggle against Batista after the 'Granma' landing began with twelve men and far fewer weapons. Despite this, Cuba went on to defeat mercenaries armed by the United States and then in October 1962, confronted the United States itself. Never did Fidel sound a note of retreat. When the OAS expelled Cuba from that organization and sought to blockade and isolate Cuba, Fidel said, in the Second Declaration of Havana : 'The duty of every revolutionary is to make the revolution. It is known that the revolution will triumph in America and throughout the world, but it is not for revolutionaries to sit in the doorways of their houses waiting for the corpse of imperialism to pass by. The role of Job doesn't suit a revolutionary.'

Increasingly after 1966 Fidel has attacked 'pseudo-revolutionaries' : those who know all the dogma, call themselves revolutionaries and communists and yet do little to further the struggle. He attacks the defeatists who believe a direct confrontation with imperialism is not yet 'ripe'; their countries are not 'ready', the masses not 'prepared'. Dogma, defeatism, sectarianism must be thrown out; action provides the only test for the revolutionary. In an attack on the Venezuelan Communist Party he said :

Anyone can give himself the name of 'eagle' without having a single feather on his back. In the same way, there are people who call themselves communists without having a communist hair on their heads. The international communist movement, to our way of thinking, is not a church. It is not a religious sect or a Masonic lodge that obliges us to follow any weakness, any deviation, that obliges us to follow a policy of mutual admiration with all kinds of reformists and pseudo-revolutionaries.

'Whoever stops to wait for ideas to triumph among the majority of the masses before initiating revolutionary action will never be a revolutionary,' Fidel said at a meeting of the Organization of Latin American Solidarity. The revolutionary must not wait for society to change itself, nor for objective conditions to be just 'right'; 'If that had been our way of thinking, we would never have initiated a revolutionary process. It was enough for the ideas to take root in a sufficient number of men for revolutionary action to be initiated, and through this action, the masses started to acquire these ideas; the masses acquired that consciousness.'

He stresses that the best education is example; that the example of men fighting will provide a rallying point, inspire hope, and suggest to others a path of action. He argues against the liberals and sectarian leftists who each in their own way equivocate and procrastinate: they are continually studying the 'whys' and 'wherefores' of everything and, in fact, do not trust the revolutionary potential of the people once an opening is provided. A strong democratic spirit flows through Fidel's speeches, for he says that the people, although they need the example of armed revolutionaries to move them to action, will carry forth the struggle and write the history of Latin America. Thus, Fidel rejects the notion common among many leftists that they must have the correct 'line' before moving:

Many times practice comes first and then theory. Our people too are an example of that. Many, the immense majority of those who today proudly call themselves Marxist-Leninists, arrived at Marxism-Leninism by way of the revolutionary struggle. To exclude, to deny, to reject *a priori* all those who from the beginning did not call themselves communists is an act of dogmatism and unqualified sectarianism. Whoever denies that it is the road of revolution which leads the people to Marxism is no Marxist, although he may call himself a communist.

A second theme that dominates Fidel's speeches and also has immediate significance for the New Left of the advanced industrial country is a vision of communist society and the new 'socialist man'. In practice, most 'communist' countries go through a stage of socialism – i.e., industrialization – and then proceed to the stage of communism where scarcity no longer exists. The social laws regulating each stage are, in the socialist society, 'from each according to his ability, to each according to his work'. In the communist society it is 'to each according to his need'. By these categories, no country is yet communist. Nonetheless, in the years after 1966, Fidel has increasingly turned his attention to the problems of how to build socialism and communism parallel to each other. In September 1966, he said: 'We will never create socialist consciousness and much less communist consciousness with a shopkeeper mentality. We will never create socialist consciousness, communist consciousness with a "dollar sign" in the minds and hearts of our men and women.' In the same speech he announced that after 1970, rents in Cuba will be non-existent. The idea is that the country should produce more and more for distribution according to need. At the same time the Cuban people must strive to build a society in which one sees one's obligation to one's brothers as the *primary* obligation; but this can never be done in a society which isn't struggling at the same time to eradicate 'dollar signs' from the hearts and minds of men.

The themes of struggle, action, and 'adventurism', and that of a vision of a communist society, both have in common the importance of example and exemplary action and the idea that the old dogmas and manuals provide no guide to the future. 'We want to build socialism and we want to build communism. Inasmuch as there is no manual, no index, no guide, since no one has traversed that path, we have the right to attempt it with our own means, our own procedures, our own methods.' And, '... We must not think that our duty is to strive so that each one of us may have his own automobile, before first concerning ourselves about whether or not each family in those countries behind us owns at least a plough ...' '... our ideal is not wealth. Our principal ideal and our duty must be to help those who were left behind.' Education, moral obligation, sacrifice, and abandonment of the goal of a consumer society are hallmarks of Fidel's speeches.

No prior models of revolution fit the situation in the United States since all socialist revolutions have taken place in nonindustrialized societies. What Fidel offers the New Left is not a model for revolutionary change in the sense of a series of steps to be copied but rather a vision of the values of a materially abundant society. Insofar as his principal concern is with the new society and the new way, Fidel differs from the other revolutionary heroes widely read by the New Left today. He provides a vision of an alternative way of organizing industrial society and the fact that Cuba has not yet arrived there does not diminish the vision. Che, Ho, Mao, Fanon, and Malcolm X have written most widely on the subject of insurrection; they provide analysis of the old society and provide strategy and tactics for its overthrow. Even Che, who was so important in formulating the ideas of the Cuban Revolution, is most known through his accounts of two insurrectionary struggles – in Cuba and in Bolivia – and in his manual on guerrilla warfare. (He of course wrote on the subject of the new man – for example, 'Man and Socialism' – but these writings are not nearly as well known or as widely read as are his writings on insurrection.) Fidel, more than any other revolutionary, provides a vision of what a communist America would be like.

Fidel differs from other revolutionary heroes in another important respect. Whereas Lenin, Trotsky, Debray, Fanon, and Ho most often wrote for party cadres and engaged in internal disputes within the revolutionary movement, Castro invariably addresses himself to the masses of the Cuban people. As we have said, his purpose is always to educate and to raise the level of political awareness. The direction of the Revolution towards the development of a new man and new values explains the form of Fidel's thought: practically everything is conveyed in *speeches*, speeches addressed to large assemblies, speeches to small groups of farmers, students, factory workers. *Fidel Castro Speaks* is meant quite literally. The new society cannot arise spontaneously but must result from the conscious effort of the people to build it. It cannot be imposed without the consent of the people; hence the emphasis on speeches meant to educate and to raise consciousness. Every speech of Fidel's is a lesson: a clear exposition of policy, analysis, and goals. He speaks often and at length – but is hardly ever demagogic. He speaks because education is the key to the new society. Cuba is an experiment and all the people must participate in it.

As nearly every journalist covering Fidel has noted, he is always on the move, and always talking with the people. His speeches represent the distillation of his thought over a given period of time and are the result of his conversations with hundreds of Cubans.

So much for the content of this collection. The role of Fidel and his speeches in the revolutionary process is also important. It usually happens something like this: Fidel enters with his entourage, is introduced, gets up, unbuckles his revolver, which he places under the lectern, and then begins to speak. At most he has a page or two of notes, yet he speaks for two, three, often four hours. Many North Americans were at first put off by the reports of Fidel's talks because of their experience with the speeches of American politicians. No one in the United States expects honesty, much less an education, from hearing a politician speak, so the thought of any leader speaking to large crowds for great lengths of time seemed appalling. But Fidel speaks on the most concrete problems facing the Cuban people, going into great detail, and providing a wealth of data. He discusses the immediate problems, suggests solutions for them, and then explains the ultimate goal which any particular reform aims towards. In all his speeches there is a tension between immediate problems and the ultimate vision. His speeches are discussed and argued about for weeks after.

Often, he speaks on a particular problem which he has investigated very intensely for weeks or months before delivering his speech. For example, in March 1962, Fidel spoke a number of times on the problems of sectarianism and party organization; his speech on 13 March of that year was just one of many in a short period of time on the same subject. On 13 March 1969, he spoke on the university in a socialist society, a subject he had been investigating from December 1968 to March 1969.

The speeches have proved to be among the most informed, sophisticated, and clear explanations of world events, economic development, and political theory to be found anywhere. Every subject, from agronomy to political economy, is discussed in the large assemblies at which Fidel speaks. Usually, on the special occasions like the 2 January, the 13 March, or the 26 July, the people come hours in advance in order to get as close to Fidel as possible. Hundreds of thousands of people, sometimes a million or more, attend these public assemblies.

There is yet another aspect to the role of Fidel's speeches. As history has sadly shown, the revolutionary process *is* reversible; a new set of rulers can come to replace the old; bureaucracy and privileged groups can replace the revolutionary determination to go to the people and learn from the people. (For example, the Soviet Union has clearly not achieved any new form of democracy and in fact the majority of the Russian people is as uninterested, bored, and uninvolved as are the masses of Americans.) Once these forces are in power, they will attempt to tranquillize and depoliticize the masses – to remove them from active participation in the affairs of the country. Fidel always seeks to avoid such anti-democratic developments. He sees education and political awareness as a critical force against the development of a privileged minority divorced from the people; the relationship between the Cuban people and the revolutionary leadership can be seen in his speeches. His directness, his willingness to deliver thorough explanations, and his absolute respect for the people is everywhere evident. At every point he seeks to explain to the people the reasons for a particular policy; to get them to understand the actions of the party and the state; to involve them in all decisions. He never uses the catch phrases or rhetoric of a demagogue, but always speaks as a teacher, in the best sense of the word. Fidel continually seeks to develop the moral, as well as the political consciousness of the people. A key tenet of the Cuban Revolution, and indeed one that sets it off from the 'People's Democracies' of Eastern Europe, is the role of moral incentives in economic development. At every stage of the revolution the point has been driven home that the aim of the revolution is to 'create wealth with political awareness, not political awareness with money or wealth'. The Cubans do not say, first we fill people's stomachs and then we talk about democracy and communism; they say the two must go hand in hand : the means must serve the ends. Communism cannot develop out of a society which uses capitalist values to grow. Moral incentives – the attempt to get people to work out of commitment to the community and not for more money – create a communist society while developing the country.

Cuba's militant international position, as well as the emphasis on moral incentives for economic development, also acts to protect the democratic nature of the revolution. The constant identification of the Cuban people with the armed struggles of other peoples serves to reinforce the idea that the revolution must never be considered won until all people are free. This identification counteracts the consumer mentality and the smugness and complacency of the Soviets and Eastern Europeans; a people, identified with armed struggle, and prepared to lend support to those struggles, is not easily swept up with interest in the latest Paris fashions. The Cuban international position, the solidarity with Latin American revolutions and the Vietnamese, continually maintains political awareness and militates against peaceful co-existence with imperialism.

The example of Cuba gives the New Left inspiration: it is living proof that a determined people and strong leadership can defeat the most powerful military forces in the world. Fidel's speeches, with their emphasis on struggle and their vision of a new society and a 'new man', speak not only to the Cuban people but also to the youth of America today.

MARTIN KENNER

I. The Revolution in Power:
From Reform to Revolution

CHAPTER 1

Overview: Economic Problems Confronting Cuba and the Underdeveloped World*

This speech provides an excellent overview of the problems confronting the new Revolutionary government and the reforms instituted to eradicate them.

In twenty-one months in power, the Revolutionary government had effected an agrarian reform that broke the back of the old Cuban ruling class. It had begun to alleviate the misery of the rural poor, eliminated corruption as a way of life in Cuba, severed its dependent relationship with the United States, began to establish an independent foreign and trade policy, and incurred the wrath of the most powerful nation in the world.

The media in the United States reacted in a hysterical and strident manner to the visit of the Cuban revolutionary leader to New York. News stories ranged from tales about Cuban diplomats plucking and cooking chickens in their hotel rooms to comparisons between Castro and Hitler because of the length and style of Castro's speeches.

This speech is a brilliant exposition of the problems and causes of economic backwardness. Fidel shows how the backward capitalist countries, and Cuba in particular, suffer in their relations with the advanced capitalist countries. Backwardness is created in the Third World hand in hand with development of the advanced countries: the depletion of natural resources, the promotion of an economy tied to a socially unprofitable export trade, the blocking of domestic industrial development, and the strengthening of the corrupt and parasitic elements of the society by the

---

* Delivered at the General Assembly of the United Nations, New York, 26 September 1960. 'Year of Agrarian Reform'.

imperial powers, all serve to create backwardness – not simply to retard growth.

In this four-and-one-half-hour speech, presented from only a page of notes, Fidel explains the history of the dispute between Cuba and the United States and presents a catalogue of the social problems confronting the Revolution; he states that any under-developed country attempting to use its resources for its own development would inevitably incur the opposition of the United States. Thus, the problems of Cuba presented here are merely a particular case of the general problem of all backward countries. As with Cuba, there is no way out of their misery short of throwing the United States out of their respective countries.

... Now, to the problem of Cuba. Perhaps some of you are well aware of the facts, perhaps others are not. It all depends on the sources of information, but, undoubtedly, the problem of Cuba, born within the last two years, is a new problem for the world. The world had not had many reasons to know that Cuba existed. For many, Cuba was something of an appendix of the United States. Even for many citizens of this country, Cuba was a colony of the United States. As far as the map was concerned, this was not the case; our country had a different colour from that of the United States. But in reality, Cuba was a colony of the United States.

How did our country become a colony of the United States? It was not because of its origins; the same men did not colonize the United States and Cuba. Cuba has a very different ethnic and cultural origin, and the difference was widened over the centuries. Cuba was the last country in America to free itself from Spanish colonial rule, to cast off, with due respect to the representative of Spain, the Spanish colonial yoke; and because it was the last, it also had to fight more fiercely.

Spain had only one small possession left in America and it defended it tooth and nail. Our people, small in numbers, scarcely a million inhabitants at that time, had to face alone, for almost thirty years, an army considered one of the strongest in Europe. Against our small population, the Spanish government mobilized an army as big as the total forces that had fought against

South American independence. Half a million Spanish soldiers fought against our people – our people with their heroic and unbreakable will to be free.

For thirty years the Cubans fought alone for their independence; thirty years of struggle that strengthened our love for freedom and independence. But Cuba was a fruit – according to a President of the United States at the beginning of the last century, John Adams – it was an apple hanging from the Spanish tree, destined to fall, as soon as it was ripe enough, into the hands of the United States. Spanish power had worn itself out in our country. Spain had neither the men nor the economic resources to continue the war in Cuba; Spain had been defeated. Apparently the apple was ripe, and the United States government held out its open hands.

Not one, but several apples fell into the hands of the United States. Puerto Rico fell – heroic Puerto Rico, which had begun its struggle for independence at the same time as Cuba. The Philippine Islands fell, and several other possessions. However, the method of dominating our country could not be the same. Our country had struggled fiercely, and thus had gained the favour of world public opinion. Therefore, the method of taking our country had to be different.

The Cubans who fought for our independence, and at that very moment were giving their blood and their lives, believed in good faith in the joint resolution of the Congress of the United States of 20 April 1898, which declared that 'Cuba is, and by right ought to be, free and independent'.

The people of the United States were sympathetic to the Cuban struggle for liberty. The joint declaration was a law adopted by the Congress of the United States by which war was declared on Spain. But that illusion was followed by a rude awakening. After two years of military occupation of our country, the unexpected happened : at the very moment that the people of Cuba, through their Constituent Assembly, were drafting the Constitution of the Republic, a new law was passed by the United States Congress, a law proposed by Senator Platt, bearing such unhappy memories for the Cubans. That law stated that the Constitution of Cuba must have an amendment, under which the United

States would be granted the right to intervene in Cuba's political affairs and, furthermore, to lease certain parts of Cuba for naval bases or coal supply stations.

In other words, under a law passed by the legislative body of a foreign country, Cuba's Constitution had to contain an amendment with those provisions. Our legislators were clearly told that if they did not accept the amendment, the occupation forces would not be withdrawn. In other words, an agreement to grant another country the right to intervene and to lease naval bases was imposed by force upon my country by the legislative body of a foreign country.

It is well, I think, for countries just entering this organization, countries just beginning their independent life, to bear in mind our history and to note any similar conditions which they may find waiting for them along their own road – and if it is not they, then those who come after them, or their children, or grandchildren, although it seems to us that we will not have to wait that long.

Then began the new colonization of our country, the acquisition of the best agricultural lands by United States firms, concessions of Cuban natural resources and mines, concessions of public utilities for purposes of exploitation, commercial concessions of all types. These concessions, when linked with the constitutional right – constitutional by force – of intervention in our country, turned it from a Spanish colony into an American colony.

Colonies do not speak. Colonies are not known until they have the opportunity to express themselves. That is why our colony and its problems were unknown to the rest of the world. In geography books, reference was made to a flag and a coat of arms. There was an island of another colour on the maps, but it was not an independent republic. Let us not deceive ourselves, since by doing so we only make ourselves ridiculous. Let no one be mistaken. There was no independent republic; there was only a colony where orders were given by the Ambassador of the United States.

We are not ashamed to have to declare this. On the contrary: we are proud to say that today no embassy rules our country; our country is ruled by its people !

Once again the Cuban people had to resort to fighting in order to achieve independence, and that independence was finally attained after seven bloody years of tyranny. Who forced this tyranny upon us? Those who in our country were nothing more than tools of the interests which dominated our country economically.

How can an unpopular régime, inimical to the interests of the people, stay in power unless it is by force? Will we have to explain to the representatives of our sister republics of Latin America what military tyrannies are? Will we have to outline to them how these tyrannies have kept themselves in power? Will we have to explain the history of several of those tyrannies, which are already classical? Will we have to say what forces, what national and international interests support them?

The military group which tyrannized our country was supported by the most reactionary elements of the nation, and, above all, by the foreign interests that dominated the economy of our country. Everybody knows, and we understand that even the government of the United States admits it, that that was the type of government favoured by the monopolies. Why? Because by the use of force, it was possible to check the demands of the people; by the use of force, it was possible to suppress strikes for improvement of living standards; by the use of force, it was possible to crush all movements on the part of the peasants to own the land they worked; by the use of force, it was possible to curb the greatest and most deeply felt aspirations of the nation.

That is why governments of force were favoured by the ruling circles of the United States. That is why governments of force stayed in power for so long, and why there are governments of force still in power in America. Naturally, it all depends on whether it is possible to secure the support of the United States.

For instance, now they say they oppose one of these governments of force: the government of Trujillo. But they do not say they are against other governments of force – that of Nicaragua, or Paraguay, for example. The Nicaraguan one is no longer a government of force; it is a monarchy that is almost as constitutional as that of the United Kingdom, where the reins of power

are handed down from father to son. The same would have occurred in my own country. It was the type of government of force
– that of Fulgencio Batista – which suited the American monopolies in Cuba, but it was not, of course, the type of government
which suited the Cuban people. And the Cuban people, at a great
cost in lives and sacrifices, overthrew that government.

What did the Revolution find
when it came to power?

What did the Revolution find when it came to power in Cuba?
What marvels did the Revolution find when it came to power in
Cuba? First of all, the Revolution found that 600,000 able Cubans
were unemployed – as many, proportionately, as were unemployed in the United States at the time of the great depression
which shook this country and which almost created a catastrophe
in the United States. That was our permanent unemployment.
Three million out of a population of somewhat over six million
did not have electric lights and did not enjoy the advantages and
comforts of electricity. Three and a half million out of a total of
slightly more than six million lived in huts, shacks, and slums,
without the slightest sanitary facilities. In the cities, rents took
almost one third of family incomes. Electricity rates and rents
were among the highest in the world. Thirty-seven and one half
per cent of our population was illiterate; seventy per cent of the
rural children had no teachers; two per cent of our population,
that is, 100,000 persons out of a total of more than six million
suffered from tuberculosis. Ninety-five per cent of the children
in rural areas were affected by parasites; the infant mortality rate
was very high, the average life span very low.

On the other hand, eighty-five per cent of the small farmers
were paying rents which came to almost thirty per cent of their
income for the use of land, while one and one half per cent of
the landowners controlled forty-six per cent of the total land area
of the nation. The proportion of hospital beds to the number of
inhabitants of the country was ridiculous when compared with
countries that have only halfway decent medical services.

Public utilities, electricity, and telephone services all belonged to United States monopolies. A major portion of the banking business, of the importing business, and the oil refineries, the greater part of the sugar production, the best land in Cuba, and the most important industries in all fields belonged to American companies. The balance of payments in the last ten years, from 1950 to 1960, had been favourable to the United States, with regard to Cuba, to the extent of one billion dollars.

This is without taking into account the hundreds of millions of dollars that were extracted from the treasury of the country by the corrupt officials of the tyranny, and which were later deposited in American or European banks.

One billion dollars in ten years. This poor and underdeveloped Caribbean country, with 600,000 unemployed, was contributing greatly to the economic development of the most highly industrialized country in the world.

That was the situation we found, and it is probably not foreign to many of the countries represented in this Assembly, because, when all is said and done, what we have said about Cuba is like a diagnostic X-ray applicable to many of the countries represented here.

What alternative was there for the Revolutionary government? To betray the people? Of course, as far as the President of the United States is concerned, we have betrayed our people. But this would certainly not have been considered so, if, instead of the Revolutionary government being true to its people, it had been loyal to the big American monopolies that exploited the economy of our country. At least, let note be taken here of the wonders the Revolution found when it came to power. They were no more and no less than the usual wonders of imperialism, which are in themselves the wonders of the free world, as far as we, the colonies, are concerned!

We surely cannot be blamed if there were 600,000 unemployed in Cuba and thirty-seven and one half per cent of the population were illiterate. We surely cannot be held responsible if two per cent of the population suffered from tuberculosis and ninety-five per cent were afflicted with parasites. Until that moment, none of us had had anything to do with the destiny of our country;

until that moment, those who had something to do with the destiny of our country were the rulers, who served the interests of the monopolies; until that moment, monopolies had been in control of our country. Did anyone hinder them? No one. Did anyone trouble them? No one. They were able to do their work and there we found the result of their work.

What was the state of our reserves when the tyrant Batista came to power? There was $500,000,000 in our national reserve, a goodly sum to have invested in the industrial development of the country. When the Revolution came to power there was only $70,000,000 in our reserves.

Was there any concern for the industrial development of our country? No. That is why we are astonished and amazed when we hear of the extraordinary concern shown by the United States government for the fate of the countries of Latin America, Africa, and Asia. We cannot overcome our amazement, because after fifty years we have the result of their concern before our eyes.

What has the Revolutionary government done? What crime has the Revolutionary government committed to deserve the treatment we have received here, and the powerful enemies that events have shown us we have?

Did problems with the United States government arise from the first moments? No. Is it perhaps that when we reached power we were imbued with the purpose of getting into international trouble? No. No revolutionary government wants international trouble when it comes to power. What a revolutionary government wants to do is concentrate its efforts on solving its own problems; what it wants to do is carry out a programme for the people, as is the desire of all governments that are interested in the progress of their country.

US attacks on the Revolution

The first unfriendly act perpetrated by the government of the United States was to throw open its doors to a gang of murderers who had left our country covered with blood. Men who had murdered hundreds of defenceless peasants, who, for many years, never tired of torturing prisoners, who killed right and left – were received in that country with open arms. To us, this was amazing. Why this unfriendly act on the part of the government of the United States towards Cuba? Why this act of hostility? At that time, we could not quite understand; now we see the reasons clearly. Was that the proper policy as regards relations between the United States and Cuba? Certainly not, because we were the injured party, inasmuch as the Batista régime remained in power with the help of tanks, planes, and arms furnished by the government of the United States; the Batista régime remained in power with the help of tanks, planes, and arms furnished by by a military mission sent by the United States government; and we trust that no official of the United States will dare to deny that truth.

Even when the Rebel army arrived in Havana, the American military mission was in the most important military camp of the city. That was a broken army, an army that had been defeated and had surrendered. We could very well have considered those foreign officers as prisoners of war since they had been there helping and training the enemies of the people. However, we did not do so. We merely asked the members of that military mission to return to their country, because, after all, we did not need their lessons; their pupils had been defeated.

I have with me a document. Do not be surprised at its appearance, for it is a torn document. It is an old military pact, by virtue of which the Batista tyranny received generous assistance from the United States government. And it is quite important to know the contents of Article 2 of this agreement:

The government of the Republic of Cuba commits itself to make efficient use of the assistance it receives from the United States, pursuant to the present agreement, in order to carry out the plans of defense accepted by both governments, pursuant to which the two governments will take part in missions which are important for the defense of the Western Hemisphere, and, unless permission is previously obtained from the government of the United States of America . . .

– I repeat: 'and unless permission is previously obtained from the government of the United States, such assistance will not be dedicated to other ends than those for which such assistance has been granted.'

That assistance was used to combat the Cuban revolutionaries; it was, therefore, approved by the government of the United States. And even when, some months before the war was over, an embargo on arms for Batista was put into effect, after more than six years of military help, once the arms embargo had been solemnly declared, the Rebel army had proof, documentary proof, that the forces of tyranny had been supplied with three hundred rockets to be fired from planes.

When our comrades living in this country laid these documents before public opinion in the United States, the government of the United States found no other explanation than to say that we were wrong, that they had not sent new supplies to the army of the tyranny, but had just changed some rockets that could not be used in their planes for another type of rocket that could – and, by the way, they were fired at us while we were in the mountains. I must say that this is a unique way of explaining a contradiction when it can be neither justified nor explained. According to the United States, then, this was not military assistance; it was probably some sort of 'technical assistance'.

Why, then, if all this existed and was a cause of resentment for our people ... because everybody knows, even the most innocent and guileless, that with the revolution that has taken place in military equipment, those weapons from the last war have become thoroughly obsolete for a modern war.

Fifty tanks or armoured cars and a few outmoded aircraft cannot defend a continent, much less a hemisphere. But, on the other hand, they are good enough to oppress unarmed peoples. They are good for what they are used for: to intimidate people and to defend monopolies. That is why these hemisphere defence pacts might better be described as 'defence pacts for the protection of United States monopolies'.

Revolutionary reforms and US retaliation

And so the Revolutionary government began to take the first steps. The first thing it did was to lower the rents paid by families by fifty per cent, a just measure, since, as I said earlier, there were families paying up to one-third of their incomes in rent. The people had been the victim of housing speculation, and city lots had also been the subject of speculation, at the expense of the entire Cuban people. But when the Revolutionary government reduced rents by fifty per cent, there were, of course, a few individuals who became upset, the few who owned those apartment buildings; but the people rushed into the streets rejoicing, as they would in any country, even here in New York, if rents were reduced by fifty per cent. This was no problem for the monopolies. Some American monopolies owned large buildings, but they were relatively few in number.

Then another law was passed, a law cancelling the concessions which had been granted by the tyranny of Batista to the telephone company, an American monopoly. Taking advantage of the fact that our people were defenceless, they had obtained valuable concessions. The Revolutionary government then cancelled these concessions and re-established normal prices for telephone services. Thus began the first conflict with the American monopolies.

The third measure was the reduction of electricity rates, which were the highest in the world. Then followed the second conflict with the American monopolies. We were beginning to appear communist; they were beginning to daub us in red because we had clashed head on with the interests of the United States monopolies.

Then followed the next law, an essential and inevitable law for our country, and a law which sooner or later will have to be adopted by all countries of the world, at least by those which have not yet adopted it: the Agrarian Reform Law. Of course, in theory, everybody agrees with the Agrarian Reform Law. Nobody will deny the need for it unless he is a fool. No one can deny that agrarian reform is one of the essential conditions for the economic development of the country. In Cuba, even the big landowners agreed about agrarian reform – only they wanted their own kind of reform, such as the one defended by many theoreticians, a reform which would not harm their interests, and, above all, one which would not be put into effect as long as it could be avoided. This is something that is well known to the economic bodies of the United Nations, something nobody even cares to discuss any more. In my country, it was absolutely necessary: more than 200,000 peasant families lived in the countryside without land on which to grow essential food crops.

Without an agrarian reform, our country would have been unable to take that step. We made an agrarian reform. Was it a radical agrarian reform? We think not. It was a reform adjusted to the needs of our development, and in keeping with our own possibilities of agricultural development. In other words, it was an agrarian reform which was to solve the problems of the landless peasants, the problem of supplying basic foodstuffs, the problem of rural unemployment, and which was to end, once and for all, the ghastly poverty which existed in the countryside of our native land.

And that is where the first major difficulty arose. In the neighbouring Republic of Guatemala a similar case had occurred. And I honestly warn my colleagues of Latin America, Africa, and Asia: whenever you set out to make a just agrarian reform, you must be ready to face a similar situation, especially if the best and largest tracts of land are owned by American monopolies, as was the case in Cuba.

It is quite possible that we may later be accused of giving bad advice in this Assembly. It is not our intention to disturb anybody's sleep. We are simply stating the facts, although the facts are sufficient to disturb everybody's sleep.

Then the problem of payment arose. Notes from the State Department rained on our government. They never asked us about our problems, not even out of sheer pity, or because of the great responsibility they had in creating these problems. They never asked us how many died of starvation in our country, or how many were suffering from tuberculosis, or how many were unemployed. No, they never asked about that. A sympathetic attitude towards our needs? Certainly not. All talks by the representatives of the government of the United States centred upon the telephone company, the electric company, and the land owned by American companies.

How could we solve the problem of payment? Of course, the first question that should have been asked was what were we going to pay with, rather than how. Can you gentlemen conceive of a poor, underdeveloped country, with 600,000 unemployed and such a large number of illiterates and sick people, a country whose treasury reserves have been exhausted, and which has contributed to the economy of a powerful country with one billion dollars in ten years – can you conceive of this country having the means to pay for the land affected by the Agrarian Reform Law, or the means to pay for it in the terms demanded?

What were the State Department aspirations regarding their affected interests? They wanted prompt, efficient, and just payment. Do you understand that language? 'Prompt, efficient, and just payment.' That means 'Pay now, in dollars, whatever we ask for our land.'

We were not one hundred per cent communist yet. We were just becoming slightly pink. We did not confiscate land; we simply proposed to pay for it in twenty years, and in the only way in which we could pay for it: in bonds, which would mature in twenty years at four and one half per cent, or be amortized yearly.

How could we pay for our land in dollars? And the amount they asked for it? It was absurd. Anyone can readily understand that, under those circumstances, we had to choose between making the agrarian reform and not making it. If we chose not to make it, the dreadful economic situation of our country would have continued indefinitely. If we decided to make it, we exposed ourselves to the hatred of the government of the powerful neighbour in the north.

We decided to go on with the agrarian reform. Of course, the limits set to *latifundia*[1] in Cuba would amaze a representative of

---

1. Referring to the plantation system of *latifundios*, or large landed estates. Most were foreign-owned or -run.

the Netherlands, for example, or of any country of Europe, because of their extension. The maximum amount of land set forth
in the Agrarian Reform Law is 400 hectares (a hectare is equal
to 10,000 square metres). In Europe, 400 hectares is practically
a *latifundium*; in Cuba, there were American monopolies
which had up to 200,000 hectares – I repeat, in case someone
thinks he has heard wrong, 200,000 hectares – an agrarian
reform law reducing the maximum limit to 400 hectares was
inadmissible.

But in our country it was not only the land that was the
property of the agrarian monopolies, but the largest and most
important mines were also owned by those monopolies. Cuba
produces, for example, a great deal of nickel. All of the nickel
was exploited by American interests, and, under the tyranny of
Batista, an American company, the Moa Bay Company, had obtained a juicy concession that in a mere five years – mark my
words, in a mere five years – it intended amortizing an investment of $120,000,000. A $120,000,000 investment amortized in
five years!

And who had given the Moa Bay Company this concession
through the intervention of the government of the United States?
Quite simply, the tyrannical government of Fulgencio Batista,
which was there to defend the interests of the monopolies. And
this is an absolutely true fact. Exempt from all taxes, what were
those companies going to leave for the Cubans? The empty,
worked-out mines, the impoverished land, and not the slightest
contribution to the economic development of our country.

And so the Revolutionary government passed a mining law
which forced those monopolies to pay a twenty-five per cent tax
on the exportation of minerals. The attitude of the Revolutionary
government already had been too bold. It had clashed with the
interests of the international electric trust; it had clashed with
interests of the international telephone trust; it had clashed with
the interests of the international mining trusts; it had clashed
with the interests of the United Fruit Company; and it had, in
clashing with these interests, clashed with the most powerful
interests of the United States, which, as you know, are very
closely linked. And that was more than the government of the

United States – or rather, the representatives of the United States monopolies – could possibly tolerate.

Then began a new period of harassment of the Revolution. Can anyone who objectively analyses the facts, who is willing to think honestly, not as the United Press or the Associated Press tell him, but to think with his head and to draw conclusions from his own reasoning and see the facts without prejudice, sincerely and honestly – would anyone who does this consider that the things which the Revolutionary government did were such as to demand the destruction of the Cuban Revolution? No. But the interests affected by the Cuban Revolution were not concerned about the Cuban case; they were not being ruined by the measures of the Cuban Revolutionary government. That was not the problem. The problem lay in the fact that those very interests owned the wealth and the natural resources of the greater part of the peoples of the world.

The attitude of the Cuban Revolution therefore had to be punished. Punitive actions of all sorts – even the destruction of those insolent people – had to follow the audacity of the Revolutionary government.

On our honour, we swear that up to that moment we had not had the opportunity even to exchange letters with the distinguished Prime Minister of the Soviet Union, Nikita Khrushchev. That is to say, that when, for the North American press and the international news agencies that supply information to the world, Cuba was already a communist government, a Red peril ninety miles from the United States with a government dominated by communists, the Revolutionary government had not even had the opportunity of establishing diplomatic and commercial relations with the Soviet Union.

But hysteria can go to any length; hysteria is capable of making the most likely and absurd claims. Of course, let no one think for a moment that we are going to intone a *mea culpa* here. There will be no *mea culpa*. We do not have to ask anyone's pardon. What we have done, we have done consciously, and above all, fully convinced of our right to do it.

The sugar quota

Then came the threats against our sugar quota, imperialism's cheap philosophy of showing generosity, egotistical and exploiting generosity; they began showing kindness towards Cuba, declaring that they were paying us a preferential price for sugar, which amounted to a subsidy on Cuban sugar – a sugar which was not so sweet for Cubans, since we were not the owners of the best sugar-producing land, nor the owners of the largest sugar mills. Furthermore, in that affirmation lay hidden the true history of Cuban sugar, of the sacrifices which had been imposed upon my country during the periods when it was economically attacked.

Formerly, it was not a question of quotas, but a question of custom tariffs. By means of one of those laws or one of those agreements, which are made between the shark and the sardine, the United States, through an agreement they called a 'reciprocity treaty', obtained a series of concessions for its products, in order to compete easily and displace from the Cuban market the products of its 'friends', the English and the French, as is often the case among 'friends'. In exchange for this, certain tariff concessions were granted our sugar, which, on the other hand, could be unilaterally changed in accordance with the will of the Congress or the government of the United States. And that is what happened. Whenever they thought it convenient for their interests, they raised the tariff, and our sugar could not enter the American market. And if it did, it entered under disadvantageous conditions. When war was near, they reduced tariffs. Of course, since Cuba was the nearest source of sugar, that supply had to be assured. Then the tariffs were lowered, and production was encouraged. During the war years, when sugar prices soared all over the world, we were selling our sugar cheaply to the United States, despite the fact that we were the only source of supply for the United States. Then the war ended, and with that came the collapse of our economy.

Errors committed here in the distribution of that product were paid for by us. Prices went up enormously at the end of World

War I. There was a tremendous encouragement of production, but then a sudden fall in prices ruined the Cuban sugar mills, which fell into the hands of – I will give you one guess – the American banks, for when Cuban nationals became bankrupt, American banks became wealthy.

So the situation continued until the thirties. Since the United States government was trying the find a formula that would reconcile its supply interests with the interests of its internal producers, it established a quota system. That quota was supposed to be based upon the traditional participation of the different sources of supply in the American market, and on the fact that our country had traditionally supplied almost fifty per cent of the United States market. However, when quotas were established, our participation was reduced to twenty-eight per cent, and the advantages which that law had granted us, the very few advantages which the law had granted us, were gradually taken away in successive laws, and, of course, the colony depended on the colonial power. The economy of the colony had been organized by the colonial power.

The colony had to be subjected to the colonial power, and if the colony took measures to free itself from the colonial power, that country would take measures to crush the colony. Conscious of the subordination of our economy to their market, the government of the United States began to issue a series of warnings that our quota would be reduced further, and, at the same time, other activities were taking place in the United States of America : the activities of counter-revolutionaries.

Many still wait for telegrams of condolence for their children murdered by US bombs

One afternoon an airplane coming from the north flew over one of the sugar refineries and dropped a bomb. This was a strange and unheard-of event, but we knew full well where the plane had come from. On another afternoon, another plane flew over our sugar-cane fields and dropped a few incendiary bombs. These events which began sporadically continued systematically.

One afternoon, when a number of American tourist agents were visiting Cuba in response to an effort made by the Revolutionary government to promote tourism as one of the sources of national income, a plane manufactured in the United States, of the type used in World War II, flew over our capital dropping pamphlets and a few grenades. Of course, some anti-aircraft guns went into action. The result was more than forty victims, between the grenades dropped by the plane and the anti-aircraft fire, because, as you know, some of the projectiles explode upon contacting any object. As I said, the result was more than forty victims. There were little girls on the street with their entrails torn out, old men and women wantonly killed. Was this the first time it had happened in our country? No. Children, old men, and old women, young men, and young women, had often been killed in the villages of Cuba by American bombs supplied to the tyrant Batista. On one occasion, eighty workers died when a mysterious explosion – too mysterious – took place in the harbour of Havana; the explosion of a ship carrying Belgian weapons, which had arrived in our country after many efforts by the United States government to prevent the Belgian government from selling arms to us.

Dozens of victims of war; eighty families orphaned by the explosions. Forty victims as a result of an airplane that brazenly flew over our territory. The authorities of the United States government denied the fact that these planes came from American territory, but the plane was now safely in a hangar in this country. When one of our magazines published a photograph of it, the United States authorities seized the plane. A version of the affair was issued to the effect that this was not very important, and that these victims had not died because of the bombs, but because of the anti-aircraft fire. Those responsible for this crime, those who had caused these deaths were wandering about peacefully in the United States where they were not even prevented from committing further acts of aggression.

May I take this opportunity to tell His Excellency, the Representative of the United States, that there are many mothers in

Cuba still awaiting their telegrams of condolence for their children murdered by the bombs of the United States.

Planes kept coming and going. But, as far as they were concerned, there was no evidence. Frankly, we don't know how they define the word evidence. The plane was there, photographed and captured, and yet we were told that the plane did not drop any bombs. It is not known how the United States authorities were so well informed.

Planes continued to fly over our territory dropping incendiary bombs. Millions and millions of pesos were lost in the burning fields of sugar cane. Many humble people of Cuba, who saw property destroyed, property that was now truly their own, suffered burns in the struggle against those persistent and tenacious bombings by pirate planes.

And then one day, while dropping a bomb on one of our sugar mills, a plane exploded in mid-air and the Revolutionary government was able to collect what was left of the pilot, who, by the way, was an American. His documents were found, and proof as to the place where the plane had taken off from. On its way to Cuba, the plane had flown between two United States military bases. This was a matter that could not be denied any longer : the planes took off from the United States. Confronted with irrefutable evidence, the United States government gave an explanation to the Cuban government. Its conduct in this case was not the same as in connection with the U-2. When it was proved that the planes were taking off from the United States, the government of the United States did not proclaim its right to burn our sugarcane fields. The United States government apologized and said it was sorry. We were lucky, after all, because after the U-2 incident the United States government did not even apologize; it proclaimed its right to carry out flights over Soviet territory. Bad luck for the Soviets !

But we do not have too many anti-aircraft batteries and the planes went on flying and bombing us until the harvest was over. When there was no more sugar cane, the bombings stopped. We were the only country in the world which had gone through a thing like this, although I do recall that at the time of his visit to Cuba, President Sukarno told us that this was not the case, for they, too, had certain problems with American planes flying over their territory. I do not know whether I have committed an indiscretion in mentioning this; I hope not.

But the truth is that in this peaceful hemisphere at least, we were a country that, without being at war with anyone, had to stand the constant attack of pirate planes. And could those planes come in and out of United States territory unmolested? Well, gentlemen, we invite you to think a little about this, and should the people of the United States learn by chance what is being said in this hall, we invite them to think about the statements made by the United States government itself, that the territory of the United States is perfectly guarded and protected against any aerial incursion, and that defence measures in the United States are infallible. It has been stated that the defences of the world they call 'free' – although as far as we are concerned it was not free until 1 January 1959 – are impregnable. If this is the case, how is it that planes, not supersonic planes, but light planes with a velocity of barely 150 miles per hour, how is it that these planes are able to fly in and out of the United States territory undetected, fly between two bases on their way out and do the same on their way in, without the United States government ever knowing that these planes are coming in and out of its national territory? This means one of two things. Either the government of the United States is lying to the people of the United States, and the United States is defenceless in the face of aerial incursions, or the United States was an accomplice of these aerial incursions.

Economic aggression

The air raids ended, and then came economic aggression. What was one of the arguments wielded by the enemies of agrarian reform? They said that agrarian reform would bring chaos to agricultural production, that production would diminish considerably, and that the government of the United States was concerned because Cuba might not be able to fulfil her commitments to the American market. The first argument – and it is appropriate that at least the new delegations in the General Assembly should become familiar with some of the arguments, because some day they may have to answer similar arguments – the first argument was that the agrarian reform meant the ruin of the country. This was not the case. If this had been so, and agricultural production had decreased, the American government would not have felt the need to carry on its economic aggression.

Did they sincerely believe in what they said when they stated that the agrarian reform would cause a drop in production? Perhaps they did. Surely it is logical for each one to believe what his mind has been conditioned to believe. It is quite possible they may have felt that without the all-powerful monopolistic companies we Cubans would be unable to produce sugar. Perhaps they were even sure we would ruin the country. But of course, if the Revolution had ruined the country, then the United States would not have had to attack us: it would have left us alone, and the United States government would have appeared as a good and honourable government, and we as people who ruined our own nation, and as a great example that revolutions should not be made because they ruin countries. Fortunately, that was not the case. There is proof that revolutions do not ruin countries, and that proof has just been furnished by the government of the United States. Among other things, it has been proved that revolutions do not ruin countries, and that imperialist governments do try to ruin countries.

Cuba had not been ruined; she therefore had to be ruined. Cuba needed new markets for its products, and we would honestly ask any delegation present if it does not want its country to sell what it produces and its exports to increase. We wanted our exports to increase, and this is what all countries wish; this must be a universal law. Only egotistical interests can oppose the universal interest in trade and commercial exchange, which surely is one of the most ancient aspirations and needs of mankind.

We wanted to sell our products and went in search of new markets. We signed a trade treaty with the Soviet Union, according to which we would sell one million tons of sugar and would purchase a certain amount of Soviet products or articles. Surely no one can say that this is an incorrect procedure. There may be some who would not do such a thing because it might displease certain interests. We really did not have to ask permission from the State Department in order to sign a trade treaty with the Soviet Union, because we considered ourselves, and we continue to consider ourselves, a truly independent and free country.

When the amount of sugar in stock began to diminish, stimulating our economy, we received a hard blow: at the request of the Executive power of the United States, Congress passed a law empowering the President or the Executive power to reduce the import quotas for Cuban sugar to whatever limits he might deem appropriate. An economic weapon was wielded against our Revolution. The justification for that attitude had already been prepared by publicity experts; the campaign had been on for a long time, because you know perfectly well that in this country monopolies and publicity are one and the same thing. The economic weapon was wielded, our sugar quota was suddenly cut by about one million tons – sugar that had already been produced and prepared for the American market – in order to deprive our country of resources for its development, and thus reduce it to a state of impotence, with the natural political consequences. Such measures were expressly banned by regional international law. Economic aggression, as all Latin American delegates here know, is expressly condemned by regional international law. However, the government of the United States violated that law, wielded its economic weapon, and cut our sugar quota by about one million tons. They could do it.

What was Cuba's defence when confronted by that reality? It could appeal to the United Nations. It could turn to the United Nations, in order to denounce political and economic aggressions, the air attacks of the pirate planes, besides the constant interference by the government of the United States in the political affairs of our country and the subversive campaigns it carries out against the Revolutionary government of Cuba.

Cuba was not the first
victim of aggression

So we turned to the United Nations. The United Nations had power to deal with these matters. The United Nations is, within the hierarchy of international organizations, the highest authority. The United Nations authority is even above that of the Organization of American States. And besides, we were interested in bringing the problem to the United Nations because we know well the economic situation that Latin America finds itself in; because we understand the state of dependence of the economy of Latin America in relation to the United States. The United Nations knew of the affair, it requested the OAS to make an investigation, and the OAS met. Very well. And what was to be expected? That the OAS would protect the country; that the OAS would condemn the political aggression against Cuba, and above all, that it would condemn the economic aggression against our country. That should have been expected. But, after all, we were a small people of the Latin-American community of nations; we were just another victim. And we were neither the first nor the last, because Mexico had already been attacked more than once militarily. In one war they tore away from Mexico a great part of its territory, and on that occasion, rather than surrender, the heroic sons of Mexico leaped to their death from the Castle of Chapultepec wrapped in the Mexican flag. These were the heroic sons of Mexico.

And that was not the only act of aggression. That was not the only time that American infantry forces trod upon Mexican soil. Nicaragua was invaded, and for seven long years was heroically defended by César Augusto Sandino. Cuba suffered intervention more than once, and so did Haiti and Santo Domingo. Guatemala also suffered intervention. Who among you could honestly deny the intervention of the United Fruit Company and the State Department of the United States when the legitimate government of Guatemala was overthrown? I understand full well that there may be some who consider it their official duty to be discreet on this matter, and who may even be willing to come here and deny this, but in their consciences they know we are simply stating the truth.

Cuba was not the first victim of aggression; Cuba was not the first country to be in danger of aggression. In this hemisphere everyone knows that the government of the United States has always imposed its own law – the law of the strongest, in virtue of which they have destroyed Puerto Rican nationhood and have imposed their domination on that friendly country – the law with which they seized and held the Panama Canal.

This was nothing new. Our country should have been defended, but it was never defended. Why? Let us get to the bottom of this matter, without merely studying the form. If we stick to the dead letter of the law, then we are protected; if we abide by reality, we have no protection whatsoever, because reality imposes itself on the law set forth in international codes, and that reality is, that a small nation attacked by a powerful country did not have any defence and was not defended.

But, on the other hand, what came out of Costa Rica? [2] A miracle of ingenious fabrication came out of Costa Rica! In Costa Rica there was no condemnation of the United States or the government of the United States – and I do wish to avoid any misunderstanding about our feelings with regard to the people of the United States. The government of the United States was not condemned in Costa Rica for the sixty air raids by pirate aircraft; it was not condemned for the economic and other aggressions of which we had been the victim. No, the Soviet Union was condemned. What an extraordinary thing! We had not been the object of any aggression from the Soviet Union; no Soviet aircraft had flown over our territory. Yet, in Costa Rica they condemned the Soviet Union. The Soviet Union only said that in the event of military aggression against our country, Soviet artillerymen, figuratively speaking, would support the attacked country.

Since when is support for a weak country, support in case of

---

2. In August 1960, the OAS met in San José, Costa Rica, and voted support for a resolution condemning communist 'penetration' in the hemisphere.

an attack by a powerful country, regarded as interference? In law there is something called an impossible condition. If a country considers that it is incapable of committing a certain crime, then it need only say so: 'there is no possibility that the Soviet Union will support Cuba, because there is no possibility that Cuba will be attacked by us.' But that principle was not established. In Costa Rica the principle was established that Soviet interference must be condemned.

And what about the air attacks on Cuba? Nothing. What about the aggressions against Cuba? Nothing.

Of course, there is something that we must remember and which should concern us all somehow. All of us, without exception, are actors in a crucial moment of history. Apparently, at times criticism does not reach us; that is, we do not become aware of the criticism and condemnation of our deeds, especially when we forget that, as we have had the privilege of being actors in this transcendental moment of history, history will someday judge us for our deeds. And when confronted with the defence-lessness of our country at the meeting in Costa Rica, we smile to ourselves, because history will judge that episode.

And I say without bitterness that it is sometimes difficult to condemn men; men are often the playthings of circumstances, and we, who know the history of our country and are, besides, exceptional witnesses of what our country is going through to-day, we understand how terrible the subordination of the economy and life in general of nations to foreign economic power is. I need only note that my country was left defenceless in Costa Rica, and something else: the interest there is in not bringing this matter back to the United Nations – perhaps because it is felt that it is easier to obtain a mechanical majority in the OAS, although this fear is not very reasonable, since mechanical majorities have often operated in the United Nations.

With all due respect to this organization, I must state here that that is why the people, our people, the people of Cuba, who have learned much and are quite up to the role they are playing, to the heroic struggle they are conducting, why our people, who have learned in the school of international events, know that in the last instance, when their rights have been denied and aggressive

forces are marshalled against them, they still have the supreme
and heroic resource of resisting when their rights are not protected by either the OAS or the UN.

We are a whole people governing a country

That is why we, the small countries, do not yet feel too sure that
our rights will be preserved; that is why we, the small countries,
whenever we decide to become free, know that we become free at
our own risk. In truth, when people are united and are defending
a just right, they can trust their own energies. We are not, as we
have been pictured, a mere group of men governing a country.
We are a whole people governing a country – a whole people
firmly united, with a great revolutionary consciousness, defending its rights. And this should be known by the enemies of the
Revolution and of Cuba, because if they ignore this fact, they will
be making a regrettable error.

These are the circumstances in which the revolutionary process has taken place in our country; that is how we found the
country and why difficulties have arisen. And yet the Cuban
Revolution is changing what was yesterday a land without hope,
a land of poverty and illiteracy, into one of the most advanced
and developed countries in this continent.

The Revolutionary government, in just twenty months, has
created 10,000 new schools. In this brief period it has doubled the
number of rural schools that had been created in fifty years. Cuba
is today the first country of America that has met all its school
needs, that has a teacher in the farthest corners of the mountains.

In this brief period of time, the Revolutionary government has
built 5,000 houses in the rural and urban areas. Fifty new towns
are being built at this moment. The most important military
fortresses today house tens of thousands of students, and, in the
coming year, our people intend to fight the great battle against
illiteracy, with the ambitious goal of teaching every single inhabitant of the country to read and write in one year, and with
that end in mind, organizations of teachers, students, and work-

ers, that is, the entire people, are preparing themselves for an intensive campaign : and Cuba will be the first country of America which, after a few months, will be able to say it does not have one single illiterate.

Today our people are receiving the assistance of hundreds of doctors who have been sent to the fields to fight against illness and parasitic ailments and to improve the sanitary conditions of the nation.

In another aspect, in the preservation of our natural resources, we can also point with pride to the fact that in only one year, in the most ambitious plan for the conservation of natural resources being carried out on this continent, including the United States of America and Canada, we have planted close to fifty million timber-yielding trees.

Youths who were unemployed, who did not attend school, have been organized by the Revolutionary government and are today being gainfully and usefully employed by the country, and at the same time being prepared for productive work.

Agricultural production in our country has been able to perform an almost unique feat, an increase in production from the very beginning. From the very start, we were able to increase agricultural production. Why? In the first place, because the Revolutionary government turned more than 10,000 agricultural workers, who formerly paid rent, into land owners, at the same time maintaining large-scale production through co-operatives. In other words, production was maintained through co-operatives, thanks to which we have been able to apply the most modern technical methods to our agricultural production, causing a marked increase in that production.

And all this social welfare work – teachers, housing, and hospitals – has been carried out without sacrificing the resources that we have earmarked for development. At this very moment the Revolutionary government is carrying out a programme of industrialization of the country, and the first plants are already being built.

We have utilized the resources of our country in a rational manner. Formerly, for instance, Cuba, a country which is mainly agricultural, imported seven times more cars than tractors. We have changed this around, and we are now importing seven times more tractors than cars.

Close to 500 million dollars were recovered from the politicians who had enriched themselves during the tyranny of Batista – close to 500 million dollars in cash and other assets was the total we were able to recover from the corrupt politicians who have been sucking the blood of our country for seven years. It is the correct investment of these assets which enables the Revolutionary government, while at the same time developing plans for industrialization and for the development of agriculture, to build houses, schools, to send teachers to the farthest corners of the country, and to give medical assistance to everyone – in other words, to carry out a true programme of social development.

The Cuban Revolution made the monopolists worry

At the Bogotá meeting, as you know, the government of the United States proposed a plan. Was it a plan for economic development? No. It was a plan for social development. What is understood by this? Well, it was a plan for building houses, building schools, and building roads. But does this settle the problem at all? How can there be a solution to the social problems without a plan for economic development? Do they want to make fools of the Latin American countries? What are families going to live on when they inhabit those houses, if those houses are really built? What shoes, what clothes are they going to wear, and what food are children going to eat when they attend those schools? Is it not known that, when a family does not have clothes or shoes for the children, the children are not sent to school? With what means are they going to pay the teachers and the doctors? How are they going to pay for the medicine? Do you want a good way of saving medicine? Improve the nutrition of the people; when they eat well you will not have to spend money on hospitals. Therefore, in view of the tremendous reality of underdevelopment, the government of the United States now comes out with a plan for social development. Of course, it is stimulating to observe the United States concerning itself with some of the problems of Latin America. Thus far they had not concerned themselves at all. What a coincidence, that they are now worried about those problems! And the fact that this con- cern emerged after the Cuban Revolution will probably be labelled by them as purely coincidental.

Thus far the monopolies have certainly not cared very much, except about exploiting the underdeveloped countries. But comes the Cuban Revolution, and suddenly the monopolies are worry- ing, and while they attack us economically, trying to crush us, they offer alms to the countries of Latin America. The countries of Latin America are offered, not the resources for social develop- ment – houses for men who have no work, schools where children will not go, and hospitals that would not. be necessary if there were enough food to eat.

After all, although some of my Latin American colleagues may feel it their duty to be discreet at the United Nations, they should all welcome a revolution such as the Cuban Revolution, which, at any rate, has forced the monopolists to return at least a small part of what they have been extracting from the natural resources and the sweat of the Latin American peoples.

Although we are not included in that aid, we are not worried; we do not get angry about things like that, because we have been settling those same problems of schools and housing and so on for quite some time. But perhaps there may be some of you who feel we are using this rostrum to make propaganda, because the Presi- dent of the United States has said that some come here for propa- ganda purposes. And, of course, all my colleagues in the United States have a standing invitation to visit Cuba. We do not close our doors to anyone, nor do we confine anyone. Any of my col- leagues in this Assembly can visit Cuba whenever he wishes, in order to see with his own eyes what is going on. You know the chapter in the Bible that speaks of Saint Thomas, who had to see in order to believe – I think it was Saint Thomas.

And, after all, we can invite any newspaperman and any mem- ber of any delegation to visit Cuba and see what a nation is capable of doing with its own resources when they are used with honesty and reason. But we are not only solving our housing and school problems, we are solving our development problems as well, because without the solution of the problems of development there can be no settlement of the social problems themselves.

Why is the US opposed
to economic development?

Why is the United States government unwilling to speak of development? It is simple: because the government of the United States does not want to oppose the monopolies, and the monopolies require natural resources and markets for the investment of their capital. That is where the great contradiction lies. That is why the real solution to this problem is not sought. That is why planning for the development of underdeveloped countries with public funds is not done.

It is good that this be stated frankly, because, after all, we, the underdeveloped countries, are a majority in this Assembly – in case anyone is unaware of this fact – and we are witnesses to what is going on in the underdeveloped countries.

Yet, the true solution of the problem is not sought, and much is said about the participation of private capital. Of course, this means markets for the investment of surplus capital, like the investment that was amortized in five years.

The government of the United States cannot propose a plan for public investment, because this would divorce it from the very reason for being the government of the United States, namely the American monopolies.

Let us not beat about the bush, the reason no real economic plan is being promoted is simply this: to preserve our lands in Latin America, Africa, and Asia for the investment of surplus capital.

Cuba will talk; US will not

Thus far we have referred to the problems of my own country and the reason why those problems have not been solved. Is it perhaps because we did not want to solve them? No. The government of

Cuba has always been ready to discuss its problems with the government of the United States, but the government of the United States has not been ready to discuss its problems with Cuba, and it must have its reasons for not doing so. The note sent by the Revolutionary government of Cuba to the government of the United States, on 27 January 1960, says the following:

The differences of opinion that may exist between the two governments that are subject to diplomatic negotiations may in fact be solved through such negotiations. The government of Cuba is ready and willing to discuss these differences openly and without reserve, and expressly declares that in its opinion there are no obstacles of any kind whatsoever which prevent such negotiations with the government and people of the United States through any of the means and instruments traditionally set up for these purposes, on the basis of mutual respect and reciprocal benefit. The government of Cuba wishes to maintain and increase diplomatic and economic relations, and feels that on this basis the traditional friendship between the Cuban and American people is indestructible.

On 22 February of this year, the Revolutionary government of Cuba states that

in accordance with this desire to renew, through diplomatic channels, the negotiations which have been initiated regarding issues outstanding between the United States and Cuba, it has decided to set up a commission with instructions to begin negotiations in Washington on a mutually agreeable date.

However, the Revolutionary government wishes to make clear that the renewal and subsequent course of such negotiations must necessarily depend on the government or the Congress of your country not taking unilateral measures which would prejudice the results of the above-mentioned negotiations, or that might be prejudicial to the economy or the people of Cuba. Needless to say, the adherence of the government of Your Excellency to this point of view would not only contribute to the improvement of relations between our respective countries, but would also reaffirm the spirit of brotherly friendship that has traditionally bound and still binds our peoples. It would also allow both governments to examine the questions that have affected the traditional relations between Cuba and the United States of America in a calm atmosphere and from a broad point of view.

What was the reply of the government of the United States?

The government of the United States cannot accept the conditions for negotiations expressed in Your Excellency's note to the effect that no measures of a unilateral character should be taken by the government of the United States that might affect the Cuban economy or the people of Cuba, be it through the Legislative or Executive branches. As was stated by President Eisenhower on January 26, the government of the United States must maintain freedom of exercise of its own sovereignty in order to take whatever measures it may deem necessary, conscious of its international commitments and obligations, for the defense of the legitimate rights and interests of its people.

In other words, the government of the United States does not deign to discuss its differences with the small country of Cuba.

What hope can the people of Cuba maintain for the solution of these problems? The facts that we have been able to note here so far conspire against the solution of these problems, and the United Nations should seriously take this into account, because the people and the government of Cuba are justifiably concerned at the aggressive turn in the policy of the United States with regard to Cuba, and it is proper that we should be well informed.

US plans subversion and war

In the first place, the government of the United States considers it has the right to promote and encourage subversion in our country.[3] The government of the United States is promoting the organization of subversive movements against the Revolutionary government of Cuba, and we wish to denounce this fact in this General Assembly; we also wish to denounce specifically the fact that, for instance, a territory which belongs to Honduras, known as Islas Cisnes, the Swan Islands, has been seized *manu militari* by the government of the United States and that American Marines are there, despite the fact that this territory belongs to

3. During the previous spring the US government prepared a plan for the violent overthrow of the Revolutionary government. In early summer, 1960, construction of a US military-CIA base in Retalhuleu, Guatemala, for the attack, was started.

Honduras. Thus, violating international law and despoiling a friendly people of a part of its territory, the United States has established a powerful radio station on one of those islands, in violation of international radio agreements, and has placed it at the disposal of the war criminals and subversive groups supported in this country; furthermore, military training is being conducted on that island, in order to promote subversion and the landing of armed forces in our country. It might be good for the delegate of Honduras in the United Nations to reaffirm his country's right to that part of the territory, but that is a matter that concerns the representative of Honduras only. What does concern us is that a part of the territory of a friendly country, seized in a piratical manner by the United States government, is being used as a base for subversion and attacks against our territory, and I ask that careful note be taken of this denunciation which we make on behalf of the government and people of Cuba.

Does the government of the United States feel it has the right to promote subversion in our country, violating all international treaties, including those relating to radio frequency? Does this mean, by chance, that the Cuban government has the right to promote subversion in the United States? Does the government of the United States believe it has the right to violate radio frequency agreements? Does this mean, by chance, that the Cuban government has the right to violate radio frequency agreements also? What right can the government of the United States have over us or over our island that permits it to act towards other nations in such a matter? Let the United States return the Swan Islands to Honduras, since it never had any jurisdiction over those islands.

But there are even more alarming circumstances for our people. It is well known that, in virtue of the Platt Amendment, imposed by force upon our people, the government of the United States assumed the right to establish naval bases on our territory, a right forcefully imposed and maintained. A naval base in the territory of any country is surely a cause for concern. First of all, there is concern over the fact that a country, which follows an aggressive and warlike international policy, has a base in the heart of our country, which brings us the risk of being involved in any international conflict, in any atomic conflict, without our having anything to do with the problem, because we have absolutely nothing to do with the problems of the United States and the crises provoked by the government of the United States. Yet, there is a base in the heart of our island which entails danger for us in case of war.

But is that the only danger? No. There is another danger that concerns us even more, since it is closer to home. The Revolutionary government of Cuba has repeatedly expressed its concern over the fact that the imperialist government of the United States may use that base, located in the heart of our national territory, as an excuse to promote an incident in order to justify an attack on our country. I repeat: the Revolutionary government of Cuba is seriously concerned – and makes known this concern – over the fact that the imperialist government of the United States of America may use a self-triggered aggression in order to justify an attack on our country. And this concern on our part is becoming increasingly greater because of the intensified aggressiveness that the United States is displaying.

For instance, I have here a United Press cable which came to my country and which reads as follows:

Admiral Arleigh Burke, United States Chief of Naval Operations, says that if Cuba attempts to take the Guantanamo Naval Base by force 'we will fight back'. In an interview for the magazine *U.S. News and World Report* Admiral Burke was asked if the navy was concerned about the situation in Cuba under Premier Fidel Castro.

'Yes, our navy is concerned – not about our base at Guantanamo, but about the whole Cuban situation,' Admiral Burke said. The Admiral added all the military services are concerned.

'Is that because of Cuba's strategic position in the Caribbean?' he was asked.

'No, not particularly,' Admiral Burke said. 'Here are a people normally very friendly to the United States, who liked our people and were also liked by us. In spite of this, an individual has appeared with a small group of fanatical Communists, determined to change all that. Castro has taught his people to hate the United States, and has done much to ruin his country.'

Admiral Burke said, 'We will react very fast if Castro makes any move against the Guantanamo base.'

'If they try to take the base by force, we will fight back,' he added.

Asked whether Soviet Premier Khrushchev's threat about retaliatory rockets gave Admiral Burke 'second thoughts about fighting in Cuba', the Admiral said:

'No, because he is not going to send his rockets. He knows quite well he will be destroyed if he does.'

He means that Russia will be destroyed.

In the first place, I must emphasize that, for this gentleman, to have increased industrial production in our country by thirty-five per cent, to have given employment to more than 200,000 Cubans, to have solved many of the social problems of our country, constitutes the ruination of our country. And in accordance with this line of reasoning, they assume the right to prepare the conditions of aggression.

So you see how conjectures are made – very dangerous conjectures, because this gentleman, in effect, thinks that in case of an attack on us we are to stand alone. This is just a conjecture by Mr Burke, but let us imagine that Mr Burke is wrong. Let us suppose, for just a moment, that Mr Burke, although an admiral, is mistaken. [VOICES OF THE SOVIET DELEGATION ARE HEARD, INCLUDING THAT OF KHRUSHCHEV] Then Admiral Burke is playing with the fate of the world in a most irresponsible manner. Admiral Burke and his aggressive, militarist clique are playing with the fate of the world, and it would really not be worth our while to worry over the fate of each of us, but we feel that we, as representatives of the various peoples of the world, have the duty to concern ourselves with the fate of the world, and we also have the duty to condemn all those who play irresponsibly with the fate of the world. They are not only playing with the fate of our people; they are playing with the fate of their people and with the fate of all the peoples of the world. Or does this Admiral Burke think we are still living in the times of the blunderbusses? Does he not realize, this Admiral Burke, that we are living in the atomic age, in an age whose disastrous and cataclysmic, destructive forces could not even be imagined by Dante or Leonardo da Vinci, with all their imagination, because this goes beyond the imagination of man. Yet, he made his conjectures, United Press International spread the news all over the world; the magazine is about to come out, hysteria is being created, the campaign is being prepared, the imaginary danger of an attack on the base is beginning to be publicized.

And this is not all. Yesterday a United States news bulletin appeared, containing some declarations by United States Senator Styles Bridges who, I believe, is a member of the Armed Services Committee of the Senate of the United States. He said:

'The United States should maintain its naval base of Guantanamo in Cuba at all costs'; and 'we must go as far as necessary to defend those gigantic installations of the United States. We have naval forces there, and we have the Marines, and if we were attacked, I would defend it, of course, because I believe it is the most important base in the Caribbean area.'

This member of the Senate Armed Forces Committee did not entirely reject the use of atomic weapons in the case of an attack against the base.

What does this mean? This means that not only is hysteria being created, not only is the atmosphere being systematically prepared, but we are even threatened with the use of atomic weapons. And, of course, among the many things that we can think of, one must ask this Mr Bridges whether he is not ashamed of himself to threaten a small country like Cuba with the use of atomic weapons.

As far as we are concerned, and with all due respect, we must tell him that the problems of the world cannot be solved by the use of threats or by sowing fear, and that our humble people, our little country, is there, what can we do about it? We are there, however much they dislike the idea, and our Revolution will go ahead, however much they dislike that. And our humble people must resign themselves to their fate. They are not afraid, nor are they shaken by this threat of the use of atomic weapons.

What does all this mean? There are many countries that have American bases on their territory, but they are not directed against the governments that made these concessions – at least, not as far as we know. Yet ours is the most tragic case. There is a base on our island territory directed against Cuba and the Revolutionary government of Cuba, in the hands of those who declare themselves enemies of our country, enemies of our Revolution, and enemies of our people. In the entire history of the world's present-day bases, the most tragic case is that of Cuba : a base imposed upon us by force, well within our territory, which is a good many miles away from the coast of the United States, an instrument used against Cuba and the Cuban people, imposed by the use of force, and a constant threat and a cause for concern to the people.

That is why we must state here that all these rumours of attacks are intended to create hysteria and prepare the conditions for an act of aggression against our country, that we have never spoken a single word implying the thought of any type of attack on the Guantanamo base, because we are the first in not wanting to give imperialism an excuse to attack us, and we state this categorically. But we also declare that from the very moment that base was turned into a threat to the security and peace of our country, a danger to our country, the Revolutionary government of Cuba has been considering very seriously requesting, within the framework of international law, the withdrawal of the naval and military forces of the United States from that portion of our national territory. And the imperialist government of the United States will have no alternative but to withdraw its forces, because how will it justify before the world its right to establish an atomic base or a base that is dangerous to our people in a part of our territory, within the well-defined limits of our island, the part of the world inhabited by the Cuban people. How can the Americans justify to the world any right to maintain and to hold sovereignty over part of our territory? How will they be able to stand before the world and justify such an arbitrary procedure? And since it will be unable to justify itself to the world, when our government requests it, within the framework of international law, the government of the United States will have to abide by the canons of international law.

But it is imperative that this Assembly be kept well informed regarding the problems of Cuba, because we have to be on the alert against deceit and confusion. We have to explain these problems very clearly, because with them go the security and the fate of our country. And that is why we want exact note to be taken of the words I have spoken, particularly when one takes into consideration the fact that the opinions or erroneous ideas of the politicians of this country as regards Cuban problems do not show any signs of improving. I have here some declarations by Mr Kennedy that would surprise anybody. On Cuba he says, 'We must use all the power of the Organization of American States to prevent Castro from interfering in other Latin American countries, and we must use all that power to return freedom to Cuba.' They are going to give freedom back to Cuba !

'We must state our intention,' he says, 'of not allowing the Soviet Union to turn Cuba into its Caribbean base, and of applying the Monroe Doctrine.' Halfway or more into the twentieth century, this gentleman speaks of the Monroe Doctrine !

'We must make Prime Minister Castro understand that we intend to defend our right to the Naval Base of Guantanamo.' He is the third who speaks of the problem. 'And we must make the Cuban people know that we sympathize with their legitimate economic aspirations ...' Why did they not feel sympathetic before? '... that we know their love of freedom, and that we shall never be happy until democracy is restored to Cuba ...' What democracy? The democracy 'made' by the imperialist monopolies of the government of the United States?

'The forces in exile that are struggling for freedom,' he says. Note this very carefully so that you will understand why there are planes flying from American territory over Cuba; pay close attention to what this gentleman has to say. 'The forces that struggle for liberty in exile and in the mountains of Cuba should be supported and assisted, and in other countries of Latin America, communism must be confined and not allowed to expand.'

If Kennedy were not an illiterate and ignorant millionaire, he would understand that it is not possible to carry out a revolution supported by landowners against the peasants in the mountains, and that every time imperialism has tried to encourage counterrevolutionary groups, the peasant militia has captured them in the course of a few days. But he seems to have read a novel or seen a Hollywood film about guerrillas, and he thinks it is possible to carry on guerrilla warfare in a country where the relations of the social forces are what they are in Cuba.

In any case, this is discouraging. Let no one think, however, that these opinions as regards Kennedy's statements indicate that we feel any sympathy towards the other one, Mr Nixon, who has made similar statements. As far as we are concerned, both lack political brains.

The case of Cuba is not an isolated one

Up to this point we have been dealing with the problem of our country, a fundamental duty of ours when coming before the United Nations, but we understand that it would be a little egotistical on our part if our concern were to be limited to our specific case alone. It is also true that we have used up the greater part of our time informing this Assembly about the Cuban case, and that there is not much time left for us to deal with the remaining questions to which we wish to refer briefly.

The case of Cuba is not an isolated one. It would be an error to think of it only as the case of Cuba. The case of Cuba is the case of all underdeveloped countries. The case of Cuba is like that of the Congo, Egypt, Algeria, Iran; like that of Panama, which wishes to have its canal; it is like that of Puerto Rico, whose national spirit they are destroying; like that of Honduras, a portion of whose territory has been alienated. In short, although we have not made specific reference to other countries, the case of Cuba is the case of all underdeveloped, colonialized countries.

The problems which we have been describing in relation to Cuba can be applied just as well to all of Latin America. The control of Latin American economic resources by the monopolies, which, when they do not own the mines directly and are in charge of extraction, as is the case with the copper of Chile, Peru, or Mexico, and with the oil of Venezuela – when this control is not exercised directly, it is because they are the owners of the public-utility companies, as is the case in Argentina, Brazil, Chile, Peru, Ecuador, and Colombia; or the owners of telephone services, which is the case of Chile, Brazil, Peru, Venezuela, Paraguay, and Bolivia; or they commercialize on our products, as is the case with coffee in Brazil, Colombia, El Salvador, Costa Rica, and Guatemala; or with the cultivation, marketing, and transportation of bananas by the United Fruit Company in Guatemala, Costa Rica, and Honduras; or with cotton in Mexico and Brazil. In other words, the monopolies control the most important industries. Woe to those countries the day they try to make an agrarian reform! They will be asked for immediate, efficient, and just payment. And if, in spite of everything, they make an agrarian reform, the representative of the friendly country who comes to the United Nations will be confined to Manhattan; they will not rent hotel space to him; insults will be heaped upon him, and it is even possible that he may be physically mistreated by the police.

The problem of Cuba is just an example of the situation in Latin America. And how long will Latin America wait for its development? It will have to wait, according to the point of view of the monopolies, until there are two Fridays in a week.

Who is going to industrialize Latin America? The monopolies? Certainly not. There is a report by the Economic Commission of the United Nations which explains how private capital, instead of going to the countries that need it most for the establishment of basic industries to contribute to their development, is being channelled preferentially to the more industrialized countries, because there, according to their beliefs, private capital finds greater security. And, of course, even the Economic Secretariat of the United Nations has had to admit that there is no possible chance for development through the investment of private capital — that is, through the monopolies.

The development of Latin America will have to be achieved through public investment, planned and granted unconditionally without any political strings attached, because, naturally, we all like to be representatives of free countries. None of us likes to represent a country that does not feel itself in full possession of its freedom.

None of us wants the independence of his country to be subjected to any interest other than that of the country itself. That is why assistance must be given without any political conditions.

That help has been denied to us does not matter. We have not asked for it. However, in the interest of and for the benefit of the Latin American peoples, we do feel duty bound, out of solidarity, to stress the fact that the assistance must be given without any political conditions whatsoever. There should be more public investments for economic development rather than for 'social development', which is the latest thing invented to hide the true need for the economic development of countries.

The problems of Latin America are similar to those of the rest of the world – to those of Africa and Asia. The world is divided up among the monopolies; the same monopolies that we find in Latin America are also found in the Middle East. There, the oil is in the hands of monopolistic companies that are controlled by France, the United States, the United Kingdom, the Netherlands – in Iran, Iraq, Saudi Arabia, Kuwait, in short, in all corners of the world. The same thing is true, for instance, in the Philippines and in Africa. The world has been divided among the monopolistic interests. Who would dare deny this historic truth? The monopolistic interests do not want to see the development of countries. What they want is to exploit the natural resources of the countries and the people themselves. And the sooner they recover or amortize the capital invested, the better.

The problems the Cuban people have had to face with the imperialistic government of the United States are the same which Saudi Arabia would face if it nationalized its oil, and this also applies to Iran or Iraq; the same problems that Egypt had when it quite justifiably nationalized the Suez Canal; the very same problems that Indonesia had when it wanted to become independent; the same surprise attacks as those against Egypt and the Congo.

Have colonialists or imperialists ever lacked a pretext when they wanted to invade a country? Never! Somehow they have always found a pretext. And which are the colonialist and imperialist countries? Four or five countries – no, four or five groups of monopolies are the owners of the wealth of the world.

If a being from another planet were to come to this Assembly, one who had read neither the *Communist Manifesto* of Karl Marx nor the cables of the United Press or the Associated Press or other monopolistic publications, if he were to ask how the world had been divided, and he saw on a map that the wealth of the world was divided among the monopolies of four or five countries, he would say, without further consideration, 'The wealth of this world has been badly distributed, the world is being exploited.'

Here in this Assembly, where the majority of the under-developed countries are represented, he would say : 'The majority of the peoples that you represent are being exploited; they have been exploited for a long time. The form of exploitation may have changed, but you are still being exploited.' That would be the verdict ...

CHAPTER 2

Economic Reform:
Cuba's Agrarian Reform*

The First Agrarian Reform Law, signed in La Plata in the Sierra Maestra on 17 May 1959, distributed land to the small farmers who cultivated food crops and tobacco and expropriated the large latifundios – turning the cattle ranches into granjas [state farms] and the cane farms into co-operatives. Since a handful of landowners had owned the lion's share of land – especially the cane-growing and cattle-grazing land – the effect was to take away from a tiny minority the control over the key productive resources of the country.

In this speech Fidel evaluates the First Agrarian Reform Law and explains why co-operatives, while a step forward over the past, retard the social development of the Revolution. He explains why keeping the large latifundios intact and not dividing up and distributing the land provided the opportunity for the mechanization of agriculture and the application of technology. More importantly, Fidel evaluates the role of the co-operatives in a society attempting to do away with privileges. The effect, he says, was to make the cane cutters, ' a great proletarian and exploited group of yesterday, cease being proletarian at the moment when the proletarian began to guide the destiny of the country'. That is, the co-operatives turned the cane cutters into property owners, employers, and businessmen, and led to the perpetuation of the speculative mentality that had long pitted man against man: hence the need to convert co-operatives into state farms.

The clear manner in which Fidel explains the historical role of

---

* Delivered at the closing of the National Congress of Cane Co-operatives, on 18 August 1962, 'Year of Planning'.

*the cane cutters, his absolute respect for them and their aspira-
tions, and the dignity that he tries to instil in them as proletarians,
all show the revolutionary character of Fidel's thought.*

In October 1963, a little more than a year after this speech was
delivered, the Second Agrarian Reform was passed. The law
limited landholdings to a maximum of 168 acres per landholder.
The Second Reform gave the state sector approximately seventy
per cent of the nation's total land, with the private sector holding the remaining thirty per cent. In terms of arable agricultural
lands the public-private ratio is closer to 60–40. Political considerations played an important part in bringing about the Second
Reform: the major domestic force against the Revolution, the
agrarian capitalist, was eliminated, and the major base of the
Revolution, the agrarian worker, was strengthened.

Delegates: We recall the history of the whole revolutionary
process in agriculture. This Congress which has just taken
place has great importance for the revolution, but perhaps its
importance is not as obvious today as it will be in the years to
come. I believe that this Congress represents a great step forward.

But it is necessary that all of you *compañeros*[1] who work in the
cane fields understand clearly why this signifies a great step forward. First of all, we ought to explain the first steps that were
taken in agriculture and why they were taken.

All of you who work in the cane plantations have a very clear
idea of what life was like in the countryside, above all on the
cane plantations.

When the Revolution triumphed, it was a fact that the first step
taken was the Agrarian Reform. You will remember when we began to speak of the Agrarian Reform, how the people immediately
began to be interested, even the workers in the cities.

It is possible that many people heard of the Agrarian Reform,
without, nevertheless, understanding what this meant. But finally
everyone realized that the reform was necessary, that the situation in the countryside could not continue, that a complete
change was needed in the conditions of life, work, and cultivation

---

1. Comrades.

of the land, that such a change would be beneficial to the *campesinos*.[2]

The Agrarian Reform is one of the most far-reaching tasks to which the Revolution set itself. It has also been one of the most difficult tasks. The problem of ownership and means of exploitation of the land is far more complex than the same problem in industry. The revolution of the system of industrial production, for example, is always much simpler than the revolution in the countryside.

In our countryside, two types of production centres existed: the large *latifundios* and the small farmers. The large *latifundios* exploited a considerable number of workers, especially the large cane *latifundios*. Among the small farmers there were certain distinct characteristics. The small farmer who was the owner of land was in the minority. Then there were the squatters, the cultivators of coffee and cocoa in the mountains, who, although they did not pay rent, always lived under the threat of eviction. There was also the farmer who paid rent, who, together with the squatters, constituted the great majority.

We were, therefore, confronted with two types of ownership of the land. There was the small farmer who worked his own land and there was the landlord who lived, in many cases, far from his lands and who employed at times hundreds of workers. The large *latifundios* like those of the United Fruit Company employed thousands of workers.

The basic outlines of the first revolutionary law that changed the system of production in the countryside were as follows: first, the liquidation of the *latifundios*; second, the liquidation of the rent system, that is to say the liberation of the *campesinos* from the rents that they were paying; third, to guarantee to the squatters the ownership of the land that they were occupying.

There remained the problem of how to make the great *latifundios* productive. It was talked about a great deal, and it was on everybody's tongue in a period when we could aspire only to partial triumphs, to partial solutions. It was a period when we

---

2. Tenant farmers, small landholders, landless rural labourers; in the past, generally the poorest of Cuban workers.

could not move forward with the Revolution on all fronts, but had to move in stages. In this period, much was said of the Agrarian Reform as simply a distribution of the lands. Many people saw the Agrarian Reform as nothing more than the distribution of land.

Fortunately, our Revolution had the good judgement and sufficient audacity to adopt a progressive system of cultivation of the land. Today that is very easy to understand.

Why we didn't divide the *latifundios*

The division of the *latifundios* could have destroyed the Revolution. Dramatic problems would have resulted from the division of these lands. First of all, there is the practical problem of dividing these lands, since all the lands have distinct characteristics. Within any *latifundio* some land is more fertile than other, some is used for one thing, some for another. From the political point of view, the easiest solution would have been the division of those lands; from the practical point of view, this would have been an inferior solution. Often what at one moment appears easiest is in the long run not the best.

The results that would have followed the division of these lands are understood by everyone. In the first place, there isn't enough land for everyone. We remember that when the agrarian law was proclaimed, someone suggested printed forms for those who wanted land. Why? Because everyone wanted land, even the people who lived in the cities.

If the *latifundios* had been divided, many workers would have been left without land, or on the other hand, the lots would have been too small for a family to subsist on.

Can you imagine, for example, a *latifundio* of one or two hundred *caballerías*[3] planted in rice, divided among three or four hundred families? Naturally, each would take possession of his parcel of land and would build his house there. Besides rice, he would wish to grow other foods and many other things. In any

---

3. About 33·2 acres per *caballería*.

rice *latifundio* the system of irrigation requires the flooding of up to thirty *caballerías*; therefore, we should have remained isolated like an island reef in the middle of flooded rice fields.

With sugar cane, more or less the same thing would have happened. With cattle it would have been even worse. The distribution of the cattle and the cattle ranches would have created one of the most serious problems of the Revolution.

First, it is hard to imagine the number of cattle that would have been sacrificed, especially with the present increase in the demand for meat. At the same time, the demand for shoes has also increased considerably, and, therefore, the demand for leather has increased.

We do not have the problem solved yet, but we have created all the conditions for the resolution of these problems. Today there is considerably less meat than the people wish to buy. It is obvious that to satisfy this demand we would have to sacrifice not only the fattened cattle, but also the cows and even the heifers and calves. In a word, if we were to kill all the cattle that the people today are able to buy, then in three or four years very few cattle would remain.

Another problem as a result of this policy would be a reduction in the number of hides available for the manufacture of shoes. You know about the difficulties in the production of shoes, nevertheless, only increased production will solve this problem. In this case, the production of meat from large animals is tied closely to the production of shoes.

Imagine the situation if we were to dispose of half the cattle we have, and could not say, like today, that year by year we can kill so many cattle, which will supply so much leather for so many pairs of shoes.

But that is not all. We have a programme for the development of the cattle herds through artificial insemination and through importation and selection of breeding stock.

To start a programme of insemination and selection in a large centre where there are hundreds of thousands of cattle does not present the same problems that would arise if there were tens or hundreds of thousands of small producers developing, for example, the beef herds. Also the breeding of hogs requires certain conditions; veterinarians, feeding houses, etc. It would be almost impossible to carry out a plan of rapid development where the land was divided into tens of thousands of farms, each with its own style, methods, and ideas. It would be the same for any programme of selection, of cultivation improvement, of irrigation. That is to say, production problems would represent an insurmountable situation.

We are not going to talk about other problems which are related to the agricultural workers, that is, to those who live in the country. If the *latifundios* had been divided, each one would have been divided, each one would have built his own *bohío* [4] on his own little piece of land; the school would have remained several kilometres from where the children live; the possibilities of electricity, suitable roads, sewage, recreation sites, and shopping centres would not have been realized.

None of the many towns that have appeared, that nevertheless are only a small part of what is really needed in the countryside, could have been built either. Bringing the comforts of city life to the countryside would never have been possible, i.e., the large school centres, artistic and cultural activities, running water, electricity, sewage, streets; in a word, everything that is done in a small town would have been impossible in the countryside, since such small towns can be built only when the land is cultivated collectively.

Besides this, the division of the land would have had other economic, political, and social consequences. It is a fact that today there is a great demand for products which as a result of drought, poor administration, and errors, agricultural production did not increase in proportion to the demand. We see, as a result, some speculation in agricultural products and more or less exorbitant prices.

Where does it occur and how does it happen? Why? Why does meat keep its price? Why do these staple articles not vary in price? Why do pork products keep their price? Why aren't three turkeys worth fifty pesos? Why don't they sell four chickens for twenty pesos in the cities? Why? Because those products come

---

4. Squatter's shack.

from the *Granjas*.[5] Because the beef which is used in the cities was raised on the *Granjas*! Because those fowl were raised on the *Granjas*! Because the agricultural products of the *Granjas* come to the towns and cities, to the workers, at reasonable and stable prices.

The nation can count on those products because they go from the production centres to the distribution centres. What are the products which become objects of speculation? They are the products cultivated on the small isolated plots.

What happened, for example, to the *malanga*[6] from Rancho Mundito in Pinar del Río, *malanga* which was sown with loans given by the Revolution, on land which was distributed by the Revolution? The *campesinos* made use of the money; they sowed and they produced, but what happened then? The Revolutionary government, in order to avoid annoyances for the independent producers, authorized the *campesinos* to sell on the open market. What happened? Everyone with a car and money went to Rancho Mundito to buy *malanga*, some for their own use, others for purposes of speculation.

The result was that the area which supplied *malanga* for the children of Havana sold 300,000 pounds of *malanga* in a single Sunday, directly to the people from the city, enough *malanga* for the children of Havana for several days.

And what was the result of this? The person who went with his car and bought a hundredweight of *malanga* was assured of the supply for his own children for several weeks. The speculator, who gained by reselling, forced families who could find no *malanga* in the stores to pay three and four times the regular price. And the children of families who had no car and who could not afford to pay three or four times the regular price had to go without.

In the face of shortages, the speculator was always present, offering much higher prices and creating difficulties for the whole population. What is even worse, the speculator was corrupting

5. A state-owned farm, in contrast to co-operatives composed of individual private landholders.

6. Farinaceous root popular in Cuba.

the *campesino*, awakening excessive ambitions, ambitions which they are not able to satisfy without causing suffering for the rest of the citizens. No individual in society can disregard the needs of others; no one can disregard others.

Anyone, then, who lives at the expense of others is acting in an anti-social and unjust way. He forgets that he needs others, because the one who produces a specific crop and wishes to sell for ten times the proper price would not like, for example, to smoke a cigar that cost him ten times more than the regular price. He would not like to pay ten times more for shoes and clothing than is just; nor would he like it if the kerosene or the medicine which he gets, or the rice, beans, salt, sugar, the thousand products which he needs to live, cost him ten times more than they should. If we forget this, we forget, in short, that we all work for others and we all need the work of others.

Who benefits from speculation?

So we see that within society articles of every type are needed – how even here at this gathering, we need electric lights and the chairs on which you are sitting. There were workers, carpenters, decorators, who organized all this. The clothes that you wear, the shoes, the room where you sleep, the meals they serve you, the trains in which you travel; they are products of the work of others. We would not have light; we would not have telephones; we would not have transportation, gasoline, clothing, or shoes if each one kept what he produced. We would have no medicine, no teachers, no doctors, no mail. We would have practically nothing, because it is an elemental truth that we are all dependent on the work of others. If someone receives ten times the just price for something he produces, then he is stealing from others.

Anyone who wishes to sell an article for ten times what it costs to produce and to buy what he uses for a just price, cannot do so without robbing the rest of the citizens. And when a bourgeois from the city comes in his automobile and offers a *campesino* ten dollars for a hundred pounds of *malanga* instead of four dollars which is more or less the proper price, a price which is in line with what other workers can pay for the article, the bourgeois corrupts the *campesino* with a price three or four times more than he thought was possible. He does this calmly, like a person doing the right thing, because he has the right to sell that food for ten dollars or even fifteen dollars; or he goes to the highway and sells three turkeys for fifty dollars.

The *campesino* does not understand these things. In his lifetime he has been concerned only with the accumulation of money, because he lived in a society where money was everything. And who are the ones who eat this high-price food? Who are the ones who eat fried turkey? The rich! The bourgeois in the cities!

When an eighty-pound pig sells for eighty dollars, what worker can afford to buy pork? The worker who earns only eighty dollars or one hundred dollars per month, so that sugar, salt, and meat can be produced cheaply for the whole nation, that worker cannot eat pork or turkey, his children cannot eat *malanga* simply because only the ones with cars and eighty or one hundred dollars have large incomes or profits and who, besides, produce absolutely nothing, can go to the countryside.

I think everyone here understands these things, especially you workers who have worked all your lives! You understand these things perfectly!

The result! The rich who remain, live well; but this is not the worst. They sow greed, ambition, corruption, and demoralization among the small farmers. The small farmer is a humble man who is a worker, not a parasite. But the parasite cannot be a parasite if along the way he is not committing acts of parasitism, sowing parasitism, and creating parasites wherever he goes. He is not satisfied with being a parasite; he must turn the *campesino* into a parasite also.

All this does not happen on a *Granja*. With all the deficiencies, with all the errors, with all the things badly done, this does not happen on a *Granja*. If there are *caballerías* of *malanga*, no bourgeois is allowed to come and offer ten dollars for one hundred pounds. No speculator can go there to buy at a higher price in order to rob the workers afterwards. The people can count on the ten *caballerías* there; all the children can count on a fair price.

In the same way, the worker of that farm has the right to buy industrial products at a fair price: cigars, tobacco, all the food which is not produced on that farm; clothing, shoes, medicines, transportation, everything is sold to him at a fair price.

I have enumerated, therefore, some distinct consequences. If the *latifundios* had been divided, not only would production have dropped in a significant way, but we would have been left without a base to develop our agricultural economy rapidly! We would have been unable to reduce unemployment in the country. Not only that; the staple commodities would have been in short supply and speculation would have been rampant.

Another thing is also very clear; it is common for a *Granja* in the Havana area to produce with hundreds of workers one to two thousand litres of milk. We can say with all certainly that if this milk were sold on the open market the people of Havana would not be assured of a supply of milk. But all this milk should not be consumed on the farm; the remainder must be used by the rest of the population, by the workers and their families who live in the cities. All the milk is not consumed on the farm; part of it is distributed and the farm worker reasons 'that milk is lacking in the city, we cannot leave the city without milk'. This could not be done if the *latifundios* had been divided, because the private producer first consumes all that he needs. After he has satisfied his own needs he sells the surplus to the highest bidder, because – imagine – he still does not understand his social obligations; the products are in their hands.

I do not wish to go into detail at this time, for example, of the problem of sending thousands of young people to study in the Soviet Union. It is much easier to make arrangements with *Granjas* or co-operatives than with six hundred individual farmers.

Rural unemployment liquidated

From every point of view, and today we see it with total clarity, it was a great thing, a great step, when the Revolution turned the *latifundios* into collective centres of production; in spite of all the difficulties, all the deficiencies at every turn, it was a great step.

You know that rural unemployment has been liquidated. You

know that the problem now is a shortage of labour in many parts of the country. Now you know all that you know that no longer have you to seize the *matulito*,[7] the *saquito*, carrying in your arms and taking by the hand your starving children – to go pick coffee or to emigrate to faraway places, or to look for a political boss who could hand out a public works job, or who would buy your vote to be cast for some shameless politician. Now it is not necessary to do that.

For that reason, those *campesinos* who, like yourselves, came from the *latifundios*, went as squatters into the precarious mountains to sow coffee. The coffee was cultivated in the mountains because the cane and cattle *latifundios* devoured all the good land, and were not interested in coffee. If there is coffee in Cuba today, it is thanks to those *campesinos*, who, during the 'dead period' (when there was no work in the cane fields) when thousands of workers were hungry, scaled the mountains. Thanks to them there is coffee.

This coffee, which was in remote places, could be picked because there were tens and hundreds of thousands of men in the countryside who were out of work.

The Revolution resolved the fundamental problem of unemployment in the countryside, resolved it because it neither distributed nor divided those *latifundios*, thereby permitting the mechanization of agriculture. But now the Revolution has another problem; who picks the coffee?

But the Revolution finds solutions for everything, because the Revolution by its own deeds draws upon fresh forces; by its own deeds finds new resources. And, like the workings of the Revolution, this itself is an extraordinary development. Tens of thousands of young people are studying, their entire expenses are paid by the nation. The Revolution mobilizes these young people, mobilizes their energy – just as it mobilized them when they went to teach in the mountains – and resolves the problems with their resources and group energy.

For this reason, the *campesinos* are not left now with no one to pick their coffee. They don't have to worry because their

7. Small bag containing personal possessions.

brothers now have work on the prairies, because the Revolution finds solutions for the problems of all. The *campesino* should not complain about the good fortune of his brothers, because he will have someone to pick the coffee.

Thus we see that despite the many shortages, and they are many, something has been done, changes have been made. As we look back on our difficulties and errors, we must apply new means. We are not yet beginning to ascend, but already we have walked part way uphill. Now we do not have the problems of the first days, the problems there were in the beginning. There are problems, yes, but problems that correspond to a stage where we have overcome many of the past evils.

Co-operatives and state farms

How did we go about organizing production in the countryside? What did we do? The *latifundios* were not divided, but collective centres of production were established. Two types appeared: the co-operatives in the cane fields; and *Granjas* in the cattle and rice *latifundios*, and on the virgin lands.

The Revolution took a bold step when it did not redistribute the *latifundios*. The two types of collective agricultural organization, the co-operatives and the *Granja*, have developed side by side.

From the cane *latifundios*, more than 600 Cane Co-operatives have been organized. From the cattle *latifundios* and virgin lands, more than 300 *Granjas* have been organized or constructed.

You all know, *compañeros*, how much interest we have shown in the meetings that have been held, the courage we have demonstrated in trying to advance the co-operatives. Who here is not aware of the initiative that was shown in placing a dairy in each co-operative, the credits that were given, the improvements that were planned, the towns, the solution of the housing problem?

Naturally, many of these things were impossible to solve in such a brief space of time, such as the problem of housing.

Many courses have been organized to produce mechanics, agricultural technicians. You know that there is not a single co-operative where many young people have not gone away to study.

These two parallel systems have been subjected to the test of reality. The co-operative is a collective centre distinct from the *Granja*. The *Granja* is like a factory, the farmer like a worker in a factory; the co-operative worker is like a member of a group of workers who works for his own benefit and not for the benefit of the nation.

It is logical that the bookkeeping of the one type would be different from the other. If the co-operative worker works for his own benefit, then he receives only the land free, not the investments. The investment, the machinery, must be paid for. Housing must also be his own responsibility. If the product is going to be his, the instruments of production, the investments, the housing, all must be paid for.

The case of the worker on the *Granja* is different. In the first place he does not have to pay for the machinery, the investments. But there is something more : the Revolution decided that housing would not have to be paid for either, nor electricity and water.

Now we see the difference. Because the worker on the *Granja* works for the benefit of the nation, he has the right to receive the instruments of production as well as all the possible benefits that the nation can give. Not so with the co-operative worker : for him there must be a charge.

During the initial stages of building the co-operative centres, therefore, credit was required for the construction of the towns. Many years of work will be required to pay for the investments, the machinery, the housing. Naturally, if this is not accompanied by high productivity, and if the people live well in the meantime, then many years will be required to pay for everything. How long cannot be known precisely.

It was logical also, on the other hand, that if the state imported 10,000 head of milk-producing cattle, they would not take them to the co-operative, but rather to the *Granjas*, where the products are for the whole nation. If we import 20,000 hogs, they too must be taken to the *Granjas*. Equipment for artificial insemination of cattle and special seeds must first be taken to the *Granjas*. If we introduce new techniques, such as hybrid corn, they must first go to the *Granjas*. We would even say that the workers on the *Granjas* should be the first to get houses, because they work for the nation as a whole while the co-operative worker works for his own benefit.

But there was also another problem which we did not have on the *Granjas*. Those who worked on the *Granjas* did not exploit anyone. Everyone was equal. But on the co-operatives, a problem existed, where a determined number of people were co-operativists (members of the co-operative who shared in the profits), what were the others? Second-class citizen workers; marginal ones. They were nothing. Since they were not co-operativists, they were workers and the co-operativists were employers. When profits were distributed, they received nothing. The co-operativists got the first houses and other advantages.

Since agriculture requires more labour at certain times of the year than at others, it is sad to think that now the rural worker is similar to the martyrs of the pre-revolutionary period of exploitation. The Revolution came, and although things are much better now than what they had been, nevertheless, this situation is hard to accept with resignation.

There remained in the countryside an outcast; he who was not a co-operativist, was nothing. Why? Because he was ashamed, he was different from others. Nevertheless his needs were the same as the others, and therefore, he ought to have the same rights.

It is true that although a great step forward had been made, that forward step did not correspond entirely to the Revolution's idea of justice.

Who had suddenly become, at times, a semi-exploiter of the work of others? Old workers! A contradiction exists here: the *latifundio* has been liquidated and this is a great forward step; but at the same time a group of proletarians, one of the most combative, most inured to war and most revolutionary – as was the cane worker – had lost their position as proletarians. The Revolution was taking a backward step.

And where were the agricultural workers who were the most revolutionary, the most long-suffering, the best fighters? They were not on the cattle *latifundios*, managed by a few labourers. Traditionally, the group with the best fighting spirit, the most revolutionary of the agricultural proletariat, was the cane worker, the workers of the cane *latifundios*. When the Revolution was becoming more proletarian; when the country moved forward to the great moment when its destiny was not in the hands of the bourgeois exploiters, nor of the imperialist filibusters; at the moment when the proletariat began to guide the destiny of the country, a great proletarian and exploited group of yesterday ceased being proletarian.

For you, *compañeros* – although the co-operative was a forward step over the past, more just than the *latifundios*, a forward step for the nation – for you, from the point of view of your class, for you from the point of view of historical importance, taking into account the class that you belong to, for you the co-operative was a backward step.

I am sure that in the mind of each one of you is indelibly engraved all of the past – the past – of leaders, of rural guards, of unscrupulous politicians, of gamblers, of *boliteros*,[8] of grafters of every type. You who have deeply engraved in your mind the memory of that hungry past, the past of suffering and humiliated workers, you would not have thought that the day would come when your children would study in a university or in foreign lands. How could a worker have thought of becoming an administrator, of coming to the capital to discuss problems, one of those who are sent from their place of work to discuss with the Ministers, with the government, to express their opinions, to participate actively in the affairs of the country? You who remember that past, I am sure, if you were asked to renounce your position as proletarians to become semi-exploiters, I am sure that you would all say: 'No, we will not renounce our proletarian position. We now, more than ever, wish to be proletarians, because in our hands is the destiny of our country. We wish to change it into a better world, without exploiters or exploited of any kind.'

That, *compañeros*, is the way we must think. To be a proletarian is an honour and title above any other in our society; more than material advantages you may be able to acquire.

Yesterday it was the owner of the *latifundio*; yesterday the

---

8. Operators of private lotteries; professional gamblers.

Yankee was the boss and made the 'shape-up'[9] every day. Today, he with the highest honour, the master of our country, is not the Yankee, nor is it the landlord exploiter. It is the proletarian !

The co-operatives have fulfilled their usefulness. They had deficiencies, great deficiencies. Each of the two types of production has been tested. Is it not correct to take one more forward step, a step that will bring together all the workers of the countryside, the workers of the *Granjas* and you [co-operativists] and those who work with you in the cane fields but who are not co-operativists?

Agricultural working-class advance

With this step, the agricultural proletariat begins to advance, becomes the most numerous sector of the working class in our country – great in size, number, and importance – because altogether, on the co-operatives, and on the *Granjas*, there are more than 250,000 workers. With this step, the Revolution will have 250,000 rural proletarians, a great and formidable force for the Revolution.

When the small independent farmer unites in order to produce more economically, he advances. For that reason, the true co-operative is one which is formed from independent producers who are not proletarians. The small farmer is the one who is attached to the land, to his small plot of ground. He has a feeling of ownership that the proletariat does not have, that the land is his world; he does not have the advanced mentality of the proletariat. When he joins with others, that is a forward step for him and for the Revolution.

Nearly 300 Agricultural Societies of Farmers have been created, resulting in the joining of lands.

Now this is a very complex problem, because the *campesino* does not have the same mentality as he who has been, or is, a worker. The *campesino* has a different outlook; he does not have

---

9. Morning assembly of workers at which the overseer chose those who would work for the day and assigned them tasks.

the same level of culture, or above all, of political consciousness which the worker has. It is necessary to march with the *campesino*, who is an ally of the working class. We must go to the *campesino* each time raising his consciousness, each time making him more revolutionary, each time more advanced. For this, it is necessary to have a correct policy. With proper leadership, the *campesino* will move spontaneously towards superior forms of production. The *campesino* cannot be socialized or co-operativized by force or compulsion.

Neither by force nor compulsion

No, that campesino must be allowed to develop little by little until, of necessity, there will no longer be any workers looking for a boss. When the *Granjas* encompass all labour, then the yoke of oxen will not do. It will be necessary to mechanize everything; then the campesino will see that by uniting forces with other *campesinos* he will have more strength, more possibilities, and will be able to produce more. Then he will march forward.

The day will come when no one will want to work for a boss. That day will come and it is now a reality in many places, when all farmers will move towards the *Granjas*, to remunerative work and to all the benefits of the *Granja*. Not the *Granja* of today, because we still lack an infinite number of things. Now there are many problems to solve, even such basic ones as housing. No, the centres which are now being created, the communities, the towns which the *campesinos* will have, the life in these communities will, in every way, be comparable to life in the cities.

Here, today, in this theatre some agricultural workers entertained us with their songs and with their artistic achievements. Thousands of instructors are being trained now to make these possibilities a reality on the *Granjas* and in the countryside, where life is isolated, tedious, often boring. They will organize the life of the future where highly productive work will alternate with many other pleasant things which will make the life of our *campesinos* much better : a healthy, happy life, a life of work, healthy diversions, sports, and recreation.

The day will come when lamps will no longer be used; the day will come when many of the things that are seen now only in the cities, will be seen on the farms as well. And that day is not so far off, not so far that you will not see it.

That is what we must think about, because that is what we must struggle for. Not now, now in the pale shadow of the future, although life today is much better than in the past, but tomorrow, a tomorrow which is not far off.

Think where we would be today, if this could have been said forty or sixty years ago when the Republic was born. Then the Revolution would not have had to dedicate a whole year to the problem of a million illiterates. Our countryside would now be full of riches, of comfort, and conveniences.

It is clear that we Cubans were not ready for this sixty years ago, and for that reason we have these problems today. Nevertheless, we can now say : we are beginning ! For this reason we will have in the future what we do not have today, what the previous generations could not do for us.

Is this, or is this not, the way a people ought to think? Is it, or is it not, the way everyone ought to think? You know that these are not simply words; you know it because now, in your children, you see that which you would have liked to have when you were children. There are many of you who say : 'What wouldn't I give to be your age today; the opportunities that you now have which I did not have !'

When parents who could not even go to school – who walked barefoot, who perhaps even saw a little brother left to die, without a doctor, without help – when they look at their children with hope, and above all with assurance as you all do, who could hesitate or doubt it, what parent today doesn't think that his child has a secure future? What parent today doesn't know that his child will have a very different future from the one he had? What parent doesn't know that his child will become all that he wishes, that he will reach the highest places in skills, in culture, and in work, that all opportunities will be open to him? Now there is no longer even the fear that so many parents have when they ask, 'What will become of my children if I lose my life?'

Thousands of young *campesinos* are now studying. If there are not more in our institutes, in our technical schools, in our universities, it is simply because most *campesinos* did not go beyond second or third grade. That is why there are not more *campesinos* in the secondary grades; that is why there are not more *campesinos* in the universities. Nevertheless, soon it will not be like this, because soon he will be able to go as far in school as he wishes.

And if there are not enough teachers? I can now say that the appeal made by the Revolutionary government for 4,500 students for the pre-vocational school of Minas del Río has met with a response of 8,000 applications.

Although our schools might have deficiencies, teachers deficient in some case and even teachers who do not teach, it will not be this way in the future, because everything is being built from the ground up. And although there are not thousands of young people from the countryside in our universities, there are thousands of young agricultural workers studying. And this year, in the next few weeks, we will have 2,000 students in the Soviet Union studying problems of administration, of machinery, of agricultural technique, and 3,500 studying problems of administration in the capital.

Therefore, these 5,500 students added to other schools of this type, which were already functioning, form a total of 6,000 young farm labourers. If we add the School of Insemination, the School of Revolutionary Instruction, and the Young Campesinos to this figure, this makes a contingent of more than 10,000 young *campesinos*. That is, 10,000 young people coming from the centres of the *Granjas* and from the old Cape Co-operatives. Ten thousand!

This gives you some idea of how opportunities are opening up everywhere for a young worker to become a technician, for a young worker to become a director of an agricultural enterprise; that now it is not the Yankee master, nor the exploiting landowner, but the young who have merit and capability. Because if there is something that we ought to understand, it is the necessity to form competent examples, to shape men, so that they will not fall into our errors and our faults.

What is it? You know! If there have been many faults, many

errors, what other way is there to overcome them? No one is born with knowledge, and many men who were called upon to a certain job that they were not able to do, were not even able to say that they did not know.

And the guilt we ourselves cannot brush aside either, because we ourselves are guilty. If within the next few years there are no perfectly capable and competent men, then we ourselves must accept the blame. But the guilt will not fall on us, because we know what we are doing. We know that in the future we will not have the difficulties, we will not lack the elementary things that we lack today.

Today, it is the bitter gift of hard work, suffering, and patience, which requires all the fortitude of revolutionaries, encouraged by a tomorrow which we know will be very different, when the masses of young people, truly prepared, become part of the task, become part of the force.

Tomorrow there may be other problems, corresponding to new stages of progress. All that is lacking today, will be abundant tomorrow. But it is not a question of days, nor of weeks, nor of months. It is a question of years!

Of course, we all wish that tomorrow were here; we all wish it immediately, but nothing like that happens in real life. The seed does not bud sooner by wishing. It always takes years. Thus, as the parents look at their children, at the little one recently born, they are not impatient. They care for him, knowing that someday they will have a man in the family. Thus, also with the faith that we have, that work today, the work of looking after the Revolution, will create tens of thousands, hundreds of thousands, yes, millions of new men for the family of Cuba.

Only with work and sacrifice

There are many things about which we ought to think seriously and responsibly. There are many evils, defects, vices against which we still must struggle in order to merit a better future, which can be accomplished only by sacrifice. We will not accomplish it by sleeping in the shade; we will not accomplish it if we are like vagabonds or loafers. Abundance of all that we wish, of all that we need, can be attained only with sweat, with work, and with sacrifice.

For that reason, *compañeros*, we must take the spirit of the Revolution and of truth to all the workers of our country. We must make them conscious of the duty of work, and of the fact that work is not a punishment but a necessity in the life of man. That which makes a man a man, and distinguishes him from the others, and makes him lord and master of nature, is work.

The vagabonds do not progress. The vagabonds will not help us to liberate ourselves from want and misery. For that reason, it is necessary to create a devotion to work, to see work as it is and not as a punishment. In the past, work was an instrument of exploitation of man. Today, it is an instrument for the redemption of man, for the elevation of man, for the progress of man.

We know that there are many things to overcome, many deficiencies, many things which grieve us, errors which grieve us, weaknesses which grieve us, carelessness which grieves us, as, for example, uncultivated lands and shortages of agricultural products caused by carelessness, because those in the front line have not been attentive, have not listened, have not paid attention to plans.

With an attentive eye on all problems, we fight to conquer them the way we resolve the problems of supplies, without stepping backward. We use as an example the problem of the supplies of those products themselves. We have thought much about this problem and have discussed what should be done. Should we give a plot of land? No. Because he who has a small plot wishes a larger plot later; his animals multiply and he no longer has three, he has ten or twenty or fifty, and the worker turns into a *latifundista*, because every herdsman must have pasture for his particular herd. No! We must not use these methods which encourage the abandonment of the obligations of work. We must not go to individualism which encourages egotism, which encourages inequalities among men; we must go to the collective.

How do we resolve the problem of housing? It is impossible now to build houses for all. It is necessary then, in order to resolve this problem, not to be too ambitious. We must spend whatever we can to resolve the problem of a place to live at least, even though that dwelling is not as good as the houses being constructed in the towns, because the housing problem cannot be solved in one year.

Each and every one of these problems must be looked after. But how? By thinking of the future, thinking of the interests of the nation, thinking of the interests of all the workers. This is how we must think, because if we are all dependent on others, if no one can depend only on himself, then we must always think of the interests of all. If one concerns himself not only with his own needs, but with the needs of others, then others will look out for the needs of the individual.

Thus, we must discuss, not with orders and commands, but with reason and truth; because faced with the truth, faced with what is reasonable, no one can oppose; faced with what is just, no one can be opposed. Always with reason, always with what is just, always discussing, always teaching, never imposing, but persuading, with you participating.

From among you must come your union leaders. Now, at last, we can reply to the question, which has been asked many times: 'Why don't we have a union?' Indeed, you will have unions, your union leaders, the Technical Advisory Councils will come from among you. In the future, more and more of you will become leaders. And finally, from you, from the mass of the proletariat, will come those who will advance the countryside. You will display the maximum interest, responsibility, sense of duty, patriotism; thinking of the nation, thinking of our great people, who, united, must march forward, who, united, must conquer their future. Thus, each time we are more aware of our social debts; each time less egotistic; each time more brotherly; each time more stripped of the dead weight of the voices of the past, to continue adapting our thinking and our actions to the present and to the future.

We trust in you, cane workers; we trust in the revolutionary spirit of the great masses. We know that you will put forth the maximum effort in the face of the present difficulties. We know that you will assert yourself in the face of weakness, the spirit of laziness, and before those who do not feel a sense of duty, those who do not understand the great truth; that work is the most honourable activity of man, the most fundamental necessity of man; that work makes men out of us.

Let us work for all, so that all will work for each one of us.

Patria o Muerte! Venceremos!

CHAPTER 3

Counter-Revolution :
'The Whole Nation On the March,
Afraid of Nothing.'*

The land reform programme had heightened foreign, i.e., American, opposition, and intensified the anxiety and the active opposition of the former ruling class of Cuba. It also served as the first real class issue that would define the political direction of the Revolution. The high degree of local autonomy involved in the implementation of the Reform Law served to separate the right from the left within the 26 July Movement. The desertion in October of a leading moderate, Major Hubert Matos, as well as the replacement in November of another leading moderate, Felipe Pazos, by Che Guevara as director of the National Bank, indicated what class politics mean: major changes created new enemies and consolidated new alliances.

The land reform broadened peasant support and alienated important parts of the bourgeoisie and the United States. This in turn created the necessity for further radicalization of the Revolution in order to prevent its being toppled by this opposition. As the example of Guatemala demonstrated, a revolution that did not arm its people would quickly be overthrown. Thus, a revolutionary cycle defines itself: economic changes that make powerful enemies, the need to defend those changes by arming the population, and then more reforms to keep pace with the rising revolutionary temper of a people who for the first time feel some power over their lives.

---

* Delivered in front of the Presidential Palace in Havana on 26 October 1959 at a rally to protest the bombing of Cuba by planes from the US.

Concretely, opposition to Castro by the United States and former Batistianos (the principal fighting opposition at that time) meant air attacks – strafing and dropping incendiary bombs – on sugar-cane fields by planes based in Florida. The United States claimed it could do nothing to stop these attacks and it refused to sell arms to the Cuban government to defend itself. The British government agreed to sell jets to the Cuban government but reneged, under American pressure, on 16 October. In September, Washington recalled its ambassador for two weeks. According to the New York Times (5 September 1959) this was done to emphasize Washington's 'displeasure' at three actions of the Cuban government: the Agrarian Reform Law, the intervention of the Cuban Telephone Company, and the reduction in rates of the Cuban Telephone Company. On 21 October Major Díaz Lanz flew a plane from Florida over Havana, dropping leaflets and incendiary bombs. In response to the heightened foreign aggression and the defections within Cuba, a popular militia, an arming of the whole population, was begun at the end of October 1959: only a government supremely confident of the support of the masses of people would dare to incorporate them into popular militias.

In this speech Fidel recalls the overwhelming odds that faced that small group of twelve men who began the armed struggle against Batista and says how much stronger the Revolution is today – that neither the forces of reaction nor the United States can overturn an armed and determined people. The confidence, the sense of struggle and determination, the sheer audacity to take on such mighty adversaries – all are part of the reason the Cuban Revolution has survived, where the reformist governments of Arbenz in Guatemala and Juan Bosch in the Dominican Republic have failed.

At this time, Fidel not only urges the people onward to victory, but he clearly identifies the Revolution with the Cuban nation and the Cuban people. 'When we speak of struggle, the people means the unredeemed masses, to whom all make promises and whom all deceive,' he had said in his trial after the abortive attack on the Moncada barracks in 1953. It is in these militant nationalistic terms that Fidel defined the Revolution in its early days: 'the

people and the nation opposed to the foreign interests.' A defini-
tion of the struggle in terms of class did not yet predominate.

... Why do they attack us? Why? That's the thing the people must ask themselves – the thing they must meditate upon not only to understand the attack itself but to understand everything else in relation to that attack. In order to understand the problems outside and inside of our country; in order to understand the aggressions from outside and the treason on the inside. Because so much of the aggression directed at us from foreign territory, like treason, has one explanation; a simple one: the Revolution. The revolutionary process rubs powerful interests the wrong way, and those interests affected by the Revolution refuse to accept it peacefully.

The people are with us

What has the Revolutionary government done? The one thing that the Revolutionary government can be accused of is of making revolutionary laws, the only thing that the Revolutionary government can be accused of is of taking revolutionary measures. Because we can expose our conduct to the light, we are able to exhibit our deeds before the eyes of the people. Why are the people with us? The people are not with us for purely sentimental reasons; the people are with the Revolutionary government because we have made revolutionary laws. Why are the peasants with the Revolutionary government? Why is the great majority of the people with the Revolutionary government? Why do the people defend the Revolutionary government? Simply because we have been defending the people, because we have been dictating revolutionary measures.

Let us publicly discuss this and once and for all, and respond to those slanderers and detractors of the Revolution, so that they will take off their masks, so that they will say that their accusations of us as communists arise because they don't have the courage to admit they are against the Revolutionary Laws. Then, as they can have nothing further to say or to accuse the Revolutionary government with ...

What must be analysed is the Revolutionary government's actions, and what the people must be asked is if they are in agreement with everything the Revolutionary government has done [SHOUTS OF 'YES, YES'] ...

I ask the people if they are or they aren't in agreement with the fact that we have established the most honourable administration they have ever known in their history [SHOUTS OF APPROVAL THROUGHOUT] ... I ask the people if they are or they aren't in agreement with the fact that the Revolutionary government has put an end to smuggling ... if they are or they aren't in agreement with the fact that the Revolutionary government has put an end to a public administration by the bottle and graft ... I ask the people if they are or are not in accord with the fact that the Revolutionary government has not gambled with the life of the country as was done before, if they are or they are not in accord with the fact that the Revolutionary government has shot the war criminals. I ask the people if they are or they are not in agreement with what the Revolutionary government has done towards recovering the wealth of the landlords who got rich during the Tyranny[1] ... if they are or they are not in agreement with the fact that the Revolutionary government has converted the Bureau of Investigation into a park and the Military Camp into a centre of learning which the people so badly need ...

I ask the people if they are or they are not in agreement with the fact that the Revolutionary government has turned the Regimental Quarters into places of learning ... if they are or they are not in agreement with the annulment of the contract the Tyranny made with the Telephone Company ... with the fact that the cost of medicines is reduced, with the fact that electric tariffs are reduced ... with the fact that 10,000 more posts have been formed for rural teachers ... I ask the people whether or not they are in agreement with the fact that a Bank of Social Security

---

1. Régime of Fulgencio Batista.

has been created ... with the fact that tourism is developing on a grand scale, a source of pride for our country ... I ask the people whether or not they agree with the fact that we have established for the workers their own unions and all the social unions which the Tyranny eliminated ... whether or not they are in agreement with the reduction of rents ... if they are in agreement with the fact that we have given boats to the fishermen so they could live off the product of their work and not be exploited ... If they are in agreement or not with the fact that the Cuban Revolution has organized Consumers Farm Co-operatives in order to change the double rates peasants had to pay for their goods ... I ask the people if they are or they are not in agreement with the Agrarian Reform. [OVATION]

The best friend of the peasants

I ask the people if they are or they are not in agreement with the fact that the peasants should own the lands they work on. With the fact that the peasants and the miners of the Zapata marshes, the Guanahacabibes Peninsula, of Belice or of Yateras, and of the other corners of Cuba should have co-operatives to sell their coal and not be victims of exploitation. If they are in agreement or not with the fact that we have constructed schools and roads and highways in every corner of Cuba. If they are in agreement or not with the fact that we have constructed houses for the peasant families and raised their standard of living. I ask the people if they are or they are not in agreement with the old system of the Rural Guard and the guards that were in the service of the large landowners and the powerful interests; [SHOUTS OF 'NO'] or if they are in agreement with the Rebel army [SHOUTS OF 'YES'] ... which is, today, the best companion and friend of the peasants because it acts with justice and because it serves exclusively the interest of the people. I ask the people if they are or are not in agreement with the fact that we have re-populated the Cuban countryside which had remained desolated thanks to the egoism and ambition of the great landowners. I ask the people if they are in agreement or not with the fact that we are searching into these lands to find natural resources for the industralization of the country. I ask the people if they are or are not in agreement with the Revolutionary government ... [SHOUTS OF 'YES'] with the fact that instead of Cadillacs what the country needs is tractors. [SHOUTS OF 'YES'] I ask the people whether they are or are not in agreement with the fact that we are planting rice here instead of importing it; planting grain, cotton; with the fact that we can produce foodstuffs here instead of importing them, in order to give work to a half million of our compatriots who don't have jobs. [APPLAUSE]

Dealing privileges and injustices a blow

I ask the people if they are or are not in agreement with the Revolutionary government's plans for industrialization. Then I ask myself what has the Revolutionary government done with which the people are not in agreement? What has the Revolutionary Government done except to increase the welfare of the people, except to defend the interest of the people, except to sacrifice itself for the homeland.

For the first time, exceptional circumstances present themselves to us. For the first time in the history of the Cuban nation – which has spanned four centuries and began with the Indians persecuted and murdered by the Conquistadores, and which then continued on to a greater stage of slavery, when men were bought and sold like beasts and which ended on the modern stage with 20,000 deaths, thousands of peasants' homes burned, thousands of peasants murdered in the name of egoism, of avarice, and of the large, powerful interests. [APPLAUSE]

In this latest stage of the history of the Cuban nation a revolutionary power surges for the first time into public life, a power which is dealing a damaging blow to all the privileges, all the injustices and has finally redeemed the tarnished manhood of men who in some cases can trace their origins back more than four centuries. It is the [Revolutionary government] which proposes the construction of what in fifty years had never been constructed: streets, aqueducts, schools, hospitals, pavements; in fifty years nothing had ever been done; the industries had never been explored. What else can the Cuban people and their Revolutionary government do if not defend Cuban interests?

They defend them in Cuba and they defend them outside of Cuba, because I ask myself and I ask the people if a posture of dignity and courage is worth while for the Cuban people to have in international organizations? [APPLAUSE] I would continue to ask the people if they are or are not in agreement with the fact that the beaches, once the exclusive privilege of a few, have now been opened up to the Cuban people regardless of colour, without stupid prejudices. I ask the people if they are or they are not in agreement with the fact that equal opportunities of employment are open to Cubans of every colour. And so we will continue, asking what has the Revolutionary government done that has not benefited its people.

Why they call us communists

But something will happen if we continue: if we plant rice we damage the foreign interests; if we produce grain we damage foreign interests; if we produce cotton we damage foreign interests; if we lower electrical tariffs we damage foreign interests; if we make a law concerning oil – which we are planning next – we damage foreign interests; if we make a Mining Law – which also will happen soon – we damage foreign interests; if we form a merchant marine we damage foreign interests, if we want to find new markets for our country, we are damaging foreign interests. If we want them to buy from us as much as we buy from them, we are damaging foreign interests. And that is the explanation for our making the Revolutionary Laws which damage national and foreign privileges; it is for that they attack us, it is for that they call us communists, it is for that they accuse us, using every possible pretext to seize our country. Perhaps the Agrarian Reform is not Cuban? Perhaps the electric tariff was not reduced by Cubans? Perhaps the proposal to create a Merchant Marine was not Cuban, or the proposal to plant rice and cotton and produce grain on our own land? Perhaps it is not

Cuban to construct houses for our workers, our peasants and their families?

It is perhaps that the reduction of medicines, many of them provided by foreign laboratories, is not a Cuban act? ... Isn't it Cuban to defend our pride? Isn't it Cuban to create 10,000 schools, double that which had been created in fifty years of the Republic? ... Isn't it Cuban to convert our forts to centres of learning? ... Isn't it Cuban to give boats to our fishermen? To give equipment to our peasants? To give rights to our workers? Perhaps it is not Cuban to proclaim the right of using Cuban products? Perhaps the measures the Revolutionary government has established are not Cuban, or aren't they the most Cuban of all? Then what do they accuse us of, these wretches? Of what are they able to accuse us of except of instituting measures beneficial to Cuba? What can they accuse us of, those insolents and cynics, of what? What do they accuse us of, those criminals, of what do they accuse us, those traitors, except of taking Cuban measures and benefiting Cuba? [APPLAUSE]

Those who aren't Cuban are the foreign monopolies

Those who aren't Cuban are the foreign monopolies. Those who aren't Cuban are the Electric Company ... and the Telephone Company ... the Fruit Company, and the Atlantic Gulf ... [SHOUTS AND APPLAUSE] ... Those which aren't Cuban are the boats which bring us products from abroad; that which isn't Cuban is most of the rice, grain, textiles, and industrial articles we have consumed. Those which aren't Cuban are those trusts which exploited our mines and obtained privileged concessions; nor were those interests Cuban which contracted out the greater part of our land, which was possibly rich in oil.

Those which weren't Cuban were the bombs which murdered our peasants during the war. Nor the weapons which murdered 20,000 of our compatriots. Those which weren't Cuban were the trainers of that mercenary army destroyed by the Revolution. Those which aren't Cuban are the bases from which they attack us, those planes and bombs and incendiaries and anti-personnel bombs which are launched against a friendly country in peacetime. That which also is not Cuban is the campaign of lies, the campaign of slanders which they direct towards us. That which isn't Cuban are those critics who defame our people and those international agencies who describe all of our country's 'horrors'.

And that is the truth, that is the truth which the people must be told; that is the truth which negates the cynics and the insulters. Because we have taken Cuban measures, their venomous campaign against our Revolution was surrounded by the same catchwords, the same lies told by all the great national and international interests, the enemies of our country.

What do the reactionaries want?

What do the forces of reaction want? Do they want, perhaps, to train our peasants and our workers? No. Look at the clamour of reaction: a clamour which pretends to represent the Authentic Party, but which it certainly doesn't represent, because the true representative of that party is Dr Carlos Prío Socarras, and he is right here with us; those voices lure us no longer, like the ranting of *La Marina* and of *Avance*. What have those newspapers done even today? One of the first things planned is to form solidarity with the traitor Hubert Matos. In the second place, they tried to toss those same communist insinuations at the Revolutionary government. In the third place they say ... 'The Revolution does not need to arm the workers and peasants to defend itself from its enemies. The proven courage and skill of the army is sufficient and better able to incarnate the moral strength of the people, of the whole country.' And further: 'If these considerations of democracy are not realized, these risky and fatiguing techniques will continue on the part of the great multitude when it is more necessary to have relaxation and serenity.' Relaxation, when the bombers criminally send their bombs against us and machine-gun our people ... [SHOUTS]

This is a good warning for those who some day will form out of the masses an Authentic Party, and will never be stopped by

these lily-livers, who are full of the intrigues of groups like *La
Marina*, and of *Avance*, and will no longer be disturbed by the
cries of reaction and the counter-revolution, who no longer will
take the same argument of Trujillo, the 'White Rose',[2] and the
international monopolies who are enemies of Cuba.

For once and for all, I say that the people will not be left in
confusion. This is a new journalistic trick paid for by the landowners ... [SHOUTS AND THE PEOPLE'S APPLAUSE]

They want an army like the one they had before

We have to think and analyse their reasons for wanting what
they want. Why do they oppose our training workers and peasants? The answer is simple: because they want a traditional
army, they want a professional army like they had before ... Because their hopes are resting on that kind of army becoming, with
the passage of time, an instrument of reaction, and they expect to
have one as ambitious, as traitorous, as the one which has just
disappeared ... They hope that a professional army will some
day be able to corrupt officials and soldiers, and at any moment
the armed forces of the Republic will be able to influence the
country's destiny, because they remember that the great privileged classes, the powerful interests of the landowners, the powers
affected by the Revolution, all these interests and privileges had
but one instrument – the army. This was the instrument of all
foreign interests and of the worst national interest; remember
that the army of Cuba had foreign trainers.

Since they know that the people are a tremendous revolutionary
force, since they know that a trained people are a people prepared to defend themselves, these men are allergic to anyone who
hints at the training of workers and peasants.

---

2. Reactionary organization which existed before the Revolution,
and which sought to destroy it.

The best allies

On the other hand, we are certain we have our best allies in the soldiering peasants and workers, that the best alliance the army could make is with the people. That the most fervent troops of the Rebel army are the peasants.

The small group of officials who allied themselves with the traitor Hubert Matos were not of that class, they were not of that type of peasant official and soldier which form the flower and the élite and the cream of the most strapping and most courageous and firmest of the Rebel army.

Those lines of gallant soldiers, who with their rifles and machine guns mount the roofs of buildings, defending the population against any attack, are the soldiers of the Sierra Maestra who once made up those columns fighting at the battlefronts ... Those soldiers are revolutionary soldiers.

Why? Because they lived in the fields, have been born and raised in the fields, and there they saw how the Rural Guard used the rifles and machetes in the service of the large landowners. There they saw the misery of our peasants, there they saw the horror of the weak and sick children, there they saw all the pure, noble and heroic sentiment of our landless peasants. For these soldiers no one would be able to threaten arms against the peasants and against the people, because those soldiers felt the Revolution deeply, they lived it and suffered for it. They pointed the way to every peasant of the country and led the Nation to triumph. Such is the reason, workers and citizens of Havana, that the rifles you carry are the rifles of the brave soldier of the Sierra Maestra. And those soldiers know, as every soldier knows, peasants of the Rebel army, they know that you, worker, you, student, you, peasant, you, Cuban man or woman, carry inside you the spirit of the Nation; those soldiers in the hours of defending the country join together with the people; they fight for the whole nation, defending her rights and her sovereignty.

They want a disarmed people

The forces of reaction don't want this. The forces of reaction want a disarmed people, a corrupted army which one day would harm the Revolution and send our country hurtling backward. And this is the seriousness of Hubert Matos' treason, because it was his primary intent to use the soldiers against the revolution, against the rights of the Cuban people. It was his primary intention to corrupt the officials against the Cuban Revolution. The forces of reaction don't want the workers and the peasants to be trained because they have nourished the hope that if all the strength of the country is in the hands of a professional army, someday they will overcome official after official and they will be able to corrupt the army and have an instrument with which they can deal crippling blows to the state as was attempted on the Tenth of March,[3] an event which will never be repeated again in our country.

Standing against this conception of a professional army and the defence of our country with professional soldiers is our revolutionary concept of defending the country with the people, with all the forces of the people, with all the arms of the people, with all the hearts of the people. And what do the traitors do? What is the first thing they do? To repeat the same slander of Trujillo, to repeat the same slander of the White Rose and the war criminals and the international monopolistic enemies of Cuba: accusing the Revolutionary government of communism.

What they are telling Trujillo is plainly: 'You're right.' And they are telling the war criminals: 'You're right.' And they are telling the great foreign monopolies: 'You are right.' And they are telling those who bomb our territory: 'You are right . . .'

The first thing they do is to wave the flag of the war criminals,

---

3. On 10 March 1952, Batista returned to power in Cuba by staging a coup. His régime was promptly recognized by the US. He suspended the constitution and delivered a new statute which concentrated all executive legislative powers in his hands.

of the Trujillistas and of the White Rose. And still they don't want us to call them traitors ...

And with all this, what is their goal? It is the goal of dividing and confusing the people, the goal of weakening the people, when they must be more unafraid than ever, when they must be stronger than ever. They are traitors who want to confuse the people, when the people must be thinking clearer than ever before, when they must be more conscious than ever before of what are their interests, and which are the interests of the enemy – those who are not sympathetic to our people.

They are traitors who adopt the sign and the flag of men like Trujillo, of war criminals and international enemy interests. And they are traitors who side with those traitors, and they are traitors who at this moment are shamefully sympathetic to those men.

They are traitors who in this moment have the boldness to try to divide our people, because the only thing they are after is the weakening of the people. Only in order to weaken the people are the powerful enemies of the Revolution attacking us. But to speak clearly, the blame for these bombs does not rest only on those who launch them, but on those who instigate them here, those like Pepin Rivero of *Diario de la Marina*, and the newspaper *Avance*. Above all those from the newspaper *Avance* who are ruled, in their journalism, by the criminal hand of the counter-revolutionaries. The blame must be laid not only upon those who throw the bombs but upon those who side with them; the blame not only on the traitors but those who are encouraging them.

Why? Why must we take these revolutionary measures? It is not harming me, it is not harming the President of the Republic, it isn't harming Raúl, it isn't harming Che, it isn't harming Camilo, nor Almeida, nor Efigenio Ameijeiras, it is harming nothing but the Revolutionary Laws, because if we had not made the Revolutionary Laws, they would have praised us. The attack is against the Revolution, the attack is against the Revolutionary measures; those are the reasons, this is why they accuse us.

Cuban measures

I have demonstrated that the measures we have taken are truly Cuban measures, which benefit solely Cubans and those who aren't Cubans are those interests opposed by the Revolutionary Laws. But I will say more. Who is carrying the Revolution forward? Who are the men who are sitting here? While I was listening to the rebel commanders on this platform, when I listened to Commandant Camilo Cienfuegos, to Commandant Guevara, to Raúl Castro, to Commandant Almeida; when I listened to the other comrades like Universo Sánchez, Efigenio Ameijeiras and others, I remembered those first days of the Revolution in the Sierra Maestra; I began to remember those difficult days, those times of tremendous difficulty, when only a small group of us remained together. I remember those days of hunger and cold, with only a cloak to protect us from the rain, without protective covering from the cold of the mountains, without shoes to wear, with only a few bullets in our rifles, pursued by a myriad of soldiers, I remember those days when the Revolution looked like it would be defeated because of our own weaknesses, because we were so few. I remember those days when a faith entered into the men assuring them they had a great and noble cause, a faith which led us forward, led us into the fighting without shrinking back, even though we were so few. I remember those days as I walk this platform because I see the pillars of those difficult hours, of those truly bitter hours. I saw the history these companions of mine wrote, I was aware that from the first day until the invasion, when a puny force of men who numbered less than a hundred – two columns under the orders of two of the companions who are speaking here today – crossed the plains of Camagüey in order to support the companions who were fighting, and thereby writing one of the most glorious pages of military history, because one day they will have to be compared with the greatest generals that history has known; but they are not generals, they are commanders, because we have abolished the generalship and the top brass of our country.

Stronger and more unified than ever

When I look at these companions I used to say, 'Where are the twelve?' Of those twelve, several fell in the fighting; the others are all here. The Revolution does not have deserters. Those who, like the traitor in the ASTA convention,[4] in the middle of our extraordinary efforts [AN EXPLOSION IS HEARD] ... that is the nine o'clock cannon ... that deserter is like the foreigner who runs to war, whose patriotism is nothing more than personal ambition, who goes to war not to elevate his country but to elevate himself. We are not really able to call them deserters, because it will be a sad day when we lose some of those companions who stemmed from the beginnings of the Revolution, who came with us in *Granma*,[5] who with us have supported all the measures, and have arrived at this point without vacillation or fear. And to see the men together with the other officials of the Rebel army, to see the commanders of the other revolutionary organizations, to see here the directors of the Student Federation, I have thought that the Revolution is stronger and more unified than ever before, because on what side will good soldiers always be? On the side of the people. [APPLAUSE]

To see here a million ardent patriots, to see a million citizens, the thought strikes me that the Revolution is stronger than ever, and the daggers they thrust at us are far from weakening us, they strengthen us.

The only importance these traitors have is that behind them are the sources of reaction: there is all the reactionary national press, the press of international oligarchy. Behind them the counter-revolution urges them on: they are no more than miserable tools, instruments whose words echo only the cry of counter-revolution, of reaction: because this is not a struggle of persons, it is a struggle of interests: of the powerful interests against the interests of the Cuban people.

---

4. American Society of Travel Agents.

5. Yacht on which Castro and his followers arrived in Cuba to begin the Revolution.

They believe they can frighten us!

For that reason the forces of reaction don't applaud Che; the forces of reaction don't applaud Camilo; the forces of reaction applaud the traitors; the forces of reaction don't applaud Almeida, they applaud the traitors; the forces of reaction don't applaud the loyal men, they applaud the traitors. The forces of reaction don't praise the men of ideals, because after them no one need look further; the forces of reaction praise and eulogize the great traitors; the forces of reaction don't applaud the steadfast men but the men who waver, the men who are cowardly, the men who sell themselves; and there are men who sell themselves for money or for flattery, or for both. Look at the shameful posture those who call us communists put themselves in! What do they do but repeat the work of the Trujillos, of the White Rose, of the war criminals, and our country's enemies. Do they believe they can frighten us? Or is it that they don't understand that we are so confident in the justice of the measures we have taken, so sure of serving our people, that only by wiping us out – not even by wiping us out – will they be able to put a stop to our ideals.

The forces of reaction, those who bombard Cuba, those who drop incendiary bombs, that today we avow are traitors, are eager for a show; they want 'fake' counter-revolutionaries and those who want this are traitors who impute to the government, to increase the confusion, the worse slanders in hundreds of newspapers, to weaken the Revolution. [APPLAUSE]

No, they don't write a word criticizing the bombs – when they do write about it, it is with a lukewarmness which bears witness to their expediency, their desire to remain healthy and to protect their position. It is impossible to separate the bombardment, the positions of those who bomb us in Havana, with the positions of those who betrayed us in Camagüey: one deserted writing a letter which was published in the press, and the other deserted writing a letter for publication with the same argument of the traitor Díaz Lanz[6]...

6. Díaz Lanz was a career officer and Chief of the Cuban Air Force. He was replaced in that position by 26 July militant Juan Almeida

The counter-revolutionary press renewed all the arguments of Díaz Lanz, accusing us of being communist, and all the arguments of Hubert Matos, which accused us of being communists. The latter's plan ended in launching bombs and the former's plan would have ended by provoking a river of blood on our soil – because the positions of both were equally slanderous and equally treacherous; and the worst part of it is the moment Matos used to make his play: when the columns were advancing in the Sierra Maestra and in the middle of the ASTA when he knew the extraordinary interest the country placed in that Travel Agents' Convention. He hoped to repress us, but when his treasonous manoeuvres were brought to light, they were defeated by the power of the people and not of the 'mob' as they said. [APPLAUSE ... SHOUTS OF 'UP AGAINST THE WALL, UP AGAINST THE WALL']

Our country has received seventy million credits in the banks and just when we are realizing our extraordinary efforts, when even the school children bring their pennies to fortify our economy; when the nation is strong everywhere, when the construction workers work nine and ten hours a day, when the workers donate a part of their earnings to the industrialization – while on the other side cables announce that our credit is being taken away – Díaz Lanz plans his bombardment and Hubert Matos interrupts the ASTA conference in order to produce a wild criminal plan. [SHOUTS OF 'TO THE FIRING SQUAD, TO THE FIRING SQUAD'] ...

This is the way they are trying to destroy the Revolution with economic threats, obstructing our plans for economic development. It is because of this. If, with our people's efforts today, with

shortly after the Agrarian Reform. He defected to the United States in June 1959, charging that communists had taken over key positions in the government and army. He testified before the United States Senate Internal Security Committee and, on 21 October, flew a plane from Florida over Havana dropping leaflets and incendiary bombs.

Major Hubert Matos was in the 26 July Movement and was in charge of carrying out the land reform programme in Camagüey Province. In October 1959, he was arrested for conspiring with landowners to block the land reform.

the sacrifices our people are making today, we advance an inch or we advance a mile, is it fair that the efforts which cost us so much sacrifice should be destroyed in a few moments by wretched traitors who strangle our economy through betrayal and terror, hoping we will perish ... hoping our fatherland will be destroyed?

But I ask myself: where do they come from? What is it they want? Perhaps they believe that the Revolution will not defend itself? Perhaps the Trujillos, the war criminals, the traitors, the foreign monopolies and enemies of Cuba believe that the Revolution will not defend itself? Don't they know by now we will remain until the last peasant of Cuba remains? Don't they understand we will remain with the last Cuban worker? Don't they understand that these people will not waver, because they are conscious, they are completely conscious of who are their enemies and who are their friends? Don't they understand that our people can no longer be confused, that each day the people are more awake? [APPLAUSE]

They have abused the generosity of the Revolution

And why do they conspire? Why do they come here with their planes, why do they have secret meetings, why do they throw bombs, why do they want to muzzle us, why do they continue their impudent counter-revolutionary campaigns? Simply because they know they are free from danger; they know they exist today thanks to the generosity of the Revolutionary Government. Conspiracy is no risk. They know that out of our solicitude we have made a generous Revolution, not a Revolution heavy-handed with its enemies ... And that has emboldened them. They know they have no problems, that they run no risks, and so they conspire together. They machine-gun, they come from Santo Domingo and wait in Trinidad. So certain fake captains have shown up on our land, and have been captured by our troops, men that aren't Cubans and for that reason bomb us; for that reason kill forty-seven defenceless victims; they believed our people were defenceless because the Revolutionary Tribunes left them alone.

They have abused the generosity of the Revolution. It doesn't bother them at all that ninety per cent of the people are with the Revolution. It doesn't bother them, and so they are disposed to machine-gun the people, bomb the people, annihilate the people. [SHOUTS OF 'AGAINST THE WALL']

And each day they get more audacious, each day more insolent, and even in the pages of their journals, dressed in women's skirts, they have written things to the effect that the Prime Minister is a criminal. [THE PEOPLE SHOUT THAT IT ISN'T TRUE] They write what they could never have written against the Dictatorship, what they could never have written against the Tyranny, they write against those who had the responsibility for directing a war which was the only one where no prisoners were assassinated or beaten; the only war in the world where the wounded were not left on the battlefield, the only war in the world where soldiers of a combative force for nearly two years gave their medicines to help the enemy wounded ...

So, boldly, and getting bolder each day, the forces of reaction promote division, promote confusion, instigate treason, mask their treason, forcing those wretches among us to abandon the cause of their people to serve its enemies ... Ah! It's because they know our interest in stabilizing the country, because they know our interest in developing the country's economy. You can see how we are embarking on a tremendous struggle to look for jobs for all our compatriots, to industrialize the country with no other help than our own people's resources. We are fighting a heroic battle against the great foreign interests who don't want us to win that battle. They don't want us to dedicate our energy to the world of the Revolution. They don't want it because they want to destroy the Revolution through terrorism and economic strangulation. But as the Revolution is not 'my' property, but the property of the people, and we are only here to interpret the wishes of the people, they make it necessary to defend the Revolution; they make it necessary to formulate a plan of defence of the Revolution and it is the people who have given us the word. And here, before all our compatriots, unified, I am going to plan

and I am going to consult with the people regarding the recon-
vening of the Revolutionary Courts. [SHOUTS AND APPLAUSE:
SAYING, 'TO THE FIRING SQUAD'] I want the citizenry to express their desires, I want the citizens to decide this question and I
want those who agree that Revolutionary Tribunals should be re-
established to raise their hands ... [THE MULTITUDE WITH
THEIR HANDS HELD HIGH, SHOUTS 'AGAINST THE WALL']
Resolved that it is necessary to defend the country from aggression, resolved that it is necessary to defend the country from an
air attack, resolved that it is necessary to defend the country from
treason, tomorrow the Council of Ministers will be reconvened
... [SHOUTS OF APPLAUSE] ... in order to discuss and to decree the law which will reestablish, for as long as the Revolutionary Tribunal deems necessary, the Revolutionary courts.
[APPLAUSE, SHOUTS OF 'AGAINST THE WALL'] And although the Tribunes will be those who decide in the end, under
the law, what shall be the punishment towards the criminals, I
will ask the people's opinion: Let them raise their hands who believe that those who invade our country merit the punishment of
the firing squad ... [SHOUTS AND APPLAUSE] ... let them
raise ... [EVERYONE RAISES HANDS TO SHOUTS 'AGAINST
THE WALL'] .... let them raise their hands who believe that
the mercenary terrorists deserve the firing squad. [SHOUTS OF
'YES', WITH THE HANDS HELD HIGH] Let them raise their
hands who believe that the fitting-out of planes to fly over our
territory and the bombing of our people deserves the penalty of
death ... And finally, let them raise their hands who believe that
traitors like Hubert Matos merit death by the firing squad.
[SHOUTS OF 'AGAINST THE WALL', AND 'FIRING SQUAD'
WITH THE HANDS HELD HIGH] ...

To defend the country from aggression

Everyone knows the efforts we have made to put an end to, to suspend, the Revolutionary Tribunals. Everyone knows that we are
sorrowed by the campaign which is directed against our country
and which must be punished by the bailiffs. Everyone knows the

efforts we have made to increase tourism, to develop that branch of our country's economy, as a part of the peaceful development of all of Cuba's riches, to give bread to Cubans, employment to Cubans. Everyone knows the efforts we have made to carry our Revolution forward, with the greatest generosity, the greatest tolerance, and the greatest kindness. Everyone knows how hard it is to leave ourselves open once more to the gang of detractors, the international cabals, to the critics who slander us, giving them the opportunity to present us before the world as cruel and insensible. Everyone knows what we have sacrificed, everyone knows the damage that has been done to our economy, above all, after the formidable event at the Travel Agents' Convention, of the tens of thousands of men whose noble goals were compromised by the work of traitors and war criminals and Cuba's enemies. Everyone knows how hard it is for us, the difficulties they planned for us, but it is certain that our country must be defended from aggression; it is certain that we are being bombarded, certain that they want to destroy us through terror and through hunger. There remains no other alternative but to defend our fatherland and we are men who do what we set out to do. [APPLAUSE] We are men who have lain close to the noblest of illusions, the noblest of dreams. We have dreamed for the time when pain and misery will be forgotten, when culture will be brought to those who have none of it, bread for those who are hungry, tranquillity and happiness to satisfy the most elemental necessities of the forgotten people of Cuba, the people with whom we are in the most accord. No one else cares about them, because while others speak of Democracy and Liberty, they forget that when you are surrounded by ignorance, by hunger, by desperation, it is oppression that they are talking about, not Democracy. The people have been oppressed all their lives by powerful interests, by the great landowners. The first right of man is the right to live, the first right of man is the right of bread for his children, the right to live by his own labours, and the right to have his own culture. [APPLAUSE]

The right to life

And here – the children who die in the fields without medical assistance don't have rights. The women who die prematurely don't have rights, the families destroyed by starvation don't have rights. Because the first right of a man is the right to his life, and everything our people have been taught in the name of false symbols and false theories pales before the forgotten men; the men for whom nobody does anything, the men for whom nobody fights. We propose to redeem them without taking bread away from anybody else. Those of us who hope to reactivate the riches and resources of our country have as our greatest desire the granting of the necessities of life for our people. We have dreamed, and we continue to dream, of a Revolution where a majority of the people over-rule a minority of egotists, status-seekers and all those unadaptable to the revolutionary reality of the country. [APPLAUSE]

We have dreamed of a Revolution where the overwhelming majority endorses the job it sets upon itself, and on the other hand we have had enough of those counter-revolutionary campaigns, of the mercenaries, of the foreigners who order gangs here, of planes which come from outside, of journalists who are full of treason and accomplices who side with them. On the other hand we have had enough of the bombing of our power supply stations, of the forty-seven victims in the cities. And since we are not disposed to permit, with impunity, the terror which would overcome our homeland, as we are not ready to permit, with impunity, the state of affairs in which each mother and each son and each wife from one end of the island to the other, with Santo Domingo over there and Florida over here, have to live like the families in the Sierra Maestra with the psychosis of planes, under the terror of machine guns and bombardments. As it is necessary to defend our homeland, as it is necessary to defend the school children, those same children whom I heard singing that hymn before this wonderful gathering. [APPLAUSE] Knowing that they must be defended, knowing we have had enough of evil, enough of those who have grown even more daring in their crimes, it is time to show the world that the Cuban people are ready to defend themselves, that the Cuban people, before they are annihilated, are ready to annihilate any enemies placed in their path. [APPLAUSE] That the Cuban people, before they are assassinated, are ready to die fighting and that the forces of re-action and counter-revolution and invaders and counter-revolutionaries coming from inside or outside, whether small or great, will confront a proud people ... [APPLAUSE] who proclaim they mean no harm to anybody. Who don't aspire to harm any people of the world, and who only want to live by their own work and by the fruits of their intelligence and the fruits of their arms; but in order to defend that desire, to fulfil their destiny in this world, in order to defend that exalted wish, that inalienable, unrenounceable right of any people, great or small, today, yesterday, or tomorrow, to defend their dreams, the Cuban people are ready to fight, the men and the women are ready to fight, the children and the old men. [APPLAUSE] Because our cause is just, because we wish to give no one harm, nor to have anyone tender harm to us ...

From this day on, we proclaim that we are afraid of nothing or no one, that we are unafraid of the measures taken against us, of the measures we have to take to destroy those who would destroy us. [APPLAUSE]

Cuba today has got the attention of the world. Cuba has got the admiration of the world and the place which Cuba occupies in the minds of the American peoples and of the world's peoples will not be abandoned. Cuba will never betray the glory and the prestige she has won in the defence of her legitimate rights. [APPLAUSE]

We are able to make a revolution because we are the kind of people we are. We could not have made one otherwise. Those who ignore history, those who have forgotten the history of other peoples, those who have not read of the advancement of humanity, from the Greek epoch until today, are the type who do not know a revolution when they see one. They are the type who try to halt a revolution and they are the type who are always crushed by the people. [APPLAUSE]

Those who adopt vacillating and cowardly stances are dragged off by the people. Other peoples would know how extraordinary and interesting the revolutionary process was if they had even a part of the great obstacles which we have had to overcome, if they had to face even a part of the powerful resources which were mobilized to crush us. We have asked the Cubans to fulfil their historic task and the Cubans fulfilled it, because with a people like the Cuban people a Revolution such as this is possible. [APPLAUSE] The faint-hearted don't matter. When have the faint-hearted ever been important in the history of a people? The vacillators don't matter. When have the vacillators been important to the history of a people? The cowards don't matter. When have the cowards ever been important in the history of a people? [APPLAUSE] What did the vacillators and the faint-hearted matter when we were only twelve men? What did it matter if they tried to prevent the Revolution when the Revolution was destined to triumph, and if those twelve men were able to carry that fight to the rest of the nation? ...

CHAPTER 4

Turn Towards Socialism:
Cuba's Socialism Proclaimed*

On 21 May 1959, in a televised speech to the Cuban nation, Fidel summarized his political outlook:

Our revolution is neither capitalist nor communist! ... We want to liberate man from dogmas, and free his economy and society, without terrorizing or binding anyone. We have been placed in a position where we must choose between capitalism which starves people, and communism which resolves the economic problem but suppresses the liberties so greatly cherished by man ... Our Revolution is not red, but olive green, the colour of the rebel army that emerged from the heart of the Sierra Maestra.

Two years later, on 15 April, just two days before the United States-sponsored invasion of Cuba, Fidel for the first time referred to the Cuban Revolution as a 'socialist revolution carried out under the very noses of the Yankees'.

Events in the intervening years had shown that a nationalist revolution had to step on the toes of US business interests, that in fact it had to be carried out against US and Western business interests and thus become anti-imperialist. The reaction of the native bourgeoisie – never truly independent since it lived off US trade and investment – together with the opposition of the US, intensified the need to socialize the economy.†

_____

* Delivered in Havana on May Day, 1961, 'Year of Education'.

† A number of books clearly explain the different facets of this process. Zeitlin and Scheer in *Cuba: Tragedy in Our Hemisphere* emphasize how Castro 'reacted' to US hostility to his reforms and was forced by this, and by the refusal of the US to grant aid, to turn further and further left. James O'Connor in *The Origins of Socialism*

The Agrarian Reform, implemented during the late summer of 1959, brought on air raids flown by former Batista air force men from air fields in Florida. They created divisions among the different wings of the 26 July movement and the need for a Popular Militia: at the same time, the United States began brandishing the economic weapon of the sugar quota. Cuba, compelled to seek out new markets, signed a trade pact with the USSR in February 1960, and began to import crude oil that summer. When Western-owned oil refineries in Cuba refused to process it – Cuba got a better price from the Soviets than from the Western oil cartel and saved vital foreign exchange because it bought the oil in exchange for sugar – the refineries were nationalized. President Eisenhower then 'declared economic war on Fidel Castro's Cuba', in the words of the Wall Street Journal (7 July 1960), 'by slashing that country's exports to the highly profitable US market by 700,000 tons.' Cuba expropriated American property and sought even closer ties with the socialist countries after the sugar quota cut. In October – in the midst of a Presidential campaign in the US in which Senator John Kennedy attacked the Republicans for letting 'Castro and his gang' turn Cuba into a Soviet 'supply depot' for Latin American revolution – the US announced an embargo on US goods to Cuba. At the same time, Cuba had begun nationalizing Cuban-owned and then United States-owned companies. Thus, by the following spring Cuba was – in its economic structure, political allies, trade patterns, and social priorities – a socialist society. By the time that Fidel declared the Cuban Revolution socialist all the strategic sectors of Cuba's industry were nationalized: sugar, petroleum refining, telephone and electric power, and cement; the state sector produced ninety per cent of Cuba's exports; state farms and co-operatives controlled the best land; the whole pattern of trade had shifted from the United States to the socialist countries. Imports from the United States declined from \$577 million in 1957 to \$2·37 million in 1961; trade

---

in Cuba and Edward Boorstein in *The Economic Transformation of Cuba*, show how the economic development of Cuba was blocked by the structure of the Cuban economy and any attempts at economic growth required a socialist takeover of the economy.

with the socialist countries accounted for over seventy per cent of Cuba's foreign trade in 1961. At the same time, the vast disparities between rich and poor, city and country, were being rapidly narrowed.

Perhaps the outstanding aspect of the run towards socialism in Cuba at that time was the plan to eradicate illiteracy, inaugurated in April 1961. One part of it, announced by Fidel a week before Kennedy launched the invasion at Playa Girón, involved moving 5,000 high school students 'into houses in the swank Miramar district of Havana once owned by Batistianos and émigrés'. The students were sons of peasants 'who cannot pay their own expenses and will be educated, fed and clothed by the government'. (New York Times, 10 April 1961.) The Times also reported that 'another group of houses around the former Biltmore Yacht and Country Club, now nationalized and made into a workers' social centre, will be used for students, as will Camp Libertad, which has been turned into a scholastic centre.' The literacy campaign also included sending 45,000 city students to the countryside to teach the peasants to read and write, and to overcome the vast differences between the urban and rural population.

The mercenaries were quickly crushed at Playa Girón. The invaders had no local base; there were no popular uprisings against the Revolution; and even the CIA, which directed the operation in the name of the Cuban people, must have realized at some point the blatant lie inherent in the operation. For the CIA did not even trust the 'leaders' of the counter-revolution – they kept them prisoner in Miami during the invasion and issued communiqués in their name.

In this May Day speech, delivered after a fifteen-hour victory parade, Fidel discusses how the old concept of patriotism had conceived of the motherland belonging to a small minority. The ruling class in the United States had misjudged Cuba, because they themselves believed in a motherland of monopolies – they identified the interest of the United States with those of the large corporations.

Whereas in Fidel's Moncada trial speech, 'History Will Absolve Me', he saw Cuba divided between those who supported the ille-

gitimate authority of Batista – who had seized power in a coup – and those who opposed it, now he sees the enemy as the foreign monopolies and their Cuban accomplices. The situation had changed. As Edward Boorstein puts it: 'The victory over Batista meant that the Cuban people had done away with the local over-seer; now they confronted the owner of the plantation – American imperialism.'

American imperialism was reflected in the policies of John F. Kennedy, who had, in his State of the Union message, set forth in the blunt language of the true believers of private enterprise, the intransigent hostility which was to characterize US policy to Cuba: 'Questions of economic and trade policy can always be nego-tiated. But communist domination in the Hemisphere can never be negotiated.'

Fidel answers that 'rights do not come from size ... Who had those notions before Kennedy? Hitler and Mussolini! They spoke the same language of force; it is the fascist language ... It is the right of might. This is the only right Kennedy advances in claim-ing the right to interfere in our country.'

The audacious and defiant tone found in Fidel's speeches re-flects the blending of military success and successful popular reform.

Distinguished visitors from Latin America and the entire world, combatants of the armed forces of the people, workers: We have had fourteen-and-a-half hours of parading. I think that only a people imbued with infinite enthusiasm is capable of enduring such tests. Nevertheless, I will try to be as brief as possible.

We are very happy over this attitude by the people. I believe that today we should outline the course to follow, analyse a little what we have done up to now, see at what point in our history we are, and what we have ahead. We have all had a chance to see the parade. Maybe we on this platform could appreciate it better than you in the square, maybe still better than those who have paraded. This May Day tells a lot; it tells a lot about what the Revolution has been so far, what it has achieved so far; but maybe it does not tell us as much as it tells our visitors.

We have been witnesses, all us Cubans, of every step taken by the Revolution, so maybe we cannot realize how much we have advanced as fully as can be understood by visitors, particularly those visitors from Latin America, where today they are still living in a world very similar to the one we lived in yesterday. It is as if they were suddenly transported from the past to the present of our Revolution, with all its extraordinary progress as compared to the past. We do not intend tonight to stress the merit of what we have done. We merely want to locate ourselves in the present.

We had a chance today to see genuine results of the Revolution on this May Day, so different from the May Days of the past. Formerly that date was the occasion for each sector of labour to set forth its demands, its aspirations for improvement, to men who were deaf to the working-class interests, men who could not even accede to those basic demands because they did not govern for the people, for the workers, for the peasants, or for the humble; they governed solely for the privileged and the dominant economic interests. Doing anything for the people would have meant harming the interests that they represented, and so they could not accede to any just demand from the people. The May Day parades of those days marked the complaints and protest of the workers.

How different today's parade has been! How different even from the first parades after the Revolution triumphed. Today's parade shows us how much we have advanced. The workers now do not have to submit themselves to those trials; the workers now do not have to implore deaf executives; the workers now are not subject to the domination of any exploiting class; the workers no longer live in a country run by men serving exploiting interests. The workers now know that everything the Revolution does, everything the government does or can do, has one goal: helping the workers, helping the people. Otherwise, there would be no explanation for the spontaneous sentiment of support for the Revolutionary government, that overflowing good will that every man and woman has expressed today.

Fruits of the Revolution are seen everywhere. The first to parade today were the children of the Camilo Cienfuegos school centre. We saw the Pioneers parade by with the smile of hope, confidence, and affection. We saw the young rebels parade by. We saw the women of the federation go by. We saw children from numberless schools created by the Revolution parade. We saw 1,000 students from the 600 sugar-cane co-operatives who are studying artificial insemination here in the capital. We saw young people, humble people, parade with their uniforms of the school where they are learning to be diplomatic representatives of the future.

We saw the pupils of the schools for young peasants of the Zapata swamps parade by, the swamps that the mercenaries chose for their attack. We saw parade thousands and thousands of peasants who are studying in the capital and who come from distant mountain areas or from cane co-operatives or from people's farms. We saw the young girls who are studying for children's club work. And every one of these groups are worthy of praise. And we also saw the work that is going into the rural areas. The volunteer teachers paraded, as well as representatives of the 100,000 young people on their way to the interior to wipe out illiteracy. Where does this strength come from? It comes from the people, and in return it is devoted to the people.

These young people are truly children of the people. When we saw them today writing with their formations 'Long Live Our Socialist Revolution' we thought how hard it would have been to have all this without a revolution; how hard for any of these children from the mountains to have paraded here today, or for any of these young people from the rural areas to have a chance to get to know the capital, or to study in any of these schools, or to parade with the joy and pride shown here today, or to march with the faith in the future shown today, because schools, university professions, art, culture, and honours were never for the children of poor families, in town or in the country. They were never for the peasant of the remote rural areas; they were never for the poor young man, black or white, of our countryside or our cities.

Art, culture, university professions, opportunities, honours, elegant clothes were the privilege of only a small minority, a minority represented today with that grace and humour shown by some worker federations in their parodies of the rich. If one remembers that we are just beginning, it is astounding to think that today more than 20,000 athletes paraded. Not to mention the most marvellous thing we had a chance to see today, that is, this armed nation, this united people, which came to attend these ceremonies.

How would it have been possible without a revolution? How can one compare this present with the past? How can one avoid emotion on seeing endless lines of workers, athletes, and militia-men parade by. At times all went by intermingled. After all, workers, athletes, and soldiers are the same thing. Anybody could understand why our people must emerge victorious in any battle. We noted the many women in the ranks of the federations. The men were in the artillery units, mortar units, anti-aircraft units, or militia battalions. The women were the wives and sisters and sweethearts of the militiamen. And those young men of the basic secondary schools, the Pioneers, who paraded by, were their sons.

And so today one can see the unity of the humble people who are fighting for the poor. Workers of every profession; manual labourers and intellectual workers; all were marching together, the writer, artist, actor, announcer, doctor, nurse, clinical employer. Marching together in great numbers under the flag of the national education workers union were the teachers, employees of the Education Ministry.

Today we have had a chance to see everything worthwhile in our country, everything produced in our country. We have understood better than ever that there are two classes of citizens, or rather there *were* two classes of citizens; the citizens who worked, produced, and created, and the citizens who lived without working or producing. These latter were parasites.

In this young, fervent nation, who did not parade today, who could not parade here today? The parasites! Today the working people paraded, everybody who produces with his hands or his brain. I do not mean that workers who did not have a chance to parade were parasites, because they had to take care of their children, or were ill, or even just did not want to parade today. I am speaking only of those who were not represented here because they could not be thought of as being among those who produce.

This is the people, the true people. He who lives as a parasite does not belong to the people. Only the invalid, the sick, the old, the children are entitled to live without working and are entitled to have us work for them and to care for them, and from the work of everyone they can be benefited. For the children, the old, the invalid, and the sick, we have the duty to work, all of us. What no moral law will ever be able to justify is for the people to work for the parasites. [APPLAUSE]

Those who paraded today were the working people who will never resign themselves to work for the parasites. In this manner our national community has understood what the Revolution is, and has understood clearly what the meaning of a revolution is in which a nation gets rid of parasites from the outside and those inside. We remember that because of the nationalization of the largest industries in the nation, and just before the US factories were nationalized, some asked: Was this factory not a Cuban factory? Why should a Cuban factory be nationalized? Well, such a factory did not belong to the people, it belonged to some man. Now they belong to the nation. [APPLAUSE]

New concept of motherland

It was the custom to talk about the motherland; there were some who had a wrong idea of the motherland. There was the mother-land of the privileged ones, of a man who has a large house, while the others live in hovels. What motherland did you have in mind, sir? A motherland where a small group lives from the work of others? A motherland of the barefoot child who is asking for alms on the street? What kind of motherland is this? A mother-land which belonged to a small minority? Or the motherland of today? The motherland of today where we have won the right to direct our own destiny, where we have learned to decide our own destiny, a motherland which will be, now and forever – as Martí wanted it – for the well-being of everyone and not a motherland for a few !

The motherland will be a place where such injustices will be eliminated. Now we have a real concept of motherland. We are willing to die for a motherland which belongs to all Cubans. [APPLAUSE] That is why the exploiting classes could not have a real concept of motherland. For them, the motherland meant their privilege to take advantage of the work of others. That is why when a Yankee monopolist ... [SHOUTS OF 'OUT!'] when a leader, or a member of the US ruling circles, talks about the motherland, they refer to the motherland of monopolies, of the large banking monopolies. And when they talk about the motherland, they are thinking about sending the blacks of the South, the workers to be killed to defend the motherland of monopolies. [APPLAUSE]

What kind of morality and what reason and what right do they have to make a black man die to defend the monopolies, the factories, and the mines of the ruling classes? What right have they to send the Puerto Rican of Latin blood, of Latin tradition, to the battlefields to defend the policy of large capitalists and monopolies? This concept of motherland and this danger to their security to which they refer is a danger only of the monopolies. You can understand what concept they have of morality, law, and rights, to send the blacks of the South and the Puerto Ricans to the battlefields to fight for them. This is their concept of motherland. That is why the people gain the real concept of the motherland only when the interests of the privileged classes are liquidated, and when a nation with its wealth becomes a nation for everyone, the wealth for everyone, and opportunity and happiness for everyone.

This happiness now belongs to those youths who paraded, and the families who know that their children can have a school, receive scholarships, and go to the best universities abroad, a privilege formerly enjoyed only by the richest. And today any family, regardless of how poor, has the opportunity to send its children to schools in the nation and abroad. Any family knows that, thanks to the Revolution, its children have all the opportunities which formerly belonged only to the rich. A nation which works for itself, whether it be in defence or in amassing wealth can achieve what the privileged few cannot.

The Revolution can win the people with its fervour and enthusiasm. The Revolution can utilize all intelligence and creative spirit and take everyone towards a path of well-being and progress. The people who spent fifteen hours here today are the same people who formerly could not spend even one hour at a public rally, or who were paid or forced to go to a public rally. These enthusiastic people are the discouraged people of yesterday. The difference is that yesterday they worked for others and today they work for themselves. [APPLAUSE]

Fight against imperialism

Think of the men who died in recent battles and decide whether a single drop of blood was worth being lost to defend the past. Consider that these workers and youths, the children of workers, fell ten or twelve days ago to defend what we have seen today. They fell to defend this enthusiasm, this hope, and this joy of today. That is why when today we saw a happy face or a smile full of hope, we thought that each smile of today was a flower over the grave of a fallen hero.

It was like giving thanks to those who gave their lives in the battle against imperialism. Without them we would not have had the May Day parade. We would not have been able to see what passed in front of us today. What would have happened to our anti-aircraft batteries, what would have happened to our cannons and our soldiers who marched here? What would have happened to our workers, wives, sisters, and factories? What would have happened if imperialism had established even a single beachhead on our territory? What would have happened if the imperialists had succeeded in taking one part of our territory, and from there, with Yankee bombs, machine guns, and planes, had launched an armed attack against us?

Let us not talk about what would have happened if the imperialists had won. There is no sadder picture than a defeated revolution. The uprising of slaves in Rome and their defeat should give us an idea of what a defeated revolution is. The commune of Paris should give us an idea of what a defeated revolution is. History tells us that a defeated revolution must pay the victors in blood. The victors not only collect the past debts but also try to collect future debts. But under certain circumstances, it is impossible to crush a revolution.

It has never happened in history that a revolutionary people who have really taken over power have been defeated. What would have happened this May Day if imperialism had won its game? That is why we were thinking of all we owed those who fell. That is why we were thinking that every smile today was like a tribute to those who made possible this hopeful day. The blood that was shed was the blood of workers and peasants, the blood of humble sons of the people, not blood of landowners, millionaires, thieves, criminals, or exploiters. The blood shed was the blood of the exploited of yesterday, the free men of today. The blood shed was humble, honest, working, creative blood – the blood of patriots, not the blood of mercenaries. It was the blood of militiamen who voluntarily came to defend the Revolution. It was spontaneously offered blood to defend an ideal.

This ideal was not the ideal with which the Yankees inculcated their mercenaries. It was not an ideal of parrots. It was not an ideal of the tongue, but of the heart. It was not an ideal of those who came to recover their lost wealth. It was not the ideal of those who always lived at the expense of others. It was not the ideal of those who sell their soul for the gold of a powerful empire.

It was the ideal of the peasants who do not want to lose their land, the blacks who do not want discrimination, the humble, those who never lived from the sweat of others, and of those who never robbed from others, an ideal that a poor man of the people can feel.

The Revolution is all for him because he was mistreated and humiliated. He defends the Revolution because the Revolution is his life. Before sacrificing this he prefers to lose his life. He knows that he may fall, but never in vain, and that the cause for which he falls will serve for millions of his brothers.

Humble, honest blood was shed by the fatherland in the struggle against the mercenaries of imperialism. But what blood, what men, did imperialism send here to establish that beachhead, to bleed our Revolution dry, to destroy our achievements, to burn our cane? It was to be a war of destruction.

US planned aggression

We can tell the people right here that at the same instant that three of our airports were being bombed, the Yankee agencies were telling the world that our airports had been attacked by planes from our own air force. They cold-bloodedly bombed our nation and told the world that the bombing was done by Cuban pilots with Cuban planes. This was done with planes on which they painted our insignia.

If nothing else, this deed should be enough to demonstrate how miserable are the actions of imperialism. It should be enough for us to realize what Yankee imperialism really is and what its press and government are. It is possible that millions have heard only the report that Cuban planes piloted by defectors had attacked our airports. This was planned; the imperialists studied the plan to bomb and the way to deceive the entire world. This should serve to keep us alert and to understand that the imperialists are capable of the most monstrous lies to cover the most monstrous deeds.

US leaders publicly confessed their participation – without that explanation which they owe the world – and this after the statements made by Kennedy that they would never participate in aggression – and saved us the effort of finding proof. Who were those who fought against the workers and peasants? We will explain.

Privileged class mercenaries

Of the first mercenaries, we can say that without counting ships' crews, there are nearly 1,000 prisoners. Concerning that 1,000 we know the following: About 800 came from well-to-do families. They had a total of 27,556 *caballerías* of land, 9,666 houses, 70 industries, 10 sugar centrals, 2 banks, and 5 mines. So 800 out of 1,000 had all that. Moreover, many belonged to exclusive clubs and many were former soldiers for Batista.

Remember, during the prisoner interrogation I asked who was

a cane cutter and only one said that he had cut cane once. That is the social composition of the invaders.

We are sure that if we ask all those here how many owned sugar centrals, there would not be even one. If we asked the combatants who died, members of the militia or soldiers of the Revolutionary army, if we compared the wealth of those who fell, surely there would be no land, no banks, no sugar centrals, or the like listed. And some of the shameless invaders said that they came to fight for ideals !

The invaders came to fight for free enterprise ! Imagine, at this time for some idiot to come here to say that he fought for free enterprise ! As if our people did not know what free enterprise was ! It was slums, unemployment, begging. One hundred thousand families working the land to turn over twenty-five per cent of their production to shareholders who never saw that land. How can they come to speak about free enterprise to a country where there was unemployment, illiteracy, and where one had to beg to get into a hospital ? The people know that free enterprise was social clubs, and bathing in mud for the children because the beaches were fenced in. The beaches were for the wealthy. One could never dream of going to Varadero,[1] for that was for a few wealthy families. One could never dream of having a son study law. That was only for the privileged. A worker could never dream that his son might become a teacher or lawyer. Ninety per cent of the sons of workers, or at least the seventy-five per cent who lived in places where there were no secondary schools, had no chance to send their children to study. Not even in a dream could the daughters of the peasants dance here or parade here.

How can one of those who never knew labour say that he came to shed the people's blood to defend free enterprise ? And they did not stop at their fathers' mention of free enterprise; they included United Fruit and the electrical company. Those were not free enterprises; they were monopolies. So when they came here they were not fighting for free enterprise; they came for the

---

1. Beach and resort area near Havana known for its beauty, formerly reserved for the upper classes.

monopolies, for monopolies do not want free enterprise. They were defending the monopolistic interests of the Yankees here and abroad. How could they tell the Cuban people that they were coming to defend free enterprise?

They also say that they came to defend the 1940 constitution. How curious! That constitution was being torn into bits with the complicity of the US Embassy, the reactionary church, and the politicians. So it is cynical for this group of privileged Batista-type tyrants, criminals, and torturers to tell the people that they were coming to defend the constitution of 1940, which has been superseded by the Revolutionary government.

1940 constitution ignored

Who represented you in the Congress? The corrupt politicians, the rich, the big landholders. There was only a handful of workers in Congress. They were always in the minority. The means of disseminating ideas were all in the hands of the rich. It was hard to learn about the horrible conditions because of that. The death of thousands of children for lack of medicine and doctors did not bother the free enterprise men. There was never an agrarian reform law because Congress was in the hands of the rich. Even though the constitution said the land must be returned to the Cubans, and even though in 1959 the 1940 constitution had been in effect nineteen years, no law took land from the Yankee monopolies, which had huge expanses.

Up to 200,000 hectares were held by some foreign monopolies. The constitution which said that land must be returned to the Cubans, as well as the law setting a limit on landholdings, were never enforced. There were teachers without employment, while children lacked schooling.

The Batista group took over through a coup sponsored by imperialism and the exploiting class; they needed such a man as Batista, so that the rural guard [2] would serve the landowners

---

2. Rural policemen or *Rurales* under Batista, known for their brutality and feared by the peasants.

against the peasants. It did not matter to them that the nation was being plundered. The landowners did not give anybody modern weapons to fight that régime; they gave arms to that bloody régime itself, not caring how it violated the constitution. The Yankees did not give arms to anybody to fight Batista. None of the fine little gentlemen fought, because they still had their Cadillacs; they had a régime that guaranteed their frivolous life. They cared nothing about politics, for they had a very good life. Now that their privileges had ended, they found a Yankee government willing to give them arms to come here and shed the blood of workers and peasants. [APPLAUSE]

Those gentlemen spoke of elections. What elections did they want? The ones of the corrupt politicians who bought votes? Those elections in which a poor person had to turn over his ballot in return for work? Those fake elections that were just a means for the exploiting class to stay in power? Those elections which were not a military coup? There are many pseudo-democracies in Latin America; what laws have they passed for the peasants? Where is nationalization of industry? Where is their agrarian reform? [APPLAUSE]

A revolution expressing the will of the people is an election every day, not every four years; it is a constant meeting with the people, like this meeting. The old politicians could never have gathered as many votes as there are people here tonight to support the Revolution. Revolution means a thorough change.

What do they want? Elections with pictures on the lamp-posts. The Revolution has exchanged the conception of pseudo-democracy for direct government by the people.

No time for elections

There had to be a period to abolish privilege. Do the people now have time for elections? No! What were the political parties? Just an expression of class interests. Here there is just one class, the humble; that class is in power, and so it is not interested in the ambition of an exploiting minority to get back in power. Those people would have no chance at all in an election. The

Revolution has no time to waste in such foolishness. There is no chance for the exploiting class to regain power. The people know that the Revolution expressed their will; the Revolution does not come to power with Yankee arms. It comes to power through the will of the people fighting against Yankee arms.

The Revolution stays in power through the people. What are the people interested in? In having the Revolution go ahead without losing a minute. Can any government in America claim to have more popular support than this one? Why should democracy be the pedantic, false democracy of the others, rather than this direct expression of the will of the people? The people go to die fighting instead of going to a poll to scratch names on paper. The Revolution has given every citizen a weapon, a weapon to every man who wanted to enter the militia. So some fool comes along to ask, since we have a majority why don't we hold elections? Because the people do not care to please fools and fine little gentlemen! The people are interested in moving forward.

They have no time to waste. The people must spend tremendous amounts of energy in preparing to meet aggression, when everybody knows we prefer to be building schools, houses, and factories. We are not warlike. The Yankees spend half of their budget on armaments; we are not warlike. We are obliged to spend that energy, because of the imperialists. We have no expansionist ambitions. We do not want to exploit any worker of another country. We are not interested in aggressive plans; we have been forced to have tanks, planes, machine guns, and a military force to defend ourselves.

The recent invasion shows how right we were to arm. At Playa Girón, they came to kill peasants and workers. Imperialism forced us to arm for defence. We have been forced to put energy and material and resources into defence, although we would prefer to put them into more schools, so that in future parades there can be more athletes and school children. If our people were not armed, they could not crush mercenaries coming with modern equipment.

The imperialists would have hurled themselves on us long ago if we had not been armed. But we prefer to die rather than surrender the country we have now. They know that. They know they will meet resistance, and so aggressive imperialism has to stop and think.

We are forced, by the threat of aggression, to proclaim to the four corners of the world : all the peoples of America should rise in indignation after the statement that one country can intervene in the affairs of another just because it is strong. Such a policy would mean that the powerful neighbour assumes the right to intervene to keep a people from governing themselves according to their own choice. It is inconceivable that there should be such miserable governments. After the aggression that killed peasants and workers, it is inconceivable that [the US] has even begun a policy of breaking with Cuba, instead of breaking with Somoza, Guatemala, or their own government in Washington that pays for planes, tanks, and arms to come here and kill peasants.

The Costa Rican government has said that, if mercenaries are executed, it will break with us. It has no reason at all for a break, so it seeks some pretext, and hits upon the excuse of 'if there are executions'. That government, in what constitutes insolent intervention, stated its disposition to break with us if any of the mercenaries are executed. It does not break with Kennedy who organized the expedition, nor with Guatemala, nor Nicaragua. We did not break with Costa Rica; we merely answered the note.

Those who promote the policy of isolating Cuba at the orders of imperialism are miserable traitors to the interests and feelings of America. [APPLAUSE] These facts show us the rotten politics that prevail in many Latin American countries, and how the Cuban Revolution has turned those corrupt forms upside down to establish new forms in this country.

New socialist constitution

To those who talk to us about the 1940 constitution, we say that the 1940 constitution is already too outdated and old for us. We have advanced beyond that short section of the 1940 constitution that was good for its time but which was never carried out. That constitution has been left behind by this revolution, which, as we

have said, is a socialist revolution. We must talk of a new constitution, yes, a new constitution, but not a bourgeois constitution,
not a constitution contributing to the domination of certain classes
by exploiting classes, but a constitution contributing to a new
social system without the exploitation of man by man. That new
social system is called Socialism, and this constitution will therefore be a socialist constitution.

Kennedy's protests

If Mr Kennedy does not like socialism, well, we do not like imperialism ! We do not like capitalism ! We have as much right to
protest over the existence of an imperialist-capitalist régime ninety
miles from our coast as he feels he has to protest over the existence of a socialist régime ninety miles from his coast. Now then,
we would not think of protesting over that, because that is the
business of the people of the United States. It would be absurd for
us to try to tell the people of the United States what system of
government they must have, for in that case we would be considering that the United States is not a sovereign nation and that
we have rights over the domestic life of the United States.

Rights do not come from size. Right does not come from one
country being bigger than another. That does not matter. We
have only limited territory, a small nation, but our right is as
respectable as that of any country, regardless of its size. It does
not occur to us to tell the people of the United States what system
of government they must have. Therefore it is absurd for Mr
Kennedy to take it into his head to tell us what kind of government he wants us to have here. That is absurd. It occurs to Mr
Kennedy to do that only because he does not have a clear concept of international law or sovereignty. Who had such notions
before Kennedy? Hitler and Mussolini !

They spoke the same language of force; it is the fascist language. We heard it in the years before Germany's attack on
Czechoslovakia. Hitler split it up because it was governed by a
progressive government. The bourgeoisie, reactionary and pro-
fascist, afraid of the advance of a socialist system, preferred even

domination by Hitler. We heard that language on the eve of the invasion of Denmark, Belgium, Poland, and so forth. It is the right of might. This is the only right Kennedy advances in claiming the right to interfere in our country.

This is a socialist régime, yes! Yes, this is a socialist régime. It is here, but the fault is not ours, the blame belongs to Columbus, the English colonizers, the Spanish colonizers. The people of the US, too, will someday get tired [of capitalism].

No threat to US

The US government says that a socialist régime here threatens US security. But what threatens the security of the North American people is the aggressive policy of the warmongers of the United States. What threatens the security of the North American family and people is the violence, that aggressive policy that ignores the sovereignty and the rights of other peoples. The one who is threatening the security of the United States is Kennedy, with that aggressive policy. That aggressive policy can give rise to a world war; and that world war can cost the lives of tens of millions of North Americans. Therefore, the one who threatens the security of the United States is not the Cuban Revolutionary government but the aggressor, the aggressive government of the United States.

We do not endanger the security of a single North American. We do not endanger the life or security of a single North American family. We, who are making co-operatives, agrarian reform, people's ranches, houses, schools, literary campaigns, and sending thousands and thousands of teachers to the interior, building hospitals, sending doctors, giving scholarships, building factories, increasing the productive capacity of our country, creating public beaches, converting fortresses into schools, and giving the people the right to a better future -- we do not endanger a single US family or a single US citizen.

The ones who endanger the lives of millions of families, of tens of millions of North Americans, are those who are playing with atomic war. It is those who, as General Cardenas said, are playing with the possibility of New York becoming a Hiroshima. The ones who are playing with atomic war, with their aggressive war, with their policy that violated the rights of people are the ones who are endangering the security of the North American nation, the security of the lives of unknown millions of North Americans.

What do the monopolists fear? Why do they say that they are not secure with a socialist revolution nearby? They are, as Khrushchev says, proving that they know their system is inferior. They do not even believe in their own system. Why don't they leave us alone when all our government wants is peace?

US refusal to negotiate

Recently, our government issued a statement that we were willing to negotiate. Why? Because we are afraid? No! We are convinced that they fear the Revolution more than we fear them. They have a mentality that does not permit them to sleep when they know that there is a revolution nearby.

Fear? No one has fear here. The people who struggle for their liberty are never frightened. The frightened ones are the wealthy. The ones who have been wealthy. We are not interested in having imperialism commit suicide at our expense. They do not care about the death of Blacks, Puerto Ricans, or Americans. But we do care about every Cuban life. We are interested in peace.

We are ready to negotiate. They say that economic conditions can be discussed, but not communism. Well, where did they get the idea we would discuss that? We would discuss economic problems. But we are not even ready to admit that these talks so much as brush a petal of a rose here. The Cuban people are capable of establishing the régime they want. We have never even thought of the possibility of discussing our régime. We will discuss only things that will not affect our sovereignty. We do want to negotiate on behalf of peace.

Those who do not worry about taking the American people to war are being led by emotions. We have no fear. If they think so, let them get over that idea. No Cuban is afraid. If they think we will discuss internal politics, let them forget that, for no one here will do that. Let them discuss all topics they want to discuss. We discussed things with the invaders, did we not? Well, we will debate with anyone. We are willing to talk. We are willing to debate. But does that mean we are aching to negotiate? Of course not. We are just taking a sensible step. Does that mean the Revolution will slow down? Of course not! We will continue, picking up speed as we can ...

Before concluding, I want to recall what I said during the Moncada trial.[3] Here is a paragraph: 'The country cannot remain on its knees imploring miracles from the golden calf. No social problem is resolved spontaneously.' At that time we expressed our views. The Revolution has followed the revolutionary ideas of those who had an important role in this struggle.

That is why when one million Cubans met to proclaim the Havana Declaration, the document expressed the essence of our Revolution, our socialist Revolution. It said that it condemned landed estates, starvation wages, illiteracy, shortage of teachers, doctors, and hospitals, discrimination, exploitation of women, oligarchies that hold our country back, governments that ignore the will of their people by obeying US orders, monopoly of news by Yankee agencies, laws that prevent the masses from organizing, and imperialist monopolies which exploit our wealth. The general assembly of the people condemns exploitation of man by man. The general assembly proclaims the following: The right to work, education, the dignity of man, civil rights for women, secure old age, artistic freedom, nationalization of monopolies, and the necessities of life. This is the programme of our socialist Revolution.

Long live the Cuban working class! Long live the Latin American sister nations! Long live the nation!

Patria o Muerte! Venceremos!

---

3. Trial of Revolutionists who followed Castro after the famous attack on the Moncada army barracks on 26 July 1953.

II. The Road to Revolution in Latin America

CHAPTER 1

The Duty of a Revolutionary is to
Make the Revolution:
The Second Declaration of Havana*

This is one of the great political documents of all time. It was presented to the Cuban people on 4 February 1962, following Cuba's expulsion from the Organization of American States. It is printed here in its entirety.

On 18 May 1895, on the eve of his death from a Spanish bullet through the heart, José Martí, apostle of our independence, said in an unfinished letter to his friend Manuel Mercado:

Now I am able to write ... I am in danger each day now of giving my life for my country and for my obligation ... to prevent before it's too late – through achieving Cuba's independence – the United States from extending its control over the Antilles and consequently falling with that much more force upon our countries of America. Whatever I have done till now, and whatever I shall do, has been with that aim ...

The people most vitally concerned with preventing the imperialist annexation of Cuba, which would make Cuba the starting point of that course – which must be blocked and which we are blocking with our blood – of annexation of our American nations to the violent and brutal North which despises them, are being hindered by lesser and public commitments from the open and avowed espousal of this sacrifice, which is being made for our and their benefit.

I have lived inside the monster and know its guts; and my sling is the sling of David.

In 1895, Martí already pointed out the danger hovering over America and called imperialism by its name: imperialism. He

---

* Delivered in Havana, Plaza de la Revolución, 4 February 1962, 'Year of Planning'.

pointed out to the people of Latin America that more than any-one, they had a stake in seeing that Cuba did not succumb to the greed of the Yankee, scornful of the peoples of Latin America. And with his own blood, shed for Cuba and America, he wrote the words which posthumously, in homage to his memory, the people of Cuba place at the head of this declaration.

Humiliation

Sixty-seven years have passed. Puerto Rico was converted into a colony and is still a colony saturated with military bases. Cuba also fell into the clutches of imperialism. Their troops occupied our territory. The Platt Amendment was imposed on our first constitution, as a humiliating clause which sanctioned the odious right of foreign intervention. Our riches passed into their hands, our history was falsified, our government and our politics were entirely moulded in the interests of the overseers; the nation was subjected to sixty years of political, economic, and cultural suffo-cation.

But Cuba rose, Cuba was able to redeem itself from the bastard guardianship. Cuba broke the chains which tied its fortunes to those of the imperialist oppressor, redeemed its riches, reclaimed its culture, and unfurled its banner as the Free Territory of America.

Now the United States will never again be able to use Cuba's strength against America, but conversely, dominating the major-ity of the other Latin American states, the United States is attempting to use the strength of America against Cuba.

What is the history of Cuba but the history of Latin America? And what is the history of Latin America but the history of Asia, Africa, and Oceania? And what is the history of all these peoples but the history of the most pitiless and cruel exploitation by im-perialism throughout the world?

At the end of the last and the beginning of the present cen-tury, a handful of economically developed nations had finished partitioning the world among themselves, subjecting to their economic and political domination two thirds of humanity, which was thus forced to work for the ruling classes of the economically advanced capitalist countries.

Privileged position

The historical circumstances which permitted certain European countries and the United States of America to attain a high level of industrial development placed them in a position to subject the rest of the world to their domination and exploitation.

What motives compelled the expansion of the industrial powers? Were they moral motives? Was it a matter of 'civilizing', as they claimed? No: they were economic reasons.

Since the discovery of America, which hurled the European conquerors across the seas to occupy and exploit lands and inhabitants of other continents, the fundamental motive for their conduct was the desire for riches. The discovery of America itself was carried out in search of shorter routes to the Orient whose goods were highly paid for in Europe.

A new social class, the merchants and the producers of manufactured articles for commerce, arose from the womb of the feudal society of lords and serfs, in the decline of the Middle Ages.

The thirst for gold was the motive which spurred the efforts of that new class. The desire for gain was the incentive for its conduct throughout history. With the growth of manufacturing and commerce, its social influence also grew. The productive forces which were developing in the womb of feudal society clashed more and more with the relationships of servitude characteristic of feudalism, with its laws, its institutions, its philosophy, its morality, its art, and its political ideology.

New philosophical and political ideas, new concepts of right and of the state were proclaimed by the intellectual representatives of the bourgeoisie, which – because they responded to the new necessities of social life – gradually entered into the consciousness of the exploited masses. They were then revolutionary ideas opposed to those outworn ideas of feudal society. The peasants, the artisans, the workers, led by the bourgeoisie, overthrew the feudal order, its philosophy, its ideas, its institutions, its laws, and the privileges of the ruling class, that is, the hereditary nobility ...

At that time, the bourgeoisie considered revolution necessary and just. It did not think that the feudal order could and should be eternal – as it now thinks of its capitalist social order. It encouraged the peasants to free themselves from feudal servitude, it turned the artisans against the medieval guilds, and demanded the right to political power. The absolute monarchs, the nobility, and the high clergy stubbornly defended their class privileges, proclaiming the divine right of kings and the immutability of the social order. To be liberal then, to proclaim the ideas of Voltaire, Diderot, or Jean Jacques Rousseau, spokesmen for bourgeois philosophy, constituted in the eyes of the ruling classes as serious a crime as it does today in the eyes of the bourgeoisie to be a socialist and to proclaim the ideas of Marx, Engels, and Lenin.

When the bourgeoisie took political power and established its capitalist mode of production on the ruins of feudal society, it was on this mode of production it erected its state, its laws, its ideas, and institutions. Those institutions sanctified, in the first instance, the essence of class rule: private property.

The new society based on the private ownership of the means of production and free competition was thus divided into two basic classes: one, the owner of the means of production, ever more modern and efficient; the other, deprived of all wealth, possessing only its labour power, of necessity sold this labour power in the market as another piece of merchandise, simply in order to live.

Productive forces

With the feudal bonds broken, the productive forces developed extraordinarily. Great factories arose in which greater and greater numbers of workers were utilized.

The most modern and technically efficient factories continually drove from the market the less efficient competitors. The cost of industrial equipment continually rose. It became necessary to accumulate more and more capital. A greater portion of production passed into a smaller number of hands. Thus arose the great capitalist enterprises and later, according to the degree and character of the association, the great industrial combines – the cartels, syndicates, trusts, and corporations, controlled by the owners of the major portion of the stock, that is to say, by the most powerful heads of industry. Free competition, characteristic of capitalism in its first phase, gave way to monopolies which entered into agreements among themselves and controlled the markets.

Exploitation

Where did the colossal quantity of resources come from which permitted a handful of monopolists to accumulate billions of dollars? Simply from the exploitation of human labour. Millions of men, forced to work for subsistence wages, produced with their strength the gigantic capital of the monopolies. From the workers came the fortunes of the privileged classes, ever richer, ever more powerful. Through the banking institutions, these classes were able to make use, not only of their own money, but that of all society. Thus was brought about the fusion of the banks with giant industry, and finance capital was born. What should they do with the great surplus of capital which was accumulating in ever greater quantities? Invade the world with it. Always in pursuit of profit, they began to seize the natural resources of all the economically weak countries and to exploit the human labour of the inhabitants, paying even more wretched wages than they were forced to pay to the workers of their own developed countries. Thus, began the territorial and economic division of the world. By 1914, eight or ten imperialist countries had subjugated territories beyond their own borders, covering more than 83,700,000 square kilometres, with a population of 970,000,000 inhabitants. They had simply divided up the world.

But as the world was limited in size and already divided down to the last corner of the earth, a clash ensued among the different monopolistic nations and struggles grew for new divisions, struggles originating in the disproportionate distribution of industrial and economic power which the various monopolistic nations had attained in their uneven development. Imperialist wars broke out which would cost humanity fifty million dead, tens of millions wounded and the destruction of incalculable material and cultural wealth. Even before this had happened, Karl Marx wrote that 'capital comes into the world dripping from head to foot through every pore with blood and mire.'

The capitalist system of production, once it had given all of which it was capable, became an abysmal obstacle to the progress of humanity. But from its origins, the bourgeoisie carried within itself its contradiction. In its womb gigantic productive instrumentalities were developed, but with time a new and vigorous social force developed : the proletariat. The proletariat which was destined to change the old and worn-out social system of capitalism into a superior socio-economic form in accordance with the historic possibilities of human society, by converting into social property those gigantic means of production which the people, and none but the people, had created and amassed by their work. At such a state of development, the productive forces made completely anachronistic and outmoded the régime which stood for private ownership and the economic subordination of millions and millions of human beings to the dictates of a small, social minority.

Rapacious wars

The interests of humanity cried out for a halt to the anarchy of capitalist production; for a halt to the waste, the economic crises, and the rapacious wars which are part of the capitalist system. The growing necessities of the human race and the possibility of satisfying them demanded the planned development of the economy and the rational utilization of means of production and natural resources.

It was inevitable that imperialism and colonialism would fall into a profound and insoluble crisis. The general crisis began with the outbreak of World War I, with the revolution of the workers and peasants which overthrew the Tsarist empire of Russia and founded, amidst the most difficult conditions of capitalist encirclement and aggression, the world's first socialist state, opening a new era in the history of humanity. From that time on, the crisis and decomposition of the imperialist system has incessantly worsened.

Imperialist powers

World War II, unleashed by the imperialist powers – and into which were dragged the Soviet Union and other criminally invaded peoples of Asia and Europe who were invaded in a criminal manner and engaged in a bloody struggle of liberation – culminated in the defeat of fascism, formation of the worldwide socialist camp and the struggle of the colonial and dependent peoples for their sovereignty. Between 1945 and 1957, more than 1,200 million human beings gained their independence in Asia and Africa. The blood shed by the people was not in vain.

The movement of the dependent and colonial peoples is a phenomenon of universal character which agitates the world and marks the final crisis of imperialism.

Cuba and Latin America are part of the world. Our problems form part of the problems engendered by the general crisis of imperialism and the struggle of the subjugated peoples – the clash between the world that is being born and the world that is dying. The odious and brutal campaign unleashed against our nation expresses the desperate, as well as futile, effort which the imperialists are making to prevent the liberation of the people. Cuba hurts the imperialists in a special way. What is it that is hidden behind the Yankee's hatred of the Cuban Revolution? What is it that rationally explains the conspiracy which unites, for the same aggressive purpose, the most powerful and richest imperialist power in the modern world and the oligarchies of an entire continent, which together are supposed to represent a population of 350 million human beings, against a small country of only seven million inhabitants, economically underdeveloped, without financial or military means to threaten the security or economy of any other country? What unites them and stirs them up in fear? What explains it is fear. Not fear of the Cuban

Revolution but fear of the Latin American revolution. Not fear of the workers, peasants, intellectuals, students, and progressive sectors of the middle strata which, by revolutionary means, have taken power in Cuba; but fear that the workers, peasants, students, intellectuals, and progressive sectors of the middle strata will, by revolutionary means, take power in the oppressed and hungry countries exploited by the Yankee monopolies and reactionary oligarchies of America; fear that the plundered people of the continent will seize the arms from the oppressors and, like Cuba, declare themselves free people of America . . .

By crushing the Cuban Revolution, they hope to dispel the fear that torments them, the spectre of the revolution that threatens them. By liquidating the Cuban Revolution, they hope to liquidate the revolutionary spirit of the people. They imagine in their delirium that Cuba is an exporter of revolutions. In their sleepless merchants' and usurers' minds there is the idea that revolutions can be bought, sold, rented, loaned, exported, and imported like some piece of merchandise. Ignorant of the objective laws that govern the development of human societies, they believe that their monopolistic, capitalistic, and semi-feudal régimes are eternal. Educated in their own reactionary ideology, a mixture of superstition, ignorance, subjectivism, pragmatism, and other mental aberrations, they have an image of the world and of the march of history conforming to their interests as exploiting classes.

They imagine that revolutions are born or die in the brains of individuals or are caused by divine laws, and, moreover, that the gods are on their side. They have always thought that way – from the devout patrician pagans of Roman slave society who hurled the early Christians to the lions at the circus, and the inquisitors of the Middle Ages who, as guardians of feudalism and absolute monarchy, burned at the stake the first representatives of the liberal thought of the nascent bourgeoisie, up to today's bishops who anathematize proletarian revolutions in defence of the bourgeois and monopolist régime.

All reactionary classes in all historical epochs, when the antagonism between exploiters and exploited reaches its highest peak, presaging the arrival of a new social régime, have turned to the worst weapons of repression and calumny against their adversaries. The primitive Christians were taken to their martyrdom accused of burning Rome and of sacrificing children on their altars. Philosophers like Giordano Bruno, reformers like Hus, and thousands of others who did not conform with the feudal order, were accused of heresy and taken by the inquisitors to be burned at the stake.

Persecution

Today, persecution rages over the proletarian fighters, and this crime brings out the worst calumnies in the monopolistic and bourgeois press. Always, in each historical period, the ruling classes have committed murder – invoking the defence of society, order, the country; 'their' society of privileged minorities and exploited majorities, 'their' class rule, maintained by blood and fire against the dispossessed; the 'country', whose fruits only they enjoy, depriving the rest of the people of those fruits, in order to suppress the revolutionaries who aspire to a new society, a just order, a country truly for all.

The march of humanity

But the evolution of history, the upward march of humanity, is not held back, nor can it be held back. The forces which impel the people, who are the real makers of history, forces determined by the material conditions of existence and aspirations to higher goals of well-being and liberty, forces which surge forth when man's progress in the fields of science, technology, and culture make it possible, are superior to the will and the terror unleashed by the ruling oligarchies.

The subjective conditions of each country – that is, the consciousness, organization, leadership – can accelerate or retard the revolution, according to their greater or lesser degree of development, but sooner or later, in each historical period, when the objective conditions mature, consciousness is acquired, the organization is formed, the leadership emerges, and the revolution takes place.

Whether this takes place peacefully or in painful birth does not depend on the revolutionaries, it depends on the reactionary forces of the old society who resist the birth of the new society engendered by the contradictions carried in the womb of the old society. The revolution is in history like the doctor who assists at the birth of a new life. It does not use the tools of force needlessly, but will use them without hesitation whenever necessary to help the birth, a birth which brings to the enslaved and exploited masses the hope of a new and better life.

Today in many countries of Latin America revolution is inevitable. That fact is not determined by anyone's will. It is determined by the horrifying conditions of exploitation in which American man lives, by the development of the revolutionary consciousness of the masses, by the world crisis of imperialism and the universal movement of struggle among subjugated peoples.

The anxiety felt today is an unmistakable symptom of rebellion. The very depths of a continent are profoundly moved, a continent which has witnessed four centuries of slave, semi-slave and feudal exploitation, beginning with its aboriginal inhabitants and the slaves brought from Africa, up to the national nuclei which emerged later: white, black, mulatto, mestizo, and Indian. Today they are made brothers by scorn, humiliation, and the Yankee yoke, and are brothers in their hope for a better tomorrow.

Exploitation remained

The peoples of America liberated themselves from Spanish colonialism at the beginning of the last century, but they did not free themselves from exploitation. The feudal landowners assumed the authority of the Spanish rulers, the Indians continued in painful servitude, the Latin American man in one form or another, continued to be a slave, and the minimum hopes of the people gave way under the power of the oligarchies and the yoke of foreign capital. This has been the truth of America – in one coloration or another, in one variation or another. Today Latin America lies beneath an imperialism, much more fierce, much more powerful, and more cruel than the Spanish colonial empire.

What is the attitude of Yankee imperialism to the objective reality of the historically inexorable Latin American revolution? To prepare to wage a colonial war against the peoples of Latin America; to create an apparatus of force, the political pretexts and the pseudo-legal instruments subscribed to by the reactionary oligarchies, to repress with blood and fire the struggle of the Latin American peoples ...

The intervention of the government of the United States in the internal politics of Latin American countries has become more open and unbridled each time.

The Inter-American Defense Council, for example, has been and is the nest where the most reactionary and pro-Yankee officers of the Latin American armies are trained to serve later as shock troops in the service of the monopolies.

The North American military missions in Latin America constitute a permanent apparatus of espionage in each nation, directly tied to the Central Intelligence Agency, inculcating in those officers the most reactionary sentiments and trying to convert the armies into instruments of its own political and economic interests.

At present, in the Panama Canal Zone, the North American high command has organized special courses to train Latin American officers to fight revolutionary guerrillas, with the aim of repressing the armed action of the peasant masses against the feudal exploitation to which they are subjected.

In the United States itself the Central Intelligence Agency has organized special schools to train Latin American agents in the most subtle forms of assassination; and in the Yankee military services the physical liquidation of the anti-imperialist leaders is an accepted policy.

It is notorious that the Yankee embassies in the different Latin American countries are organizing, instructing, and equipping fascist bands to spread terror and to attack labour, student, and intellectual organizations. These bands, into which they recruit the sons of the oligarchies, *lumpen*, and people of the lowest character, have already perpetrated a series of aggressive acts against the mass movements.

Santo Domingo

Nothing is more evident and unequivocal about the intentions of imperialism than its recent conduct in the events in Santo Domingo. Without any kind of justification, without even making use of diplomatic relations with that republic, the United States, after stationing its warships before the Dominican capital, declared with its usual arrogance that if Balaguer's government sought military aid, it would land troops in Santo Domingo to quell the insurgence of the Dominican people. That Balaguer's power was absolutely spurious, that each sovereign country of Latin America should have the right to resolve its internal problems without foreign intervention, that there exist international norms and world opinions, that there even exists an OAS,[1] did not count at all in the considerations of the United States.

What did count were its designs for holding back the Dominican revolution, for its reinstating its odious policy of landing Marines, with no more basis or prerequisite for establishing this new piratical concept of law than a tyrannical, illegitimate, crisis-ridden ruler's simple request. The significance of this should not escape the peoples of Latin America. In Latin America there are more than enough rulers who are ready to use Yankee troops against their own people when they find themselves in a crisis.

US policy

North American imperialism's declared policy of sending soldiers to fight against the revolutionary movement of any country in Latin America, that is, to kill workers, students, peasants, Latin

1. Organization of American States, US dominated Latin American Regional organization of all American states except Canada, and after the Punta del Este meeting, Cuba.

American men and women, has no other objective than the continued maintenance of its monopolistic interests and the privileges
of the traitorous oligarchies which support it.

It can now be clearly seen that the military pacts signed by the
government of the United States with Latin American governments – often secret pacts and always behind the backs of the
people – invoking hypothetical foreign dangers which did not
exist, had the sole and exclusive object of preventing the struggle
of the people; they were pacts against the people, against the
only danger – the internal danger of the liberation movements
that would imperil Yankee interests. It was not without reason
that the people asked themselves: Why so many military agreements? Why the shipments of arms which, even though technically outmoded for modern war, are nevertheless efficient for
smashing strikes, repressing popular demonstrations, staining the
land with blood? Why the military missions, the pact of Rio de
Janeiro and the thousand and one international conferences?

Since the end of World War II, the nations of Latin America
have been impoverished more and more, their exports have less
and less value, their imports cost more, the per capita income
falls, the awful rate of infant mortality does not decrease, the
number of illiterates is higher, the people lack jobs, land, adequate housing, schools, hospitals, means of communication, and
means of life. On the other hand, North American investments
exceed ten billion dollars. Latin America, moreover, provides
cheap raw materials, and is the buyer of expensive finished articles. The United States trades with Latin America like the first
Spanish conquerors, who bartered mirrors and trinkets for gold
and silver. To guard that torrent of riches, to gain over more control of Latin America's resources and to exploit its suffering
peoples – that is what is hidden behind the military pacts, the
military missions, and Washington's diplomatic lobbying ...

This policy of gradual strangulation of the sovereignty of the
Latin American nations, and of a free hand to intervene in their
internal affairs, culminated in the recent meeting of foreign ministers at Punta del Este. Yankee imperialism gathered the ministers
together to wrest from them – through political pressure and un-
precedented economic blackmail in collusion with a group of the

most discredited rulers of this continent – the renunciation of the national sovereignty of our peoples and the consecration of the odious Yankee right to intervention in the internal affairs of Latin America; the submission of the peoples completely to the will of the United States of North America, against which all our great men, from Bolívar to Sandino, fought. Neither the government of the United States, nor the representatives of the exploiting oligarchies, nor the big reactionary press, in the pay of the monopolies and feudal lords, concealed this, but openly demanded agreements which constituted formal suppression of the right of self-determination of our peoples; abolishing it with a stroke of the pen at the most infamous conspiracy in the memory of this continent.

Behind closed doors, in repugnant and unlawful meetings, the Yankee minister of colonies dedicated entire days to beating down the resistance and scruples of some ministers, bringing into play the millions of the Yankee treasury in an undisguised buy-and selling of votes. A handful of representatives of the oligarchies (of countries which together barely add up to a third of the continent's population) imposed agreements that served up to the Yankee master on a silver platter, the head of a principle which cost the blood of all our countries since the wars of independence. The Pyrrhic character of such sad and fraudulent deeds of imperialism, their moral failure, the broken unanimity, and the universal scandal do not diminish the grave danger which agreements imposed at such a price have brought so close to the peoples of Latin America. At that evil conclave Cuba's thundering voice was raised without weakness or fear, to indict, before all the peoples of America and the world, the monstrous attempt, and to defend with a virility and dignity which will be clear in the annals of history, not only Cuba's rights but the deserted rights of all our sister nations of the American Continent. The word of Cuba could find no echo in that house-broken majority, but neither could it find a refutation; only impotent silence greeted its demolishing arguments and the clearness and courage of its words. But Cuba did not speak for the ministers, Cuba spoke for the people and for history, where its words will be echoed and answered.

At Punta del Este a great ideological battle unfolded between the Cuban Revolution and Yankee imperialism. Who did they represent there, for whom did each speak? Cuba represented the people; the United States represented the monopolies. Cuba spoke for America's exploited masses; the United States for the exploiting, oligarchical, and imperialist interests; Cuba for sovereignty; the United States for intervention; Cuba for the nationalization of foreign enterprises; the United States for new investments of foreign capital. Cuba for culture; the United States for ignorance. Cuba for agrarian reform; the United States for great landed estates. Cuba for the industrialization of America; the United States for underdevelopment. Cuba for creative work; the United States for sabotage and counter-revolutionary terror practised by its agents – the destruction of sugar-cane fields and factories, the bombing by their pirate planes of the labour of a peaceful people. Cuba for the murdered teachers; the United States for the assassins. Cuba for bread; the United States for hunger. Cuba for equality; the United States for privilege and discrimination. Cuba for the truth; the United States for lies. Cuba for liberation; the United States for oppression. Cuba for the bright future of humanity; the United States for the past without hope. Cuba for the heroes who fell at Girón to save the country from foreign domination; the United States for mercenaries and traitors who serve the foreigner against their country. Cuba for peace among peoples; the United States for aggression and war. Cuba for socialism; the United States for capitalism . . .

The agreements obtained by the United States through methods so shameful that the entire world criticizes them, do not diminish but increase the morality and justice of Cuba's stand, which exposes the sell-out and treason of the oligarchies to the national interests and shows the people the road to liberation. It reveals the corruption of the exploiting classes for whom their representatives spoke at Punta del Este. The OAS was revealed for what it really is – a Yankee Ministry of Colonies, a military alliance, an apparatus of repression against the liberation movements of the Latin American peoples.

Cuba has lived three years of the Revolution under the incessant harassment of Yankee intervention in our internal affairs. Pirate airplanes coming from the United States, dropping incendiaries, have burned millions of *arrobas* [2] of sugar cane; acts of international sabotage perpetrated by Yankee agents, like the explosion of the ship *La Coubre*, have cost dozens of Cuban lives; thousands of North American weapons have been dropped by parachute by the US military services onto our territory to promote subversion; hundreds of tons of explosive materials and bombs have been secretly landed on our coast from North American launches to promote sabotage and terrorism; a Cuban worker was tortured on the naval base of Guantanamo and deprived of his life with no due process before or any explanation later; our sugar quota was abruptly cut and an embargo proclaimed on parts and raw materials for factories and North American construction machinery in order to ruin our economy. Cuban ports and installations have been surprise-attacked by armed ships and bombers from bases prepared by the United States. Mercenary troops, organized and trained in countries of Central America by the same government, have in a warlike manner invaded our territories, escorted by ships of the Yankee fleet and with aerial support from foreign bases, causing much loss of life as well as material wealth; counter-revolutionary Cubans are being trained in the US army and new plans of aggression against Cuba are being made. All this has been going on incessantly for three years, before the eyes of the whole continent – and the OAS was not aware of it.

The ministers meet in Punta del Este and do not even admonish the US government nor the governments who are material accomplices to these aggressions. They expel Cuba, the Latin American victim, the aggrieved nation.

The United States has military pacts with nations of all the continents; military blocs with whatever fascist, militarist, and reactionary government there is in the world: NATO, SEATO, and CENTO, to which we now have to add the OAS; it intervenes in Laos, in Vietnam, in Korea, in Formosa, in Berlin. It openly sends ships to Santo Domingo in order to impose its law, its will, and announces its proposal to use its NATO allies to

2. Dry measure of about twenty-five pounds.

block commerce with Cuba. And the OAS is not aware! The ministers meet and expel Cuba, which has no military pacts with any country. Thus the government that organizes subversion throughout the world and forges military alliances on four continents, forces the expulsion of Cuba, accusing her of no less than subversion and having ties beyond the continent.

Cuba's record

Cuba, the Latin American nation which has made landowners of more than 100,000 small farmers, provided year-round employment on state farms and co-operatives to all agricultural workers, transformed forts into schools, given 70,000 scholarships to university, secondary, and technological students, created lecture halls for the entire child population, totally liquidated illiteracy, quadrupled medical services, nationalized foreign interests, suppressed the abusive system which turned housing into a means of exploiting people, virtually eliminated unemployment, suppressed discrimination due to race or sex, ridded itself of gambling, vice, and administrative corruption, armed the people, made the enjoyment of human rights a living reality by freeing man and woman from exploitation, lack of culture, and social inequality, which has liberated itself from all foreign tutelage, acquired full sovereignty, and established the foundations for the development of its economy in order to no longer be a country producing only one crop and exporting only raw materials, is expelled from the Organization of American States by governments which have not achieved for their people one of these objectives. How will they be able to justify their conduct before the peoples of the Americas and the world? How will they be able to deny that in their concept the policy of land, of bread, of work, of health, of liberty, of equality, of culture, of accelerated development of the economy, of national dignity, of full self-determination and sovereignty, is incompatible with the hemisphere?

The people think very differently, the people think that the only thing incompatible with the destiny of Latin America is misery, feudal exploitation, illiteracy, starvation wages, unemployment, the policy of repression against the masses of workers, peasants, and students, discrimination against women, Negroes, Indians, mestizos, oppression by the oligarchies, the plundering of their wealth by the Yankee monopolists, the moral stagnation of their intellectuals and artists, the ruin of the small producers of foreign competition, economic underdevelopment, peoples without roads, without hospitals, without housing, without schools, without industries, the submission to imperialism, the renunciation of national sovereignty, and the betrayal of the country ...

How can the imperialists make understood their conduct and condemnatory attitude towards Cuba? With what words and what arguments are they going to speak to those whom, all the while exploiting, they ignored for so long?

The imperialist record

Those who study the problems of America are accustomed to ask: what country has concentrated upon – for the purpose of remedying – the situation of the idle, the poor, the Indians, the Blacks, and the helpless infants, this immense number of infants – thirty million in 1950 (which will be fifty million in eight more years). Yes, what country?

Thirty-two million Indians – like the Andes mountains – form the backbone of the entire American continent. It is clear that for those who considered the Indian more as a thing than a person, this mass of humanity does not count, did not count and, they thought, never would count. Of course, since they were considered a brute labour force, they had to be used like a yoke of oxen or a tractor.

How – under what oath – could anyone believe in any benefit, in any 'Alliance for Progress' with imperialism, when under its saintly protection, its killings, its persecutions, the natives of the South of the continent, like those of Patagonia, still live under strips of canvas as did their ancestors at the time the discoverers came almost 500 years ago? Where are those great races which populated northern Argentina, Paraguay, and Bolivia, such as the Guarani who were savagely decimated, hunted like animals,

and buried in the depths of the jungle? Where is that reservoir
of indigenous stock – whose extinction is continually hastened –
which could have served as a base for a great American civilization? Across the Paraguayan swamps and desolate Bolivian high-
lands, deeper into itself, America has driven these primitive,
melancholy races, brutalized by alcohol and narcotics to which
they became addicted in order at least to survive in the subhuman conditions – not only of nutrition – in which they live.
Where does a chain of hands stretch out almost in vain, yet still
stretching out across centuries, over the Andean peaks and slopes,
along great rivers and in the shadowy forests, uniting their miseries with those of others who are slowly perishing. Where do
hands stretch out to Brazilian tribes and those of the North of
the continent and the coasts, until in the most incredible and
wild confines of the Amazon jungle or mountain ranges of Perija,
Venezuela's hundred thousand indigent are reached, then to the
isolated Vapicharnas, who await their end, now almost definitely
lost to the human race, in the hot regions of the Guianas? Yes,
all these thirty-two million Indians, who extend from the United
States border to the limits of the Southern hemisphere, and the
forty-five million mestizos, who for the most part differ little
from the Indians; all these natives, this formidable reservoir of
labour, whose rights have been trampled on, yes, what can imperialism offer them? How can these people, ignored so long, be
made to believe in any benefit to come from such bloodstained
hands?

Entire tribes which live unclothed; others which are supposed
to be cannibalistic; others whose members die like flies upon their
first contact with the conquering civilization; others which are
banished, that is, thrown off their lands, pushed to the point of
squatting in the jungles, mountains, or most distant reaches of
the prairies where not even the smallest particle of culture, light,
bread, nor anything penetrates.

In what 'alliance' – other than one for their own more rapid
extermination – are these native races going to believe, these races
who have been flogged for centuries, shot so their lands could be
taken, beaten to death by the thousands for not working faster
in their exploited labour for imperialism?

'Alliance' for Blacks

And to the Black? What 'alliance' can the system of lynching and brutal exclusion of the Black offer to the fifteen million Negroes and fourteen million mulattoes of Latin America, who know with horror and rage that their brothers in the North cannot ride in the same vehicles as their white compatriots, nor attend the same schools, nor even die in the same hospitals?

How are these disinherited racial groups going to believe in this imperialism, in its benefits or in any 'alliance' with it which is not for lynching and exploiting them as slaves? Those masses who have not been permitted even modestly to enjoy any cultural, social, or professional benefits, who – even when they are in the majority or number millions – are persecuted by the imperialists in Ku Klux Klan costumes, are ghettoed in the most unsanitary neighbourhoods, in the least comfortable tenements built expressly for them, are shoved into the most menial occupations, the hardest labour and the least lucrative professions. They cannot presume to reach the universities, advanced academies and private schools.

What 'Alliance for Progress' can serve as encouragement to those 107 million men and women of our America, the backbone of labour in the cities and fields, whose dark skin – black, mestizo, mulatto, Indian – inspires scorn in the new colonialists? How are they – who with bitter impotence have seen how in Panama there is one wage scale for Yankees and another for Panamanians, who are regarded as an inferior race – going to put any trust in the supposed Alliance? . . .

What can the workers hope for, with their starvation wages, the hardest jobs, the most miserable conditions, lack of nutrition, illness, and all the evils which foster misery?

What words can be said, what benefits can the imperialists offer to the copper, tin, iron, coal miners who cough up their lungs for the profits of merciless foreign masters, and to the fathers and sons of the lumberjacks and rubber-plantation workers, to the harvesters of the fruit plantations, to the workers in the coffee and sugar mills, to the peons on the pampas and plains who forfeit their health and lives to amass the fortunes of the exploiters?

What can those vast masses – who produce the wealth, who create the values, who aid in bringing forth a new world in all places – expect? What can they expect from imperialism, that greedy mouth, that greedy hand, with no other face than misery, but the most absolute destitution and death, cold and unrecorded in the end?

What can this class, which has changed the course of history, which in other places has revolutionized the world, which is the vanguard of all the humble and exploited, what can it expect from imperialism, its most irreconcilable enemy?

And to teachers, professors, professionals, intellectuals, poets, and artists, what can imperialism offer? What kind of benefits, what chance for a better and more equitable life, what purpose, what inducement, what desire to excel, to gain mastery beyond the first simple steps, can it offer to those who devotedly care for the generations of children and young people on whom imperialism will later gorge itself? What can it offer to these people who live on degrading wages in most countries, who almost everywhere suffer restrictions on their right of political and social expression, whose economic future doesn't exceed the bare limits of their shaky resources and compensation, who are buried in a grey life without prospects which ends with a pension that does not even meet half the cost of living? What 'benefits' or 'alliances' can imperialism offer them? . . .

If imperialism provides sources of aid to the professions, arts, and publications, it is always well understood that their products must reflect its interests, aims, and 'nothingness'. On the other hand, the novels which attempt to reflect the reality of the world of imperialism's rapacious deeds; the poems aspiring to protest against its enslavement, its interference in life, in thought, in the very bodies of nations and peoples; and the militant arts which in their expression try to capture the forms and content of imperialism's aggression and the constant pressure on every progressive living and breathing thing and on all that is revolutionary, which teaches, which – full of light and conscience, of clarity and beauty – tries to guide men and peoples to better destinies, to the highest summits of life and justice – all these meet imperialism's severest censure. They run into obstacles, condemnation, and McCarthyite persecution. Its presses are closed to them; their names are barred from its columns of print and a campaign of the most atrocious silence is imposed against them – which is another contradiction of imperialism. For it is then that the writer, poet, painter, sculptor, the creator in any material, the scientist, begins truly to live in the tongue of the people, in the heart of millions of men throughout the world. Imperialism puts everything backward, deforms it, diverts it into its own channels for profit, to multiply its dollars; buying words or paintings or stutterings or turning into silence the expression of revolutionists, of progressive men, of those who struggle for the people and their needs.

We cannot forget, in this sad picture, the underprivileged children, the neglected, the futureless children of America.

America, a continent with a high birth rate, also has a high death rate. The mortality of children under a year old in eleven countries a few years ago was over 125 per 1,000 and in seventeen others it stood at 90 children per 1,000. In 102 nations of the world, on the other hand, the rate is 51. In Latin America, then, there die, sadly neglected, 74 out of a 1,000 in the first year after birth. In some Latin American countries that rate reaches 300 per 1,000; thousands and thousands of children up to seven years old die of incredible diseases in America; diarrhoeas, pneumonias, malnutrition, hunger. Thousands and thousands are sick without hospital treatment, medicines; thousands and thousands walking about, victims of endemic cretinism, malaria, trachoma, and other diseases caused by contamination, lack of water, and other necessities. Diseases of this nature are common among those Latin American countries where thousands and thousands of children are in agony, children of outcasts, children of the poor and of the petty bourgeoisie with a hard life and precarious means. The statistics, which would be redundant here, are blood-curdling. Any official publication of the international organizations gathers them by the hundreds.

Mass illiteracy

Regarding education, one becomes indignant merely to think of what America lacks on the cultural level. While the United States has a level of eight or nine years of schooling for those in its population who are fifteen years and older, Latin America, plundered and pauperized by the US, *has a level of less than one year of approved schooling* in the same age group.

It makes one even more angry to know that of the children between five and fourteen years old, only twenty per cent are enrolled in a school in some countries, and in those of the highest level, sixty per cent. That is to say, more than half the children of Latin America do not go to school. But the pain continues to grow when we learn that enrolment in the first three grades comprises more than eighty per cent of those enrolled; and that in the sixth grade the enrolment fluctuates from a bare *six* to twenty-two pupils for each hundred who began in the first grade. Even in those countries which believe they have taken care of their children, pupil dropouts between the first and sixth grade averages seventy-three per cent. In Cuba, before the Revolution, it was seventy-four per cent. In Colombia, a 'representative democracy', it is seventy-eight per cent. And if one looks closely at the countryside only one per cent of the children reach the fifth grade in the best of cases.

When one investigates this disastrous student absenteeism, there is one cause which explains it: the economy of misery. Lack of schools, lack of teachers, lack of family resources, child labour. In the last analysis – imperialism and its product of oppression and backwardness.

The summary of this nightmare which torments America, from one end to the other, is that on this continent of almost 200 million human beings, two thirds are Indians, mestizos, and Blacks – the 'discriminated against'; on this continent of semi-colonies about four persons per minute die of hunger, of curable illness or premature old age, 5,500 per day, two million per year, ten million each five years. These deaths could easily be avoided, but nevertheless they take place. Two thirds of the Latin American population lives briefly and lives under constant threat of death. A holocaust of lives, which in fifteen years has caused twice the number of deaths of World War I ... it still rages. Meanwhile, from Latin America a continuous torrent of money flows to the United States: some $4,000 a minute, $5 million a day, $2 billion a year, $10 billion every five years. For each thousand dollars which leave us, there remains one corpse. A thousand dollars per corpse: that is the price of what is called imperialism! A *thousand dollars per death, four deaths every minute!*

Punta del Este

But why did they meet at Punta del Este despite this American reality? Perhaps to bring a single drop of hope? No!

The people know that at Punta del Este the ministers, who expelled Cuba, met to renounce national sovereignty; that the government of the United States went there not only to establish the basis for aggression against Cuba, but the basis for intervention against the people's liberation movements in any American nation; that the United States is preparing a bloody drama for Latin America; that just as the exploiting oligarchies now renounce the principle of sovereignty, they will not hesitate to solicit intervention of Yankee troops against their own people, and that for this end the North American delegation proposed a watchdog committee against subversion in the Inter-American Defense Council, with executive powers, and the adoption of collective measures. Subversion for the Yankee imperialists is the struggle of hungry people for bread, the struggle of peasants for land, the struggle of the peoples against imperialist exploitation.

A 'watchdog committee' with executive powers in the Inter-American Defense Council means a continental repressive force against the peoples under the command of the Pentagon. 'Collective measures' means the landing of Yankee Marines in any country of America.

To the accusation that Cuba wants to export its revolution, we reply: Revolutions are not exported, they are made by the people ...

What Cuba can give to the people, and has already given, is its example.

And what does the Cuban Revolution teach? That revolution is possible, that the people can make it, that in the contemporary world there are no forces capable of halting the liberation movement of the peoples.

Our triumph would never have been feasible if the Revolution itself had not been inexorably destined to arise out of existing conditions in our socio-economic reality, a reality which exists to an even greater degree in a good number of Latin American countries.

It inevitably occurs that in the nations where the control of the Yankee monopolies is strongest, the exploitation of the oligarchy cruellest, and the situation of the labouring and peasant masses most unbearable, the political power appears most solid. The state of siege becomes habitual. Every manifestation of discontent by the masses is repressed by force. The democratic path is closed completely. The brutal character of dictatorship, the form of rule adopted by the ruling classes, reveals itself more clearly than ever. It is then that the revolutionary explosion of the peoples becomes inevitable.

Although it is true that in those underdeveloped countries of America the working class is generally relatively small, there is a social class which, because of the subhuman conditions in which it lives, constitutes a potential force that, led by the workers and the revolutionary intellectuals, has a decisive importance in the struggle for national liberation – the peasants ...

In our countries are two conditions: an underdeveloped industry and an agrarian régime of feudal character. That is why, with all the hardships of the conditions of life of the urban workers, the rural population lives in even more horrible conditions of oppression and exploitation; but it is also, with exceptions, the absolute majority sector, at times exceeding seventy per cent of the Latin American population.

Discounting the landlords, who often reside in the cities, the rest of that great mass gains its livelihood working as peons on the *haciendas*[3] for the most miserable wages, or work the land under conditions of exploitation which in no manner puts the Middle Ages to shame. These circumstances determine that in Latin America the poor rural population constitutes a tremendous potential revolutionary force.

The armies, built and equipped for conventional war, which are the force on which the power of the exploiting classes rests, become absolutely impotent when they have to confront the irregular struggle of the peasants on their own terrain. They lose ten men for each revolutionary fighter who falls. Demoralization spreads rapidly among them from having to face an invisible and invincible enemy who does not offer them the opportunity of showing off their academy tactics and their braggadocio which they use so much in military displays to curb the city workers and the students.

The initial struggle by small combat units is incessantly fed by new forces, the mass movement begins to loosen its bonds, the old order little by little begins to break into a thousand pieces, and that is the moment when the working class and the urban masses decide the battle.

What is it that from the beginning of the struggle of those first nuclei makes them invincible, regardless of the numbers, power, the resources of their enemies? It is the aid of the people, and they will be able to count on that help of the people on an ever-growing scale.

Role of peasants

But the peasantry is a class which, because of the uncultured state in which it is kept and the isolation in which it lives, needs the revolutionary and political leadership of the working class and the revolutionary intellectuals, for without them it would not by itself be able to plunge into the struggle and achieve victory.

In the actual historic conditions of Latin America, the national

---

3. Large farms or plantations.

bourgeoisie cannot lead the anti-feudal and anti-imperialist struggle. Experience shows that in our nations that class, even when its interests are in contradiction to those of Yankee imperialism, has been incapable of confronting it, for it is paralysed by fear of social revolution and frightened by the cry of the exploited masses.

Facing the dilemma of imperialism or revolution, only its most progressive strata will be with the people.

The actual world correlation of forces and the universal movement for the liberation of the colonial and dependent peoples points out to the working class and the revolutionary intellectuals of Latin America their true role, which is to place themselves resolutely in the vanguard of the struggle against imperialism and feudalism.

Imperialism, utilizing the great movie monopolies, its wire services, its periodicals, books, and reactionary newspapers, resorts to the most subtle lies to sow divisionism and inculcate fear and superstition among the most ignorant people with regard to revolutionary ideas which can and should frighten only the powerful exploiters with their worldly interests and privileges.

Divisionism, a product of all kinds of prejudices, false ideas and lies; sectarianism, dogmatism, a lack of broadness in analysing the role of each social layer, its parties, organizations, and leaders, all make difficult the necessary unity of action of the democratic and progressive forces of our peoples. They are defects of growth, infantile sicknesses of the revolutionary movement which must be left behind. In the anti-feudal and anti-imperialist struggle it is possible to bring the majority of the people resolutely behind goals of liberation which unite the spirit of the working class, the peasants, the intellectual workers, the petty bourgeoisie and the most progressive layers of the national bourgeoisie. These sectors comprise the immense majority of the population and join together great social forces capable of sweeping out the imperialist and reactionary feudal rule. In that broad movement they can and must struggle together for the good of our nations, for the good of our peoples, and for the good of America. There is a place for all progressives, from the old militant Marxist to the sincere

Catholic who has nothing to do with the Yankee monopolists and the feudal lords of the land.

That movement would pull along with itself the most progressive elements of the armed forces, those also humiliated by the Yankee military missions, the betrayal of national interests by the feudal oligarchies and the sacrifice of the national sovereignty to Washington's dictates.

Where the roads for the peoples are closed, where the repression of workers and peasants is fierce, where the rule of the Yankee monopolists is strongest, the first and most important task is to understand that it is neither honourable nor correct to beguile people with the fallacious and convenient illusion of uprooting – by legal means which don't exist and won't exist – ruling classes who are entrenched in all the state positions, monopolizing education, owning all media of information, possessing infinite financial resources – a power which the monopolies and oligarchies will defend with blood and fire and with the might of their police and armies.

The duty of revolutionaries

The duty of every revolutionary is to make the revolution. It is known that the revolution will triumph in America and throughout the world, but it is not for revolutionaries to sit in the doorways of their houses waiting for the corpse of imperialism to pass by. The role of Job doesn't suit a revolutionary. Each year that the liberation of America is speeded up will mean the lives of millions of children saved, millions of intelligences saved for culture, an infinite quantity of pain spared the people. Even if the Yankee imperialists prepare a bloody drama for America, they will not succeed in crushing the peoples' struggles, they will only arouse universal hatred against themselves. And such a drama will also mark the death of their greedy and carnivorous system.

Unity

No nation in Latin America is weak – because each forms part of a family of 200 million brothers, who suffer the same miseries, who harbour the same sentiments, who have the same energy, who dream about the same better future and who count upon the solidarity of all honest men and women throughout the world.

Great as was the epic of Latin American Independence, heroic as was that struggle, today's generation of Latin Americans is called upon to engage in an epic which is even greater and more decisive for humanity. For that struggle was for liberation from Spanish colonial power, from a decadent Spain invaded by the armies of Napoleon. Today the call for struggle is for liberation from the most powerful world imperialist centre, from the strongest force of world imperialism and to render humanity a greater service than that rendered by our predecessors.

But this struggle, to a greater extent than the earlier one, will be waged by the masses, will be carried out by the people; the people are going to play a much more important role now than then, the leaders are less important and will be less important in this struggle than in the one before.

This epic before us is going to be written by the hungry Indian masses, the peasants without land, the exploited workers. It is going to be written by the progressive masses, the honest and brilliant intellectuals, who so greatly abound in our suffering Latin American countries. Struggles of masses and ideas. An epic which will be carried forward by our people, despised and mal-treated by imperialism, our people, unreckoned with till today, who are now beginning to shake off their slumber. Imperialism considered us a weak and submissive flock; and now it begins to be terrified of that flock; a gigantic flock of 200 million Latin Americans in whom Yankee monopoly capitalism now sees its gravediggers.

This toiling humanity, inhumanly exploited, these paupers, controlled by the whip and overseer, have not been reckoned with or have been little reckoned with. From the dawn of independence their fate has been the same: Indians, gauchos, mestizos, zambos, quadroons, whites without property or income, all this human mass which formed the ranks of the 'nation', which never reaped any benefits, which fell by the millions, which was cut into bits, which won independence from the mother country for the bourgeoisie, which was shut out from its share of the rewards, which continued to occupy the lowest step on the ladder of social benefits, which continued to die of hunger, curable diseases and neglect, because for them there were never enough essentials of life – ordinary bread, a hospital bed, the medicine which cures, the hand which aids – their fate has been all the same.

But now from one end of the continent to the other they are signalling with clarity that the hour has come – the hour of their redemption. Now this anonymous mass, this America of colour, sombre, taciturn America, which all over the continent sings with the same sadness and disillusionment, now this mass is beginning to enter conclusively into its own history, is beginning to write it with its own blood, is beginning to suffer and die for it ...

Because now in the fields and mountains of America, on its slopes and prairies and in its jungles, in the wilderness or in the traffic of cities, this world is beginning with full cause to erupt. Anxious hands are stretched forth, ready to die for what is theirs, to win those rights which were laughed at by one and all for 500 years. Yes, now history will have to take the poor of America into account, the exploited and spurned of Latin America, who have decided to begin writing history for themselves for all time. Already they can be seen on the roads, on foot, day after day, in endless marches of hundreds of kilometres to the governmental 'eminences', to obtain their rights.

Already they can be seen armed with stones, sticks, machetes, in one direction and another, each day, occupying lands, sinking hooks into the land which belongs to them and defending it with their lives. They can be seen carrying signs, slogans, flags; letting them flap in the mountain or prairie winds. And the wave of anger, of demands for justice, of claims for rights, which is beginning to sweep the lands of Latin America, will not stop. That wave will swell with every passing day. For that wave is composed of the greatest number, the majorities in every respect, those whose labour amasses the wealth and turns the wheels of history.

Now, they are awakening from the long, brutalizing sleep to which they had been subjected.

For this great humanity has said, 'Enough!' and has begun to march. And their giant march will not be halted until they conquer true independence – for which they have vainly died more than once. Today, however, those who die will die like the Cubans at Playa Girón. They will die for their own true and never-to-be-surrendered independence.

Patria o Muerte! Venceremos!

THE PEOPLE OF CUBA
Havana, Cuba
Free Territory of America
4 February 1962

The National General Assembly of the People of Cuba resolves that this Declaration be known as the Second Declaration of Havana, translated into the major languages and distributed throughout the world. It also resolves to urge all the friends of the Cuban Revolution in Latin America that it be widely distributed among the worker, peasant, student and intellectual masses of this continent.

CHAPTER 2

Sino-Soviet Split: 'Division in the Face of the Enemy Was Never a Revolutionary or Intelligent Strategy'*

The Caribbean Crisis in the fall of 1964, and the bombing of North Vietnam in February 1965, created real concern in the smaller socialist countries about Soviet intentions and about the splits in the socialist camp. While polemics flew between the Soviet Union and China, US warplanes flew over Cuba and Vietnam and warships sailed off their coasts.

Cubans felt that their ultimate survival depended upon the success of other revolutions in Latin America. With Cuba under the pressure of the US embargo and politically isolated in the hemisphere, Fidel's answer was the Second Declaration of Havana – a document that supported armed revolutionary struggles in Latin America. This document was in direct conflict with the Soviet line of peaceful co-existence and further rejected the Soviet assertion that the Latin American bourgeoisie was capable of leading the revolutionary struggle. From the perspective of Cuba the choice was quite limited: either encourage revolutions on the mainland and break the US blockade, or the Cuban Revolution would have to surrender to US policy-makers. That was the choice, although the Soviets pretended otherwise.

Nevertheless, the Cuban policy in 1965 and early 1966 was to unify the left – both internationally and within Latin America. Indicative of this was the visit to Cuba in March, 1956 of Juliano – a peasant leader from north-east Brazil who advocated armed struggle – and the General Secretary of the Brazilian Communist

---

* Delivered at the University of Havana, 13 March 1965, 'Year of Agriculture', in commemoration of the Eighth Anniversary of the student attack on the Presidential Palace.

Party, Prestes. *The tensions between the Soviet Union and the People's Republic of China which were marked by the withdrawal of Soviet technicians from China in late 1960; by Khrushchev's scathing attack on the Albanian Communists in October 1961; by the polemics between China and the Soviet-leaning Yugoslavian and Italian Communist Parties in 1962–3; and by the hostile reception that greeted Wu-Hsiu-Shuan's remarks at a Party Congress in East Berlin in January 1965, greatly affected the smaller socialist countries like Cuba and North Vietnam.*

During the Caribbean Crisis in October 1963, the Soviet Union, without consulting the Cuban government, withdrew missiles it had placed in Cuba. It did this before the United States had met any of the Cuban demands. These included: an end to the economic blockade; an end to all subversive activities sponsored by the US; an end to pirate attacks emanating from the US and Puerto Rico; an end to violations of Cuban air and naval space by US warplanes and warships; and withdrawal from the naval base at Guantanamo.

The Chinese were very critical of Soviet actions. Mao stated: 'We neither requested the installation of missile bases, nor do we oppose their dismantling. But we do oppose the sacrifice of the sovereignty of a country in connection with commitments made to imperialism. That is one hundred per cent conciliation, Munich pure and simple.' China had real fears about Soviet accommodations with the United States and its allies. During the Himalayan crisis Khrushchev chose to remain neutral; later Nehru stated, on more than one occasion: we can count on Soviet MIGs 'to defend the threatened borders'.

Comrade professors and university students and students from other centres who are present here:

Today is the Eighth Anniversary of the 13 March,[1] and the Sixth Anniversary of its commemoration, the sixth meeting to commemorate the date that we have held on this stairway of the

---

1. The date, in 1957, when members of the Student Directorate attacked the Presidential Palace.

University. It has become a tradition, a duty for all, for the comrades of the Revolution and the University students.

With the years certain changes have been taking place in the University, changes that are reflected in the composition of our students. The first year, almost all who met here had been comrades of José Antonio Echeverria,[2] comrades of all those who fought on that day, many of them active participants in the struggle of the University students against the Batista régime.

After six years many of those students have graduated, many are already working on different fronts of the Revolution. Naturally, the student ranks and the University stairway are today full of younger comrades who have been entering the University during these years. Many young faces can be seen among the students here tonight.

I said to the comrades : 'The students here seem very young to me – are they university students?' And they told me, yes, that they were university students except some 2,000 exemplary students from pre-university and secondary schools. [AN INTERRUPTION – 'TECHNICAL STUDENTS TOO'] But don't you consider yourselves pre-university students? – [CRIES OF 'YES!'] So why do you protest? And there are also a number of students from the Teachers Institute here.

Comrade Armando [Hart, Minister of Education] took advantage of my question to say, somewhat ironically, that we don't take into account that it is no longer our contemporaries who are here in the university. And I said, 'That's right, unfortunately.'

The really important thing is that we do not lose our youthful spirit and that the young people do not lose the revolutionary spirit. I think this is the point where we must always meet, without regard to age ... And the Revolution still has much to do. It still has a great deal to do. The Revolution has powerful enemies, and primarily one powerful enemy, Yankee imperialism. This enemy threatens us and will threaten us for some time to come. This enemy will not easily resign itself – although it has no alternative – to the revolutionary successes of our people. This enemy,

---

2. A leader of the Student Directorate, Echeverria, was killed in the attack on the Presidential Palace.

not here, but thousands of miles from here, is attacking other countries as it is criminally attacking the people of North Vietnam and the revolutionary people of South Vietnam.

This enemy is intervening in the Congo. It sends its ships, its Marines, and its planes to any corner of the world. It takes advantage of divisions among the revolutionaries, of the lamentable divisions that exist in the socialist camp. Unfortunately, they calculate, analyse, and take advantage of everything that can weaken the revolutionary front.

That is to say, that circumstances exist that involve dangers for us all, for us and for other nations in parts of the world that fight for their independence and freedom. Dangers are not lacking.

I am not going to speak at length about the problems related to the differences and divisions in the socialist camp. We don't even know when we may have to speak of this at length, because the problem is not to speak just for the sake of speaking; the problem is to speak in order to say something. The problem is to speak when, by speaking or talking or saying something, there is a positive and useful result and not a result that is positive and useful only to imperialism and the enemies of the people.

We'd rather not have to face such bitter circumstances. As far as talk is concerned, enough and more than enough has been said already. As far as division is concerned, unfortunately, enough and more than is necessary has been said, more than suits the interests of the people and what, unfortunately, is useful to the interests of the enemies of the people.

But for us, small countries, that do not base ourselves on the strength of armies of millions of men, or on the strength of atomic power, small countries like Vietnam and Cuba, we have enough instinct to see with serenity and to understand that these divisions and differences that weaken the strength of the socialist camp hurt no one more than us who are in special situations: here, ninety miles from the Yankee empire; there, attacked by Yankee planes.

Here it's not a question of analysing the problems under dispute theoretically or philosophically, but of recognizing the great truth: that in the face of an enemy that attacks, in the face of an enemy that becomes more and more aggressive, there is no justification for division; division doesn't make sense; there is no reason for division.

And at any time in history, at any period, of mankind, since the first revolutionary appeared in the world, since revolutions became social phenomena in which the masses acted instinctively, until the time revolutions were made consciously, became tasks and phenomena fully understood by the people – which took place when Marxism arose – division in the face of the enemy was never a correct strategy, it was never revolutionary strategy, was never intelligent strategy.

And in this revolutionary process we have all, from the beginning, been educated in the idea that everything that divides weakens, that everything that separates us is bad: bad for our people and good for imperialism.

And the mass of our people understood the need for unity from the first moment and unity became an essential question for the revolution, unity became the cry of the masses, unity became a slogan of the whole people.

And we ask ourselves whether imperialism has disappeared; we ask ourselves if the imperialists are not attacking North Vietnam; we ask ourselves whether in North Vietnam men and women of the people are not dying.

And who can be made to think or to believe that division is proper or useful? Perhaps it's not seen that the imperialists are advancing in North Vietnam? Perhaps it's not seen that the tactic the imperialists are following there is to smash the revolutionary movement in South Vietnam, attacking North Vietnam first under the pretext of the attacks being in reprisal, later arrogating to themselves the right to attack whenever they want to, and continuing to use masses of planes against the fighters of South Vietnam.

What is the situation at this moment? The imperialists are talking about a naval blockade, landing their Marines in South Vietnam, sending aircraft carriers, mobilizing masses of planes to smash the revolutionary movement in South Vietnam; to attack, with every available means of war, the guerrillas in South Vietnam. They are reserving the right to attack North Vietnam whenever it seems best to them, carrying on this kind of aerial war, without any sacrifice on their part, bombing with hundreds of planes and even sending their helicopters to rescue the pilots of the downed planes.

Doubtless the imperialists want a comfortable kind of struggle! Doubtless the imperialists want a kind of war with only industrial losses! That is – 'so many planes lost'. Doubtless the people of South Vietnam and of North Vietnam suffer all this! And suffer it in their own flesh because there are men and women there who die, in South Vietnam and in North Vietnam, victims of the US strafing and victims of the US bombing.

And they don't hesitate in the least to declare that they propose to continue all that because even the attacks on North Vietnam have not had the effect of overcoming the divisions within the socialist family. And who doubts that this division encourages the imperialists? Who doubts that to face the enemy with a united front would make them hesitate, make them pause and think before launching their adventurous attacks and their barefaced intervention in that part of the world? Who is to be convinced of this? With what reason, with what logic? And who benefits from this? The imperialists! And who are the victims? The Vietnamese! And what suffers? The prestige of socialism, the prestige of the international communist movement, of the international revolutionary movement! And this truly hurts us! Because for us the liberation movement is not a demagogic word but a slogan that we have always felt deeply!

This is because we are a small country that does not aspire to become the navel of the world; because we are a small country that does not aspire to become the revolutionary centre of the world. And when we speak of these problems, we speak with absolute sincerity and we speak disinterestedly. We did not win revolutionary power in bourgeois elections but by fighting with weapons in hand: we speak in the name of a people who for six years irrevocably and unhesitatingly resisted the ambushes and the threats of imperialism.

We speak in the name of a people who, for the sake of the strength of the revolutionary movement, for the sake of the strength of the socialist camp, for the sake of the firmness and the determination to defend the Revolution against the imperialists, did not hesitate. We are a people who did not hesitate to risk the danger of thermonuclear war, of a nuclear attack, when in our country and on our territory – with the full and absolute right that we have never abjured, an absolutely legitimate act that we will never regret – we agreed to the installation of thermonuclear strategic missiles on our territory. And, not only did we agree that they should be brought here, but we disagreed that they should be taken away. And I think that this is no secret to anyone.

We are a country and a nation, in whose name I speak, that receives no Yankee credits, or Food for Peace, and we haven't the slightest relation with the imperialists. Which means that in the matter of revolutionary conviction and sincerity no one taught us anything, just as no one taught our liberators of 1895 and 1868 the path of independence and of dignity. We are the people of the First and Second Declarations of Havana, which we didn't copy from any document but which were the pure expression of the spirit of our people, deeply revolutionary and highly internationalist.

As this has been the feeling and the thinking of our Revolution, proven as often as was necessary, proven without hesitation of any kind, without yielding in any way, without contradictions of any type, we have the right to ask – as many other peoples must ask – who benefits from these disagreements if not our enemies?

And of course we have full right, the full and absolute right, that I don't think anyone will dare question, to proscribe such dissensions and such Byzantine battles from our country and our people.

And it should be known that it is our Party which directs the propaganda here, that it is our Party which gives guidance here, that this is a question that comes under our jurisdiction! And if we don't want the apple of discord to come here, because we simply don't want it here, then none can smuggle it in. Our enemies, our only enemies, are the Yankee imperialists. Our only insuperable contradiction is with Yankee imperialists. The only enemy against whom we are ready to break our lances, is imperialism.

As far as anything else is concerned, we don't understand any other language; we don't understand the language of division. Before the concrete case of a country attacked by imperialism, like Vietnam, we have one position. We don't act, as perhaps some think, as perhaps above all the imperialists think, on the basis of 'when you see your neighbour's house on fire, you throw water on your own roof' – in reality, the way we act is, when we see our neighbour's house on fire, we want to share this difficulty.

We are not people to be frightened by these events; rather we are kindled to action by them. And we have one position. We are in favour of giving Vietnam all the aid that may be necessary, we are in favour of this aid being arms and men, we are in favour of the socialist camp running the risks that may be necessary for Vietnam.

We are quite aware of the fact that in case of any serious international complication we will be one of the first targets of imperialism, but this does not worry us and has never worried us. And we don't keep quiet or act like simpletons in order that our lives be spared.

This is, in all frankness, and all sincerity, our reasoned, dispassionate stand, emanating from our legitimate and inviolable right to take measures and to act in the way we believe most correct and most revolutionary – and let no one harbour the illusion that they can give us lessons on revolution.

I hope that no one commits errors of underestimation by ignoring the peculiarities of our people, because Yankee imperialism has committed lots of errors of this kind. One of its characteristics was disdain for others, disdain for and underestimation of small nations. And imperialism has committed great colossal errors of underestimation in respect to our revolutionary people. It would be regrettable if others committed similar errors. Our sincere policy has been and is that of uniting, because we are not and will never be satellites of anyone. And in this whole problem we have taken a very dispassionate, very honest and very sincere position.

This is not the time to go through papers and files. I believe that as long as we have imperialism in front of us, attacking, it would be ridiculous for us here to do as in the fable, argue whether they are greyhounds or hound dogs, whether they are made of paper or of iron.

Let us leave the papers and files and documents to history, let history be the one to say who acted well or badly, to say who was right and who was wrong, let history show what each thought, what each did, what each said – but let it be history. Because it would be humiliating to wash dirty linen in front of our enemies, enemies who are attacking, and who are attacking not the most powerful but the smallest and weakest.

We have many things to do. We have ahead of us many very difficult, very hard tasks. Millions of tons of sugar to be cut to defeat the imperialist blockade, and they are not cut with papers, but with toil, with sweat, with the machete.

The dangers that lie in wait for us are great, but they are not fought with Byzantine disagreements and academic charlatanry. No, they are fought with revolutionary firmness, revolutionary integrity, the readiness to fight. The imperialist enemy is not fought effectively anywhere in the world when revolutionaries are divided, insulting each other, and attacking each other, but only with unity and cohesion in the revolutionary ranks. And to those who may not believe that this is the correct tactic for the international communist movement, we say that for us here on our small island, on our territory, in a front-line trench ninety miles from the imperialists, it is the correct tactic. And we will adjust our line and our conduct to this way of thinking.

I believe that we honour our dead comrades, that we honour those who have fallen, from the first to the last one, in a worthy way, because this Revolution was born out of the rebellious spirit of a whole people, out of the progressive and revolutionary spirit of a whole nation, out of the dignity of a whole people, because this struggle which today is interlaced and entwined with the struggle of other peoples of the world against imperialism began almost a century ago. It began with the first men who took up arms against colonialism and against the exploitation of our country, and it has followed this course, followed this line, and our people have never abandoned this line, never betrayed it. They have followed this firm and clear line. That is their spirit, that is their tradition.

On this path all the worthy men of this land have come together and in the long struggle many good men of this land have died. The first were not Marxist-Leninists. Carlos Manuel de Cespedes was not. Martí was not, because in the time in which he lived, and under the historic conditions in which he developed his magnificent struggle, he could not be one. In those days we would have been like them, today they would have been like us, because what was decisive in each period was the revolutionary spirit of our people, the task of our people at each moment. And what can be said is this, that from that time until now the road has been long and the evolution of our revolutionary thinking has been long. At the beginning of the second half of the past century it was not the tasks of the proletarian revolution that were raised in our country, it was the fight for independence against the Spanish colonial power.

And this independence came to life at a time when a much greater and more fearful power arose – Yankee imperialism. The struggle against this power became the great historic task of our nation. To win independence from this power, to resist its attacks and to keep high the banner of the Revolution, became the great task of our nation in this century. This became the great task of our people, coinciding with similar tasks of other peoples on this same continent and in Africa and Asia and Oceania, wherever people are struggling with increasing determination against colonialism and against imperialism.

There has always been one sole path and one revolutionary line. Many heroes, many patriots, many martyrs have followed this path and this line. And those who have carried this banner forward, those who have followed this line, represent the will of all and are under obligation not only to present and future generations, but also to the past generations that took part in the struggle.

And so on a day like today when we remember those who have died, we think that there is only one sense, that there is essentially only one idea, which consoles and compensates absolutely, and that is that the men who have fallen, the men who have died, did not die in vain.

Other times, in other periods, from this same stairway, the

memory of the dead was recalled, but with sadness, with pain, with despair under the insupportable idea that those sacrifices had not yet born fruit. When at a time like this, in circumstances like these, on a day like today, we recall those comrades, all symbolized in the name 'José Antonio Echeverria', we have the consoling idea, the tranquillity and the satisfaction of knowing that their sacrifice was not in vain.

In the progress of our revolution, in the ascendant march of our people on the road of history, on the road of revolutionary thinking, on the road of the extraordinary evolution of our ideas, the men who fought for this, the men who sacrificed for this, take on flesh and blood.

And you, the young people of today, must feel yourselves the followers of those men, the standard bearers of those men, those who have taken up their banner, who continue the advance, who are marching forward on the ascendant road of our people, in the glorious history of our country.

You are the new revolutionary wave and we are sure that you will know how to act and that you will be worthy standard bearers of José Antonio Echeverria and his comrades.

Patria o Muerte! Venceremos!

CHAPTER 3

The Latin American Communist Parties
and Revolution: 'Their Attitude towards
the Guerrilla Struggle will define the
Communists in Latin America.'*

*The United States escalation of the war in Vietnam, its military
intervention in the Dominican Republic and the subsequent development of a rationale for US military intervention throughout
Latin America has had a profound influence on Cuba's policy
towards the strategy of armed revolutionary struggle. Experience
had clearly shown that the United States would not allow a
socialist government to exist in Latin America if it could help it.
After the United States had Cuba expelled from the OAS in 1962,
President John Kennedy stated that 'the concept of Marxism-
Leninism is incompatible with the inter-American system'. Cuba
existed because it defended itself; the Dominican Republic and
Guatemala had failed to form popular militias to resist United
States actions.*

*In the early years of the Revolution, between 1959 and 1962,
the Cuban leadership basically supported a broad spectrum of
Latin American political forces ranging from left-wing to moderate nationalist forces, including Quadros of Brazil. Yet the policies
of Washington meant to isolate Cuba. Its expulsion from the
OAS in 1962 precipitated a series of military coups in Latin
America – in Argentina, Brazil, Bolivia, Peru – as Washington
forced its colonies to take a hard line in terms of Cuba. The frail-
ness of a third alternative – a nationalist-capitalist one – became*

---

* Delivered at the University of Havana, 13 March 1967, 'Year of
Heroic Vietnam', in commemoration of the Tenth Anniversary of the
student attack on the Presidential Palace.

increasingly apparent. The choice was clearly between socialism and United States domination.

In 1962, as Cuba grew closer to the Soviet Union and as it began organizing its own united socialist party, the Cuban leadership began shifting its support more and more towards the official Communist Parties (perhaps hoping they would take the revolutionary road as some did temporarily) and the left-wing nationalists (e.g., MIR of Venezuela and Peru). During this period there was a continuous 'ambiguity' in Cuban policy: the Cubans called for an aggressive, armed revolutionary strategy, yet supported the Communist Parties who had no pretension in this direction.

While the Latin American Communist Parties are frequently militantly active in trade unions, and to a much lesser extent in peasant movements on the level of the masses, at the upper levels the party leaders continually subordinate the party to 'progressive forces', i.e., bourgeois régimes or parties. The Communist Parties are thus, at best, militant pressure groups – not groups oriented toward taking power. Frequently this is, however, enough to put them 'outside the law' – and they join the armed struggle. But again, this is not – at least at the leadership level – an attempt to 'seize power' but rather a means of retaining legality and parliamentary rights.

In Bolivia, the Communist Party rejected a revolutionary strategy even after the Barrientos military coup and refused to support Che Guevara and the guerrilla forces. Since 1965 the Communist Party of Venezuela has been calling for a 'democratic peace' – a return to legality in exchange for ending the armed struggle. It is this policy of the PCV, as well as their tendency to concentrate their forces in the city and underestimate the strength of the peasantry, that Fidel attacks in this speech.

Beginning in the latter part of 1966, the Cuban revolutionary leadership definitely shifted its support away from the 'official' communists towards the active militants conducting armed guerrilla warfare – whether they were nationalists, communists, or independent revolutionaries. The Tri-Continental Conference, held in the beginning of 1966, contained a preponderance of 'official' communists. Yet, increasingly in that year, Fidel called for an aggressive revolutionary strategy. In May, Cuba directed *a series of polemics at Yugoslavia – attacking that country for not aiding revolutionary movements – and in numerous speeches that year (e.g., May Day and 26 July) he made it clear that the existence of socialism in Cuba depended on socialist revolutions in other countries. This shift must be seen in conjunction with the emphasis in Cuba on example, moral incentives, the necessity of struggle, and the moral values of revolution.*

In August 1966, Fidel said that revolutions in Latin America would be made 'with a party or without it'. In this speech, as the title indicates, he makes clear, as he had in his other 13 March speeches, that it is deeds and not dogma or party labels that determine the true revolutionaries.

Can we explain the insinuations of the oligarchies, and those of the Venezuelan oligarchy in particular, in blaming Cuba for revolutionary actions in their countries? And what of the insinuations made by the rightist leadership of the Communist Party of Venezuela? What preceded it and what gave rise to it? How can it be explained? It is necessary to make a brief résumé of the history of the revolutionary struggle in Venezuela.

Struggle in Venezuela

First : a few months prior to the triumph of the Cuban Revolution, there was a formidable popular movement in Venezuela, that overthrew the Pérez Jimenez régime. Participating in this movement were many popular forces, among them the Communist Party of Venezuela. And a young newspaper man was especially outstanding : Fabricio Ojeda, who was President of the Patriotic Council that ousted Pérez Jimenez. However, that victory of the people of Venezuela was frustrated, because from that moment the Partido Acción Democrática which at one time had played a certain revolutionary role, a certain role in the anti-imperialist struggle, that had mass support, not in the capital – because naturally the most advanced sectors had majority support in the capital – this party had particularly broad support in extensive regions of the interior of the country, and began to act as a fundamental factor in hindering the maturing and development of the Venezuelan revolutionary movement.

Betancourt won some elections, coming up with a ridiculous minority in the capital and getting his majority in the interior of the country – similar to what sometimes happened in our country. And from the moment it was sworn in, that government dedicated itself to developing a clear policy of conciliation, kowtowing to imperialism, and defending imperialist interests in Venezuela. Naturally, it became one of the instruments of US policy.

There began to be repression of the revolutionary movement; repression of the workers, of the students, of the revolutionaries. Those repressions became more and more brutal, and the first massacres of students and the general population took place in Caracas. Betancourt felt a deep resentment towards the people of the capital; he could not pardon that lack of support, the affront he had been given by the population of Caracas.

We remember when, in the early days of the Revolution, we visited this sister nation. In the Plaza del Silencio there, we spoke at a gigantic assembly of 300,000 people. When we mentioned the name of Betancourt – as was our courtesy obligation to the president-elect – a great hiss came up out of that great mass. Since we were visitors in the country, this put us in a rather embarrassing situation and I even felt compelled to protest, saying that I had not mentioned a man's name so that people would boo him, but that it was simply my duty to make official reference to him who was about to assume the presidency as a result of elections. In this way, the people of Caracas demonstrated themselves furiously anti-Betancourtist. And this feeling of scorn in the capital of Venezuela, which was the vanguard in the struggle for the overthrow of Pérez Jimenez, was thus shown. This, naturally, contributed in no small way to the extraordinary hate Betancourt felt for the popular masses of the capital of Venezuela.

And soon, just as soon as the repression had become intolerably brutal, supporters of the armed struggle arose. One of the first of these was the Movement of the Revolutionary Left, organized by a group of progressive leaders who had broken off from the official party, Acción Democrática, and organized this movement.

They began to prepare for armed struggle. Similarly, the Communist Party began to prepare for armed struggle.

At first, it was thought that the extreme right-wing elements in the army would surely overthrow Betancourt; and at first these organizations set about their preparations with the idea that the struggle would have to be against a reactionary military government. But the sharpening of repression, which increasingly characterized Betancourt's policy, made these organizations cease to regard their efforts as directed against the Betancourt régime itself, which was becoming increasingly repressive and brutal in its dealings with the people...

And so the first moves began. The Third Congress of the Communist Party of Venezuela approved the road of armed struggle for the revolution in Venezuela. Other dissident forces from different parties also began preparations for armed struggle. Among these was a sector of the political party to which Fabricio Ojeda belonged. And Fabricio Ojeda, friend of Cuba, friend of our Revolution – like so many Venezuelans – one day resigned his position as member of Parliament and went into the mountains to organize a guerrilla movement.

Several years passed. Undoubtedly the Venezuelan revolutionaries, as in all revolutions in every part of the world, made a number of errors in their conception of the struggle, a number of errors of strategic and of a tactical nature. Different factors contributed to these errors. One of these was the fact that the revolutionary movement was very strong in the capital, and on the other hand – as has or had happened in many other countries in Latin America, and for this the Communist Parties are to blame – the revolutionary movement was weak in the country. Why? Because the Marxist Parties concentrated their attention mainly on the city, on the workers' movement, which is, of course, quite correct. But in many cases – for naturally all these generalities have their exceptions – they greatly underestimated the importance of the peasantry as a revolutionary force.

As the official party of Venezuela was strong in the countryside and the parties of the left were weak there, although strong in the capital, for a long time the leadership of the Venezuelan revolutionary movement overestimated the importance of the capital and the struggle in the capital and underestimated the importance of the guerrilla movement.

But not only this. Venezuela was one of the countries – or *the* country in recent times – where the revolutionary movement had the greatest influence in the ranks of the professional army. Many young Venezuelan army officers openly showed their sympathy for the revolutionary movement, even in its most radical form, inspired in Marxist concepts. So the force of the revolutionary movement was strongly felt in the ranks of the army. And this led to another conceptual error; to a downgrading of the guerrilla movement in favour of great hopes in a military uprising.

They accuse us of promoting subversion, they accuse the Cubans of directing the armed revolutionary movement in Venezuela. And if we Cubans had had anything to do with the leadership of that revolutionary movement, we would never have fallen, and that revolutionary movement would never have fallen, into those two major conceptual errors. [APPLAUSE] Why? Because it is the revolutionaries, they and only they, who decide, who are able to determine their general strategy and their specific tactics. And the revolutionaries always do that, always! In Venezuela, as in all other countries, their criteria – and these criteria may often be mistaken – are only rectified as a consequence of the process itself, of the experience of the process itself, of the blows received in the process. It is not we, the Cuban revolutionaries or leaders, who tell them what they must do; it is their own experience. And the best teachers of revolutionaries in every country of Latin America – as it was in Cuba – the best teachers, the great teachers, were the setbacks.

And naturally the Venezuelan revolutionary movement suffered many setbacks, as revolutionary movements in all parts of the world have always suffered setbacks, and Latin America's movement logically had to go through a long apprenticeship. Today it can be affirmed that that movement has learned a great deal, not from Cuba, but from its own experience, from the blows it has received. And therefore that more experienced revolutionary movement is growing and consolidating itself, and the rulers are showing themselves unable to crush it. They are impotent to crush it in Guatemala, unable to crush it in Colombia, unable to crush it in Venezuela.

But reverses always take a toll; they frequently take a toll in desertions from the revolutionary ranks by the weakest, the least tenacious, the least persevering, in a word, the least revolutionary.

Directing the guerrillas from the city is an absurdity

Apart from erroneous strategic conceptions in themselves, these erroneous conceptions in turn gave rise to serious errors of a practical nature: the guerrillas found themselves abandoned and deprived of the most elementary resources. The revolutionary leadership of the Party was trying to direct the guerrillas from the city, from the capital. What ought to have been done was not done – what a daring and truly revolutionary leadership would have done, what the leadership of the great and historic contemporary movements that have triumphed has done – is, go up to the mountains with the guerrillas to lead the war from the battlefield, to lead the war from the mountains. It is absurd and almost criminal – we don't call it a hundred-per-cent criminal because it is a question of ignorance more than of wilful fraud – to try to direct guerrillas from the city. The two experiences are so different, so utterly distinct, the two settings so completely dissimilar, that the greatest insanity – a painfully bloody insanity – that can be committed is to try to direct guerrillas from the city. And the guerrillas were not really seen as a force that could be developed to take revolutionary power in countries such as ours, but rather as an instrument of agitation, a tool for political manoeuvring, for negotiation. Underestimation of the guerrillas led to the errors committed subsequently.

And in Venezuela the guerrillas were constantly being ordered to cease fire, and that is madness! A guerrilla contingent that agrees to a truce in fighting is one condemned to defeat.

A guerrilla contingent can agree to a truce of one or two days as we did on some sectors of our front in order to return prisoners to the Red Cross. As a matter of principle, a guerrilla contingent must never agree to a truce of any other kind. The men get used to the quietude of the camp, a weakening and demoralization of forces sets in. But the commanders of the city-led guerrillas constantly received orders to make truces, more and more truces. That was happening in Venezuela.

And naturally as a result of an inept leadership, blows and setbacks followed in succession. Nevertheless, in spite of the errors in leadership, in spite of the conceptual errors, the government could not eliminate the guerrillas. Yet what the repressive and pro-imperialist forces of Betancourt and Leoni could not achieve was very nearly achieved thanks to the ineptitude of the revolutionary leadership.

The leaders of the Communist Party of Venezuela began to speak of a democratic peace. 'What is this about democratic peace?' many people asked. 'What is this about democratic peace?' we, the leaders of the Cuban Revolution ask ourselves. We did not understand. We did not understand but, nevertheless, we wanted to understand. 'What does this mean?' we asked some Venezuelan leaders. As a reply we received the same old worn-out and elaborate theory of a tactic, a manoeuvre – by no means an abandonment of the war : No ! No ! It was only a manoeuvre to broaden the base, to destroy the régime, to weaken and undermine it.

And, of course, we by no means considered this a correct point of view. Nevertheless, we had hope and confidence, in spite of the fact that a democratic peace seemed absurd, ridiculous. For only a revolutionary movement that is winning the war can speak of peace, because then it can begin to mobilize national opinion in favour of a peace that can only be won by winning the revolution. Then one can mobilize people's spirits, public opinion, the people and their desire for peace on the only possible foundation; the defeat of the tyranny and of exploitation. But to speak of peace when the war is being lost is precisely to concede peace by defeat.

In the history of revolutionary movements, the words democratic peace were mentioned for the first time after the victory of the Bolshevik Revolution in 1917. The new Revolution launched a campaign for a democratic peace, that is, peace in the midst of World War, a peace without annexations or conquests of any type. And the new Soviet power launched this campaign and struggled for a peace without annexation or conquests: a victorious revolutionary power that did not want to continue participating in that imperialist slaughter.

In silence we have withstood a campaign of defamation

So the slogan of democratic peace was launched. And we asked ourselves: 'What similarity can there be between that historic situation, between that victorious proletariat in the first socialist revolution, and the situation of a revolutionary leadership that has been unable to lead the armed struggle to victory?'

However, in reality, behind their explanations, lay deceit. Deceit! They told us that their democratic peace was a manoeuvre, but that the struggle would be stepped up, guerrilla warfare would be stepped up. Nevertheless, they were lying. In reality, the intention was to abandon the armed struggle and they were simply preparing the way.

How did we learn about these things, these truths? How did we confirm them? We would have preferred not to air this matter publicly; as a matter of fact, during many weeks and months we have silently borne a defamatory campaign waged by the rightist leadership of the Communist Party of Venezuela, which voiced accusations against us in various Communist Party congresses, and sent letters to various Latin American Communist Parties, accusing Cuba of interfering in their internal affairs and of supporting and fomenting factionalism.

We would have preferred not to discuss this matter; however, it has become unhappily impossible to avoid doing so. In order to answer the imputations of pro-imperialist oligarchies and of renegade communists, since both are intimately related, we find ourselves obliged to clarify and answer these charges, reserving the right to do this at the opportune moment and in a more detailed form, in a document which our Party will draw up when it deems convenient. Recent events in Venezuela have made this necessary.

A letter from Fabricio Ojeda

I have mentioned Fabricio Ojeda's name, his clean record, his participation in the overthrow of Pérez Jimenez, the rarely seen phenomenon of his resignation from office when he gave up his parliamentary immunity, relinquished his parliamentary privileges, to go into the mountains. A rare case in a politician in our America. Fabricio was ignominiously assassinated on 21 June 1966. Sixteen days earlier, on 4 June 1966, Fabricio wrote a letter, the letter was addressed to me and was probably one of the last things he ever wrote. And that letter, which I have kept without knowing that I would need to reveal its contents one day, goes as follows:

My dear friend:

Here, all of the time, as always, attempting to overcome the burden of temporary difficulties in order to wage the struggle on a more serious and precise basis; we have made some advances towards this end. The fundamental step has been that of going directly to the solution of the problems of leadership, the structuring of our national organizations, such as the FLN[1] Executive Committee and the Executive Command of the FALN[2]; starting points for a general reorganization of the movement's entire structure. To this end we are working intensely. We intend to hold a national FLN-FALN conference as soon as possible which, as a constituent power, will devote itself to a study and analysis of the situation, to establishing strategy and tactics, political and military lines and to defining the effective constitution of our directing organism at all levels. In this way the liberation movement will break out of its present state of stagnation, overcome differences, and clarify its historic potential, in addition to consolidating the factor indispensable to further progress, revolutionary unity of the revolutionary forces.

---

1. Frente de Liberación Nacional, National Liberation Front.
2. Fuerzas Armadas de Liberación Nacional, Armed Forces of National Liberation.

Our project of restructuring the struggle on new bases has forced us to define certain important questions. The first of these is the provisional restructuring of the présent directing organism of the national FLN-FALN. In this regard, we have decided to increase the number of nuclei in the existing leadership, which has produced a critical situation within the Communist Party of Venezuela. This includes the sanctioning of Comrade Douglas Bravo by the majority of the Political Bureau of the Party, who have removed him from this organism, accusing him of an attitude of anti-Party factionalism.

The second question of importance is the decision to confront any circumstance whatsoever in order to bring all revolutionary forces together with the purpose of incrementing the war of national liberation as the only means of advancing towards the conquest of power and the achievement of national independence, taking into account the objective conditions prevailing in the country and the peculiarities of the Venezuelan process.

In both areas we have made advances. Steps are being taken to set up a unified FLN-FALN command. This will be led by myself as President in charge of the FLN, together with the First Commander of the FALN, Douglas Bravo. A leader from the MIR[3] will join us this week as Secretary-General.

The General Command of the FALN now includes the commanding officers of the guerrilla fronts. This new form was arrived at after an analysis of the present situation of these organisms, since it was considered that a nucleus of three members of the FALN General Command that was still active was insufficient for general military leadership, since the other members of the Command have either been taken prisoner or are abroad. In relation to the unification of the revolutionary forces for the purpose of advancing the war of national liberation, a unified commission will be designated to study and draw up the theoretical material on strategy, tactics, and the political and military line of the movement to be presented for discussion in the coming FLN-FALN national conference.

The incorporation of the MIR into the directing organizations and the preparatory work for the conference are steps of great significance, since in this way a period of internal discussion on present differences will begin replacing diatribe in our talks, and opening up truly democratic roads for the ideological and political unity of the revolutionary movement.

---

3. Movimiento de la Izquierda Revolucionaria, Movement of the Revolutionary Left.

Nonetheless, a new breach has been opened in our ranks by the disciplinary measures taken by the majority of the Political Bureau of the Communist Party of Venezuela.

In respect to this new problem, I have been informed that the intermediate and basic sectors, including those in the Central Committee itself, have been reacting against the sanction imposed on Comrade Douglas ...

Already certain documents have been circulated which expressly state this reaction. In my opinion, the disciplinary measures taken by the majority of the Political Bureau correspond to problems of a truly ideological and political nature, to profound questions, which they have attempted to cover up by talking of methods or supposed errors on the part of Comrade Douglas and other comrades whose ideas on strategy and tactics of our revolutionary process coincide with his. The fact is that within the Communist Party of Venezuela two important currents are being debated.

One of these is held by a minority in the base of the Party but is very prevalent among the members of the Political Bureau and the Central Committee. Its essence is as follows: Present developments permit the revolutionary movement to take the initiative on the political front. Nonetheless, the FALN must order the guerrillas and the UTC [Tactical Combat Units] to fall back. It does not mean simply another truce but rather something more profound; it means diverting the form of struggle. That is, a new tactical period begins, which in place of combining all forms of struggle, would suspend guerrilla and UTC operations. The guerrillas and the UTC should make an orderly retreat and the revolutionary movement introduce a change in tactics. Several conditions are indispensable, to maintain unity and internal cohesion, to maintain iron discipline, and to support and aid the directing nucleus. To achieve these ends the Party and the Young Communists must act in two ways. First, employ persuasion, using every kind of reasoning and political arguments in support of the new tactical changes, discussing matters calmly with all who must be convinced. Second, carry on an active campaign against adventurist tendencies and provocations. (This is a synthesis of two documents presented to this organization by prominent members of the Political Bureau.)

The other, held by a majority of the base of the Party, but with little support among members of the leadership of higher organizations, is headed by Comrade Douglas Bravo, who not only opposes the alteration of plans and the changes in tactics, but who presents strong criticisms of the way that the revolutionary struggle has been carried out.

It is quite obvious that the crux of these differences is the question of armed struggle, which a group of leaders within the Communist Party of Venezuela has opposed since the very beginning.

There is no doubt that the sanctioning of Comrade Douglas is the beginning of these alterations, and that these are designed to eliminate, by means of disciplinary actions, any who oppose a new tactical period which, rather than combining all forms of struggle, would choose to suspend all action by the guerrillas and the Tactical Units.

In a situation like this, the decision to enlarge the integral organizations of leadership by incorporating the most responsible and firm cadres is a step forward of great magnitude.

The majority of the Political Bureau has opposed this measure and has proceeded to repudiate us publicly, denying the validity and legitimate nature of the groups already formed.

We have, however, remained firm and we have been pleased to note that a great body of opinion has formed in support of our cause, in the guerrilla fronts and in the intermediate organizations, as well as at the base of the Communist Party of Venezuela. In addition, some members of the Central Committee, parties within the FLN and urban units of the FALN have lent their support.

A period of clarification of ideology and definition of the revolutionary road has begun. There is one unfavourable transitory factor involved in this situation and which places us in a rather difficult spot. That is the problem of economic resources, since it has been the Political Bureau which has exercised control over this sector ...

Until now all funds for the revolutionary movement have been centralized in that organization and used to further their policies – that is, to snuff out guerrilla centres by economic means.

The letter ends as follows:

Our guerrilla fighters have maintained a high state of morale and there is gigantic resolution in our movement. We are conscious that the present picture is full of difficulties but we are sure that these will be overcome within a short time. Truth will be borne in on the sceptics and then a bright future will appear on our horizon. Not one step backward, not even to gain speed!

The bearer can give more details and better explain some things.

We go forward, towards victory. To fight until victory. A warm embrace from your friend, Fabricio Ojeda.

[APPLAUSE]

Sixteen days later Fabricio was arrested and vilely assassinated by the henchmen of the tyranny oppressing Venezuela, precisely when these steps for organization and restructuring which he speaks about in his letter were being taken.

One can say, well, this was the opinion of a respected, worthy, valiant comrade, but is it proof? Is this enough to guarantee his words? Of course, for us who knew Fabicio well, there is no doubt: the integrity with which this letter is written, its serenity, are guarantees of its author's honesty. But, in addition, some documents which came to our hands verified what Fabricio had said, one hundred per cent; documents which were distributed among the militants of the Communist Party of Venezuela for discussion; documents which, without any doubt, indicate and at the same time explain the policy followed in recent times by the government of Venezuela.

One of the documents is written by Pompeyo Marquéz, Teodoro Petkoff and Freddy Muñoz and in essence says the following in its main lines:

First. Some changes have taken place which force the revolutionary movement to revise certain aspects of its tactics in a fundamental way regarding the armed struggle.

In broad outline the situation is the following: the armed struggle has suffered several blows and has weakened. The revolutionary movement at present is not in a condition to continue the frontal and open attacks on its enemies. The armed apparatus of the Party has been severely damaged; a bloody and brutal repression is affecting the ability of the revolutionary movement to organize, unify, and mobilize the broad masses and give an adequate riposte to government policy.

Due to the continual reverses and blows suffered, to its own weakness which impedes successful actions, the armed struggle, by not taking appropriate measures to safeguard its instruments, could lose the role it has played in the recent past, in which it offered a perspective of revolutionary transformation to the masses. In reality, it is not playing this role at present and its future depends on the measures we take today.

The weak armed operations which do nothing but repeat similar former operations without attaining progress of true significance, are:

a) making political action difficult and impeding the regrouping of forces against the Betancourt 'gorillas';

b) letting the Betancourt 'gorilla' clique maintain its alliances;

c) acting as a brake and preventing the rapid decomposition of its broad base;

d) wiping out convictions, faith in the correct general strategy of the revolutionary movement, whose basis was set down in the Third Congress of the PCV[4] and was later strengthened in the successive plenaries of the CC.[5]

Second. Consequently, the Party must undertake a retrenchment on the military front and recommend the suspension of armed actions in favour of proceeding to a regrouping of its forces and their preparation for a new revolutionary stage which must be qualitatively superior to those existing up to now.

Until recovery has been attained in a fundamental sense, and until some advance is achieved in the promotion of new forces and the regrouping of nationalist sectors, all operations of the FALN must cease.

This military retrenchment must be accompanied by a political offensive which will permit us to cover the retrenchment, alleviate the pressures of repression and recover the political initiative.

In short, it is not a new truce, but something deeper; – textually what Fabricio explained – it is a temporary about-face in the forms of struggle, that is, suspending the actions of the guerrillas and the UTC and giving political initiative priority ...

This is, in essence, the position taken in this document by Pompeyo Marquéz, Teodoro Petkoff and Freddy Muñoz. At the same time, other leaders sent a similar document to the Party, this time signed by Guillermo García Ponce and other leaders. It is, in essence, the same with some slight variations. They themselves explain these differences in the introduction.

It reads:

Document enclosed. We present this to you, comrades, in order to arrive at opinions in a more collective way. However, you will receive not one, but two documents – this one and another.

4. Communist Party of Venezuela.
5. Central Committee.

'As you will note, the resolutions and conclusions are the same: retrenchment of the guerrillas and of the UTC, as well as a change of tactics towards an emphasis on political acts. There are, therefore, no differences on fundamental decisions; there is full unity on the essence of the problems. The motivations, the reasons for the change in forms of struggle for a specific period are also the same. Nevertheless, there is one shade of difference; our document places prime importance on political motivations and secondary importance on setbacks conceived as a reason for change.

'For the other comrades this order is reversed. First: the blows received constitute a very important factor, but we should not change our tactics for this reason. Setbacks help us to become aware of the changes that we ought to introduce, but they form part of a concrete and principally political reality which has forced us to make a certain change in course. The truth of the matter is that we should have retrenched before receiving the blows.

In other words, and in essence, Pompeyo, Teodoro, and Freddy Muñoz speak of retrenchment because of receiving blows. And they say: 'Yes, yes, very well, we're in agreement. There is only one fundamental difference: we should have retrenched even before receiving the blows. Second, upon giving prime importance to political elements, we emphasize one of the peculiarities of the present situation; namely, while the guerrillas and the UTC are in retrenchment, the revolutionary movement can take the offensive on the political front where all militants, organizations, etc. of the Party and the UTC can place the weight of their activity in a high combative spirit, free of all passivity and terrorist attempts.'

Further on, the document reads:

The need for a retrenchment of the FALN: The events transpiring permit the revolutionary movement to take the initiative on the political front; nevertheless, it will be necessary for the FALN to order a retrenchment of the guerrillas and the UTC. This will not be a new truce, but something deeper; an attempt to change the forms of struggle, that is, to open a new tactical period in which, instead of combining all forms of struggle, guerrilla and UTC actions will be suspended. Prime importance will be taken by political events; a grouping of the leftist organization; promotion of new forces of struggle against 'Betancourtism'; unity, organization, and mobilization of the popular masses; alliance with nationalist sectors of the

Armed Forces; action by the workers on behalf of their demands; struggle against repression; etc.

The only thing they didn't put in was the colloquy, the electoral struggle, which they obviously did not insert here because they intended to insert it later on.

'As long as no new political situation occurs and while material conditions improve, the guerrillas and the UTC should retrench.' Retrenchment meant disappearance, dissolution, since they kept them retrenched practically all the time.

The document continues: 'In this sense, it should be recommended that the FALN publish a manifesto giving the political reasons for the retrenchment of the guerrillas and the UTC.'

And finally, the worn-out litany, the classic cliché, the glib phrase, the diatribe.

'In particular it is necessary to watch the uncontrollable groups – the difficult, the bellicose, the rebels – and also to defend actively the policy, tactics, and leadership of the Communist Youth and the Communist Party from the attacks of the anarcho-adventurist MIR group.'

If only they had as much imagination for revolutionary action as they have for glibness and diatribe! [APPLAUSE] 'In order to prevent tactical changes from being presented in an adulterated form by US and "Betancourtist" policies, and to prevent the enemy from taking advantage of any insufficiently formulated proposal or excess of information, it will be necessary to pay special attention to propaganda and, in general, to all written matter.'

Violation of agreements

The Communist Party was not the only one constituting the FALN; at least two or three other organizations were also members. One of them was the Movement of the Revolutionary Left (MIR), which was one of the first organizations to initiate the struggle. The FALN also included the forces represented by Fabricio Ojeda which came from – if I remember the name correctly – the Partido Unión Republicana, as well as the Communist Party and several organizations of fighting men.

Notice how these allies are not mentioned in the two documents; rather, they are mentioned, but only to accuse them of adventurism, anarcho-adventurism. Not one word is said about the sector represented by Fabricio Ojeda. No! They do not recognize the right of other organizations to participate in the formulation of policy; they launch the policy, and publish it, as an order. Not only do they violate the agreements taken in a Party Congress, which should be inviolate, but they also refuse to recognize the forces that in all loyalty had been fighting side by side with the Party.

They not only disregarded the agreements adopted by the Congress, they disregard their allies, the militants, the combatants, and the guerrilla fighters and begin talking of discipline and imposition of discipline.

And what happened? The principal guerrilla chief – among them, the most respected one, who from within the Communist Party from the very beginning, since 1959, was in charge of the military section, organizing cadres for armed struggle, who remained in the mountains for years and fought many victorious battles, not great ones but hard-fought ones, to the extent of his own forces and all the while harassed by continuous orders of truce and more truce – and along with him a large number of guerrilla commanders reacted against the line. We can see how Fabricio and his followers rejected that conception. The MIR, and with them the fighters of El Bachiller front, rejected that defeatist conception. And the Party's best men, the most courageous, the most experienced men, those who had carried the heavist load in the struggle, refused to accept such a defeatist conception.

That was the state of affairs. Out of three organizations, two remained in the struggle. Some of the first leaders of the MIR deserted, but the majority, represented by Sáez Mérida, who upon being taken prisoner was replaced by Americo Martín – who now heads the MIR fighters at El Bachiller – maintained their position in favour of armed struggle and continued their ideological line until he died. And Douglas and the most respected guerrilla commanders maintained theirs. On what basis can we be accused of fomenting divisionism within the Venezuelan Party?

What can be used as a base to blame Cuba for problems resulting only and exclusively from an inefficient political leadership?

We have the right to express our solidarity with the fighters

From the point of view of principles, revolutionary theory, revolutionary dignity, and our revolutionary experience, could we ever accept the theses of official leadership, the theses expounded in these documents? No! Never! Because, had we been men with little faith in the Revolution, we would have given up the fight following our first setback at the Moncada Barracks, [APPLAUSE] or when our little army landed from the 'Granma' only to be dispersed three days later, and only seven of us were able to reunite. Thousands, or rather millions of reasons could have been used as a pretext to say that we were wrong and that those who said that it was impossible to fight that army, those great forces, were right. However, three weeks later, on 17 January, we, who at the end of December had barely reunited our forces, carried out our first successful attack on an army post, killing its occupants. Five days later we were fighting again; this time against the parachutists.

These first two successful actions were followed by intense persecution and several cases of treason that came close to bringing about our destruction. Twenty men, practically isolated from the rest of the country, pursued by thousands of soldiers. Even under such conditions of hardship we maintained our faith in carrying our fight to victory. And – as many of you may recall – when during the April Strike our movement was dealt a disastrous blow we would have had plenty of reasons, similar to these, to give up our struggle.

Many letters were written. One of them, entitled 'A Letter to a Patriot' urged us to give up the fight. However, that crisis in the revolutionary movement was overcome in less than four months when 10,000 soldiers armed with cannon were sent against 300 guerrilla fighters only to meet a disastrous defeat. They were defeated due to our experience, because we had lived through a revolutionary struggle from its very inception. How could we docilely accept the defeatist pronouncements of those guilty of faulty development in the revolutionary movement, of those who were incapable of leading that armed struggle?

The only correct thing to be done by those who had failed, by those who did not have the capacity to lead, was not to court martial and expel those who had shown the capacity to defeat the enemy on the field of battle, but rather to resign. It was the only honest, correct thing to do; to take the responsibility for defeat and to turn the leadership of the Party over to those who had proved their capacity to carry on the war.

Why should we be forced to accept such a thesis? It is not incumbent upon us to decide the problems of strategy or tactics for the Venezuelan revolutionary movement. Nobody has ever asked us to make any decisions on such problems nor have we ever attempted to do so. But we do have an inalienable right, and that is the right to think, the right to have an opinion, the right to express our sympathy and solidarity with the fighters. And it was not possible that we, revolutionaries – having to choose between capitulators, between defeatists, and men determined to convert to reality the watchword of 'make our country free or die for Venezuela', [APPLAUSE] men who were not a group of theorizing charlatans, but a group of combatants – it was impossible for us, as an elemental question of revolutionary principle and morality, to do other than express our solidarity with those combatants.

Our history, the history of our country, a history full of beautiful examples, tells us of an unforgettable episode from our wars of independence when, in 1878, after ten years of war, a great many – even the majority – of the leaders of the revolutionary movement decided to ask for a truce, and the Peace of Zanjón was signed after ten years of heroic struggle. Our most brilliant general refused to accept that peace and drew up the famous Protest of Baraguá. [APPLAUSE]

Douglas Bravo has voiced a sort of 'Baragua Protest'

How many things our history has taught us! Are there many things more admirable from the pages of Cuba's history than that rebellious and noble gesture, full of greatness and dignity, with which Antonio Maceo asked for an interview with Martínez Campos and declared that he would not accept peace with the Spaniards? In a gesture which won him immortality in the eyes of past, present, and future generations, immortality before world opinion, after ten years of war!

How can we consider Douglas Bravo a common divisionist, a common adventurer, a commonly ambitious person, if Douglas Bravo has made within the sector of the revolutionary movement deriving from the Party, has declared a kind of Protest of Baragua against the Peace of Zanjón which defeatist leadership wanted to impose on the Party?

For this reason he has our support and solidarity. And we have the inalienable right to express with all honesty what we think and what we feel. He did not side with the capitulators; he sided with the combatants. Acceptance of the capitulationist theory would have meant that we, as well, would have had to deny our solidarity to Americo Martín and the combatants of the MIR who are fighting in the mountains of El Bachiller; it would have meant denying our solidarity to Fabricio Ojeda and his comrades. Proof that the capitulators were wrong and proof that their theory amounted to handling the revolutionary struggle of Venezuela over to the pro-imperialist government of Leoni on a silver platter is that, in spite of this virtual treason, the pro-imperialist government of Leoni, aided by Yankee officials, supported by and supplied with Yankee weapons, has not been able to crush the heroic and unvanquished guerrillas that fight in the western mountains of Venezuela and in the mountains of El Bachiller. [PROLONGED APPLAUSE]

It was on 7 November 1965 that the defeatists signed the document that I read to you before; we are already in mid-March 1967. If the defeatists have been right, the government of

Venezuela would not have found itself obliged to take desperate suppressive steps in view of the upsurge of the guerrilla movement, and it would long since have wiped out the last fighter. In this case, then, it will not be necessary to wait for time to prove the fighters right; time is already proving them right. Any one of those fronts, in the western mountains or in El Bachiller, has at least as many, or more, men and weapons as did our columns when they were considered invincible in the Sierra Maestra.

And the sell-out, traitorous oligarchy that rules Venezuela will not be able to crush those fighters; that is why it is so frantically seeking guilty parties and advocating aggressions against Cuba, against the revolutionary example constituted by this country.

In the name of what revolutionary principles, reasons, or fundamentals were we obliged to say that the defeatists were right, to say that the rightist, capitulationist current was correct? In the name of Marxism-Leninism? No! We would never have been able to say they were right in the name of Marxism-Leninism. In the name of the international communist movement? Were we perhaps obligated by the fact that it was a question of the leadership of a communist party? Is this the conception we are supposed to have of the international communist movement? To us the international communist movement is in the first place just that, a movement of communists, of revolutionary fighters. And those who are not revolutionary fighters cannot be called Communists! [APPLAUSE]

We conceive of Marxism as revolutionary thinking and action. Those who do not possess a truly revolutionary spirit cannot be called Communists.

There are some who call themselves revolutionaries who are not

Anyone can give himself the name of 'eagle' without having a single feather on his back. In the same way, there are people who call themselves communists without having a communist hair on their heads. The international communist movement, to our way of thinking, is not a church. It is not a religious sect or a Masonic lodge that obliges us to hallow any weakness, any deviation; that obliges us to follow a policy of mutual admiration with all kinds of reformists and pseudo-revolutionaries.

Our stand regarding Communist Parties will be based on strictly revolutionary principles. The parties that have a line without hesitations and capitulationism, the parties that in our opinion have a consistent revolutionary line, will receive our support in all circumstances; but the parties that entrench themselves behind the name of communists or Marxists and believe themselves to have a monopoly on revolutionary sentiment – what they really monopolize is reformism – will not be treated by us as revolutionary parties. And if in any country those who call themselves communists do not know how to fulfil their duty, we will support those who, without calling themselves communists, conduct themselves like real communists in action and in struggle. For every true revolutionary, who bears within him the revolutionary spirit, revolutionary vocation, will always come to Marxism! It is impossible for a man, travelling the road of revolution, not to arrive at Marxism! And every revolutionary on the continent who is deserving of the name will arrive at the Marxist conception of society! What is important are the revolutionaries, those who are capable of making revolution and developing themselves in revolutionary theory.

Many times practice comes first and then theory. Our people too, are an example of that. Many, the immense majority of those who today proudly call themselves Marxist-Leninists, arrived at Marxism-Leninism by way of the revolutionary struggle. To exclude, to deny, to reject *a priori* all those who from the beginning did not call themselves communists is an act of dogmatism and unqualified sectarianism. Whoever denies that it is the road of revolution which leads the people to Marxism is no Marxist, although he may call himself a communist.

This will be our line of conduct. It is the line that has guided our conduct in relations with the revolutionary movements.

At the Tri-Continental Conference in Havana, representatives of revolutionary organizations of the three continents met. Some called themselves communists and others did not. What defines a communist is his attitude towards the oligarchies, his attitude towards exploitation, his attitude towards imperialism; and on this continent, his attitude towards the armed revolutionary movements. What will define the communists of this continent is their attitude towards the guerrilla movement in Guatemala, in Colombia, and in Venezuela. No one who claims to call himself communist will support the rightist official leadership opposing Douglas Bravo. Communist Parties must differentiate between the guerrillas who are fighting in Venezuela and the defeatists who wish to renounce the struggle, who in practice wish to give up the guerrilla movement. And this will be a dividing line, for we are arriving at the time of definitions, not by anyone's whims, but by the force of the process itself, of historical events themselves.

Those who condemn the guerrillas for the simple reason of sect or dogma, in the spirit of freemasonry, cannot consider themselves revolutionaries.

One must ask the revolutionary guerrillas in Guatemala, Colombia, or any other country, who, in their opinion, are the revolutionaries; who, in their opinion are those who show them solidarity; who are their real supporters, the Venezuelan guerrillas or the defeatists? For those who fight in Venezuela, those who force the imperialists to use up part of their resources against them, who bear their share of imperialist bombs, aid those who are fighting in Guatemala or Colombia. Those who fight in the mountains of Venezuela are the only real and possible allies of those who are fighting in the mountains of Colombia and in the mountains of Guatemala ...

Our policy is clear. We recognize only revolutionaries as representatives of the people. We do not consider any of those oligarchic and traitorous governments that broke with Cuba, following orders from the Yankee embassy, as representatives of their peoples. Only one of those governments, which is not a socialist government, but whose international position deserves our respect – only one of those governments deserves such respect – and that is the government of Mexico.

What is our diplomatic position with the other governments? We will not re-establish diplomatic relations with any of those governments that obeyed imperialist orders; we have no interest in doing so; we have no desire to do so. We will only establish diplomatic relations with revolutionary governments in those countries; and, therefore, with governments that show they are independent. Re-establish relations so that they can break them the day after tomorrow following a simple indication from the State Department? No. We do not like to waste our time on such foolishness. Economic relations with those oligarchies, when they were the ones that broke with us? We are not interested in re-establishing relations until there are revolutionary governments leading those countries.

We will not give financial aid to any oligarchy to put down the revolutionary movement with blood. And whoever, no matter who, aids those oligarchies where guerrillas are fighting will be helping to suppress the revolution, for repressive wars are carried on not only with weapons but also with the millions of dollars used for purchasing the weapons and for paying the mercenary armies.

An unmistakable proof of the lack of independence of those governments is to be found in the recent case of Colombia, where at 6 a.m. a few days ago, because of a guerrilla attack against a train, they arrested the General Secretary of the Communist Party of Colombia and all the leaders of that Party who were found in their customary places. They did not hesitate a bit because, at that very moment, a delegation of high Soviet officials was present for the signing of a commercial, cultural, and financial agreement with the Lleras Restrepo government; that same day, it was said there was to be an interview between Lleras Restrepo and the high Soviet officials. And that same day not only did they arrest the Communist leadership but they also attacked, according to the wire service dispatches, the offices of the news agency TASS. What a friendly spirit those oligarchies have! What an independent spirit those puppets have! There is reciprocity for you! That is a proof of the lack of independence, of the hypocrisy of the international policy of those puppet governments...

You see how the Venezuelan puppets talk, with their demands that the USSR withdraw from the Tri-Continental Organization, that the USSR do no less than virtually break with Cuba, the 'dead-end street', to enter through the wide, expansive, and friendly door of the Venezuelan government, the government that has slaughtered more communists than any other on this continent!

As for us, we are Marxist-Leninist: let others do as they please. We will never re-establish relations with such a government!

They have broken relations with us, we have not broken relations with anyone. The German Federal Republic even broke with us because we recognized the German Democratic Republic. But we did not waver; as a matter of principle, even though it affected our economic interests, we recognized the German Democratic Republic. All is not rose-coloured in the revolutionary world. Complaints and more complaints are repeated because of contradictory attitudes. While one country is being condemned for reopening relations with Federal Germany, there is a rush to seek relations with oligarchies of the sort of Leoni and company. A principled position in everything, a principled position in Asia, but a principled position in Latin America, too.

Let us condemn the imperialist aggression against Vietnam; let us condemn the crime that the Yankee imperialists are committing today against Vietnam and let us condemn it with all our might and all our heart! But let us condemn, starting right now, the future Vietnams in Latin America, let us condemn, starting right now, the future imperialist aggressions in Latin America!

What would the Vietnamese revolutionaries think if we were to send delegations to South Vietnam to deal with the Saigon puppet government? What would those who are fighting in the mountains of America think were we to seek close relations with the puppets of the future Yankee aggressions and interventions of this continent?

The Leoni of today, the Lleras Restrepo of today, will be the Ngo Dinh Diem and the Cao Ky of tomorrow; they will be on the end of the string of governments that have passed through South Vietnam merely to justify the imperialist aggressions, just to legalize the interventions of the Yankee Marines.

And all of them, imperialists and puppets, join in a conspiracy against our revolutionary, socialist nation, which is as it is not because we have imported revolution from any other country, but rather because we have generated it on our own soil and under our own skies.

There are some who speak of supposed cases of fatalism, but there is no fatalism that can hold back this Revolution, not the ninety-mile fatalism, or any other kind of fatalism! This Revolution that sprang from nothing at all; this Revolution that sprang from a tiny group of men who for whole years lived in conditions of encirclement by the enemy, where nothing could get through, is a Revolution which has its own particular right to exist. It is a Revolution – understand this well, all puppets, oligarchs, shilly-shalliers and pseudo-revolutionaries of all stripes – it is a Revolution which no one or nothing will be able to crush or halt! [PROLONGED APPLAUSE] And this Revolution will maintain its position of absolute independence, that kind of independence to which all people capable of fighting for it are entitled, that kind of independence all honourable people are entitled to have.

We proclaim it to the world: This Revolution will hold true to its path, this Revolution will follow its own line, this Revolution will never be anybody's satellite or 'yes-man'. It will never ask anybody's permission to maintain its own position either in matters of ideology, or on domestic or foreign affairs; proudly and courageously our people are ready to face the future, whatever that future may hold.

Today we work with feverish enthusiasm, with more enthusiasm than ever before; and we are advancing in our national development, in the development of our economy more impetuously than at any other time in the past eight years. Great ideological battles are being won on all fronts, in all respects, and we will confidently hold true to our ideological path, with the confidence of true revolutionaries, with confidence in our people and in our masses.

Perhaps, if it had not been necessary to deal with the subjects I have been concerned with tonight, it would have been necessary to talk about this profound, incredible revolution that is taking place in the awareness of our people. We look to the future serenely and confidently, as we face any eventuality. We are aware that this struggle will not and cannot be easy, that we live on a continent in full revolutionary ferment, in the midst of a score of peoples who are waking up to reality, who are already fighting or are getting ready to do so. We realize that threats of all kinds will be hurled at us, and conspiracies will be organized against us, and possibly even aggression by the dozen will be launched against us. Very well, from this very moment we declare ourselves invincible. [APPLAUSE]

An invasion of this country ... this is practically what Señor Leoni proposed or insinuates. He does not now call for sanctions because of the international situation, but he wishes to start building up his dossier; in short, it is perfectly clear that once they are through in Vietnam it will be time for them to ask for sanctions and war against us. No wonder the first person he talked with was 'His Highness', the Yankee ambassador in Caracas. Very well: now or at any other time, while they attack Vietnam or after they are defeated in Vietnam – because they will be defeated, they are going to be defeated in their aggression against the heroic people of North Vietnam and they are going to be defeated in their aggression against the heroic people of South Vietnam, led by the National Liberation Front, whose position and policy the Cuban Party supports without any vacillation. [APPLAUSE] There is no doubt whatsoever that they will defeat the imperialists – if they think they will find a pushover here, let them know that they will find here at least one Stalingrad plus 3.6 Vietnams; [APPLAUSE] and besides, half a dozen more Vietnams on the rest of the continent. Let them take note of that as of now ! And as far as we are concerned, we base ourselves on mathematical calculations, on numbers of men, on the volume of fire, and on a fire that burns hotter than that of arms; the fire in the hearts and the fire of the valour of an entire people ! [APPLAUSE] ...

CHAPTER 4

The Role of Armed Struggle:
'Our People have No Other Path to
Liberation than that of Armed Struggle.'*

*In this speech Fidel makes clear that the fundamental road open
to revolutionaries is that of armed struggle. He tells the veterans
of Playa Girón and the Cuban people that this is the principal
road because the imperialists will allow no other means of change.
Therefore the Cubans, in following their international obligations, must expect retaliation for such support. In this he cites
the example of Vietnam – a nation paying the price, but defeating
the United States.*

*This speech is important because of its clear exposition of the
internationalist position of the Cuban Revolution. In order to
understand both its foreign policy and its domestic economic
development policies, one must first understand the moral basis
for the Revolution. Fidel quotes approvingly 'Humanity comes
before one's own country', and in this speech makes clear the
link between the values espoused in the development of Cuba
and their international consequences.*

*Thus, in this speech, as well as in the funeral oration of Che,
one sees the necessary link between the domestic policy of development with moral incentives, and the foreign policy of armed
revolution. For this reason, Che Guevara, fallen guerrilla hero and
exponent of moral incentives, is extolled as the image for youth
in Cuba.*

... The population of Latin America is growing, but the economy
is not; the population is growing, but food production is not.

---

* Delivered at the 'Chaplin' Theatre on the Sixth Anniversary of
Playa Giron, 19 April 1967, 'Year of Heroic Vietnam'.

And imperialism is driven to increase its exploitation, to be even more avaricious as a result of its war policy, its aggression, its repression of the revolutionary movement, its economic situation, that is, the shrinkage of US gold reserves and its unfavourable trade balance. As a result of its adventures, as a result of its policies, as a result, among other things, of its criminal war in Vietnam, it has been forced to deplete Latin America's resources more and more. And it has been increasingly unable to give the slightest economic aid to those countries.

What is the inevitable outcome? What is the significance of the fact that, throughout a continent of 230 million inhabitants, the population is growing faster than food production? What will be the only outcome? What must the inevitable outcome be?

What will be the inevitable outcome of a situation in which misery and hunger lead year by year to more misery and hunger? Can there be any other outcome than that of revolution? And that is the spectre; more than a spectre, the reality, that haunts the short-sighted, the blind, those who believed that this situation of hunger and misery could be solved in co-operation with the imperialists, the exploiters, those who bear the main responsibility for that situation of misery.

Those are facts that cannot be concealed and that lead to the only possible outcome – revolution. And this revolution is the outcome of a historical need, not the result of caprice or personal will. No one will be able to impose that revolution, as no one will be able to prevent it; for that revolution is the outcome of a vital necessity. It is the only path open to the peoples of Latin America. And that is what our Revolution has declared since the first day; that is what our Revolution stated in the First Declaration of Havana, and in each of the statements made in the course of these years. We have said, and we have firmly believed and passionately defended the premise, that this revolution, in the situation of present-day Latin America, can come only from the armed struggle of the peoples.

And is it the people who voluntarily choose that road? Do the peoples have the alternative of choosing between one road and another? No!

It is imperialism, it is the bloody dictatorship of the oligarchs and exploiters who do not and will not calmly relinquish their privileges, who will not docilely hand over the reins of society to the exploited. Moreover, the exploiters dominate not only the economic resources; they dominate the armed institutions, they dominate the means of communications, they monopolize television, radio, printing presses, the immense majority of the newspapers, most educational and cultural institutions. And the revolutionary organizations are unarmed. What sort of arms can they rely on to try to gain revolutionary power by peaceful means, if the arms supposedly available in such a conflict are never within the reach of revolutionaries?

Our people have no other path to liberation than that of armed struggle

It is not only a question of repression. The oligarchies, the exploiting classes, create the conditions to keep the revolutionaries and the exploited from having access to power. And thus far history has shown us a *single* road – our own history of today and yesterday and always, the history of the peoples who have made their revolutions. It has shown us that the peoples who have achieved any progress, any freedom, have not done so by humbling themselves, by placing their necks in the yoke. The peoples have found themselves forced to struggle; they have had to struggle. They have had to fight not because they like to spill blood, not because they like war, but because they are faced with the alternative of slavery or sacrifice; they are forced to pay for their freedom and justice with their blood and sacrifice.

Historically, this is the alternative that the exploiters have imposed upon the exploited, the oppressors upon the oppressed, the slavemasters upon the slaves: exploitation, oppression, slavery – or sacrifice. The road is not chosen by the peoples, gentlemen; the peoples only follow the roads imposed upon them by their oppressors and exploiters. And to us it is clear. We have defended this viewpoint with conviction, with tenacity and even with passion; our peoples unfortunately have no other road to liberation than that of struggle.

And the facts increasingly show that we are right. Awareness of that truth is growing on this continent, awareness of that truth is becoming more palpable with every day that passes. The peoples begin to inspire fear when they begin to find out the truth, when they begin to discover the truth of their situation.

We, too, were inoffensive vassals, we, too, were among the defenceless and the oppressed. Our people were just that until they began to discover the truth of their situation, until they began to discover their road. Today it seems almost inexplicable to all of us how it was possible for all that savagery, all that injustice, all that heartless exploitation, to maintain itself for so long; how it was possible for that entire social order to exist defended by a mercenary army, defended by tiny squads of soldiers and rural guards. All of that was possible while the entire people believed in the myth that the prevailing force could not be overcome, that the prevailing force was invincible. That system was maintained more – much more! – by myth and lie than by the actual force that defended it. And suppose our oldest comrades – I don't mean old in years, but those with most experience in the guerrilla fighting – suppose that our comrades who took part in that struggle were placed back on 11 March 1952, after the coup d'état, with all that they know today, with all their present understanding and knowledge, even if it were without a single bullet, without a single rifle. Suppose they were placed in that situation, which can only be utterly imaginary, of course, and were asked: how long do you thing this situation will last? No one would feel that seven years of oppression and bloodshed would lie ahead. Only a few would doubt – almost no one would doubt with what they know today – that the revolutionary armed struggle in our country would have begun on 12 March, if not on the eleventh or even on the tenth itself. [APPLAUSE] And it would have been sufficient – yes, sufficient! – to take away the rifles of a pair of those rural guards to begin the revolutionary struggle: just a pair! ... They would have wiped out one of those hired killers by hitting him with a stone or giving him a good crack on the neck. And I know, I have the conviction, that with what has been learned, with what is known and understood today, the struggle would have begun the next day.

However, we know all that now. What a long time it took us to find that out. What a long time it took us to understand that truth! A long time, that is, from a revolutionary standpoint. When the myth of the invincibility of that army fell away, when the lie was destroyed, the counter-revolutionaries then fell into another myth, into another lie. They were unable to distinguish between the power of exploitation and injustice and the power of the Revolution.

They went so far as to think that it could be just as easy to destroy a revolution as it had been to destroy exploitation and oppression. And then it took time, it took years to establish another truth: the truth that, just as it is possible to destroy a system of exploitation and injustice, it is absolutely impossible to destroy a revolution, no matter by what means. [APPLAUSE]

The imperialists, the CIA, learned that lesson very well. They learned that gimmicks and mercenary bands are worthless against a revolution, that guerrilla tactics get absolutely nowhere against a revolution. For a revolution is defended by the people, a revolution is defended by armed workers and peasants. That's why the imperialists live in a constant state of trauma and see spectres everywhere.

How is it possible, that with all their ultra-modern weapons and resources and equipment, with the absolute impunity with which they have been able to carry out their crimes on a world scale, they are unable to get a counter-revolutionary movement going? And how is it, nevertheless, that revolutionary movements arise everywhere and the imperialists are unable to crush them?

And so a revolutionary movement arose in South Vietnam. To crush it they organized a huge mercenary army, a puppet army, with all kinds of modern weapons and equipment to crush the revolutionary movement of the peasants and workers of Vietnam, to crush the guerrillas. But the more the counter-revolutionary army grew in numbers, the more the guerrilla movement grew in strength and power.

Vietnam has been a great lesson
to the world, to revolutionaries,
but also to the imperialists

They came to have an army of 400,000 men, but it was insufficient; they began to send special troops, first a few hundred, then several thousand, but these were insufficient; then they began to send tens of thousands of Yankee soldiers, but that was not enough either; they sent in mercenary troops from half a dozen nations, but it wasn't enough; they have used tactical aviation, they have used strategic aviation against the South and against the North, and nevertheless, what have they achieved? Two years have already gone by since they began their massive bombings and what have they achieved?

That is a lesson the imperialists will have to learn, whether they like it or not.

We have said on other occasions, and we will have to repeat it many more times, that the people of Vietnam have given the world, the revolutionaries, and also the imperialists, a supreme lesson, a lesson they cannot ignore. The imperialists have seen that there are limits to their might; they have seen that despite their industrial and military resources they have been unable to crush the revolutionary movement in a country many times smaller than the United States. Not with mercenary troops nor with the complicity of the mercenary armies of several countries, nor with their own troops, nor with their own sea- and air-power have they been able to crush the revolution. They have, it is true, caused much pain and sacrifice, they have spilled much blood, but they are further than ever from defeating the revolutionary movement in Vietnam.

The situation of the imperialist aggressors is worsening. The consequences in domestic politics, the moral and economic consequences, are increasingly difficult to ignore. One of these consequences is the resistance of the people of the United States itself, who just a few days ago staged one of the biggest demonstrations[1] that has ever been seen there, precisely against the

1. 15 April: Mobilization to End the War in Vietnam.

brutal and criminal war being waged by the imperialists in Vietnam.

And one more ally – a most estimable one at that – is arising right there among the people of the United States. It is really interesting from a historic standpoint, from the point of view of the course of events nowadays, that there – right in the heart of New York – hundreds of thousands of citizens joined together under that watchword. The representatives of the movement against racial discrimination were present in considerable numbers with posters saying that the war being waged by the imperialists against the Vietnamese people is inspired in the same feelings that lead to the oppression of black people in the United States.

That is, the victims of exploitation and discrimination in the United States have realized that their own cause has an ally in the Vietnamese who are fighting and dying for their homeland. It is really impressive to see hundreds of thousands of US citizens marching through New York, some of them with pictures of Ho Chi Minh, among others. And something even more enlightening: along with the pictures of Ho Chi Minh and some of the martyrs in the civil rights cause, the news dispatches reported that there were also pictures of Che Guevara. [LENGTHY APPLAUSE]

The people of the United States will see more clearly as the people's revolutionary struggle grows

This is an indication to us, to revolutionaries, that, sooner or later, among the exploited sectors of the United States, among those who suffer discrimination under that system, among the poor of the United States, among the students of the United States, and even among the progressive and intellectual sectors of the United States – and there are many of these who are fully aware of the brutality of imperialist policies – among the progressive sectors of the United States, and among the people themselves – whose awareness will awaken more and more – the world revolutionary movement, and in particular the Latin American revolutionary movement, will have – sooner or later – a mighty ally.

Imperialist interests, the interests of the small minority of monopolists who rule the United States, attempt to persuade the people of that country that the liberating revolution of the peoples goes against their interests, but the people of the United States will come to see with increasing clarity who represents the most vital interests of the people of the US, whether the revolutionaries of the liberation movements or the imperialists who are spending nearly 100,000 million dollars in war-mongering adventures, who spend more all the time. It is a fact that the US war budget, already over fifty billion dollars several years ago, has grown considerably larger in recent years with the war in Vietnam and its escalation.

Who pays for these expenditures? Who pays for these adventures? Where does the money come from? It is true that a part comes from the labour of the peoples exploited by the monopolists, but a large amount is also extracted from the sweat of US workers. Not only do the imperialists squander the fruits of the labour of the people of the United States on war adventures and brutal crimes, they also divest the US people of a good part of the fruits of their labour in order to augment their monopoly capital and to foot bloody wars in defence of these monopoly interests. And they squander not only the money of the people of the United States, but also their blood, and they are threatening to cause greater bloodshed with each passing day.

This universal revolutionary and anti-imperialist awareness is growing, both outside the United States, and within.

This lesson, of course, has not been learned by the people of the United States from speeches or pamphlets. No ! It has been a costly lesson; it has been a costly lesson for the peoples; it has cost the Vietnamese people much blood, it has cost Dominican blood, and unfortunately, it will cost still more blood, of these peoples, and of others.

In other words, the peoples of the world have had to pay the cost of imperialist barbarity so that the people of the United States might open their eyes. And the people of the United States will open their eyes; they will open them more and more as the revolutionary struggle of the people grows, and as the imperialists become increasingly impotent and increasingly battered by the revolutionary movement not only in Vietnam, but, as Che said, in two, three, four, five, ad infinitum, Vietnams. [APPLAUSE]

The imperialist press has attempted to distort some of the ideas expressed in Che's splendid message to the peoples of the world, opining that this message proposes the destruction of the United States. Nothing could be further from the truth. The message very clearly expresses the idea that revolutionary strategy aims at the destruction, not of the United States, but at the destruction of the imperialist domination of the United States of America.

Let the imperialists not attempt to confuse the people of the United States, the nation of the United States – which is not composed of imperialists only – with the imperialists themselves. And what is perfectly clear in the message of Major Ernesto Guevara is the proposition that revolutionary strategy be directed towards the destruction of imperialist domination.

This means that once imperialist domination is destroyed, and, above all, imperialist domination of Latin America, imperialism as a system will disappear. In other words, the liberation of Latin America will constitute a decisive step in the liberation of the world from its worst enemy – US imperialism.

And it is a clear and evident fact that revolutionary awareness is growing in Latin America, and, as this awareness develops, events also develop; and as events develop, revolutionary awareness develops. There is no longer one, nor two, nor three, but four guerrilla movements already developing with steadily increasing strength; four guerrilla movements that the oligarchies are clearly unable to crush: the Guatemalan guerrilla movement in Central America, [APPLAUSE] the guerrilla movements of Colombia and Venezuela [APPLAUSE] and the guerrilla movement of Bolivia, [APPLAUSE] all in process of development, slowly at first, but with constantly increasing energy and momentum.

The combatants of the revolutionary movement of this contingent have been gaining experience, and the peoples have been opening their minds to the truth.

The pusillanimous, the weak-spirited, the pseudo-revolutionaries who thought that the first setbacks meant that revolution had failed and that armed struggle was futile must wake up to a new reality.

No blow, no setback has ever destroyed the faith, tenacity, and firmness of true revolutionaries, nor will it ever, in any country. In some cases, development will be more accelerated than in others.

It is worthy of note that, in Colombia, for example, important actions are being carried out; the revolutionaries attack military convoys being carried on important railway lines, take towns, or engage in intense, hours-long combat in the mountains, victorious combat in which the repressive forces suffer numerous losses. The strength of the guerrilla movement in Colombia is apparent in equal measure in different regions of the country.

As to Venezuela, Señor Leoni became a laughing stock recently at the Punta del Este Conference when he insisted that the Venezuelan guerrillas were little more than an invention of the press, that they did not really exist.

How often have they affirmed that the guerrillas have been wiped out? Yet, despite ironclad censorship of the press, everyone knows that the guerrilla movement is growing in Venezuela and that heavily-armed detachments are inspiring fear in the régime, and fear in its soldiers. No matter how they try to hide it, they cannot deny that the guerrilla columns under the command of Douglas Bravo [APPLAUSE] have victoriously penetrated not only the Falcon zone, but the state of Lara as well, or that, despite offensive operations by the army, the guerrilla forces in El Bachiller are firmly holding their positions under the leadership of Americo Martín [APPLAUSE] . . .

We have learned recently through the news services that the army situated heavy artillery before El Bachiller mountains, from where it carried out an intense bombardment of the mountains.

There are enough old guerrilla fighters present here, and not only old guerrilla fighters, but also others who learned the art of war while hunting down bands of counter-revolutionaries, to know, as anyone who has had guerrilla experience knows, that nothing is more ridiculous than firing a battery of cannons against mountains. If it is ridiculous to shoot from planes that can drop hundreds and thousands of bombs without even one falling anywhere near a guerrilla fighter, of what use is artillery against guerrillas?

And when one reads such news he asks himself, who are they trying to fool? Are they trying to fool Leoni? Or are the 'Green Beret' advisers fooling the army? Are they all trying to fool each other? Or are they trying to fool the people? But who on earth are they going to make believe that this is anything other than an act of desperation, an absurdity, an incredible stupidity!

It is a sign of impotence, of inability to crush the guerrilla movement.

And, according to what can be deduced from the press dispatches of the news services, the guerrilla movement in Bolivia grows in strength and combativity. According to what we have read, in a matter of just a few weeks, the guerrillas, in a series of fulminating attacks, have caused the repressive troops of the régime more than forty losses including dead, wounded, and prisoners – despite the fact that specially-trained 'anti-guerrilla' troops are being used against them.

The fact is that these specially trained troops are effective for repression of the people in the streets, for wholesale assassination of workers, for attacks on miners, but when they have to confront the guerrillas in the mountains they are totally useless, perfectly inept, and their fate – like that of the mercenaries in Vietnam – will be to die like insects. [APPLAUSE]

Increasing numbers of 'Green Berets' are being used in Guatemala, Colombia, and Venezuela and, according to news from Bolivia, the imperialists have recently sent about 1,000 'Green Berets' to that country. Airline travellers between Panama and Bolivia have told of flights on which as many as fifty Yankee tourists – very odd tourists, who travel under 'superiors' and are met at the different airports by others like themselves – arrive and fill the hotels, while in the Ministry of the Interior, the Ministry of Defence, the various repressive bodies, at Army Headquarters, etc., very little effort is made to conceal the presence of these special troops of the US Army.

The imperialists, of course, try to conceal the magnitude of their intervention in Bolivia. They speak of planeloads of arms being sent and of military instructors who are sent in accordance with agreements that existed before the upsurge of the guerrilla movement, but the fact is that armaments have been taken in by plane and close to 1,000 specially trained troops have been sent via different routes to Bolivia.

This illustrates the panic, the desperation, the fear, and the dead-end road of the imperialists. Because, above and beyond the hundreds of thousands of soldiers they already have in Vietnam and the thousands that still occupy Dominican territory, they are now obliged to mobilize more and more soldiers to send against the different guerrilla fronts in Latin America in a shameless intervention that is, it is logical to assume, the beginning of another imperialist adventure.

Of course, they won't have too many experts to send, because the Vietnamese have put many of the 'Green Beret' experts out of commission. And if the imperialists send increasing numbers of 'Green Berets' against the guerrilla movements, so much the worse for the 'Green Berets'! Not only because the revolutionaries are going to settle accounts with them, but also because this will serve to accelerate and strengthen solidarity among the peoples of the world to fight at the side of the revolutionaries! [APPLAUSE]

The internationalist scope and nature of this revolutionary struggle of all the peoples against the Yankee imperialist – the enemy – was superbly described by Che in his message.

Awareness grows. Revolutionary theses gain ground; they are gaining ever-increasing support and an ever-increasing number of adepts, while the conformist, reformist, submissive, and pseudo-revolutionary theses are being increasingly rejected and grow steadily weaker.

We have not the shadow of a doubt that all of this is a simple matter of time, and that the vacillators, those who prefer to come to terms, and the pseudo-revolutionaries, will be swept away in this struggle. As the truth of the peoples makes headway, there will be no one left who will heed any charlatan who advises him to bow his head and accept the yoke. This is clear. The peoples of this continent are becoming more and more aware of the reality of their situation ...

... We want to convert our work to wealth and welfare for our own people and for other peoples. We want to work for ourselves and to help others. We are aware of the dangers, but we are not discouraged, they will not reduce our enthusiasm one iota.

Our country, our people, and our future are important, but still more important are our 230 million Latin American brothers! [APPLAUSE] All of America is important. The future of this continent is important! But the whole world is still more important! And if, as someone in the past century – when Marxist ideas had not yet taken root in the minds of hundreds of millions of human beings – said: 'Humanity comes before one's own country,' we internationalist revolutionaries will always say: we love our country, we love the welfare of our people, we love the riches that we create with our own hands, but humanity comes before our country! May the heroes who died at Girón, fighting for their country, and fighting for humanity, live forever!

Patria o Muerte! Venceremos! [APPLAUSE AND SHOUTS OF 'VIVA']

CHAPTER 5

'Whoever Stops to Wait for Ideas to Triumph among the Majority of the Masses before Initiating Revolutionary Action will never be a Revolutionary.'*

Despite the close trade ties between the USSR and Cuba, Fidel has remained apart from the strict Soviet stance on world affairs. The Caribbean Crisis, the bombing of socialist North Vietnam, the Sino-Soviet dispute, and the class collaborationist position of official Communist Parties in Latin America all caused intensive points of friction between the USSR and Cuba. In 1965, Fidel had rebuked both parties in the Sino-Soviet dispute ('Division in the face of the enemy was never a revolutionary or intelligent strategy', II, 2). In 1966, he had become critical of the official Communist Parties for their failure to push armed struggle and of the Soviet Union for its seeking close ties with the Latin American oligarchies.

As noted in the introductory note to 'Their attitude towards the guerrilla struggle will define the communists in Latin America' (II, 3), the Tri-Continental Conference in Havana in 1966 had a predominance of official Communist Parties. Shortly thereafter, Fidel became increasingly critical of these Parties. In the summer of 1967 the founding conference of the Organization for Latin American Solidarity (OLAS) met in Havana. As the following text of Fidel's address to the closing of that conference makes clear, Cuba and the majority of delegates present had clearly split with the coexistence, 'democratic peace', parliamentary strategy

---

* Delivered in Havana at the closing of the First Conference of OLAS at the 'Chaplin' Theatre, 10 August 1967, 'Year of Heroic Vietnam'.

of the official Communist Parties. This split was clear earlier, however, as exemplified in the previous two speeches.

The significance of this speech is that it intended to inaugurate a new International that would break down the traditional cold-war categories. This new International would include Communist Parties – indeed, the Cubans were represented by the Cuban Communist Party – but would not be exclusively made up of official Communist Parties nor would the fact of being a Communist Party lead to automatic membership. Certainly, the Venezuelan Communist Party was excluded. The text was of actions, and not words or party affiliation. Thus, after fifty years, the revolutionary capital of Latin America shifted from Moscow to Havana.

Nevertheless, the Cubans have never tried to force a line on any group in Latin America. The Chinese split in the early sixties did not create an international realignment of parties to the degree that the Cuban-led OLAS grouping did. While OLAS has not functioned as a tight, disciplined, political grouping, it did give important moral support and international attention to the small guerrilla bands in various Latin American countries.

The break with the official communists involved an analysis of revolutionary strategy. Whereas the communist line viewed the national bourgeoisie as a progressive force, a force capable of leading Latin American nations to independence from the United States, the OLAS forces generally held that historical experience had shown the weakness of the national bourgeoisie, e.g., the failures of Quadros and Goulart in Brazil. Arbenz in Guatemala, and Bosch in the Dominican Republic. Analysis had shown that the deep penetration of US capital in Latin America had created a predominantly 'comprador' middle class, that is, a class tied to the US as managers, lawyers, and franchise dealers of US-owned firms. Therefore, they believed the middle class incapable of leading an independent struggle against the United States, given their economic and political dependence on the United States. Given the polarization of forces, and the historically proven impossibility of reform, the OLAS forces believed that armed struggle was the 'fundamental' road to power. Their analysis led to the conclusion that since the enemy is international and not national, the revolutionary front must be international. Hence, Che's call for 'two, three, many Vietnams' meant the creation of many fronts of attack.

The OLAS conference and Fidel's speech to that conference show the Cuban emphasis on struggle, their rejection of electoral politics, and their essentially non-sectarian manner of unifying all those who are actually fighting against imperialism.

Whoever stops to wait for ideas to triumph among the majority of the masses before initiating revolutionary action will never be a revolutionary. For, what is the difference between such a revolutionary and a *latifundium*-owner, a wealthy bourgeois? Nothing!

Humanity will, of course, change; human society will, of course, continue to develop – in spite of human beings and the errors of human beings. But that is not a revolutionary attitude.

If that had been our way of thinking, we would never have initiated a revolutionary process. It was enough for the ideas to take root in a sufficient number of men for revolutionary action to be initiated, and, through this action, the masses started to acquire these ideas; the masses acquired that consciousness.

It is obvious that in Latin America there are already in many places a number of men who are convinced of such ideas, and that have started revolutionary action. And what distinguished the true revolutionary from the false revolutionary is precisely this: one acts to move the masses, the other waits for the masses to have a conscience already before starting to act.

And there is a series of principles that one should not expect to be accepted without an argument, but which are essential truths, accepted by the majority, with reservations on the part of a few. That Byzantine discussion about the ways and means of struggle, whether it should be peaceful or non-peaceful, armed or unarmed: the essence of that discussion – which we call Byzantine because it is like the argument between two deaf-and-dumb people – is that it distinguishes those who want to promote the revolution from those who do not want to promote it, those who want to curb it from those who want to promote it. Let no one be fooled.

Different words have been used: if the road [of the armed

struggle] is the only one, if the road is not the only one, if it is the exclusive one, if it is not the exclusive one. And the Conference has been very clear in this respect. It does not say *only* road, although it might just have well said only road: it says fundamental road, and the other forms of struggle must be subordinated to it: in the long run, the only road. To use the word 'only', even though this meaning of the word be understood – the true meaning – might lead to errors about the imminence of the struggle.

That is why we understand that the Declaration, by calling it the fundamental road, the road that must be taken in the long run, is the correct formulation. If we wish to express our way of thinking, and that of our Party and our people, let no one harbour any illusions about seizing power by peaceful means in any country in this continent, let no one harbour any illusions. Anyone trying to tell such a thing to the masses will be completely deceiving.

This does not mean that one has to go out and grab a rifle, and start fighting tomorrow, anywhere. That is not the question. It is a question of ideological conflict between those who want to make revolution and those who do not want to make it. It is the conflict between those who want to make it and those who want to curb it. Because, essentially, anybody can tell whether or not it is possible, whether or not conditions are ripe, to take up arms.

No one can be sectarian, so dogmatic, as to say that one has to go out and grab a rifle tomorrow, anywhere. And we ourselves do not doubt that there are some countries in which this task is not an immediate task, but we are convinced that it will be their task in the long run.

There are some who have put forward even more radical theses than those of Cuba; that we Cubans believe such and such a country doesn't have conditions for armed struggle, and that we're wrong. But the funny thing is that it has been claimed in some cases by representatives who are not quite in favour of the theses for armed struggle. We will not be angered by this. We prefer them to make mistakes trying to make revolution without the right conditions than to have them make the mistake of never making revolution. I hope no one will make a mistake! But nobody who really wants to fight will ever have differences with us, and those who do not want to fight ever will always have discrepancies with us.

We understand very well the essence of the matter, and it is the conflict between those who want to advance the revolution and those who are deadly enemies of the ideas of the revolution. A whole series of factors have contributed to these positions.

Dogma

This does not always mean that it is enough to have a correct position and that is all. No, even among those who really want to make revolution many mistakes are made; there are still many weaknesses, that is true. But logically we will never have deep contradictions with any one – no matter his mistakes – who honestly has a revolutionary position. It is our understanding that revolutionary thought must take a new course; it is our understanding that we must leave behind old vices, sectarian positions of all kinds and the positions of those who believe they have a monopoly on the revolution or on revolutionary theory. And poor theory, how it has had to suffer in these processes; poor theory, how it has been abused, and how it is still being abused! And all these years have taught us to meditate more, analyse better. We no longer accept any 'self-evident' truths. 'Self-evident' truths are a part of bourgeois philosophy. A whole series of old clichés should be abolished. Marxist literature itself, revolutionary political literature itself should be renewed, because by repeating clichés, phraseology, and verbiage that have been repeated for thirty-five years you don't win over anyone; you don't win over anyone. [APPLAUSE]

There are times when political documents called Marxist give the impression that you go to the archives and ask for a form: form fourteen, form thirteen, form twelve, they are all alike, with the same empty words, which logically is a language incapable of expressing real situations. And many times the documents are divorced from real life. And many people are told that this is Marxism ... and in what way is this different from catechism, and in what way is it different from a litany, from a rosary?

And everyone that poses as a Marxist feels almost obligated to go around looking for this or that manifesto. And you read twenty-five manifestos of twenty-five different organizations, and they are all alike, copied from the same standard; no one is convinced by any of them.

And nothing is further from the thought and style of the founder of Marxism than empty talk, than putting a strait jacket on ideas, because Marx was, undoubtedly, one of the greatest and most brilliant writers of all time. But, worse than the phrases are the ideas they convey. Meaningless phrases are bad, of course, but so are the supposed meanings of certain phrases. Because there are these that are forty years old; the famous thesis about the role of the national bourgeoisies for example. How hard it has been to become convinced, finally, that this idea does not apply on this continent; how much paper, how many phrases, how much empty talk has been wasted waiting for a liberal, progressive, anti-imperialist bourgeoisie.

And we ask ourselves if there is anybody who, at this time, can believe that any bourgeoisie on this continent is playing a revolutionary role.

All these ideas have been gaining strength, have been maintained for a long time – a long series of theses.

I am not going to say that the revolutionary movement and the communist movement in general have ceased to play a role – even an important role – in the history of the revolutionary process and of revolutionary ideas in Latin America. The communist movement developed method, style, and, in some aspects, even took on the characteristics of a religion. And we sincerely believe that the character should be left behind.

Of course to some of these 'illustrious revolutionary thinkers' we are only adventurous petit-bourgeois without revolutionary maturity. We are lucky that the Revolution came before maturity! Because at the end, the mature ones, the over-mature, have matured so much that they are rotten. [APPLAUSE]

But we consider ours a Marxist-Leninist Party, we consider ours a Communist Party. And this is not a problem of words, it is a problem of facts.

We do not consider ourselves teachers, we do not consider

ourselves to have drawn the guiding lines, as some people say. But we have the right to consider ours a Marxist-Leninist Party, a Communist Party.

We are deeply satisfied, and it is with great joy, not nostalgia, with happiness, not sadness, that we see the ranks of the revolutionary movement increasing, the revolutionary organizations multiplying. Marxist-Leninist spirit making headway – that is, Marxist-Leninist ideas – and we felt deeply satisfied when the final resolution of this Conference proclaimed that the revolutionary movement in Latin America is being guided by Marxist-Leninist ideas.

Judge all revolutionaries by their actions

This means that convert-like narrow-mindedness must be overcome. And we, in our Communist Party, will fight to overcome that narrow concept, that narrow-mindedness. And we must say that, as a Marxist-Leninist Party, we belong to OLAS; as a Marxist-Leninist Party we belong not to a small group within the revolutionary movement, but to an organization which comprises all true revolutionaries, and we will not be prejudiced against any revolutionary.

That is, there is a much wider movement on this continent than the movement constituted simply by the Communist Parties of Latin America, we are a part of that wide movement, and that we shall judge the conduct of organizations not by what they say they are, but by what they prove they are, by what they do, by their conduct.

And we feel very satisfied that our Party has wholeheartedly entered into this wider movement, the movement that has just held this first Conference.

Guerrillas must be directed from the countryside

The importance of the guerrilla, the vanguard role of the guerrilla. Much could be said about the guerrilla, but it is not possible to do so in a meeting like this. But guerrilla experiences in this continent have taught us many things – among them the terrible mistake, the absurd concept that the guerrilla movement could be directed from the cities.

That is the reason for the thesis that political and military commands must be united.

This is the reason for our conviction that it is not only a stupidity but also a crime to want to direct the guerrillas from the city. And we have had the opportunity to appreciate the consequences of this absurdity many times. And it is necessary that these ideas be overcome, and this is why we consider the resolution of this Conference of great importance.

The guerrilla is bound to be the nucleus of the revolutionary movement. This does not mean that the guerrilla movement can rise without any previous work; it does not mean that the guerrilla movement is something that can exist without political direction. No! We do not deny the role of the leading organizations, we do not deny the role of the political organizations. The guerrilla is organized by a political movement, by a political organization. What we believe incompatible with correct ideas of guerrilla struggle is the idea of directing the guerrilla from the cities. And in the conditions of our continent it will be very difficult to suppress the role of the guerrilla.

There are some who ask themselves if it is possible in any country of Latin America to achieve power without armed struggle. And, of course, theoretically, hypothetically, when a great part of the continent has been liberated there would be nothing surprising, if under those conditions, a revolution succeeds without opposition – but this would be an exception. However, this does not mean that the revolution is going to succeed in any country without a struggle. The blood of the revolutionaries of a specific country may not be shed, but their victory will only be possible thanks to the efforts, the sacrifices, and the blood of the revolutionaries of a whole continent.

It would therefore be false to say that they had a revolution there without a struggle. That will always be a lie. And I believe that it is not correct for any revolutionary to wait with arms crossed until all the other peoples struggle and create the conditions for victory for him without struggle. That will never be an attribute of revolutionaries.

To those who believe that peaceful transition is possible in some countries of this continent, we say to them that we cannot understand what kind of peaceful transition they refer to, unless it is to a peaceful transition in agreement with imperialism. Because in order to achieve victory by peaceful means, if in practice such a thing were possible considering that the mechanisms of the bourgeoisie, the oligarchies, and imperialism control all the means for peaceful struggle . . . [the media for influencing opinion]. And then you hear a revolutionary say: They crushed us, they organized two hundred radio programmes, so and so many newspapers, so and so many magazines, so and so many TV shows, so and so many of this and so and so many of the other. And one wants to ask him: What did you expect? That they would put TV, the radio, the magazines, the newspapers, the printing shops, all this at your disposal? Or are you unaware that precisely those are the instruments of the ruling class to crush the revolutions?

They complain that the bourgeoisie and the oligarchies crush them with their campaigns, as if that is a surprise to anyone. The first thing that a revolutionary has to understand is that the ruling classes have organized the state in such a way as to maintain themselves in power by all possible means. And they use not only arms, not only physical instruments, not only guns, but all possible instruments of influence, to deceive, to confuse.

And those who believe that they are going to win against the imperialists in elections are just plain naïve; and those who believe that the day will come when they will take over through elections are super-naïve. It is necessary to have been present in a revolutionary process and to know just what the repressive apparatus is by which the ruling classes maintain the status quo, just how much one has to struggle, just how difficult it is.

This does not imply the negation of forms of struggle. When someone writes a manifesto in a newspaper, attends a demonstration, holds a rally, propagates an idea, they may be using the so-called famous legal means. We must do away with that differentiation between legal or illegal means, and call them revolutionary or non-revolutionary means.

The revolutionary, in pursuit of his ideal and revolutionary aims, uses various methods. The essence of the question is whether the masses will be led to believe that the revolutionary movement, that socialism, can take over power without a struggle, that it can take over power peacefully. And that is a lie! And those who assert anywhere in Latin America that they will take over power peacefully will be deceiving the masses.

We are talking about conditions in Latin America. We don't want to involve ourselves in any other problems, which are already large enough, of those of other revolutionary organizations in other countries such as those of Europe. We are addressing Latin America. And of course, if they would only confine their mistakes to themselves ... but no ...! they try to encourage the same mistakes in those who are already mistaken on this continent! And to such an extent that part of the so-called revolutionary press has made attacks against Cuba for our revolutionary stand in Latin America. That's a fine thing! They don't know how to be revolutionaries over there, yet they want to teach us how to be revolutionaries over here.

But we are not anxious to start arguments. We already have enough to think about. But of course, we will not overlook the direct or indirect, the overt or covert attacks of some neo-Social Democrats of Europe.

And these are clear ideas. We are absolutely convinced that, in the long run, there is only one solution, as expressed in the Resolution : the role of the guerrilla in Latin America.

Does this mean that if a garrison rises in rebellion because there are some revolutionaries in it we should not support the rebellion because it is not a guerrilla struggle? No! What is stupid is to think, as one organization did, that the revolution would be made with the rebellion of garrisons only. What is stupid is to bring about a rebellion in a garrison, and afterwards let it be crushed by overpowering force, as has happened on some occasions.

New situations arise, new situations may arise – we do not deny that. For example, in Santo Domingo, a typical case came up of a military uprising that started acquiring a revolutionary character.

But of course, this doesn't mean that the revolutionary movement must be on the look-out for what may come up, for what may take place. Nobody was able to foresee, nobody was able to estimate the form, the character that the revolutionary movement acquired, especially after the imperialist intervention.

In other words, by stressing the role of the guerrilla as an immediate task in all those countries where true conditions exist, we do not discard other forms of armed revolutionary struggle.

The revolutionary movement must be in a position to take advantage of, and even support, any expression of struggle that may arise and develop or that may strengthen the positions of the revolutionaries. What I do not believe is that anyone who considers himself a revolutionary will wait for a garrison to rebel in order to make a revolution. I do not believe that there can be any revolutionary dreaming of making a revolution with the rebellion of garrisons.

This uprising of military units may constitute a factor, one of the unforeseeable factors that may arise; but no really serious revolutionary movement would begin with these eventualities as a starting point.

Guerrilla warfare is the main form of struggle, but that does not exclude all other expressions of armed struggle that may arise.

Case of Venezuela

And it is necessary – it is very necessary – that these ideas be clarified, because we have had very bitter experiences; not the blows or reverses of a military order, but the frustrations of a political nature, the consequences – in the long run sad and disastrous, for the revolutionary movement – of wrong concepts. The most painful case was that of Venezuela.

In Venezuela the revolutionary movement was growing, and

the revolutionary movement has had to pay dearly for the absurd concept of wanting to lead the guerrilla warfare from the city, of wanting to use the guerrilla movement as an instrument for political manoeuvres, of wanting to use the guerrilla movement as an instrument of low politics. These are the consequences that may be derived from incorrect attitudes, from wrong attitudes and, in many occasions, from immoral attitudes.

And the case of Venezuela is a very worthwhile case to take under consideration, because if we do not learn from the lessons of Venezuela, we never will learn.

Of course, the guerrilla movement in Venezuela is far from being crushed, in spite of treason. And we, gentlemen, have every right to use the word treason.

We know that there are some that do not like it; a few will even feel offended. I wish that some day they will be convinced that they have no reason to be offended unless they carry in their hearts the seeds of treason.

The case of Venezuela is eloquent in many aspects, because in Venezuela a group – which was in the leadership of a party with all these wrong concepts – almost achieved what neither imperialism nor the repressive forces of the régime could achieve.

The Party,[1] or rather not the Party but the rightest leadership of the Venezuelan Party, has come to adopt practically the position of an enemy of revolutionaries, of an instrument of imperialism and the oligarchy. And I do not say this for the sake of talking; I am not a slanderer, I am not a defamer.

We have some unfinished business with that group of traitors. We are not encouragers of polemics; we have not been inciters of conflicts; far from that, for a long time we have silently borne the publication of a series of documents and a whole series of attacks from that rightist leadership, in the same degree as that leadership forsook the guerrilla fighters and took the road of conciliation and submission.

We were the victims of deceit. First they spoke to us about a strange thing – for many of these problems began with a series

---

1. Communist Party of Venezuela, i.e., Soviet-oriented party.

of strange things – they began to talk of democratic peace. And we would say: 'What the devil does democratic peace mean? What does that mean? It is strange, very strange.' But they would say: 'No, that is a revolutionary slogan to widen the front, to join forces, to set up a broad front.' 'A broad front?' 'Well, a broad theoretical front, who could oppose that? No, trust us.'

Then, after a few months, they began to speak of tactical retreats. Tactical retreats? How strange is all that!

Because if they had told us the truth we might have disagreed, we might have doubted, anything, but never . . .

A tactical retreat: that is what they said to the militants, they said that to the people.

The tactical retreat was followed by an attempt to end the struggle, an attempt to suppress the guerrilla movement. Because anyone knows that in a guerrilla movement there is no tactical retreat; because a guerrilla that retreats is like an airplane that cuts the engine in midflight; it falls to the ground. Such a tactical retreat must have been conjured up by those genius inventors of high-flown revolutionary theories. Whoever has an idea of what a guerrilla is, and begins to listen to talk of retreat by the guerrillas, says: 'This man is talking a lot of nonsense. A guerrilla can be totally withdrawn, but he cannot retreat.'

Bit by bit they began unmasking themselves, until one day they completely unmasked themselves, and said: 'Let's have an election' and they became electoralists.

But even before they declared themselves in favour of elections, they committed one of the most vile deeds that a revolutionary party can commit: they began to act as informers, as public accusers of the guerrillas. They took advantage of the case of Iribarren Borges and with that episode took the opportunity to openly and publicly accuse the guerrilla movement, practically throwing it into the jaws of the beasts of the régime. The government had the weapons and the soldiers with which to pursue the guerrillas who would not retreat. The so-called Party, or the rightist leadership of a Party which had taken command, took charge of arming, both morally and politically, the repressive forces that persecuted the guerrilla forces.

We must ask ourselves honestly, how could we, a revolutionary party, in the name of any argument, of any castle- or convent-intrigue, ignore the attitude of a party that was trying to morally arm the repressive forces that persecuted the guerrilla forces.

Then came the phraseology. They began accusations, saying that we were creating divisions. That we were guilty of creating divisions!

It wasn't a case of a group of charlatans. They were talking about a group of guerrillas that had been in the mountains for years, combatants who had gone into the mountains and had been completely abandoned, had been forgotten. But can a revolutionary say: 'Yes, once more you are correct, you who have been deceiving us, who began speaking to us about this and about that, and then afterwards did something else'?

And, naturally we publicly expressed our condemnation, after a series of statements had already been issued by the right-wing leadership against our Party, condemning it in a treacherous manner, using the Iribarren incident to spread calumnies and to attack revolutionaries.

Logically that provoked the airy and indignant protest of that right-wing leadership, which made us the butt of a series of tirades. They did not answer a single one of our arguments, they were unable to answer even one, and they wrote a maudlin reply: to the effect that we were ignoble, that we had attacked an underground party, that we were fighting a most combative, a most heroic anti-imperialist organization. And they drafted a reply against us.

Why has it been necessary to bring that reply here? Because that document became the argument of a gang, a whole gang of detractors and slanderers of the Cuban Revolution. And that incident served for the beginning of a real international conspiracy against the Cuban Revolution, a real conspiracy against our Revolution.

In the first place, there has been a deliberate attempt to distort our views. Furthermore, these gentlemen of the rightist leadership of the Communist Party of Venezuela had a goal, and they pursued it in a very immoral manner. Once, when Leoni's administration was trying to establish diplomatic relations with the Soviet Union, we were asked what we thought of it; these gentlemen were also asked, and they responded negatively to the idea.

Why do these gentlemen resort to this argument and drag in a problem that was not being discussed with them? This is very clear; this forms part of the plot, of the conspiracy in which they and their fellows are participating with imperialism in order to create a serious conflict between the Cuban Revolution and the socialist countries. It is unquestionable that this argument is one of the lowest, most despicable, most treacherous, and most provocative. It pretended to present a contradiction between our position and our trade with capitalist countries. Furthermore, this argument, until recently, was not only openly published – for the capitalist press published it, and the letter was published by the counter-revolutionary organizations – but this low argument was also employed *sotto voce* in small groups by the conspirators and detractors of the Cuban Revolution.

Cuba's trade policy

In the first place, they are lying when they state that Cuba is opposed to trade. In every international body, in every economic conference, in all the organizations in which Cuba has taken part as a State, we have constantly denounced the imperialist policy of blockade, and we have denounced the acts of the government of the United States against our country as a violation of free trade and of the right of all countries to trade with each other. Cuba has inflexibly maintained that position at all times; that has been a policy pursued by our country which the facts throughout the history of the commercial relations of our country can bear out. Our position does not refer to commerce; it never referred to commerce. And that position of ours is known by the Soviet people; we have stated our viewpoint to them.

We refer to the problem of financial and technical help of any socialist State to the Latin American oligarchies. Let these things not be confused; do not try to confuse one thing with another;

do not ever try to confuse one thing with the other. Some socialist States even offered dollar loans to Mr Lleras Restrepo because he was in difficulties with the International Monetary Fund.

And we asked ourselves: How can this be? This is absurd! Dollar loans to an oligarchic government . . . That is repressing the guerrillas, that is persecuting and assassinating guerrillas. And the war is carried out with money – among other things – because the oligarchies have nothing with which to wage war except money, with which they pay mercenary forces.

And such things seem absurd to us – as does everything that implies financial and technical aid to any of those countries that are repressing the revolutionary movement, countries that are accomplices in the imperialist blockade against Cuba, which we condemn. It is unfortunate that we have to go into this problem in detail, but, naturally, it is the number-one argument employed by this gang.

And it is logical. Cuba is a small country against which the United States practises a cruel blockade. At Gran Tierra we explained to some of those present here how the imperialists do everything within their power to prevent our obtaining even such insignificant things as a handful of seeds of a kind of rice, cotton or anything else, seeds of any kind of grain, of vegetables, any kind at all.

No one can imagine to what lengths the imperialists go to extend their economic blockade against our country. And all those governments are accomplices, all those governments have violated the most elemental principles of free trade, the rights of peoples to trade freely; those governments help imperialism in its attempts to starve the people of Cuba.

And if that is true, if that is the case, and if internationalism exists, if solidarity is not a word worthy of respect, the least that we can expect of any state of the socialist camp is that it will lend no financial or technical assistance of any type to those governments.

It is truly repugnant that this vile argument is used to test the revolutionary steadfastness of this country, or to provoke conflicts with it. And, truly, this nation's steadfastness, its policy based on principle, its decision to act in a responsible way, yes!

carefully, yes! to prevent wherever possible polemics and conflicts. Yes! but never believe under any circumstances, no matter
how difficult it may be, that in the face of any problem, no
matter how great, will they be able to put our dignity and our
revolutionary consciousness up against the wall! Because if we
were that, if that is the kind of leadership our party had, we
would have surrendered long ago in the face of the great and
mortal dangers – the dangers engendered by imperialism, by our
firm political position.

And it is equally repugnant that they try to find a contradiction
between this position and Cuba's commercial policy with the
capitalist world. The imperialists have tried to break us with the
blockade. And the question is not what countries we do trade
with, but with how many countries throughout the wide world
do we not trade with simply because, one by one, and under
the incessant and growing pressure of the imperialists, they break
trade relations with us.

We have never broken off those relations. Imperialism has
taken care of that, in the same way that it has seen to it that,
one by one, they break off diplomatic relations with Cuba. We
have never broken off with anybody. They are weapons imperialism has used against the Cuban Revolution, in diplomatic
relations, in commercial relations.

And it is worthwhile, to speak about commercial relations,
for some of the mafia – and I cannot define, in any other way,
those who attack our Revolution in such a slanderous and base
fashion, without any serious and powerful argument – have
spoken of our not breaking off diplomatic relations with the State
of Israel. Neither did our country break off relations with
Albania when a great number of countries from the socialist
camp did; we did not break off relations with Federal Germany,
but Federal Germany did not want to accept our establishing
relations with the German Democratic Republic. And even though
we knew that the consequences would be the breaking-off of
diplomatic and commercial relations, this country had not the
slightest hesitation of being among the first to establish
diplomatic relations with the German Democratic Republic.
[APPLAUSE] And this country has never hesitated in the least

to put our political principles above economic interest, for if this were not so we would have found a million reasons to reconcile ourselves with imperialism a long time ago, more so in these times when it has become quite fashionable to do so.

The slightest insinuation of our following a sordid policy of interests in our international stand is to forget what this country has paid for its unyielding stands, its solidarity with a great number of countries – Algeria among them – notwithstanding the fact that this gave another country – which was one of the biggest buyers of Cuban sugar – an excuse to justify the pressures exercised by imperialism against them and to stop buying our sugar. And many are the facts.

And our people always saw, and we thought that every one understood quite clearly, that each time an imperialist pressure against anyone selling or buying from us failed, it was a victory of our Revolution in the face of the blockade. And we always saw as an expression of the attitude – in a certain sense of self-defence – and we have spoken publicly about it, we have spoken about it in the Plaza de la Revolución quite recently – how Europe could not accept and why it could not accept imperialist pressure, why Europe offered resistance, why Europe, in spite of its economic and industrial development, has to resist the competition of Yankee monopolies, Yankee imperialist attempts to take over the economy of those countries and how, owing to a question of interest, it was impossible to accept imperialist pressure; and because Cuba paid, and paid promptly, and because Cuba was a growing market, the imperialists had utterly failed in having the whole capitalist world break off – as they wished – commercial relations with Cuba.

What has this to do with our arguments? What has it to do with our statements? If imperialists had succeeded, the road of the Revolution would have been much more difficult.

Do we trade with the socialist camp? Yes, a trade which is practically all barter, the so-called clearing currency, which has a value only in the country with which the agreement is signed. And if there are things that the country may need, such as medicines of a certain kind, things essential for the life of our people and the trade organizations in any socialist country say

'We do not have it', we must look for them in other markets and pay in the currency of that country. And it is here that imperialism tries to crush us. And if we have bought medicines in capitalist countries, because we cannot get them or any similar product in a socialist country, to save the lives of sick people, of children, to reduce – as we have reduced – the child mortality rate, the mortality rate in general, and attain the position Cuba has today – for instance in public health and in many other fields – apparently we are criminals, we apparently are people without principles, we apparently are immoral, we apparently are the opposite of what we proclaim.

And they have done the same thing concerning the breaking off of relations with the State of Israel. I expect no one to have the slightest doubt about what has been the position of Cuba in that painful problem; a position of principle, an uncompromising position, a firm position. It is just that we do not like petty subterfuges.

What is Israel? A State which is an instrument of Yankee imperialism, the instigator, the protector, of that State. And that is why I ask those of the mafia, those who intend to slander Cuba with those arguments, why don't they break relations with the United States? It just happens that if we are not obedient 'yes-men', we are immoral, we are a people without principles, we are a people full of ideological contradictions ... And all this is but part of a repugnant conspiracy to create a conflict between the Cuban Revolution and the states of the socialist camp.

We are not instigators of conflicts, we do not seek unnecessarily, gratuitously, to create conflicts of that nature. I believe that in a high degree, facing a powerful enemy, the interdependence among the movements, the parties, the revolutionary states, will grow.

We may very much want it, a country as small as ours, without having any possibility of economic autarchy, in need principally of the arms to defend ourselves from Yankee imperialists. No one can imagine us acting in an irresponsible manner and creating problems that can be avoided. But between that position and that attitude of Cuba, and the idea that this country can be intimidated with provocations of that sort, there is a profound abyss.

And actually at the bottom of this there is a conspiracy of these elements of the reactionary mafia within the revolutionary movement and Yankee imperialism, a conspiracy to create a conflict between our Revolution and the States of the socialist camp. Because, in fact, what they attempt, what they demand, what they urge, is that the socialist camp also join in the imperialist blockade against Cuba.

We do not deliberately search out conflict, problems, difficult situations. That will never be the attitude of the Revolution. They'll never see an irresponsible, absurd attitude adopted by the Revolution, no! But neither will they see the Revolution hesitating, the Revolution giving up; they'll never see the Revolution yielding one iota of its principles! For *Patria o Muerte* has many meanings. It means being revolutionaries until death, it means being a proud people until death! And the fact that we speak about *Patria o Muerte* does not mean that we have a sense of fatalism. It is the expression of determination. When we say 'death', we mean that not only we would be dead, but many of our enemies would be dead, as well. Kill our people? All the soldiers of Yankee imperialism could not do it! [PROLONGED APPLAUSE]

These facts, these attitudes are calling us all to order; they are calling us all to reason, to clarify things. These attitudes are the result not of development, but of the deterioration of revolutionary ideas and of a revolutionary conscience.

The resolutions of OLAS do not mean that everything is done. They do not mean that the struggle is past. The Tri-Continental, also, had resolutions, and there were those who signed the resolutions and forgot all about them afterwards.

There must be a struggle. We have to struggle. And the statement that Cuba wants to set itself up as an arbiter, a head, a leader is more than ridiculous. No! And I am going to tell you what we really think: There is no reason why there should be leading peoples or leading men!

It is leading ideas that are needed! And revolutionary ideas will be the true and only guide of our peoples. We fight for our ideas! We defend ideas! But to defend ideas does not mean the pretension to lead anyone. They are our ideas and we defend them, the revolutionary ideas. But nothing more ridiculous, because the world does not need countries that lead, parties that lead, men that lead. The world, and above all our Latin American world, needs ideas that lead.

And the ideas will open the road. We know the process. At the beginning, when a few began to think about the idea of an armed struggle in our country and we began to struggle, very few believed in this possibility – very few. And for a long time we were very few. And afterwards, little by little, these ideas began to gain prestige, began to acquire conscience, and the moment came when everybody believed and the Revolution won.

How difficult it was to get the idea accepted that the struggle of the people against modern professional armies was possible in order to make a revolution! And when that was finally demonstrated, after the triumph of the Revolution, what happened? Everybody believed in this truth in such a way that the counter-revolutionaries also believed that it was also a truth for them, and then followed the organization of guerrilla groups and counter-revolutionary gangs, and even the most gentle, the most peaceful of the counter-revolutionaries, the most charlatan of counter-revolutionary park-benchers, grabbed for, joined a gang and took to the hills. Then it became necessary to show them they were mistaken, that that kind of action was a revolutionary action to be used against the oligarchies; but a counter-revolution of oligarchs, a guerrilla warfare of oligarchs and of reactionaries against a social revolution is impossible.

And how difficult it was! Until we finally showed them that this was true. We have had to point out more than once that it is impossible for oligarchs to defend themselves against the people's struggle; and that it is impossible for the people to be defeated by counter-revolutionary guerrilla gangs. And the CIA knows that. Do you know who are probably the most convinced of the effectiveness of armed revolutionary guerrilla warfare and of the incapacity of the oligarchies to oppose the armed guerrilla struggle of the people? Do you know who? The CIA, Johnson,

MacNamara, Dean Rusk, Yankee imperialism. They are the most convinced.

And one would ask oneself: How is it possible that these counter-revolutionaries let themselves be deceived and dragged into the armed revolutionary struggle against the Revolution if it is impossible to win? And it is, gentlemen, we are forced to admit, that these counter-revolutionaries are more consistent than many who call themselves super-revolutionaries.

They are most consistent. They wrongly believe in that and let themselves be dragged ... Naturally, afterwards they say what they say, always, that is a rule without exception! that they had been fooled, that they had been deceived, that they believed that the army, that militia ... All that. For us it is a broken record: we know that ...

And, logically, the ideas in our country have had to develop dialectically, in the struggle, in conflicts. And it will be the same in every country, and no country will be freed from this conflict of ideas. These conflicts of ideas survive even in Cuba. No, the fact that we have a revolutionary people does not mean that there are no antagonisms, no contradictions. Here we find the contradiction the counter-revolution and imperialism, and there are also contradictions with those who share the ideas of the reactionary gentlemen of the Venezuelan Party.

And in this country we also have our micro-fraction – we can't call it a fraction, because it has no volume, it has no size, it has no possibilities, it has nothing – it is a micro-fraction that has existed. Where does that micro-fraction come from? From the old resentful sectarians. Because our Revolution has its history; our Revolution has its history. I said that at the beginning very few believed; afterwards many believed.

Our Revolution went through the process, it passed through the process of sectarianism, and the sectarians created serious problems for us, with their ferocious opportunism, with their inexorable policy of persecution against many people; they brought corruption into the Revolution. And naturally, the Revolution with its methods, its patience, made the criticism; it was generous, it was generous with that sectarianism.

And not only that. We had to be careful to prevent sectarianism from creating neo-sectarianism in the ranks of the Revolution, and that was also prevented. But some sectarian elements held on, they swallowed their resentment, and each time they have had a chance they have expressed it. There are those who never believed in the Revolution unless it was in an opportunist way, trying to profit by the efforts of the revolutionary people, trying to climb high in a shameful way. They never believed in Revolution, they haven't learned in eight years, nor in ten years, and they will never learn.

Let it be clearly understood; I am not referring to old communists, because the worst expression of sectarianism and of the activities of those sectarians has been trying to involve the concept of old communists with their pseudo-revolutionary attitudes.

We have to say that the Revolution counts and always counted on the support of the real communists in this country.

But logically, at the time of sectarianism, many cowards who had deserted the ranks of the old party turned up again. Opportunism, sectarianism, brings all this; isolated from the masses, it tries to create forces by means of favouritism. And then followed the incomes, and more incomes, and more incomes, and the privileges.

Logically, afterwards, when the Revolution put a brake on sectarianism, it prevented the expressions of sectarianism, it prevented the expressions of sectarianism of another kind, because that has always been our stand, that has always been the stand of the revolutionary leadership, it has always tried to find the best solution, has tried to always overcome those problems with the characteristic style of our Revolution, without incurring excesses of any type, preferring to sin by omission than by excess.

And here we have our micro-fraction, made up of old sectarian groups, which are not the same as old communists. And I repeat, the greatest harm is that they have tried, although in vain, to instil their unhealthy ideas, their resentful ideas, into the old and tried revolutionaries. They were the ones who, for example, at the time of the October Crisis, thought that we should have let Yankee imperialism inspect us, search us from head to foot, let the planes fly over low, in fact everything. They have been systematically opposed to all the concepts of the Revolution, to the most pure and sincere revolutionary attitudes of our people; to our concepts of socialism, of communism, of everything.

That is, no one will be exempt. And this micro-fraction has the same attitudes of this larger group; this micro-fraction constitutes a new form of counter-revolutionary activity, in that it has the same goals as Alfa,[2] as Faria, as Pompeyo and Company; the same as MacNamara, Johnson, and all those people.

Now the CIA has a new thesis; why does it want to prepare so many personal attacks and so many other things? Its thesis now is that Castro has to be eliminated in order to destroy the Revolution, because imperialism is losing ground. At the beginning it wanted to do away with everything revolutionary; now, the more it loses ground, the more frightened it gets. Now its thesis is to moderate the line of the Revolution, to change its course so that Cuba will take a more moderate position – and, in this, Alfa, Johnson, Faria, the micro-fractionists, and similar political groups coincide. And they are harbouring illusions.

Really, I'm not interested in buying an insurance policy; I don't care what they believe. Let them believe what they want; I don't want to be indebted to our enemies for their ceasing to consider me a true enemy; I don't want to be indebted to them for their not doing whatever they want to. They have their rights, they are in their rights. I do not intend to buy any insurance policy.

But, to all of you, I think it is unnecessary to say that the line of this Revolution is not the Castro line; it is the line of a people, it is the line of a leading group that has a real revolutionary history. [LONG APPLAUSE] And it is the natural line of this Revolution!

The counter-revolutionaries encourage one another; their international organization has been encouraged, greatly encouraged, by the idea that insurmountable antagonisms may develop, insurmountable conflicts between the Cuban Revolution and the socialist camp. Really, the only thing that we can say is that it

2. Alfa 66, Cuban exile counter-revolutionary organization which has conducted terrorist raids against Cuban towns.

is an honour for our Revolution that our enemies think so much about it; likewise, it must be an honour for all Latin American revolutionaries that imperialism has given so much attention to the problem of OLAS. They issued threats, they postponed the OLAS conference, they said they were going to do a lot of things, they 'were going to clean the place up', and that this meeting could not take place. And the OLAS conference has been held – a true representation of a genuine revolutionary movement, whose ideas are solid because they are based on reality. OLAS is the interpreter of tomorrow's history, interpreter of the future, because OLAS[3] is a wave of the future, symbol of the revolutionary waves sweeping a continent of 250 million. This continent is pregnant with revolution. Sooner or later, it will be born. Its birth may be more or less complicated, but it is inevitable.

We do not have the slightest doubt. There will be victories, there will be reverses, there will be advances, there will be retreats; but the arrival of a new era, the victory of the peoples in the face of injustice, in the face of exploitation, in the face of oligarchy, in the face of imperialism, whatever the mistakes that man makes, whatever the mistaken ideas that may be obstacles on the road : it is inevitable.

We have spoken to you with complete and absolute frankness; we know that the true revolutionaries will always be in 'solidarity' with Cuba; we know that no true revolutionary, that no true communist on this continent, nor among our people, will ever let himself be induced to take those positions which would lead him to an alliance with imperialism; which would make him go hand in hand with the imperialist masters against the Cuban Revolution and against the Latin American Revolution.

We do not condemn anyone *a priori*, we do not close the doors to anyone *en masse*, in a block; we express our ideas, we defend our ideas, we debate these ideas. And we have absolute confidence in the revolutionaries, in the true revolutionaries, in the true communists.

Those will not fail the revolution, the same as our Revolution

---

3. *Olas* means 'waves' in Spanish. – Ed.

will never fail the revolutionary movement of Latin America.
[APPLAUSE]

We don't know what awaits us, what vicissitudes, what
dangers, what struggles. But we are prepared, and every day we
try to better prepare ourselves, and every day we will be better
and better prepared.

But one thing we can say: we are calm, we feel safe, this little
island will always be a revolutionary wall of granite and against
it all conspiracies, all intrigues, and all aggressions will be
smashed. And high upon this wall there will fly forever a
banner with the legend:

Patria o Muerte! Venceremos! [APPLAUSE]

CHAPTER 6

Eulogy for Che Guevara*

Che Guevara was murdered at the order of the Bolivian military leaders in co-operation with the United States military on 9 October 1967, while fulfilling his international responsibilities as a true communist.

Che was an incomparable soldier. Che was an incomparable leader. Che was, from a military point of view, extraordinarily courageous, extraordinarily aggressive. If, as a guerrilla, he had his Achilles' heel, it was this excessively aggressive quality, his absolute contempt for danger.

The enemy believes it can draw certain conclusions from his death. Che was a master of warfare! He was a virtuoso in the art of guerrilla struggle! And he showed that an infinite number of times. But he showed it especially in two extraordinary deeds. One of these was in the invasion, in which he led a column, a column pursued by thousands of enemy soldiers, over flat and absolutely unknown terrain, carrying out – together with Camilo – an extraordinary military accomplishment. He also showed it in his lightning campaign in Las Villas Province, especially in the audacious attack on the city of Santa Clara, entering, with a column of barely 300 men, a city defended by tanks, artillery, and several thousand infantry soldiers.

These two heroic deeds stamped him as an extraordinarily capable leader, as a master, as a virtuoso in the art of revolutionary war. However, now, after his heroic and glorious death, some attempt to deny the truth or value of his concepts, his guerrilla theories.

---

* Eulogy delivered by Fidel Castro in memory of Major Ernesto Che Guevara, at the Plaza de la Revolución, on 18 October 1967, 'Year of Heroic Vietnam'.

The master may die – especially when he is a virtuoso in an art as dangerous as revolutionary struggle – but what will surely never die is the art to which he dedicated his life, the art to which he dedicated his intelligence.

What is so strange about the fact that this master died in combat? What is stranger is that he did not die in combat on one of the innumerable occasions when he risked his life during our revolutionary struggle. And many times it was necessary to take steps to keep him from losing his life in actions of minor significance.

And so it was in combat – in one of the many battles he fought – that he lost his life. We do not have sufficient evidence to enable us to make deductions about what circumstances preceded that combat, to imagine how far he may have acted in an excessively aggressive way, but – we repeat – if, as a guerrilla, he had an Achilles' heel, that Achilles' heel was his excessive daring, his complete contempt for danger.

And this is where we can hardly agree with him, since we consider that his life, his experience, his capacity as a seasoned leader, his prestige and everything his life signified were more valuable, incomparably more valuable than he himself, perhaps, believed.

His conduct may have been profoundly influenced by the idea that men have a relative value in history, the idea that causes are not defeated when men fall, that the powerful march of history cannot and will not be halted when leaders fall.

That that is true, there is no doubt about it. It shows his faith in men, his faith in ideas, his faith in examples. However – as I said a few days ago – with all our hearts we would have liked to see him as a forger of victories, to see victories forged under his leadership, since men of his experience, men of his calibre, of his really unique capacity, are not common.

We have a full understanding of the value of his example. We are absolutely convinced that many men will strive to live up to his example, that men like him will emerge from the heart of the peoples.

It is not easy to find a person with all the virtues that were combined in him. It is not easy for a person, spontaneously, to develop a personality like his. I would say that he is one of those men who are difficult to match and virtually impossible to surpass. But I would also say that the examples of men like him contribute to the appearance of men of the same ilk.

In Che, we not only admire the fighter, the man capable of performing great feats. And what he did, what he was doing, the very fact of his rising, with a handful of men, against the army of the ruling class – trained by Yankee advisers, sent in by Yankee imperialism, and backed by the oligarchies of all neighbouring countries – in itself constitutes an extraordinary feat.

Millions of hands will stretch out to take up arms

And if we search the pages of history it is likely that we will find no other case in which a leader with such a limited number of men has set about a task of such import, a case in which a leader with such a limited number of men has set out to fight against such large forces. Such proof of confidence in himself, such proof of confidence in the peoples, such proof of faith in men's capacity to fight, can be looked for in the pages of history – but the like of it will never be found.

And he fell.

The enemy believes it has defeated his ideas, his guerrilla concepts, his points of view on revolutionary armed struggle. And what they accomplished, by a stroke of luck, was to eliminate him physically; what they accomplished was to gain an accidental advantage that an enemy may gain in war. And we do not know to what degree that stroke of luck, that stroke of fortune, was helped along, in a battle like many others, by that characteristic of which we spoke before – his excessive aggressiveness, his absolute disdain for danger.

This also happened in our War of Independence. In a battle at Dos Ríos they killed the Apostle of our Independence. In a battle at Punta Brava they killed Antonio Maceo, a veteran of hundreds of battles. Countless leaders, countless patriots of our

War of Independence were killed in similar battles. And, never-theless, that did not spell defeat for the Cuban cause.

The death of Che – as we said a few days ago – is a hard blow for the revolutionary movement, in that it deprives it, without a doubt, of its most experienced and able leader.

But those who are boasting of victory are mistaken. They are mistaken when they think that his death is the end of his ideas, the end of his tactics, the end of his guerrilla concepts, the end of his theses. For the man who fell, as a mortal man, as a man who faced bullets time and again, as a soldier, as a leader, is a thousand times more able than those who killed him by a stroke of luck.

However, how must revolutionaries face this serious setback? How must we face this loss? If Che had to express an opinion on this point, what would it be? He gave his opinion, he ex-pressed that opinion quite clearly when he wrote in his Message to the Latin American Conference of Solidarity that, if death surprised him anywhere, it would be welcome as long as his battle cry had reached a receptive ear and another hand stretched out to take up his rifle.

And his battle cry will reach not just one receptive ear, but millions of receptive ears! And not one hand but millions of hands will stretch out to take up arms!

New leaders will emerge. And the men – of the receptive ears and the outstretched hands – will need leaders who emerge from the ranks of the people, just as leaders have emerged in all revo-lutions.

Those hands will not have available a leader of Che's extra-ordinary experience and enormous ability. Those leaders will be formed in the process of struggle; those leaders will emerge from among the millions of receptive ears, from the millions of hands that will sooner or later stretch out to take up arms.

It isn't that we feel that his death will necessarily have im-mediate repercussions in the practical sphere of revolutionary struggle, that his death will necessarily have immediate reper-cussions in the practical sphere of development of the struggle. The fact is that when Che took up arms again he was not think-ing of an immediate victory; he was not thinking of a speedy victory against the forces of the oligarchies and of imperialism. As an experienced fighter, he was prepared for a prolonged struggle of five, ten, fifteen, or twenty years if necessary. He was ready to fight for five, ten, fifteen, twenty years, or all his life if need be!

Che's extraordinary personality was made up of virtues which are rarely found together

And within this time perspective, his death – or rather his example – will have tremendous repercussions. The force of that example will be invincible.

Those who cling to the idea of luck try in vain to deny his experience and his capacity as a leader. Che was an extraordinarily able military leader. But when we remember Che, when we think of Che, we do not think fundamentally of his military virtues. No! Warfare is a means and not an end; warfare is a tool of revolutionaries. The important thing is the revolution; the important thing is the revolutionary cause, revolutionary ideas, revolutionary objectives, revolutionary sentiments, revolutionary virtues!

And it is in this field, in the field of ideas, in the field of sentiments, in the field of revolutionary virtues, in the field of intelligence, that – apart from his military virtues – we feel the tremendous loss that his death means to the revolutionary movement.

Che has become a model of what men should be, not only for our people but also for people everywhere in Latin America. Che carried to its highest expression revolutionary stoicism, the revolutionary spirit of sacrifice, revolutionary combativeness, the revolutionary's spirit of work. Che brought the ideas of Marxism-Leninism to their freshest, purest, most revolutionary expression. No other man of our time has carried the spirit of proletarian internationalism to its highest possible level, as Che did.

And in the future, when an example of a proletarian internationalist is spoken of, when an example of a proletarian internationalist is sought, that example, high above any other, will be Che's example! National flags, prejudices, chauvinism, and egoism had disappeared from his mind and heart. And he was ready to shed his generous blood spontaneously and immediately, on behalf of any people, for the cause of any people!

And thus, his blood fell on our soil when he was wounded in several battles; and his blood was shed in Bolivia, for the redemption of the exploited and the oppressed. That blood was shed for the sake of all the exploited and all the oppressed; that blood was shed for all the peoples of America and for the people of Vietnam, because while fighting there in Bolivia, fighting against the oligarchies and imperialism, he knew that he was offering Vietnam the highest possible expression of his solidarity!

It is for this reason, comrades of the Revolution, that we must face the future with optimism. And in Che's example we will always find inspiration, inspiration in struggle, inspiration in tenacity, inspiration in intransigence towards the enemy, inspiration in internationalist sentiment!

Therefore, after tonight's impressive ceremony, after this incredible demonstration of multitudinous recognition – incredible for its magnitude, discipline, and spirit of devotion – that demonstrates that our people are a sensitive, grateful people who know how to honour the memory of the brave who die in combat, and that our people recognize those who serve them, that demonstrates the people's solidarity with the revolutionary struggle and how this people will raise aloft and maintain ever higher aloft their revolutionary banners and revolutionary principles – in these moments of remembrance let us lift our spirits with optimism in the future, with absolute optimism in the final victory of the peoples, and say to Che and to the heroes who fought and died with him: Ever onward to victory!

Patria o Muerte! Venceremos!

III. The Cuban Road to Communism

1. Capitalist and Communist Development: 'A Hundred and Fifty Years of Accumulated Misery.'

2. Socialist Consciousness: 'Communism Cannot be Built in One Country in the Midst of an Underdeveloped World.'

3. 'We will Never Build a Communist Conscience with a Dollar Sign in the Minds and Hearts of Men.'

4. 'Communism will be Abundance without Egotism: On Intellectual Property.'

CHAPTER 1

Capitalist and Communist Development: 'A Hundred and Fifty Years of Accumulated Misery.'*

In 1966 the subject of Fidel's speeches turned dramatically to the subject of how best to build socialism and communism parallel to one another: how, in the process of industrializing and developing the country, to begin to build a 'new man'. The discussion centred on the role of moral as opposed to material incentives in the building of communism. Moral incentives assume the interest and enthusiasm of the masses and aim at creating communist consciousness while building the material foundation for communism. In short, moral incentives appeal to man's sense of obligation to his fellow man and to the community. Material incentives seek to have men work harder by giving incentives of higher pay. They appeal to man's selfishness and depend on a belief in the virtues of egotistic, individualistic, acquisitive man – in a man that 'behaves as a wolf to other men', as Fidel says. Essentially the Cuban line maintained that there were no compromises with bourgeois society. On the international level, the idea of moral incentives, i.e., of a society based on the recognition of mutual dependence and brotherhood, had as its corollary the necessity for active solidarity with those engaged in armed struggle against imperialism. Che had said that 'to build communism, you must build the new man as well as the new economic base'. Exemplary acts, sacrifice, and brotherhood are the common denominators of moral incentives at home and aggressive internationalism abroad. Subsequent speeches in this section discuss the new socialist man.

---

* Speech in the 'Chaplin' Theatre on the Fifth Anniversary of Playa Girón, 19 April 1966, 'Year of Solidarity'.

The international context for this emphasis, in 1966, was the intensification of US aggression in Vietnam (solidarity with that country is mentioned in nearly every speech); the unilateral Russian dealings with the United States regarding Cuba during the Caribbean crisis; the nasty polemics between Cuba and China in early 1966 regarding the cutback of China's rice exports to Cuba; the Soviet's extension of credit to the oligarchies of Latin America; and the increasingly apparent failure of the official Latin American Communist parties to initiate and support revolutionary actions. In November 1966, Che Guevara opened another front against imperialism, in Bolivia – following his own call to the Tri-Continental earlier that year to 'create two, three, many Vietnams' – without the support of the Bolivian Communist Party.

In this speech, made on the anniversary of Cuba's victory at Playa Girón, Fidel discusses the differences between capitalist and socialist development. He describes how the Alliance for Progress has not and cannot solve the real problems of Latin America and that in fact, by facilitating private investment, it retards its development. This speech, together with the United Nations speech, provide an historical context in which to view socialist revolutions and debates on strategy for a revolution.

Our Revolution and our people stand firm against imperialist power, its political influence, its long experience in aggression, crime, subversion, and piracy – an experience with which many peoples of other continents are also familiar. And that is a task for revolutionaries, for genuine revolutionaries.

And if our people have taken that road, it is because they are capable of following such a road, in that historic mission which has fallen to our country in this epoch. Our country, the last to free itself from the Spanish colonial yoke – since the other nations of this Continent preceded us by almost a century – waged alone its battle in the heroic Ten Years' War and in the War for Independence, and carried on armed struggle for almost thirty years to achieve an independence which was stolen from us at the last minute. But to our country belongs the glory of being the first to achieve its second and true independence.

That this is clearly true is shown by the example of Santo Domingo, militarily occupied by Yankee troops, in the same style that they might occupy any farm or *latifundium*, as if they were the lords and masters of this Continent. We see this truth in the history of the Central American countries – in the history, for example, of Guatemala, whose revolutionary government was liquidated by a Girón-type aggression with the complicity of a Batista-type army.

We see it in the situation of almost all the countries of South America where the United States removes and sets up governments at will; countries unable to say, as we do, that they have achieved definite independence; countries which, having freed themselves from Spain a century and a half ago, spent one hundred years working mainly for the English imperialists, or rather for European imperialism, and another half-century working for Yankee imperialism. One hundred and fifty years of history!

And while many nations were developing, were becoming industrialized, our Latin American nations straggled behind and became poorer and poorer. And the gap separating the industrialized countries from Latin America grew wider. Population also grew. But resources, wealth, and industry did not grow; the population increased more than did food production.

A hundred and fifty years of accumulated misery! During that century and a half, Cuba spent one hundred years toiling and struggling to free herself from Spanish colonialism. And then during more than half a century, we worked for the Yankee imperialists, the corrupt politicians, and the privileged few who squandered the resources of this country for almost sixty years.

They built few factories. The privileged of this country and the corrupt politicians bought country estates, built mansions, deposited millions in foreign banks. And meanwhile, in the countryside, the men who cut the cane and produced the sugar, the men who, in other words, produced the country's foreign exchange, lived in huts and hovels. They never saw cement, nor electric lights, nor running water, nor streets, nor parks. They worked for such a long time and received such an insignificant share of the national product, while our capital city grew and grew. A drive

258 The Cuban Road to Communism

along Fifth Avenue is sufficient to see where a good part of the sweat of the workers of this country was invested.

And undoubtedly, we are making the best possible use of those palatial mansions; it is a fact that today we have tens of thousands of students living in those houses. But what we lack are cement factories; what we lack are fertilizer factories; what they did not leave us were industries, except for a few entirely dependent upon imported raw materials, and the sugar mills, the newest of which is more than thirty years old, because in the last thirty years not a single new sugar mill has been built. And many of those industries are old and almost dilapidated.

They did not even leave us an advanced mechanized agriculture. They did not, nor could they, because the workers had opposed mechanization, since under capitalism the introduction of machinery is opposed by the workers as it takes away their jobs and leaves them to starve. Neither cane-loading machines, nor cane harvesters, nor cane-conditioning centres, nor bulk loading facilities; not one of these modern labour-saving techniques would they have been able to introduce into our country.

Total identification of the people
with their resources

Today, the fight of our country is for the introduction of those techniques. It does not occur to anyone in this country today to consider a machine his enemy. Today, when there is total identification of the people with their resources; today, when there is complete identification of the labourer with the fruits of his labour; today, when hundreds of thousands of men and women mobilize to increase production, it would not occur to anyone to consider a machine his enemy. For that reason, capitalism and imperialism left us a backward agriculture. They could neither introduce machines, nor did they need to introduce machines. For cutting cane, they counted on the immense army of seasonally unemployed who anxiously awaited the harvest months in order to pay off debts they had contracted during the dead season and eat enough to survive. There was an abundance of cheap labour.

And when the workers got together to make demands, seeking improvements in their miserable living conditions, there was the rural guard. For it must be said that these soldiers of the privileged class also knew how to handle the machete, but not exactly to cut cane; they knew how to handle the machete to beat the farmers, the workers, the unfortunate.

What a difference! And how can this difference be understood by those who are accustomed to seeing that the role of weapons has been to defend the powerful, the privileged, and the rich? The imperialists are accustomed to creating armies of parasites to serve the exploiters and when have they ever seen an army wield the machete to cut cane, to produce, to increase the wealth of the people? How could they ever understand the power of the Revolution?

In our countryside, there still exists much of the poverty they left us. But it is a fact that there is no longer a dead season. That affliction has disappeared from our country forever: the dead season has died.

It is a fact that there is practically not a single corner of our country without a school, nor is there a region of our country without a hospital. We are now, in education as well as in medical care, without doubt the foremost country of this continent, including the US.

But there is still much poverty; there still exist many inadequate dwellings. Thousands of kilometres of roads and hundreds of thousands of houses must be built, as well as electrical installations and water supplies. And that, naturally, cannot be achieved in a few years, especially in a country that produces about one third of the cement it could use at this time.

And before the Revolution there was an excess of cement which, naturally, was not employed in building highways in the mountains, nor bridges in the interior of the country, because when they built a highway, it was like the Vía Blanca, that is, a highway that crosses regions where there is practically no agriculture, and that leads from Havana to Varadero. Did they ever build a highway all the way to Baracoa, as the Revolution has done, with constructions that are truly impressive because of the technical solutions devised for the laying of a highway over such difficult terrain? Were highways like that constructed before in the province of Oriente? Of course not! Rural housing programmes? Unheard of!

A large part of the cement produced in this country was used for building weekend country homes. Today the supply of cement is insufficient. And although some cement is imported, it is still not enough. Everyone needs cement – all the municipal governments and everyone else – not just those dedicated to public works but those in agriculture and in water projects as well. Everywhere we hear the same thing. 'We need cement'. And unfortunately cement factories cannot be built in a few weeks. Our new cement factories – the first being built in Nuevitas, the second in Las Villas, and the Santiago de Cuba plant is being enlarged – will double our cement production. However, even when our cement production has been doubled, what are two million tons of cement for our needs? A third factory is already being considered. To begin to solve part of our problem, we must necessarily plan to double, triple, or quadruple the amount of cement that we have today.

The road is long and patience is needed. This is the road of any underdeveloped country. But at least since the triumph of the Revolution, well done or not, better or worse, our work no longer benefits the foreigner. We no longer work for a privileged class. Even though it has been necessary to create everything, to begin everything from zero, it was necessary to overthrow the rotting bourgeois state in order to build anew. The country had to be completely revolutionized. It was necessary to do away with the old and to rebuild. And this task had to be carried out with new men, the great majority of whom lacked experience.

We work to create legions of technicians

Our country suffered from a true poverty of technical personnel. And part of the technical personnel – of what little technical personnel this country had – was identified with the interests affected by the Revolution. It was necessary to begin to prepare cadres. And this also takes years. In spite of the efforts made, legions of new technicians have not yet entered production; it will take us a few years but we will get there. We will reach the goal because we have not wasted time, having set about this task from the very beginning. In some activities in some fields, tens of thousands are already prepared. The triumph of the Revolution found almost 10,000 unemployed teachers. All those teachers were given jobs and this did not solve the problem. There weren't enough teachers. Special courses had to be organized in order to send teachers to the mountains and there were still not enough.

Last year almost 1,000 teachers were graduated from our Pedagogical Institute. Part of these went to the mountains to replace the teachers who had spent five years in this service and those left were too few to fill the needs. The workers' technological institutes needed teachers and the Army needed teachers, too.

Thousands of soldiers are studying in accelerated courses, because as our military techniques increase and modernize, the knowledge needed also increases. There are not enough teachers. These thousands of men need teachers, as do the thousands of workers who study in the technological institutes and as also do practically all the factories of the country, all the state farms. But there are not enough teachers. Nevertheless, more than 20,000 young men and women are in teacher-training schools. And we do not want to rush them, we do not want to interrupt their studies to solve immediate problems; we prefer to wait until they have acquired sufficient preparation to be the kind of teachers that we want to produce. An enormous effort is being made in agriculture, but our agriculture also lacks an adequate number of technicians. Nevertheless, approximately 20,000 students are enrolled in our agricultural technological institutes.

Before 1970, those 20,000 will have graduated, as will more than 20,000 teachers, and, in addition, by 1970, we shall have some 30,000 new students being trained as teachers, and another 30,000 students in the agricultural technological institutes. That is, our country is moving forward with a huge number of people who are receiving training precisely in order to regain the ground lost during more than a century and in order to attain levels of economic development which we had not been able to reach before.

Where do we stand today? We strive to have the greatest possible number of young people in our universities. If 10,000 enroll, it seems few to us; if 20,000 enroll, they are still too few. Nevertheless, when one reads the news reports about the situation in the universities in other countries of Latin America, the case is different. The number of university students is limited, and problems exist in many countries of Latin America because of this limitation on the number of students who can enter the universities. What future can these economically underdeveloped, technically backward countries have if they close the doors of their universities? For not only do the university graduates have difficulties in getting jobs, but a large number of them emigrate to the United States seeking employment. How can these countries overcome their underdevelopment and their poverty if they close the doors of their universities?

Who can know this better than we? Who can better understand the enormous need for technicians?

Of course a social system which is totally unconcerned with the health of its people does not need many doctors. In countries where practically no medical service exists, there are more than enough doctors, who always tend to concentrate in the big cities.

In countries full of large land-holdings, where agriculture is under a feudal-type régime, agronomists are not needed, veterinarians are not needed, mechanical engineers are not needed.

Our need for mechanical engineers is constantly present. Why? Because the need constantly arises for machines, machines of every kind: machines for fertilizing, clearing, and cultivating; machines for cutting, cleaning, and transporting sugar cane. And our need for mechanical engineers is evident; our need for hydraulic engineers is evident; for civil engineers, electrical engineers, architects, chemists, and research workers. Our need for pedagogues, university professors, professors for pre-university and technological institutes; our need for skilled workers in industry, in production, for the development of the country, for the fulfilling of its social needs, is constantly arising. Because that is precisely the task of the Revolution; to develop the country in every way, to develop the country materially and culturally.

In our system no one works to make profits for any individual;

we work to satisfy the needs of the people, to enrich the country, to raise the productivity of labour. Every citizen of this country is today concerned with increasing labour productivity; every citizen in this country is, logically, interested in raising and multiplying the productivity of a rural worker, of a caneworker, of a construction worker, of a mineworker, a transport worker, a fisherman, because our resources will increase and it will be possible to take care of the most pressing needs of the people in the same measure as labour productivity increases.

These are the things that make our case different from that of the other Latin American nations. We are ahead of them. And in a world where the population increases more rapidly than the output of foodstuffs, how will the underdeveloped nations be able to face this tremendous problem without Revolution, without doing precisely what we are doing?

Today, for example, some press reports mention the five years of the 'Alliance for Progress'. The 'Alliance for Progress', is, in part, a result of the imperialist defeat at Playa Girón. The 'Alliance for Progress' appeared after Playa Girón. The imperialists decided to set up a programme which – they said – was aimed at solving the problems of Latin America so that no more revolutions such as Cuba's would take place.

Imperialist remedies cannot be true remedies

But what remedies does imperialism wish to apply to those ills? It seeks to apply imperialist remedies, capitalist remedies. And, logically, imperialist remedies cannot be remedies at all, because it was precisely imperialist remedies that led those countries into the present state of affairs.

But they said they were going to lend money to build roads, schools, waterworks, and housing, and at the same time that the 'good and noble' US investors were going to invest money in these countries to develop their economies.

And today, the press stories have it that up to now the 'Alliance for Progress' had been a disappointment but, nevertheless, certain amounts had been invested. And they said, for example, that the United States had lent 5,000 million dollars; that, in addition, private investors had invested 9,000 million dollars in Latin America, and that the respective governments had invested an indefinite number of thousands of millions of dollars.

But they said that a good deal of the money lent had been squandered, that some of the 'Alliance for Progress' aid had been used, in a country like Brazil, to buy things such as confetti for Christmas – confetti are tiny pieces of paper that are tossed, I suppose that confetti is not the same as 'confite' [sweets] that is today, money spent on trivial things.

They also reported that some governments had said they were going to make some reforms, but that the reforms they had made were very few. Yet the following was the most interesting part : that sixty per cent of the aid had been loaned to pay back foreign debts, in other words, that sixty out of each hundred dollars of that so-called aid given by the imperialists was destined to pay debts to those same imperialists and to contract new debts with them.

And it was precisely the dispatches of the Yankee news agencies which spoke of the failure of the 'Alliance for Progress', and many Latin American governments of the servile type, unconditional supporters of imperialism, are evidently so disillusioned that at every meeting of the representatives of those governments they seem to have got together for the purpose of asking, requesting, and demanding help, stating that practically no help has been given them.

Many of them give examples of what the imperialists do : they lend one dollar and then cut the price two dollars on the products that they buy from Latin America.

The imperialists possess what they call strategic reserves of copper, tin, of various products, and every now and then they dump these reserves on the market. When it's tin, Bolivia collapses. When it's copper, the bottom falls out of Chile, and so on. When they're not doing this, they dump great stocks of cotton, causing crises in half a dozen cotton-exporting countries, and so on.

Five years have elapsed since Girón. Naturally, we have difficulties; we have a difficult road to travel. This is evident. But at least we're moving forward: we work for the future; we face all these difficulties and we are sure that we are going to overcome them.

Five years after Girón, the other countries of Latin America admit their defeat, their disillusionment, their pessimism. What happens in those countries does not happen in Cuba. In those countries people work so that a minority of the population may eat well, and very well indeed, while the rest must shift for themselves.

In those countries there is no rationing, because there is another traditional type of rationing: unemployment and a lack of purchasing power among the masses. In those countries when an item becomes scarce, its price doubles or triples or quadruples or quintuples, and then the workers, or those sectors of the population which have limited resources, can buy absolutely nothing, while the rich minorities can buy absolutely anything they want.

This is taken care of by the law of supply and demand: when there is a scarcity of any item, the masses must do without it.

We have a different situation because we consider it necessary to attend to the needs of every citizen. It is true that we have rationing, and we will have it on certain items for a few more years, but nobody in this country can say that he doesn't have the money to buy what is allotted to him on the rationing card. If anyone does say that, it's of his own free choice: it means that he doesn't want to work.

There is work of one type or another for everyone. The Revolutionary state has never denied assistance to any family with problems. There is not one single family in this country that can say it is neglected, as least not after having gone to ask for help from the Revolution.

And when we say the Cuban Revolution, we are speaking of the Revolution in Latin America. And when we speak of the revolution in Latin America we are speaking of revolution on a universal scale, the revolution of the peoples of Asia, Africa and of Europe. Here, as a symbol of what this Revolution means and what the other revolutions of other heroic peoples mean, we have a delegation from the heroic people of Korea, whose outstanding leader, Comrade Kim Il Sung, [APPLAUSE] sent today a very friendly message of solidarity, for the celebration of the victory of Girón. Kim Il Sung is one of the most distinguished, brilliant, and heroic socialist leaders in the world today, and his story, perhaps, because he is the leader of a small nation, is not sufficiently known. It is one of the most splendid stories that a revolutionary has written in the cause of socialism.

For us this message of solidarity has extraordinary value, because Korea, in the same way as the heroic people of Vietnam, [APPLAUSE] knows what the imperialists are. Just as the people of Vietnam are doing today, the people of Korea also heroically faced the armies of Yankee imperialism and inflicted severe defeats upon them.

Our nation has good examples to follow in the peoples of Korea and Vietnam. They are heroic peoples, heroic parties, which in spite of their small geographic size have confronted the imperialist monster and have written pages of extraordinary heroism.

We are not denying the heroism of any people. The heroic peoples of the world are many, both of large and small nations. But naturally we look with great sympathy upon those men who at a given hour taught the peoples of the world that, regardless of size, it is possible to fight against the imperialists and to withstand the imperialists' aggressions.

The imperialists are cowards. They like to be merciless with small nations, while at the same time they tremble at the possibility of coming to blows with the great powers.

In the United States there are many senators and leaders who talk every day about aggressions against Cuba and invasions of Cuba, because they imagine they are going to have 'easy pickings' here. And really, we are not interested in persuading them to the contrary.

We know that aggressions are not defeated by words but by weapons. We know that we are not going to save ourselves from the dangers of an invasion by scaring the imperialists. We confront the dangers of an invasion, or the consequences of any invasion, by preparing ourselves, constantly preparing ourselves ! And we will not stop preparing ourselves for one single minute.

I said that there wasn't enough cement, that the resources we require are many, but nevertheless, the country does not scrimp on the resources channelled into defence. It does not scrimp on the resources that it channels into strengthening the Revolution. And therefore I said that we do not seek to frighten the imperialists, because that would be ridiculous. And it is without any desire to frighten when I say that they are going to find a very hard bone to gnaw here. [APPLAUSE] We know this, because they will have to face the entire people everywhere, everywhere! Because if the imperialists believe that with the swarm of parasites that they have there they could get this country moving they are mistaken! If they believe that with that plague of parasites they are going to cut the sugar cane of this country, and get their transport, industries, mines, and agriculture on the move with those who have never sweated their shirts, no! When they bring in all that plague, supposing that they do arrive, supposing they got in, and supposing that they had one whole stone, left to sit on, [LAUGHTER] supposing all this, then on top of everything they would say to the Yankees: 'Good, now send us some maids.' Because if the day should come when the Yankees had them installed here in some houses (which would have to be imaginary), on top of everything else they would ask for some maids because they have never soaked a shirt with sweat.

Ah! but those who cut cane, those who work, those who create with their hands, those who make this country move by their work, all these, all, will be wielding something, but not tools to work for the imperialists, but weapons to kill them! And here, if the imperialists set foot in this country, the first decree will be that decree, like Bolívar's, which declared war to the death against the enemy. And there won't be one healthy imperialist's head left within reach of our hands. Pilots who bomb here, pilots who drop a bomb on this country, [SHOUTS] might as well commit *hara-kiri* in the air, because they are not going to last even three minutes on the ground. If the imperialists should one day bomb this country, if the imperialists should set foot in this country, they will learn that there will not be any imperialist prisoners around here; none will escape; the first decree will be, like the decree of Bolívar in the struggle for independence, a war to the death against every imperialist or puppet-imperialist enemy that may tread this land. [APPLAUSE]

And today, on the Fifth Anniversary of Girón, when we have come here to commemorate the victory and to pay tribute to the memory of our dead, there is no better day than this to tell our enemies what awaits them, and that the generosity of Girón will not be repeated, neither with mercenary invaders nor with imperialist invaders, because we do not want war, we do not want the destruction of our wealth, we do not want the destruction of the fruits of our labour, but if they touch a single hair of ours, a single hair, they will have to kill us all, down to the last revolutionary citizen of this country, because we know that pirates have to be dealt with as pirates, that bandits have to be dealt with as bandits.

And we are a small country but against this country, against its dignity, against its integrity ... this country which is the first one to conquer true independence, the vanguard of America, an example for all the other countries of this Continent; this country which defies imperialism and all its might and marches forward, does so because it is ready to do so, because it is ready to march ahead, because it is certain that it will march ahead, because no one can prevent us from doing so. And if they attack us, they will be smashed by that integrity and that heroism. Because we will be martyrs, like those of Girón, rather than the slaves of anyone!

Patria o Muerte! Venceremos! [OVATION]

CHAPTER 2

Socialist Consciousness: 'Communism Cannot be Built in One Country in the Midst of an Underdeveloped World.'*

This speech exemplifies the importance of internationalism in the Cuban road to communism, and the central role of moral education – in both foreign and domestic struggles – in moving towards communism. It must be viewed in the context of the criticisms of Castro by the 'mature' Marxist-Leninists who had called him an adventurer when he went into the Sierra Maestra, and now, when he called for the active support of Third World Revolutions, when he claimed the right of Cuba to follow its own timetable in moving towards communism, and when he insisted on the primacy of moral over material incentives – now, they called him a utopian. The Yugoslavian press, the official Communist Parties of Latin America, and the 'experts' from Eastern Europe failed to understand the essential message of Fidel; i.e., if you want to have a communist society some day you had better use norms consistent with it in guiding your everyday tasks. ('We cannot encourage or even permit selfish attitudes among men if we don't want man to be guided by the instinct of selfishness.')

Communism is not going to come about by some cataclysmic act; socialist society must break with the past – it must reject the acquisitive egotistical individualism of Western capitalism and Eastern European communism – and this cannot be done by asking men to work harder for greater material rewards and by failing to align oneself with comrades fighting against imperialism. Communism will be the result of shared experiences, accumulated over time. In this sense, Castro appears far more realistic

_____

* Delivered at the Plaza de la Revolución, Havana, May Day, 1966, 'Year of Solidarity'.

and tough-minded than the Marxist-Leninists of the Soviet school.

Fidel rejects the old, mechanical schemes for building socialism which have been so counter-productive in Eastern Europe and the Soviet Union. The ideas put forth by the Soviet bureaucrats were not very different from those of General Motors and Ford: pay high salaries to encourage greater productivity. In the Eastern countries, the end result has been not only the emergence of new exploitative strata, but equally important, a population in which large sectors are thoroughly imbued with acquisitive, individualistic values. The communism of the Eastern European countries is largely an ideology devoid of content, irrelevant to the values that guide people's lives. The Cubans on the other hand do not merely exhort each other to 'be' good communists. They know that subjective factors such as political consciousness spring from the social structure and are shaped and realized by a certain technological base. They also realize that political ideas and social norms shape the types of social structure that emerge. The Cuban road to socialism is a dialectical approach which embraces the necessity of developing the economic and technical basis of society through the education, in communist norms, of the individuals participating in that process.

In this speech Castro maintains the right of Cuba to determine its own path to communism. He rejects the idea of pat formulas and fixed timetables. He attacks those who believe that communism and socialism can be built independently of each other – that is, those who did not realize the moral necessity of moral incentives and the imperative of expanding the area of free social services as rapidly as possible – and he attacks those who believe that communism can be built in one country while others are still languishing in poverty: communism refers not only to objective social structures but to an advanced state of consciousness in the people.

Fidel's presentation of this idea to the Cuban people demonstrates the interconnection between internationalism and moral incentives:

... we ask ourselves whether, in the midst of a world full of misery, we will be able to think tomorrow only of ourselves, only and exclusively of ourselves, to live in superabundance with our tens of

*thousands of agricultural engineers, teachers, with our super-de-
veloped technology. How will we be able to live in that superabundance – resulting from communism based on abundance, or superabundance – while we see around us other peoples who, by not having
had the opportunity or the good fortune to make a revolution in the
epoch in which we are making ours, within ten years, be living
even more miserably than they are living today?*

*This is the lesson of Cuba and Castro: the creation of a new man
'capable of thinking of other human beings, men who are willing
to deprive themselves in order to give, instead of giving to themselves by depriving others'.*

   *These ideas and modes of development are revolutionary – even
within the majority of 'socialist' countries. Thus, as Fidel observes
at the end of this speech, Cuba can rely, at the moment, only on
its own strength, especially when it observes the terrible aggression against Vietnam.*

Comrade guests;
Cane cutters of the Millionaire Brigades;
Workers:
If I am not mistaken, this is the eighth May Day since the
triumph of the Revolution. And I do not believe that anyone
among those who have witnessed this parade can doubt that this
has unquestionably been the most colourful, the most enthusiastic, and the greatest in the numbers of workers present.

   Why does the joy of this date constantly increase among the
masses, how do the May Days of our revolutionary epoch differ
from former ones? Those who cannot or do not want to understand revolutions should have the opportunity to witness a May
Day celebration such as this. For the masses of our country the
concept of work and of the worker has changed profoundly. To
the same extent that the revolutionary consciousness of our
people has grown, the idea of work and the honour of being a
worker are felt and understood by ever-growing sectors of our
population.

   In our country, work is no longer – nor will it ever be again –
a means of enriching a privileged minority; in our country, work

is no longer – nor will it ever be again – a means of exploitation. The sweat of the men and women of our country will never again serve the privileged or the exploiters.

But it is not true that because of this, as a result of the Revolution, we shall have fewer millionaires in this country. Now, we have more millionaires! But they are not millionaires in the old sense of those who amassed hundreds of thousands of pesos and came to possess fortunes of millions of pesos, and even tens of millions of pesos, drawn from the blood and the sweat of the people. And there is no way to become a millionaire, nor has there ever been in any epoch of history, other than the exploitation of labour, because no one by his own work alone can produce sufficient wealth to accumulate millions of pesos.

Our millionaires of today are not those who exploit the work of others, but those who by their own work are capable of cutting a million *arrobas* of sugar cane – as is the case of the cane cutters present here, honoured guests of this celebration. [PROLONGED APPLAUSE] We have here more than 3,000 cane cutters, members of a brigade that have surpassed the goal of a million *arrobas* and earned the title of millionaire cane cutters. They are not millionaires whose fortune is gained at the expense of others; but millionaires by their own work. They are millionaires because their contribution to the wealth of the country can be measured in millions of pesos. Personally, not one of them, not a single worker, will ever be a millionaire – according to the old monetary concept – nor does he need to be. But, on the other hand, they will make the people millionaires; they will make ours a multi-millionaire country.

In the past the millionaires were different. There were only a few, and they did not cut cane or shed a drop of sweat. The millionaires were precisely those who did not work but made others work for them. Yes, there were a few millionaires, but the nation was poor, the people were poor. To justify their right to exploit the nation, they alleged that without their intelligence, their leadership, and their management, society couldn't function.

They alleged that they contributed their intelligence and their experience as businessmen to society. They also affirmed that man was a kind of animal motivated by selfish interests, that only unwholesome self-interest could make him put forth his best efforts, and that, in the fierce struggle of man against man, society would progress, a society guided by the most vulgar egoism. They believed that the people were devoid of any virtues; they believed that men were incapable of any disinterested and generous sentiments; they conceived of human beings as wild beasts, beasts in both senses; capable of devouring each other and unable to function without the privileged minority of exploiters.

The need to rebuild everything in a country

But in fact, our people are functioning without that minority and have not gone under in its absence. In spite of its absence and all that the Yankee imperialists have done in their attempt to destroy our people our country has not moved backward.

It is true that that minority had accumulated, not intelligence, but experience; they had accumulated all the shrewdness of which they were capable. They had learned the art of deception, of exploitation, of robbery; they had had the opportunity to manage businesses, factories, sugar mills, huge landholdings, all kinds of businesses. And it is true that no workers managed or learned to manage a sugar mill, a factory or a farm. It is true that when a revolution takes place in a country such as ours, the first thing that may happen is that those gentlemen lose their ownership of the nation's basic means of production, but a people do not acquire overnight all the experience required to replace that exploiting minority and their experience.

The reactionaries' greatest hope for the failure of revolutions is based on the notion that the exploited, the workers and farmers, will be unable to run the nation. And this is, at the same time, one of the important contradictions in a revolution; that is – as we have said on more than one occasion – the need to rebuild everything in a country, to rebuild its administration from top to bottom, to completely rebuild its armed forces, to completely rebuild its economic structure, to replace those who were in charge of public institutions, factories, and all centres of production, with the very limited or even nonexistent experience which the workers possess during the earliest stages.

But while it is indeed true that experience, as well as a good part of administrative and productive techniques and knowledge, were possessed by a minority, it was certainly not true that the country's intelligence was to be found exclusively in the brains of the minority. Much more intelligence is to be found among the masses of the people, much more potential capacity, much more energy, and far greater ability to move the country forward.

The fact that after seven years, or after seven anniversaries of the Revolution, the strength of our working people and of the Cuban Revolution has grown so considerably, shows that those early obstacles, as well as the most difficult stages have been overcome. For this reason, because it was necessary to train the people, it was undeniably correct for the Revolution to concern itself, fundamentally, with the development of education, with raising the standards of instruction and of culture and the technical level of our people.

Today, after seven years, during which it has been necessary to remake everything, we no longer have the old capitalist and bourgeois state. No! We now have the new socialist state! While it is true enough that in the first stages this state was not, nor could it be, very efficient, it is also true that the new state still retained many reminders of the past and was permeated by the influence and the participation of some members of that minority who never would have been able to adapt to the Revolution. And it is also true, that, to say the least, the spirit of that class was a considerable factor in the low level of efficiency of the new socialist state. Today, no one can doubt that the new state has been constantly stripping away those reminders of the past, removing those elements which were unworthy of the confidence of the Revolution and the people. The state has been eliminating more and more that bourgeois or petit-bourgeois spirit, and has begun to be incomparably more efficient. Furthermore, it is without doubt infinitely more efficient than our nation's prerevolutionary state.

Anyone who is capable of dispassionate and objective analysis will see that in all administrative fields our efficiency is increasing year by year, month by month, and day by day. And who can doubt our efficiency in creating the new Revolutionary Armed Forces in spite of the fact that when the war ended none of our guerrilla fighters even knew how to drill, stand at attention, salute, give commands to a platoon, company, battalion, or division! Who can doubt that the Revolution was faced with the need for a strong army to defend itself from its imperialist enemies? Not 'to maintain the revolutionary régime or to oppress the people' as the imperialist detractors of our Revolution write in their libellous, mercenary press. Because when there is identification between the revolutionary power and the people, as exists in a country such as ours when a revolution, a new social system, has such support from the masses, it does not need to arm itself in order to maintain this system or uphold this power!

This power would have no reason for existence if it were not the power of the people and for the people. It is precisely this which characterizes a socialist state, a socialist Revolution; the very opposite of what happens in the capitalist society, in the capitalist state. That state was an instrument of power in the hands of a minority; to maintain the great masses of the population in ignorance and poverty; exploited, oppressed, and living in misery.

The Revolution is the power of the great majority of the people instead of an insignificant minority. But this minority, so weak and insignificant, did not need anything like our armed strength because our reason for building up the Revolutionary Armed Forces is essentially the need to defend ourselves from a powerful foreign enemy.

In the past the possibilities of work for women were extremely limited

If there's something that really catches one's attention in these May Day parades, and especially in this one, it is the process of integration of women into the labour force.

In the past the possibilities of work for women were extremely limited. In this sense, discrimination certainly existed. But aside from this, it was logical that in a country where there were hundreds of thousands of men without work there would be little or no work opportunities for women. We already know what kind of work was reserved for women in the capitalist society. We know how prevalent was the custom among the bourgeoisie of hiring working-class women, pressed by necessity to work in amusements, in bars, as just one more kind of commercial attraction. We know of the considerable numbers of women in our country who were forced into the most lamentable form of survival, that is, prostitution. We know that our bourgeoisie had established many brothels in this country; brothels in every Cuban city, brothels for the Yankee tourists, for the Yankee Marines, in Havana, in Guantanamo. We know also that the bourgeoisie of the region of Guantanamo were so ingratiating that they not only supplied the Marines with brothels but also, on many occasions, with their own daughters. In Guantanamo many stories are known about all this and about the parties that went on at the Naval Base. Many of those people sent their daughters to those parties. In any event, it can be concluded that this type of work is one of the types that capitalist society – all capitalist societies – reserves for women. It was not possible, of course, to eradicate this evil from our country in one day. But we can say with pride and with satisfaction that just as the Revolution has eradicated other vices, such as gambling, for example, just as the Revolution has rid the country of beggars, just as there are no longer poverty-stricken children roaming in the streets (and there is no capitalist society in which there are no beggars, homeless children, brothels, gambling, vice and corruption of all kinds), the Revolution has also eradicated practically all prostitution from our country. Today a tremendous number of dignified and decent activities are accessible to Cuban women. Many thousands of Cuban women have gone into public health work during these years of the Revolution. Many thousands of young women have become nurses and nurses' aides, assistants in the field of medicine in general. Thousands of women work in the scholarship students' centres. Other thousands of women, tens of thousands, are teaching. Today the number of women who go into technological institutes and technical training centres is incomparably greater.

The fact that the number of women studying in the School of Medicine almost equals the number of men, will serve to illustrate the idea. Thousands of women are working in day nurseries and thousands are working not only in these public service jobs, but also in the production of material goods.

Women are working, for example, in the planting of seedlings in tree nurseries, or planting coffee seedlings. The whole poultry plan of four million – now we have somewhat over four million laying hens, and by the end of this year we will have 5,800,000 hens in order to cover our needs all year round – this entire important branch of our nation's food production is manned by women workers. Hundreds of poultry centres are managed by women.

Women have joined agricultural production in other activities, such as vegetable production, the raising of calves, and rabbit breeding. In short, new job opportunities are constantly opening up, in which an extraordinary number of women have found decent, remunerative, and satisfying employment.

Because that was the agonizing worry of the immense majority of our people. How to get a job? How to earn a living? It is really incredible how men suffer in capitalist society over this vital question, this elemental matter of how to assure oneself of a job in order to earn a decent living.

Therefore, on a day like today, this phenomenon of which I am speaking can be understood directly as we see the composition of our labour force. But there is something more: the women of our country are not only entering production work *en masse*, but are turning out to be workers of high efficiency, and we have heard many commentaries in praise of the work of our women, their sense of responsibility and their lack of absenteeism.

For this reason, the Revolution is making efforts to create more day nurseries, more schools, to establish more school cafeterias, to make it constantly easier for women to work. But when we speak of making it easier for women to work in production, this does not mean simply that society wishes to help women, not only that. Society has a duty to help women, but at the same time society helps itself considerably by helping women, because it means more and more hands joining in the production of goods and services for all the people.

As it is known, one of the means to make it possible for women to work is the creation of day nurseries. The women workers themselves pay certain amounts, in accordance with their income, for their children's care in the nurseries. But the women who have entered agricultural production have the added benefit that they do not have to pay for the day nursery. [APPLAUSE]

No woman will have to pay for her children's day nursery

And it is the intention of the Revolutionary government that by the end of this year, that is to say by next year, no woman worker will have to pay for her children's day nursery. We believe that this will contribute to encouraging Cuban women to work, and we also believe that this is just. Society profits from the work of every woman. Society profits in the same measure that it helps the mother. It profits to the same degree that permits women to receive full wages, without having to utilize a part to pay expenses, such as a day nursery.

If today, for example, all education is free : if there are approximately 150,000 young people and children in public boarding schools without paying a cent, if all medical services in the national hospitals are free; if a large part of our population no longer pay any rent since they have completed the five years of rent payment under the Urban Reform Law; [APPLAUSE] if more than 100,000 farmers have received deeds to their land without charge; if any person in our country who is destitute may obtain State help for the asking; if all these things are true, then why should we charge for day nurseries?

Of course, we have not yet attained communism, and at the beginning we believed that those services should be paid for. Nevertheless, experience has shown more and more the multiplying power of the work of the people, the multiplying creative power of the working people. And we have learned, for example, that the entire nation profits from the incorporation of thousands, of hundreds of thousands, say of a million women into production : if each one of those million women produces the value of 1,000 pesos per year, a million women means a 1,000 million pesos in created wealth. And what does it matter if society forgoes receiving the part that they pay for day nurseries?

As a matter of logic, I repeat, everything cannot be free, because this can only happen in a society which has reached the stage we conceive of as communism. But, of course, although formulas are talked about – socialist formulas and communist formulas – and it is said, according to the formulas, that in socialist society each gives according to his ability and receives according to his work, I ask myself what we should do in this stage, when we are building socialism, in the case of a family. For example, a woman who is left a widow with seven children, whose ability to work is small and who, receiving in accordance with her capacity, would never be able to feed and clothe those seven children. Can the socialist state ignore the fate of that woman's seven children? Can they be permitted to grow up barefoot, with rickets, and undernourished, simply because we are going to apply the formula of paying this woman according to her capacity, forgetting her needs and hoping that communism will arrive so that we can apply the formula of needs? No! We cannot wait for it. The woman would be the loser, the children would be losers, and this would be cruel. But, in addition, society itself would be the loser, since it is interested in producing healthy citizens and in providing all human beings with what they need in order to live decently, especially the children. [APPLAUSE]

This shows, then, that no formula is always applicable to the letter, and that, generally, in political and social matters, formulas are always bad.

We believe that these problems of socialism and communism must be pondered, reflected upon, studied, analysed, and investigated a great deal.

It could be said that while industrial technique and science in general have developed at an incredible pace, the social sciences remain undeveloped. We hear formulas and read manuals, but nothing teaches better than a revolution that, while we must appreciate and evaluate the importance of the experience of other peoples, each country must make an effort – not to copy – but to contribute to those undeveloped sciences; the political and social sciences.

We are developing our ideas. We understand that Marxist-Leninist thought requires unceasing development; we understand that some stagnation has taken place in this field, and we even see that formulas that can, in our opinion, lead to deviation from the essence of Marxism–Leninism are widely accepted.

Socialism and communism should be constructed parallel to one another

We believe that the construction and development of socialism and the advance towards a superior society, the communist society, must necessarily have its laws and its methods, and that, of course, these methods may in no way be the same methods of those of the capitalist society. We do not believe that methods and laws are subject to blind law or automatic regulations; we believe that they must be based more and more on the capacity of the peoples to plan, to master the processes of production, to foresee, in short, to control and dominate those laws and not be simply helpless objects of those laws.

Of course, this Plaza de la Revolución is not a class in political economy, nor do I pretend to be an authority on these matters. Much more honestly, I should say that I consider myself an apprentice, a student interested in these problems.

On one occasion, when the Central Committee was organized, we said that we did not believe that communism could be built entirely independent of the construction of socialism. That communism and socialism should be constructed, in a certain sense, parallel with one another. To invent a process and to say, 'Up to this point we are building socialism, and at this point we are building communism' can be an error, a great error. Because obviously, among other things, in our eagerness to reach our goals, we must not renounce or endanger the development and the formation of the communist man.

When I expressed this idea – not the pronouncement of a

teacher, nor an apostle, nor a professor, nor an authority on revolutionary theory, nor much less a kind of petty ideological Pope – some were surprised, and more than a few readers of manuals were astonished. More than a few people – they weren't counted, but I estimate their number based upon the number of those who have been intrigued by this statement, people accustomed to having the ideas in their minds as well ordered as the clothes in their closets – even became disturbed at these statements, and I do not doubt that some asked themselves if perhaps we weren't somewhat sacrilegious.

And, of course, I believe that in this category the worst of sacrileges – and when I speak of sacrilege, the catechism I was taught as a child comes out, at least in words. . . . The worst of sacrileges (and it would seem that Marx also studied catechism, since he often employs this type of terminology, which, of course, is not copied but is something that I have observed in my reading of Marx) – the worst of sacrileges is stagnation in thinking. 'Thinking that stagnates is thinking that "rots".'

And we must not permit our thinking to stagnate, much less to rot. When we made these statements, we were simply asking certain questions, about which we must all meditate and which we must all study a great deal.

There are certain aspects of our own Cuban experience which teach us that this attitude may be very healthy – as our experience in making the Agrarian Reform in Cuba, for example, which differed in its method from all the classic and traditional canons, in that while we made all the tenant and renting farmers proprietors of the land they worked, we did not divide the *latifundia* into fractions, creating a system of *minifundia*, but reserved those lands for factory-type, large-scale production. If we hadn't done this – in a country that depends and will depend upon its agriculture for the solution of its fundamental problems and as the basis of resources for its development – we could not have carried out the plans for the development of our agricultural production which will have such impressive results. And this isn't being done precisely with those small machines we saw passing by here today. They were too insignificant to reflect our potential, both in quality and in quantity, in agricultural machinery.

Because just a little while ago, the announcer – whom we can justly excuse, not only because he is a good announcer but also a good worker and a good voluntary worker, and we can't expect him to know everything about tractors or ploughs – spoke of the powerful three-disc plough. The truth is that these are the sorriest ploughs we have!

In our agriculture we have 17,000-pound harrows – and we are steadily increasing their number – which are pulled by powerful tractors. We have agricultural machinery of such quality and in such quantities that considerable organizational efforts must be made for their operation on a national scale.

Thanks to the use – as I was saying – of technique and machinery, our country can surely achieve extraordinary success in agriculture. And if anyone doubts this he can reflect on the fact that in the technological institutes alone we have 20,000 young people studying agriculture at this moment, and by 1970 we will have graduated these 20,000 and will have 40,000 more studying.

This means that we are advancing, but behind us a much more powerful force, a technical force of incredible magnitude, advances to consolidate and strengthen the positions we attain.

None of these things, which constitute such a great hope for the nation, could have been realized if we had fallen back on the classic formula of dividing up large landholdings, cattle ranches, sugar plantations, and other large farm lands. We would not even have been able to achieve that which has been achieved in the countryside, where, as a result of only limited development, unemployment has totally disappeared.

No one can graduate as a revolutionary by copying

And the millionaire cane cutters present here [APPLAUSE] can testify better than anyone else to the fact that, in the past, rural workers only worked from three to four months. And even during those three or four months, they had less work in any one day than they have now on any working day the whole year round.

We would not have been able to solve the problem of unemployment.

We must say that our Revolution suffered during its first years from diverse tendencies to copy, to be mechanistic. We copied from one or another brother country and then the country we had copied from later changed that system because it didn't work. Imagine the consequences of such copying! Copying is always bad. To copy in life, to copy in the Revolution is comparable to copying in an examination. And no one can graduate as a revolutionary by copying others.

But, fortunately, we did not copy in the matter of Agrarian Reform. And we will always consider that a very wise move, because it saved us from a great mistake.

Different economic and political formulas are elaborated in different countries, and, logically, some people have more experience than others. And I repeat that we must not underestimate nor, much less, ignore experience. But just as we must guard against ignoring experience, we must also guard against mechanically copying formulas.

There is talk about the building of communism in some countries. Even more, when one country stated that it was ready to begin the building of communism, not a few communist parties followed suit by repeating that communism was going to be built. Nevertheless, we modestly think that it is still to be considered and answered whether, in a world divided between industrialized and underdeveloped countries, between countries with a high labour productivity and countries without any labour productivity whatsoever, any nation can undertake the building of communism in a single country, without productive forces and technology being first developed in the rest of the underdeveloped countries of the world.

Because, while repeating once more that I consider myself no more than an apprentice in revolution, I believe that socialism can be built in a single country and that communism can be built to a certain degree. But communism, as a formula of absolute abundance, in the midst of an underdeveloped world, cannot be built in a single country, without running the risk, involuntarily and unintentionally, in future years, of immensely rich countries

284 The Cuban Road to Communism

finding themselves trading and dealing with immensely poor countries. Some people in communism and other people in loin-clothes! And we ask ourselves – we who wish the best for our people, who wish that not a single child in this country grow up without all the proteins and vitamins and minerals and generally indispensable foodstuffs, we who wish them all to receive a complete education, we ask ourselves whether, in the midst of a world full of misery, we will be able to think tomorrow only of ourselves, only and exclusively of ourselves, to live in superabundance with our tens of thousands of agricultural engineers, teachers, with our super-developed technology. How will we be able to live in that superabundance – resulting from communism based on abundance, or superabundance – while we see around us other peoples who, by not having had the opportunity or the good fortune to make a revolution in the epoch in which we are making ours, will, within ten years, be living even more miserably than they are living today.

And I believe we should aspire to higher levels of food supply for our people, as well as education for our people, so that our citizens may develop both physically and mentally, and we should satisfy our needs for medical care and housing.

We do not need very much in order to achieve this. I am sure that with our country's natural resources, plus work and the use of technology, it will not be long before we reach those levels. But from there on, we must not think that our duty is to strive so that each one of us may have his own automobile, before first concerning ourselves about whether or not each family in those countries which are behind us owns at least a plough.

Our present duty as a poor, underdeveloped country, is to make the maximum effort to rid ourselves of poverty, misery, and underdevelopment. But in the future we must not think of great affluence while other peoples still need our help. We must begin now to educate our children in the idea that tomorrow, when all our pressing needs are supplied, our goal will be more than simple affluence. Our ideal is not wealth. Our principle ideal and our duty must be to help those people who were left behind. [PRO-LONGED APPLAUSE]

Let us educate our people in this concept of our international duty, so that within ten years not one person in this country will say that he does not have more because we are helping someone else, but instead, so that we will have a type of man capable of thinking of other human beings, men who are willing to deprive themselves in order to give, instead of giving to themselves by depriving others.

And if in future years, some of our people should still think this way, it would be without a doubt, because we, leaders of the people, have not been able to educate our people politically. It would be because our Party had been unable to teach the deep sense of internationalism, without which no one may be called a Marxist-Leninist and without which even this May Day, International Workers' Day, would have no meaning; it would be meaningless without that profound and permanent sense of international duty. [APPLAUSE]

That is why we feel such deep satisfaction; satisfaction with the internationalist emphasis that our workers gave to their International Day, so that Vietnam and the Dominican Republic have been the centre of this impressive celebration. [PROLONGED APPLAUSE] This shows that our Party is doing well and that it is educating our people in the profoundest meaning of international duty. And the idea that we are brothers, of the same flesh and blood as the other peoples of the world, suffering the exploitation and aggression of the imperialists, continues to grow within the heart of each one of the sons of this country.

Dining rooms for school children

I expressed these thoughts because I saw the need to explain them. Of course, we have not arrived, nor will we for some time, and we will delay still longer in reaching the highest level of what we might call a communist way of life to the degree that the rest of the world delays in this march. And, therefore, everything cannot be given away without cost, although we do believe that those things which are essential to a human being – health, adequate nutrition, physical and mental education, cultural development, housing, all those things essential to man – must be provided as soon as possible from the resources of the whole society with the goods that society produces. Thus we can say that within ten years we shall have sufficient school lunchrooms so that all the children of the country may eat without cost at school. The shoes and clothing they receive, as well as their toys, should not depend on whether the mother has ten children and can do little work, but rather on the needs of the child as a human being. The same applies to the health of the child and to housing. And what is true of children should also be true of every person who, because of old age, is incapable of working. In ten years we should be able to say: This elderly person should not lack the necessities of life just because he is old and cannot work and because he belongs to a family of a worker with low earning capacity. Why should an elderly person, who needs food and clothing, suffer because his son, on whom he depends, has low earning capacity? And if we were to apply the socialist formula in that particular case, the elderly person would strive. In ten years, we should be able to say that not only every worker who retires should receive a pension, but every man or woman in our country, because he or she is a human being and is too old to work, should also have the right to receive a pension from society, regardless of whether or not he or she has belonged to this or that sector of industry, but because of the greater merit of belonging to the human race, because of the greater merit of belonging to our society. Within ten years the worker, in fact, should be freed of economic family burdens, so that the aged person who lives with him may not be a burden, in the economic sense of the word, even when that worker would never consider it a burden to care for his mother's or father's uncle, grandfather, or other relative.

Nor would any elderly person have to feel ashamed of needing aid, when this society, from its total resources, its production, is able to give every child, every old person, in short, every person unable to work, everything he needs.

That is to say, the nation's economically inactive population should be able to live in accordance with this inherently communist formula. If we incorporate the entire active population into the working class, if we are capable of organizing our human resources in such a way that the entire active population can be creative and productive, if we are able to provide a million women with work, and to elevate the productivity of our work by means of technology, and if young people and students work a number of weeks in the year as part of their education, so that next year we can mobilize some 200,000 young people for six weeks during the springtime, the critical period in agriculture, this will practically assure the fulfilment of our goals in the field of agriculture. [APPLAUSE] If we can do all this, then in ten years we will not only be able to say that no worker will pay rent, but that all workers will be able to enjoy completely whatever they earn from their work. We will be able to apply the socialist formula to the worker; and to his children, his parents and to the old people. Economically, we should apply the communist formula, thereby providing for them according to their needs and not according to the capacity of the family's wage-earner. [APPLAUSE]

Two and one half million people are now studying

This aspiration explains why some things are provided without charge. One thing that is being provided free of charge this year in the University is textbooks. And technical books will be sold at cost to all those who want and need them. How is this possible? By means of a principle that we can sum up in the expression, 'Inexpensive books and expensive beer'.

We know that everyone likes beer, or almost everyone. And the beer being made now is of very good quality. But technology is more important to us. It is far more important for us to possess technical skill in our work so that we may increase productivity than it is to consume beer. Free books for students and books at cost for others, and expensive beer. And so, books are subsidized by the sale of beer.

In this way, whoever drinks beer not only experiences a moment of pleasure on a summer afternoon but also has the satisfaction of knowing that he is contributing to the development of technology and culture. [APPLAUSE]

It is clear that the Revolution has not only liberated the worker from exploitation, it has not only eradicated forever the system by which man and his work capacity are bought and sold as merchandise, but the Revolution has also made an extraordinary effort to promote the educational development of the whole nation.

At this moment, almost forty per cent of our country's population is studying; 1,300,000 children, some 250,000 young people in technological institutes, secondary and pre-university schools, and 28,000 university students. And, in addition, 900,000 adults in improvement courses.

So that there are two and a half million persons in all who are studying in this country. Farewell, illusions of the enemy! Because as ignorance and deficient education were instruments used by the capitalist oppressors and exploiters, farewell to their illusions that a people that devotes itself, as a whole, to improvement, study, organization, arming itself, and working can ever be made to return to that past! Impossible!

This is not just a phrase; it is something so logical and clear, as clear as day, that this can never happen again.

Our enemies amuse themselves spinning tales and fabricating intrigues. But they do it to console themselves. And, after all, if they want to console themselves, let them do it. One McCloskey – or whatever the devil his name is – one of those imbeciles who are forever making declarations in the name of the US government, said that an awful situation exists in Cuba, full of tension, a terrible, terrible crisis! Poor devil!

Sometimes we ask ourselves if he really believes this or if he wants people to think he really believes it. Perhaps he believes it. This would not be surprising. They believed a lot of things at the time of Playa Girón; and afterwards they did a lot of lamenting, and they are still lamenting.

What did those fools believe? That as soon as the fair-haired boys of the country-club set got here, the boys of the Yacht Club, the Biltmore Club, and all those other clubs, sons of big landowners and millionaires – not millionaire cane cutters, but millionaires who made fortunes stealing from the people – [APPLAUSE] that this mercenary band of playboys would land here and everyone would hail them as their liberators and carry them on their shoulders and turn everything over to them: the factories, the houses, rent from the land, their women and children, so that the gambling houses, the houses of prostitution, and the vice centres could be reopened. What did those fools imagine? Have they no idea of what a liberated people are like? Have they any idea of what the suffering of the masses was, the hunger, the insecurity and above all the constant fear? Because in that monstrous society, if a man died, if a dispossessed worker died, what became of his wife, his parents, his children? The least that could happen was that his daughter would be sold into prostitution and his son exploited.

And what did they believe, those who have not the least concept of a free people? Idiots, imbeciles, charlatans. They believed that at the first sign of the landing of the enslavers, the slaves would come running, to fall at their feet to have their chains put on again. They still think our people long for their chains. No! For those who want chains, those few who want chains – but not chains for themselves, since they never worked, they were never slaves but enslavers – for those who want chains not for themselves, but for others, we have opened the doors wide, so that they may leave the country.

The imperialists count those who want chains for others, but not for themselves, saying that such and such a number left the country. The imperialists always count those who leave but never those who stay. And they exaggerated about the ones who go. They say that there are a million who want to go. But it is not we who limit the number of those who leave; it is they. They have counted all the relatives and friends of those who are already in the US and say 'a million!' And there are many there who put acquaintances' names on the list, names of people who, when they are asked here if they want to go, answer, 'Not on your life.' It appears that these are the calculations they make. They don't calculate the Puerto Ricans who went to the United States, they don't say how they close the doors to immigrants from other countries so that they can try to attract the greatest number to come from Cuba and make propaganda. But we don't lose, we win. It is not a million, nor a half a million. We calculate that somewhere between 100,000 and 200,000 people would go, because they have relatives in the United States, because they let themselves be seduced by the song of the imperialist siren, or because they are incapable of perceiving and feeling the warmth and greatness of a Revolution. During the War of Independence in the United States, an estimated 100,000 to 200,000 colonists who did not want that independence emigrated to Canada.

But it is not we who are placing restrictions: it is not we who oblige people to wait here for months. It is they. Once already we challenged them, saying: open the doors, hypocrites! Open the doors, cynics! It is not we but you who keep the doors closed so that you can make propaganda of it. And they opened the doors. Now we ask them: 'Why don't you take everyone out of here who wants to go, once and for all? For each one who goes, we will have that much more in resources for giving a scholarship to the son of a farm worker, or a cane cutter.' [APPLAUSE] ...

And in the coming year we are going to distribute 20,000 scholarships among the families of sugar cane workers who still live in shacks in very difficult conditions.

Twenty thousand scholarships! We will continue working for a more united, homogeneous, enthusiastic, and revolutionary people. We will have a people who are more and more *Patria o Muerte*.

Everyone who has ever had to cook at some time – especially housewives – knows that when you want to clean rice or beans, you put them in water, stir it and all the dirt floats to the top. In this same way the imperialists – let it be said, once and for all – committed a strategic error. In their eagerness to rob technicians from us, in their eagerness to make propaganda campaigns, they facilitated the emigration from this country of the very class they relied on to make counter-revolution. They took away the counter-revolutionary class; they took almost all of them. Let them take the few remaining, once and for all! Let them take them! We challenge that idiot who spoke on behalf of the government of the United States to take away, once and for all, those who want to go. It is not we who set the limits, it is they. [SHOUTS FROM THE PUBLIC]

A long time ago we unmasked them. Now we cannot unmask them any more since they practically have no mask left to remove. As I said, they had this type of illusion about the Revolution, about its strength, about revolutionary unity. Never has the Revolution been stronger, nor more united; never has the Revolution been more invincible, more unshakeable; never have the perspectives of the Revolution with respect to progress, organization, and work been better than at this moment.

To tell the truth, this does not frighten or discourage us; it teaches and prepares us. It strengthens our spirit. And we know that with what we have we are a very hard bone to gnaw on. [APPLAUSE]

But we cannot but feel indignant when viewing the aggressive, savage, and criminal actions of the imperialists against the people of Vietnam: the criminal, repugnant, and cowardly aggression; piratical aggression that places Mr Johnson among the worst criminals that humanity has ever known, among the worst pirates.

What is the difference between the Yankee savagery in Vietnam and what the Nazis did, when they annexed Austria, or when they cut Czechoslovakia into pieces or when they invaded Poland?

We know well the fruits of that savagely aggressive policy.

Even farther away, thousands of miles away, in the very heart of Asia, the imperialists use hundreds of airplanes in bombing raids which slaughter women and children, waging chemical warfare against no less than a socialist country. And they do it with considerable impunity, considerable impunity!

For whatever causes or motives, the imperialists are showing tremendous aggressiveness, criminal aggressiveness.

And we know the imperialists well for the cowards and opportunists they are. This is why they vent their fury and commit all manner of savage acts.

And they will continue to do it – we said this at the time of the October Crisis – they will continue as long as they can get away with it, as long as they are not stopped.

And we believe, really, that peace would be much better preserved by letting the imperialists know what they can do and what they can't do. [APPLAUSE] In the long run, letting them do as they please, letting them carry out their piratical and vandal actions, does not contribute to peace. This is an enormous error. It contributes to increasing the danger of war!

The crimes of Vietnam and Santo Domingo are upon the conscience of Johnson. Not Johnson – Johnson is only a representative of the financial oligarchy – of Yankee imperialism, and these crimes and vandalisms are upon their guilty consciences.

Are they perhaps trying to intimidate the peoples by this? Are they trying to frighten the peoples? Well, here is a good example: the example of Cuba. Vandalism, far from frightening the peoples, prepares them for the struggle! [PROLONGED APPLAUSE] Imperialist vandalism makes our people firmer and more decided: it shows us all the criminal and savage essence of imperialism, it strengthens the people's hatred and their indignation, and it prepares them for the struggle. This is what they gain by their vandalism in Vietnam, in Santo Domingo, and in all the places in the world under imperialist attack, and among that host of nations is our people, our Revolution!

Today, International Workers' Day, our thoughts are entirely with those peoples who are fighting: our homage of solidarity to Vietnam, Santo Domingo, and all revolutionary fighters in Asia, Africa, and Latin America.

Today our people comply in an exemplary manner with their international duty and conscience, placing in the centre of their minds and hearts the struggle of the heroic peoples who are fighting and will defeat the imperialists. Because all the peoples, united, carrying out the battle cry of Karl Marx, uniting in combat against imperialism, helping and supporting each other, will be stronger than the imperialists!

Let us cry out more fervently today than ever: Long live the heroic people of Vietnam! [SHOUTS OF 'VIVA'] Long live the heroic people of Santo Domingo! [SHOUTS OF 'VIVA'] Long live proletarian internationalism! [SHOUTS OF 'VIVA'] Long live Marxism-Leninism! [SHOUTS OF 'VIVA']

Patria o Muerte! Venceremos! [OVATION]

CHAPTER 3

'We will Never Build a Communist Conscience with a Dollar Sign in the Minds and Hearts of Men.'*

Central to the development of communism in Cuba is the extension of free services to the people. In this speech Fidel announces an urban reform whereby rent will be abolished after 1970. This reform serves two purposes: it spreads the material benefits of the Revolution among the people, and it contributes towards building a communist consciousness. Fidel states that 'if we want a people who remove the "dollar sign" from their minds and from their hearts, we must have men who have got rid of their own mental "dollar signs".' It was not any particular reform that won over the masses of Cubans to the Revolution; rather, it was the accumulated effect of many actions that made the people feel like human beings for the first time. Thus, people will die for the moral benefits of the Revolution, not for any particular material gain. Free services are the other side of the coin of voluntary labour – both stem from a sense of community and collective responsibility that negates the liberal ideals of competition.

We said that we are going to pass a new law so that, starting in 1970, rent for housing will be practically nonexistent.

Some of the Comrades of the Urban Reform Office became concerned and asked if the advance announcement of this law might not cause a relaxation in rent payments. It does not seem so to me. On the contrary, it is known that the Urban Reform Law denied the right to stop paying rent at the expiration of five years to those people who would normally have been included in that category

---

* Speech made at the ceremony marking the Sixth Anniversary of the CDR, 28 September 1966, 'Year of Solidarity'.

but had not kept up their rent payments. The people know that the Revolution can never – without exception – reward irresponsibility. So, those who do not fulfil this obligation will be the only citizens of this country who continue to pay rent after 1970. This solution in regard to housing will be an important step forward for the Revolution. It will imply the virtual suppression of an entire agency dedicated to collecting rent and it will mean a considerable reduction in office workers. And we hope that very few citizens of this country will have to endure the shame of admitting, after 1970, that they are still paying rent because they did not fulfil their obligations.

We believe, naturally, that an opportunity to bring his payments up to date should be given to anyone who has lagged behind in making payments. We believe that everyone should be given an opportunity to enjoy the new right, including those who have been paying through salary attachments. In short, we should give an opportunity to all who say : 'I want, finally, to become a person who fulfils his obligations, in order to be able to have the same rights as others.'

What would be most convenient for the country is that a minimum of citizens and, if possible, none, pay rent for housing by that date.

Some may question the financial aspects of this type of revolutionary law and I say, sincerely, that I believe this Urban Reform Law to be a truly revolutionary law. The financial implications of this law, with a view towards 1970, will be virtually nil for a country such as ours, if we attain the pace of development that we have projected. The seventy or eighty million pesos that will no longer be collected by 1970 will mean practically nothing if we are able to fulfil our plans for economic development. Much greater amounts, incomparably greater amounts than these, will be represented by the growth that we attain in our economy. [APPLAUSE]

There is something that distinguishes revolutionaries from non-revolutionaries, and that is their attitude towards the future, their attitude towards the great goals and the great objectives to be achieved. I will say that anyone who does not have an attitude of

combat, of confidence in the people and their strength, of confidence in the people and their enormous capacity for struggle,
work, and creativity, will never be a revolutionary! [SHOUTS
FROM THE AUDIENCE: 'SHAKE THE TREE, FIDEL! WE
STILL HAVE A FEW ROTTEN ORANGES LEFT']

Some remain, some remain. But we must be able to recognize
the 'rotten oranges'.

[A COMMENT FROM THE AUDIENCE]

Who says he's unemployed?

I was saying that this man's attitude before obstacles and difficulties, his attitude towards effort, that serves as a yardstick to
gauge the mettle of a revolutionary. The optimistic, revolutionary
attitude will no doubt be challenged by calculating critics, by
those whose attitude towards life is entirely metaphysical, who add
and subtract, but come out wrong on the total – which is the sum
of will power, courage, and determination; it is the sum total of
the moral factors with which the peoples have always undertaken
– and accomplished – the great tasks in the history of mankind.

Those who resign themselves to a minimum effort will always
take fright, be intimidated. When there is talk of great tasks, great
projects and great goals; when there is talk of giving something to
the people, these weak-hearted men will never be able to give the
people anything but small advantages, small successes. They take
fright simply because they are unable to comprehend what the
people are doing by the huge task of organization required, by the
enormous push that the work of the Revolution demands. These
puny men remind us of those who, in the past, faced by the
struggle required to attain the extremely difficult goal by overthrowing that system of exploitation and tyranny, said that it was
impossible and that it was only a dream of adventurers and madmen.

There are often some who vacillate when faced by the great
tasks, and among the vacillators, we will find the first opportunists.
We have not the slightest doubt that, with the effort made by the
people, with the effort we must make in the coming years, this
people, with its strength and with its sweat, will be capable of
creating riches incomparably superior to whatever financial losses
may be involved in the fact that the people stop paying rent in
1970. With the other criterion, we would never have arrived at any

rent-cut, and one of the first things the Revolution did was to reduce rents – in many cases as much as fifty per cent. Everyone is familiar with the anguish, the bitterness, and the feeling of insecurity that existed under the former system : the suffering of having to pay rent – in many cases as much as half the salary earned – for a small house or a small apartment. Everyone remembers the common dream : to one day have a home of one's own. We all remember those commercial firms that, in order to sell soap or newspapers, raffled off a small house each month. And how many men, in the country and in the cities, saved those soap coupons in the hope that – as one out of every thousand, or one out of every million – he would be lucky enough to win a house !

A 'financier', a pure economist, a metaphysician of revolutions would have said, 'Careful ! Rents shouldn't be lowered one cent. Think of it from a financial standpoint, from an economic standpoint, think of the pesos involved . . .' Such persons have 'dollar signs' in their heads and they want the people, also, to have 'dollar signs' in their hearts and heads. But if we want a people who remove the 'dollar sign' from their minds and from their hearts, we must have men who have got rid of their own mental 'dollar signs'. Those persons would have said, 'No !' and they would have added up accounts. We would have asked them then :

For what reason do you ask the people to make a revolution ? By chance, for purely metaphysical reasons ? For what reason are you going to ask the people to struggle and even die in defence of the Revolution ?

Could we expect the people to believe, to be simple *a priori* believers in all of that ? Or was it necessary, in the first place, to demonstrate the Revolution was on the side of the people, that the Revolution was against the interests of the rich, that the Revolution, with no hesitation whatsoever, sacrificed the interests of the privileged minorities for the sake of the interests of the people ? Such people would not have made even one revolutionary law. In the name of those principles they would have proposed to go on charging the farmers rent; in the name of the same principles they would have continued to charge the farmers interest on loans; they would have charged for medical and hospital care; they would have charged school fees; they would have charged for the boarding schools that are now completely free, all in the name of a metaphysical approach to life. They would never have had the people's enthusiasm, the masses' enthusiasm, which is the prime factor, the basic factor, for a people to advance, for a people to build, for a people to be able to develop. And that enthusiasm on the part of the people, that support for the Revolution, is something that can be measured in terms incomparably superior to the adding and subtracting of the metaphysicians.

Of course the Revolution was unable to give the people all that they needed : the people could not be given what the Revolution did not have to give. But the Revolution did give the people all that it could; the Revolution has sought to give the people all that it had to give. It has sought, above all, to create confidence among the people and a sense of security in regard to the future.

We have spoken in the name of socialism, we have spoken in the name of communism, but we will never create socialist consciousness and much less communist consciousness with a storekeeper mentality.

We will never create socialist consciousness, communist consciousness with a 'dollar sign' in the minds and hearts of our men and women. And if we ask ourselves the reason for the attitude of the people in all parts of the country – in the cities and in the rural areas, on the loneliest mountain – the reason for their firmness in support of the Revolution, it is because the Revolution has created confidence and a sense of security among the people. It has created the conviction that everything can be accomplished by work and struggle.

It is not because the Revolution has filled all the material needs of the people. No. But a great part of the moral needs of this people has been filled by the Revolution.

Something that cannot be counted or calculated : moral benefits

Many people wonder why there is such enthusiasm among the masses, why such reactions arise in individuals everywhere. And there is something that can't be calculated mathematically, simply by multiplying and dividing, by adding and subtracting – and that is the moral benefits that the Revolution has meant for the people, what feeling for the first time like human beings, like men and women in the fullest sense of the word, has meant for every man and woman in this country; what it has meant for millions of men and women in this country to cease being nothing in order to become something. For in the old society where just a handful were everything, millions of beings were nothing, millions of human beings didn't count for a thing.

Was there any hope for the family in the face of illness, death, unemployment, poverty? None! If someone got sick, what was to happen to the family? In the case of a farmer with eight or ten children who was struck down by illness, what was to happen to his family? If he were to die, what was to happen to his wife and children? If he were out of work, what was to happen to his wife and children? If he had a house but didn't have money at the end of the month, what was to happen to his meagre furniture? What was to happen to his relatives? What hope did he have that his children would have a better life? None! Was there any hope of learning to read and write? None! Was there any hope that his children would reach the sixth grade? None! That they would reach an institute? None? Or a university? Out of the question! [APPLAUSE] And today throughout the length and breadth of the land there's not one father, there's not one mother who doesn't feel justified, confident in saying: 'This one is going to study such and such: the other one is going to study something else.' And they say it with absolute confidence.

There's not one family, one farmer, one single worker, one common man in our country that doesn't feel security in the face of death, accidents, illness, in the face of anything. And all this has been creating in our citizens a sense of their own worth. This has been creating in them a sense of their own dignity.

Today in the rural areas of our country, you no longer see pairs of rural guards with their machetes, with their big horses. No! You no longer see anyone with a gun as a symbol of authority. No! You no longer see a single man or woman in the countryside who sees power as a thing apart, authority as a thing apart, the State as a thing apart. For today these men and women are the

authority. They are the ones who have the weapons in their hands
– more and better weapons than those rural guards had ! Today
they are the power. But not just in words or in theory, but in fact,
in reality. There's no farmer regardless of age who doesn't have his
weapon there in his company or in his battalion. There's no farmer
who doesn't have there the means for defending his rights, for
defending his Revolution. And this has created a moral fortitude
that cannot be measured in terms of numerals. For those are the
things that have made the people identify with the Revolution.
Those things have made the people mobilize to carry out every
task, to answer every appeal of the Revolution of any kind whatsoever.

This shows how men are capable of responding conscientiously,
how men are capable of responding to moral factors. The people
have received many material benefits, but they have also received
great moral benefits. I am sure that if many simple people of this
country were to be asked: 'What are you most grateful to the
Revolution for? Your low rent? Your steady job? What are you
most grateful to the Revolution for – the material benefits you've
received or the moral benefits that you've received?' I'm sure that
many, perhaps the great majority would say: 'What I'm most
grateful to the Revolution for and the reason I'm willing to die for
the Revolution, is that since the Revolution I've felt like a human
being. I've felt like a man of dignity. I've felt that I amount to
something among my people, that I am somebody in my country.
I've felt as I never felt in the past.'

And we have to encourage these feelings of social worth in our
people. We have to encourage these moral factors in the people,
besides making an effort to satisfy their material needs.

We are making a Revolution, but we're only halfway along the
road in that Revolution. We've advanced a great deal since the
first day of this Revolution. People have divided into revolutionaries and reactionaries depending on whether they have clung to
the past or looked towards the future. And the people have kept
moving ahead, kept growing in awareness, kept raising their
political level.

Difficult struggles had to be waged against reactionary ideas.
And we've been moving forward from that stage.

Yesterday's ideological positions may not be so advanced today

But we have new stages before us. And once more, we will find reactionary ideas in our way, ideas that might have been revolutionary ten years ago, yet can be perfectly reactionary today. The ideological positions of yesterday may not be sufficiently advanced when confronted with the ideological positions of today. Today we see beyond them, we are not satisfied with drops in the bucket, we are not satisfied with a Revolution by halves; we believe in the people, we believe in man.

And these things that the Revolution does, these ideas in relation to housing, medical services, education, in relation to everything that is given the people – without the need for payment, without the need for 'dollar signs' in the head and bills in the pocket – tend to gradually create a more advanced social consciousness in the people, tend to create different property values in the people, a different regard for material possessions, a different regard for man's work.

We do not believe in Utopia. We do not believe that this can be done overnight. We do not believe that this consciousness can be developed in just a few years, but we do believe that it will never be created if we do not struggle unceasingly in this direction, if we do not advance incessantly on this path.

We wish to call ourselves revolutionaries, but the term 'revolutionary' encompasses more and more; each day it has new facets. Dialectics should also be applied to the conception of a revolutionary. We cannot call ourselves revolutionaries if we do not truly and consistently aspire to a better society.

We have not the slightest doubt that everything that is being done is superior to the past. We have no doubt that all the possibilities that have been developed, that all the rights that the people have been receiving, and all the benefits obtained, are superior to what existed in the past. But we cannot be satisfied. Of course, it is far easier to appeal to their feelings of solidarity, to their feelings of generosity and, clearly, many things can still be solved with money. Clearly, even now, a factory can 'hijack' workers from another factory, by offering money. With higher wages, any work centre can lure workers from another centre, in what is truly a piratical action.

In the reality of matters as they stand, many men and women, for a series of reasons – economic, social, or from lack of conscience – still cannot bring themselves to turn down the opportunity to receive something more for themselves. But those who wish to solve problems by appealing to personal selfishness, by appealing to individualistic effort, forgetful of society, are acting in a reactionary manner, conspiring, although inspired by the best intentions in the world, against the possibilities of creating a truly socialist spirit, a truly communist spirit in the people. They will be conspiring against the effort to create an awareness in the people of the possibility of a way of life in which men, acting and working in unison, will be able to give each individual member of society much more than he could ever attain on a solitary path, left to his own resources.

We will never stop fighting individualist trends

There are always those who pander to the selfishness of others. But those of us who call ourselves revolutionaries should never relax the fight against such individualistic trends. We must always encourage the generosity and solidarity of the men and women of our nation.

Those who believe in every Cuban there is a potential 'Sancho Panza' forget the lesson that the Revolution has taught us: that among the people there are many more 'Quixotes' than 'Panzas'. They forget what the Revolution has taught us about our people.

And for those who never believed in the people, who had no faith in them in the past, how can we expect them to believe in the people today, or to begin believing in the future? Those who have no faith in the moral virtues of the peoples of the world can never be leaders, can never lead a people forward. For man does not live by bread alone.

And if we recall those moments in the past that were difficult, and perilous for us, we must also recall the people's attitudes. It was clear on those occasions that the people were prepared to die rather than surrender. To die before giving up ! And willingness to die rather than surrender signifies that a human being is motivated by much more than mere biological instincts; that a human being is motivated by something higher than simple 'animal appetite'.

And those who think that man is more animal than human are offending the memory of those who, in every epoch of Cuban history, have taught us what a human being really is. They offend the memory of the countless heroic men who have fought for this country, from the time of the War of 1868 – whose centennial we will soon celebrate – when tens of thousands of Cubans went forth to the battlefields. They offend the memory of the many revolutionary combatants who have given their lives for this country.
[PROLONGED APPLAUSE]

Consider those who fought in the difficult days of our own revolutionary struggle (the times we know best, since we experienced them); those in the cities who risked their lives daily during those difficult days, ruthlessly persecuted; those in the mountains, sweaty and hungry, their clothing tattered, weighed down by heavy packs, who marched day after day, month after month, and year after year to fight and to die. What were their motivations? Were 'animal appetites' by chance behind their struggles? Were they motivated by selfish instincts? Or did an idea, a cause, a moral factor lie behind that strength, that capacity for finding followers, that quality which was able to arouse a whole people when the day arrived?

And when we are asked how we won the war we can answer like Ignacio Agramonte: With pride, with honour, with morality!
[PROLONGED APPLAUSE]

And these factors are the ones which mobilize our people today throughout the entire nation. They will enable us to win today's battles, and to reach tomorrow's goals.

The number-reckoners will find that such factors, which they have never taken into account, have more force than all their figures. The number-reckoners – and there are those who act in good faith and those who do not – must also one day recognize this reality, for our people are on the march, our people are advancing.

We may not reach every goal now, nor tomorrow, but we are getting nearer and nearer to the time when the facts will show exactly what our people are capable of producing, even though faced with difficulties which the imperialist enemy forces upon us; even though faced with difficulties which underdevelopment bequeathed us, such as the widespread illiteracy and great ignorance that existed in our country; even though faced with any number of adverse conditions, any number of reverses stemming from our enemy or from nature itself.

This year, for example, an unexpected hurricane that came in the spring – an extremely rare phenomenon – devastated practically all the early crops in the western provinces of the nation. Barely three years ago, at about this time of year, a hurricane caused great loss of life and enormous material damage in Oriente province. We all recall this very well. At this very moment, another hurricane is following the same path as Hurricane Flora [of 1963], advancing directly towards the easternmost region of our country. We are not yet sure whether within thirty-six hours we may be feeling the lash of yet another natural disaster such as the one on that occasion.

These are the adversities that nature itself has imposed on us. Plans have been made without taking the possibility of hurricanes into account. We must lay our plans thinking in terms of one, two, or even three hurricanes a year. We must learn to take into account not just those factors that are predictable, but the unpredictable as well. It would be truly unfortunate, and we should suffer heavy losses if a hurricane should devastate the eastern provinces at this time, just when coffee harvesting is in progress, just when a great many roads and hydraulic projects are under construction. It would indeed be grave, but nonetheless if another 'Flora' should pass through Oriente province, we are certain that, this time, the victims would be incomparably fewer in number. Though many lives were saved in 1963 due to the great mobilization made then, this time everyone would be evacuated many hours beforehand from all places where the flooding waters might reach. This time, the material damage would also be greatly reduced, but we must learn to take into account such natural disasters. It would seem that hurricanes have been especially attacking Oriente province where there had not been a hurricane for twenty or thirty years. 'Flora' passed through that area in 1963; in 1964, it was 'Cleo', and now in 1966 there is another hurricane headed towards that region.

We have to confront not only imperialists but also hurricanes

Does that mean that we are going to get discouraged? [CRIES OF 'NO!'] Does it mean that we are going to stop developing our plans in Oriente province? [VOICES ANSWER 'NO!'] No! If the hurricane comes through here tomorrow, the day after tomorrow we will start all over again! [APPLAUSE]

And that's not all. Since we know that these hurricanes harry us year after year, we must work to have production meet our needs even though there is a hurricane, or two or three. We are working to this end. The countryside must remain just as if these phenomena had never happened.

We know, for instance, that hurricanes mow down banana plantations. 'Flora' destroyed hundreds of *caballerías* in Oriente Province, but they were replanted. Now we have twice as many as we had when 'Flora' attacked us. But if a hurricane lashes Oriente and destroys the banana plantations, and if another crosses Havana Province and does likewise, then we must have banana plantations in Oriente, Camagüey, Las Villas, Matanzas, Havana and Pinar del Río.

Root vegetable, citrus fruit, and other basic plantations must exist in all provinces. Last June's hurricane destroyed ninety per cent of the grapefruit crop on the Isle of Pines, and literally did not leave a single mango or avocado in the Province of Havana, the eastern area of Pinar del Río or the western area of Matanzas.

This represents a setback not only for our domestic consumption but also for our exports, since if we supply our foreign market one year and not the next we may come to be considered an unreliable source of supply.

Hence the same policy must be in force with our citrus plantations. We must have them in all provinces and in such quantity
that they allow us not only to fulfil our needs, but also to meet our
foreign commitments and to build up reserves! Reserves are important.

Great tasks confront us, but I can assure you that there is
enthusiasm for these tasks. I can assure you because I have seen
it: I have encountered enormous enthusiasm for these tasks
throughout the length and breadth of the country. And that must
be our attitude. Ours as well as yours.

Whenever you hear someone say: 'I don't know,' look upon
him with suspicion. Whenever you hear someone say: 'I cannot,'
look upon him with suspicion. Whenever you hear someone say:
'It is too much,' look upon him with reservations: because what
we all have to say is: 'Yes, we can do it! And whatever we don't
know, we'll learn!' We must say that nothing is too much for us!

Experience has taught us that whenever we think we are doing
too much, we can still do a little more. Many past experiences have
shown us that when we have said, 'This far,' reality has proved
that we can go much further.

And that is the only revolutionary attitude. And the revolutionary, by his character, influences events. The non-revolutionary,
the resigned, the conformist, the defeatist, plans ahead for ten or
fifteen years. But not all are like him.

Why ten years if it can be accomplished in three? If we can
solve many, many problems within three years, why take ten?
That is the right attitude: a fighting attitude, a challenging atti-
tute towards obstacles, towards the tasks to be fulfilled.

And this type of man is coming to the fore everywhere. Some of
our comrades have great ability for choosing cadres. And already
we find here and there what they called the 'little cadres', many of
them young men with a tremendous – tremendous – determination to face problems and solve them, men who never stand still.
And this is the type of man we must promote.

Sometimes we find people who are good, refined, decent, and
who don't want to hurt anybody! Well . . . I'm not saying this is
wrong, a man should not be cruel: an administrator, a man with
responsibilities, must not be cruel. Of course he must find it pain-

ful to hurt anyone. I agree! We must feel sorry for individuals, but we must feel sorrier for the people! We must feel sorrier for the people! What is one to do? Nobody enjoys having to replace a man in a job; it is always a painful thing to do. Nothing is more painful or unpleasant but a man must be told: 'You are not doing a good job, you must be replaced.'

Very few people recognize the truth, very few. Out of every ten persons, you may meet one who will say: 'That is true.'

A duty of the Revolution: to promote those who are worth it

How difficult it is for man to maintain a spirit of self-criticism and really understand when he is doing things wrong! And, in general, it is necessary to replace people who are functioning badly, even when they really think they are doing wrong! And, in general, it is necessary to replace people who are functioning badly, even when they really think they are doing well. This is painful. But we are not revolutionaries if we do not know how to overcome our reluctance when faced with embarrassment that must be suffered, because, in its essence, it is a cowardly attitude. It is painful to have to tell someone: 'You are not working properly, you will have to be replaced.' And it is absolutely necessary, Comrades, it is the duty of the Revolution to promote all who work well. By promoting all who work well, I do not mean that everyone is to be replaced, because there will always be twenty to say, 'This one is no good.' And quite often it is the one who is least useful who says that no one else is any good. We should not compromise, but we must have the good sense to be able to evaluate work done and to select capable cadres who can carry forward this militant, aggressive, dynamic policy, people who are tireless, indefatigable, who, at any time, day or night, are ready and willing to face problems.

And fortunately, we already have a number of comrades of this type: serious, responsible, constant workers. Ah, but we must carry this policy to the farthest corner of the country, promoting the most capable! Society requires that the most capable be placed in charge of all tasks. This is what society needs and this is what the Revolution needs – so that they may respond to this spirit, so that they may respond to this drive. Because this thing is growing every day, it is becoming stronger every day, it is becoming more devastating every day. Men who are tired cannot follow this rhythm: those who lack enthusiasm, who are lukewarm or cowardly, cannot follow this pace. The Revolution causes considerable wear and tear. There are what may be termed people who are 'worn out'. Some say: 'This one has burnt himself out'; another will remark: 'This one has fizzled out,' and there are others who have simply exhausted their capacity. Well, the Revolution can retire anyone; what is more, the Revolution can offer generous retirement to any revolutionary who has tired; it is better to have a retired revolutionary than a tired man trying to act like a revolutionary. [APPLAUSE]

And the truth is that we should be very clear about this. If someone is tired, let him retire; but he must not be permitted to become a brake, an obstacle, a hindrance. There is much to be done, and this is work for revolutionaries. It is not enough to have been a revolutionary yesterday, we must know how to be revolutionary today, and how to be revolutionaries tomorrow. And it is even possible to be revolutionary merely by not being an obstacle.

Let the new cadres come forward; let there be room for the new generations of men. Promote the most capable; let no one cling to honours, to responsible posts, for this has always proved to be very costly to the peoples. Let new generations come, better than we; let new generations come, more apt than we, and we shall gladly hand them the vanguard posts; but what we will never do is stop being revolutionaries; we will never be content with half a Revolution; we will never resign ourselves to the minimum, but will always demand the maximum; we will never stop halfway along the road.

We believe that we have the right to call ourselves revolutionaries, but we will not have this right the day we abandon the march forward.

The conformists may be satisfied with the minimum; we seek the maximum. The Revolution moves forward; but it has scarcely begun. The work of the Revolution has scarcely begun. But our people will have the historic right to call themselves revolutionary. History will give them this right because they won't be satisfied with the minimum, but will fight for the maximum. They will fight to advance as far as possible. Of that, we are absolutely confident.

But confidence in the people didn't arise today, when the people have more than proven what they are capable of, when they have more than proven that we were not mistaken. Before any of this had happened, before a rally like this – and like all the others that have been held in the Plaza de la Revolución – had ever taken place here, we believed in the people. And we know that we can ask anything of our people. We know that they will go as far as any people can go, and that they are as revolutionary as any people can be. Our people will make their Revolution, their Revolution which is also our Revolution, our Revolution, our road. This does not mean that we disparage the experiences of others, that we underestimate the merits of any other people. But we have deep convictions about what we have, and what we must do. And the only revolutionary thing to do is to make our Revolution. [APPLAUSE]

There are servile spirits, tame spirits. There are people here who become offended when we say 'Make our Revolution!' They become offended when we say that the people will make our Revolution. They consider it a kind of sin, a kind of Marxist-Leninist sacrilege.

But we won't waste time on such elaborate discussions, because we'll be making our Revolution, because it's a law of universal history and it's a law of our history.

And those who don't want us to make our Revolution will share the fate of all pseudo-revolutionaries or counter-revolutionaries or reactionaries. Because some of those submissive, servile, tamed spirits get together to make the same criticisms of the Revolution as those made by the counter-revolutionaries. They use the same arguments against the Revolution as those used by the counter-revolutionaries. There was a saying in Rome that: There is only one step from the Capitol to the Tarpeian Rock. Of course, we don't need any Tarpeian Rock, because any little stream of water will carry away that rubbish. That is, the rubbish exists – let's call a spade a spade – but it will meet the same fate as the back-sliders and the pseudo-revolutionaries and even – if they go too far – the same fate as the counter-revolutionaries. We'll make our Marxist-Leninist Revolution! Our Socialist, our Communist Revolution! We don't say we'll reach socialism, but rather, via the path of socialism, we'll reach communism! [PROLONGED APPLAUSE] And we'll reach communism by the road of Marxism-Leninism! We'll reach communism through a revolutionary and scientific interpretation of reality. We won't reach communism by the road of capitalism, because nobody will ever reach communism by following the road of capitalism! [APPLAUSE]

Nor will we always take the easiest road. Sometimes we'll take the hardest roads. We won't sacrifice our aspirations to reach communism by looking for the easy way. As builders of a new society, we know that any construction is difficult, especially when it has to be erected on the debris of a still-recent past . . .

We know that any historic work, any work of historical creation, is difficult. We know that it is a steep climb, that the going is hard on the way up. And we shall head for the highest peak, along difficult paths; not always looking for the easy way, because at times the easy way leads to failure.

We shall march forward, fighting all the way, because without fighting nothing is achieved, nothing is created. We shall march forward making great efforts, because without effort no goal is reached. With effort we have come this far, and with effort we shall go much further. And we shall arrive with energy, with enthusiasm, with fervour, with security, with confidence as yesterday; as in the very first years of the Revolution, because if we had faith then, we have much more reason for faith today. We shall go forward with the people, with the masses, with their revolutionary vanguard, with their Party the vanguard! with the best, the most resolute, the most capable, the most revolutionary. And the question of deciding who is the most revolutionary will not be up to us, it will be left to the people to say, the people, always. And the decision of the people will be based on deeds and not on words, and the people will decide because only they can judge. Only the people will be capable of taking that step, of carrying forward this work.

Today you came here with torches to symbolize the Technical Revolution, and with machetes. Those machetes must be sharpened because in the next cane-cutting harvest, they must cut a lot of cane! Those machetes will have to work strenuously in our fields.

You have made a perfect interpretation of the essence of this hour: technology and work; you have eloquently interpreted the watchword of this moment, of this year, of these years. We must turn to creative work, turn our efforts towards our fields. And – something of prime importance – we, all of us, at times, seem to be too attached to the capital; at times, it seems to us, that the capital has an undue influence on all of us.

You, ladies and gentlemen of the capital, should not feel slighted by this. You, ladies and gentlemen of the capital should not feel that it is a bad thing to be from the capital. Many of you were born in this capital, but the Revolution was born in every part of the country, not only in the capital. This government was born in every part of the country, not just in the capital, and the country consists of more than the capital.

An enormous effort is being made in our fields, on the plains, in the mountains of our country. I sincerely believe that we, the majority of us, should spend the major part of our time in the interior of the country, working there, engaged in the economic battle, the agricultural battle, engaged in the battle for production. [THE CROWD SHOUTS SOMETHING TO HIM]

Are the machetes heavy for you? What did you say?

[THE CROWD SHOUTS AGAIN]

If we start lowering production quotas, we're not going to win the battle that way. [THE CROWD SHOUTS SOMETHING TO HIM AGAIN]

I agree that if the quotas are too high, it is necessary to reconsider them; but an attitude that demands a reduction in quotas is not an attitude conducive to winning the economic battle. [APPLAUSE] I repeat that it is our duty to keep in mind the differing capacities of different people. But these years are for achievement, for increasing production. These years are for increasing productivity. And all of us, absolutely all of us, ought to promise ourselves, to pledge ourselves to elevate productivity, elevate production.

The day will come when, with less than half of today's effort, we will produce ten times as much as we are now producing. And when that day arrives, as its advent approaches closer and closer, as the fruits of our efforts increase more and more, the quotas will seem less and less high.

You, comrades of the CDR,[1] I was saying that you have interpreted the attitude of this moment, of this moment when large masses are joining in the work of production, when tens of thousand of women are engaging in different undertakings. We have been proposing and advocating that those activities should be chosen that are more easily performed by women.

We have already found many places in the country, in the people's stores, for example, where women are working. They are engaged in all sorts of activities everywhere. There is practically no state poultry farm in this country that is not being run by women. We should try to make it so that the inclusion of women in production is not geared to compensating for the lack of productivity by men, and compensating for a fall in production, but to increasing production. This is something we proposed at the Congress. And we ought to direct that effort, and we are doing so, towards those activities that women can perform well. We will always oppose the employment of women in jobs which they are, physically, virtually incapable of performing. The activities that women can perform are numerous, and we are planning along these lines.

The people and the party have great confidence in the CDR

Not only will we incorporate great numbers of women into production, into activities suitable for women, but we will also incorporate great numbers of machines. We repeat that the solu-

---

1. Committee for the Defence of the Revolution. A mass organization which performs such tasks as organizing the campaign against polio, promoting rallies, and helping local government in maintaining parks and buildings.

tion to the problem lies in the utilization of machines; not in the physical exertion of workers.

We will still have to depend on physical exertion in many cases because we still don't have enough machines and yet we must develop the country, we must develop agriculture, we must increase production. And if the only way we can do it now is by increased physical exertion, then let us exert ourselves more. In the future – the near future – we will use machines and, in time, more machines. [APPLAUSE] We will mechanize all activities that can be mechanized. Above all, in the countryside, we will gradually eliminate a whole series of operations.

Let me give you an example. Every year workers in our country loaded forty-five million tons of cane; they lifted it stalk by stalk from the ground up to the cane cart; forty-five million tons of cane! And you know what lifting cane means. Many persons say that they would rather cut than lift. Every year, our sugar-cane workers manually loaded over forty million tons of sugar cane, stalk by stalk. With mechanization, the bulk of that work is already being done by cane-lifts. Very soon not one stalk will have to be picked up manually. What does this mean? It means that we will have saved our workers the gigantic, the huge task of loading forty-five million tons of sugar cane by hand every year.

That example holds for many other fields. As we introduce mechanization, we will be increasing productivity and eliminating arduous physical work, as in the example I have just mentioned . . .

Long Live the Committees for the Defence of the Revolution!
Patria o Muerte! Venceremos! [OVATION]

CHAPTER 4

'Communism will be Abundance without Egoism: On Intellectual Property.'*

In this speech Fidel contrasts the pre-revolutionary society's property fetish with the Revolution's attitude towards property. In particular, he discusses intellectual property. Whereas in the old society everything that could be contained and sold became a commodity, even knowledge which could benefit man, in socialist society intellectual property, like all property, becomes the possession of the community and not of the entrepreneur who can package and sell it. No one should have to pay for patents and copyrights any more than we should have to pay the inventors of the alphabet or of numbers, or the first man to use a stick to knock fruit off of a tree. Therefore, he announces that Cuba will share with the world its technical knowledge and at the same time feel free to reproduce technical books from the US without regard to copyright.

... Radio, television, movies, the press, magazines, apparently we do not know how to use them as efficiently as we could, just as we previously didn't know how to utilize practically anything else as efficiently as we could.

But, fortunately, we have been learning in these years, and therefore we are beginning to understand how to do things better. And we also hope that in the area of providing information to the people we are also learning and are going to improve.

So many things! Speaking of any one of these deficiencies recalls something we were able to prove in the mountains of Oriente not long ago: with all the publishing houses we have in this

---

* Delivered on 29 April 1967, 'Year of Heroic Vietnam'.

country, with all the workers who work in these publishing houses, with all the paper that they use, not one single book has been published in this country for the farmers. And you went into a store in the mountains and found books on philosophy. This does not in any way mean that philosophy is something to be underestimated, but those farmers were not about to study matters of deep philosophy. They were interested in books on agriculture, books on mechanization, books on a whole series of subjects. One day I asked a man in charge of a store what kind of books he had and which ones were sold. The answer was: 'Well, we have a lot of books by Marx and Angel.' 'Marx and Angel? Ah, I see, Marx and Engels.'

So there were books on political philosophy, books of every kind, and we asked ourselves: 'What are these books doing here?' And the problem was simply that no books were printed in this country for our farmers. Nor for our students either, for that matter.

Fortunately, this is now practically a thing of the past and for quite some time now all the books our students needed have been printed and a Book Institute has been organized that is doing a great deal of printing, taking full advantage of the abundant human resources and machinery we have at hand in the printing field. And perhaps we shall also learn to make better use of our paper.

At times, millions of copies of certain works were printed only to be submitted – as Marx would say – to the devastating criticism of moths and mice – since there was no demand for them and they were simply stored.

Should it surprise us then that many of the things accomplished by our people today are not publicized, when not even many of the great accomplishments of humanity were publicized, when even elementary matters of agricultural technology were not made available to our agricultural workers and farmers, and technical matters were not brought before our students, nor did our students have textbooks?

Intellectual property

Of course, the solution was not an easy one. It became necessary to make a decision that we considered revolutionary. There exists a thing known as 'intellectual property'. In these matters of property we are increasingly less experienced. In the past, everything was 'property, property, and more property'. No other concept was better known, more publicized, or more sacred than that of private property. Everything was private. Possibly the ground on which you are now sitting was once very 'private'. The houses, the land, the mountains, the sky, the sea, everything was private – even the sea, the seas surrounding Cuba, because every vessel that crossed those seas was a private vessel.

Well, these are all becoming things of the past. Our entire new generation is becoming more and more familiar with a different concept of property and is beginning to look upon those things as goods of general use and as goods that belong to the whole of society. The air, it is true, could not be said to be private, for the simple reason that there was no way to get hold of all of it and enclose it in a carafe. Had it been feasible, the air would have been taken over in the same way that the landgrabbers took over the land. But better the air in their control than food. Air was available to everyone, because it could not be bottled up, but food was not available to all because the land that produced it was not in the hands of the people.

Among all of the other things that were appropriated, there was one, very *sui generis*, called intellectual property. You will say : but that is abstract property. Yes, it is abstract property. And strangely enough, air could not be bottled up, yet, nevertheless, something as abstract as intellectual property could be shut up in a kind of bottle.

What do we mean by intellectual property? It is well enough understood. But, in case anyone is not familiar with it, it is, simply, the property of anything that emanates from the intelligence of individuals, of a group of individuals – a book, for example; any book of a technical nature, or a novel.

I want to make it quite clear – because I do not want to earn the enmity of the intellectuals; in the first place, because it would be unjustified enmity – that this should by no means be taken as disregard for the merit, the value, even the right to survive of those who produce this type of spiritual goods. Very well. But, what happens? Those property rights over intellectual possessions – following custom, following a system that prevailed in the world until very recently, following the influence of the whole capitalist concept of society – those intellectual possessions were subject to purchase and sale.

And, naturally, some – and, in general, many – of the creative intellects were badly paid; many have gone hungry. Anyone who reads, for example, the biography of Balzac, who was one of the great novelists of the last century, must be moved by the poverty in which that good man lived. In general, many of the great creative minds have gone hungry because they had no backing. Many products of the intellect have been highly valued years after the death of their authors. Many men whose works have gained fame and immortality later were completely ignored while they lived.

Persons producing works of intellect have generally lived in poverty. They have lacked the support of society and have often had to sell their intellectual productions at any price .

And in what circumstances, in what conditions, did we find ourselves? We were an underdeveloped country, completely lacking in technical knowledge, a country lacking technology and technicians; a country that had to begin by taking on the task of teaching one million citizens to read and write; a country that had to begin establishing technical schools, technological institutes, schools of all kinds from primary to university level; a country that had to undertake the training of tens of thousands, of hundreds of thousands of skilled workers and technicians in order to emerge from poverty and underdevelopment; a country that had to make up the centuries of backwardness that burdened us. When a country like ours sets itself the task of recovering all that lost time, when it proposes to create better living conditions for the people, when it proposes to overcome poverty and underdevelopment, it must then invest every cent, a large part of its limited resources, in construction, in purchasing means of production, factories, equipment. At the same time that we had to make countless investments, we were faced with the difficulties in educating the people.

Why? Because as our citizens learned to read and write, as all children began to attend school, as the number of sixth-grade graduates topped the 50,000 mark and reached 60,000, 70,000 and 80,000, as more students entered the technological institutes and the universities, and as we aspired to defeat underdevelopment and ignorance, we needed an ever-increasing number of books. And books were – and are – very costly.

Knowledge is the patrimony of mankind

Because of the existing copyright concepts, we found that, in order to satisfy the demand for books, we had to spend tens of millions of pesos on their purchase, often paying for them most dearly. But in practice it is very difficult to determine exactly what is copyright; copyright belonged no longer to the authors but to those who had paid hard cash on the market for these products of the intellect, at any price, generally a low one. Those who exercised a monopoly over books had the right to sell them at the price they deemed suitable. We had to arrive at a decision, a defiant one, indeed, but a fair one. Our country, in fact, decided to disallow copyrights.

What does this mean? We feel that technical knowledge ought to be the patrimony of all mankind. To our way of thinking, whatever is created by man's intelligence ought to be the patrimony of all men.

Who pays royalties to Cervantes and to Shakespeare? Who pays the inventors of the alphabet; who pays the inventors of numbers, arithmetic, mathematics? In one way or another, all of mankind has benefited from, and made use of, those creations of the intellect that man has forged throughout history. When the first primitive man took a stick in his hand to knock down a piece of fruit from a tree, mankind began to benefit from a creation of the intelligence : when the first human being emitted a grunt that was the precursor of a future language, mankind began to make use of that product of man's intelligence.

That is, all, or rather the vast majority of man's creations have been amassed throughout thousands of years. And all mankind feels entitled to enjoy those creations of the intellect; everyone feels entitled to enjoy all that past generations have produced in other periods of history. How is it possible today to deny man, hundreds of thousands of human beings – no, not hundreds of thousands, but hundreds of millions and thousands of millions of human beings, who live in poverty, in underdevelopment, to deny access to technology to those thousands of millions of human beings who need it for something as elemental as feeding themselves, something as elemental as living?

Naturally, to adopt such a decision generally involves incurring the enmity of those whose interests are affected. Often copyrights are ignored, and it is done secretly, surreptitiously, without admitting it. We are not going to adopt that procedure. We state that we consider all technical knowledge the heritage of all mankind and especially of those peoples that have been exploited. Because where is there hunger, underdevelopment, ignorance, a lack of technical knowledge? Right there, in all those regions of the world where men were criminally exploited for centuries of colonialism and imperialism.

Technical books are generally printed in developed countries. And then the poor countries, the countries that have been exploited for centuries, have virtually no access to that technical knowledge, when for centuries they have been stripped of many of the resources with which, equipped with modern technology, they could have been developed.

In the United States there are many thousands of technical books. We have begun by announcing an end to intellectual copyrights on all technical books from the United States. And we state our unequivocal right to reprint all US technical books that we feel will be useful to us.

It is clear that we don't have to offer any excuses to justify this. We feel justified in printing US technical books, entitled to this, at least, in compensation for the harm they have tried to do this country. Well, then, we will bypass copyright in relation to the

United States; but we, independent of those circumstances, consider as a right of our people – of all the underdeveloped peoples – the use of all technical knowledge that is available throughout the world, and we therefore consider ourselves entitled to print any book of a technical nature that we need for our development, that we need in the training of our technicians.

And what will we give in exchange? We feel it a duty of society to help, to stimulate. We feel it a duty of society to protect all intellectual creators. I don't mean protect them; perhaps that is not the correct concept. We feel that our intellectual creators must take their place in society with all the rights of outstanding workers.

Cuba can and is willing to compensate all its intellectual creators; but, at the same time, it renounces – renounces internationally – all the copyrights that it is entitled to.

Not many technical books are published in this country, but, for example, we have produced a great deal of music that is enjoyed all over the world.

And in the future, in all intellectual fields, our people will produce more and more. As of now, we announce our renunciation of all copyrights relating to our intellectual property and, with Cuban intellectual producers protected by the Cuban government, our country renounces all its copyrights relating to intellectual property. That is, our books may be reprinted freely in any part of the world, while we, on the other hand, assume the right to do the same. If all countries did the same, humanity would be the beneficiary.

However, this is utopian. It is impossible to think that a capitalist country would do this. But if all countries did exactly the same, in exchange for the books that each country created, for the books published, or rather written in a given country, that country, by renouncing its copyrights to those books, could acquire the rights to the books written in every other country of the world.

Naturally, we cannot assume that this will happen. But, for our part we can state that this will be our stand on the problem of copyrights. And we believe that it is correct to state this frankly, no matter who may be discomfited.

We can, naturally, come to mutually convenient agreements with any country, they sending us their books published in large editions, and we sending them our books published in large editions. Any type of exchange of already published books, any type of agreement of this sort, we can do perfectly well, meeting the convenience of any country. But this will be the policy that we shall follow. We shall do the same with what are called 'patents'. We, for our part, it is true, have not yet invented great things or many things, and it is not a matter of our planning to become inventors, but any gadget that we do invent will be at the disposal of all humanity, as well as any success in the technical field, any success in the agricultural field.

And it should be said that we have high hopes in these fields. Yes, we expect to have considerable success. It will not be long before many people in many parts of the world will have to turn their eyes towards what we are doing here, to see how this country, situated in a tropical zone, solves many of the agricultural problems still unsolved in other tropical countries of the world. Because, above all, poverty has been mainly confined to the tropical countries; there are practically no tropical countries in the so-called developed areas of the world. And we, beyond any possibility of doubt, will be in the vanguard of agriculture among the tropical zones of the world and our solutions, our techniques, will be available to all who care to learn from them.

It is known, for example, that our Institute of Sugar Cane Investigations is carrying on research to obtain new and improved cane varieties. Very well: each time that we obtain a new variety of cane, we, a cane-producing country, will put this knowledge at the disposal of every other cane-producing country interested in that variety. We shall not stoop to weak and miserly egoism.

Competition belongs to a world of hunger

No ! We shall not concern ourselves with questions of competition.

If in the poultry sector, for example, we develop a variety of fowl that lays more eggs than another or produces more meat than another, this knowledge will be placed at the disposal of all other peoples. If with the massive programmes we are carrying out in livestock genetics, we obtain superior specimens, new breeds of animals or, within existing breeds varieties with singular characteristic, this knowledge will be placed at the disposal of all who need it, and even the means to acquire these specimens – by artificial insemination or by any other method. This holds true for any field of competition.

Because the concept of competition belongs to a world of hunger, because competition belongs to an underdeveloped world, because competition belongs to a world where hunger and poverty have become institutions. Because, what is competition, after all? It is that fight among producers of one same product for a limited market. When competition appears, the fight appears, too; it is not the fight to feed all the needy, but the fight to feed those who are able to buy. In our country there were surpluses of many products, because production was geared not to needs, but to the market. People without a penny in their pockets didn't count. There could be surpluses of coffee, milk, meat, and citrus fruits: anything, because how were people without money going to buy?

And in the midst of the job scarcities, in the midst of the chaos, anarchy, and limitations of a capitalist economy, there could be surpluses of anything; because there was a greater surplus of unemployed than of goods, a surplus of those without either a penny in their pockets or the means to earn one, and who, consequently, didn't count. Hundreds of millions of people in this world live in poverty and suffer malnutrition.

This idea of competition will have to disappear in tomorrow's world. Because, just as our people produce today not for the market but for their needs – that is, domestically, we attempt to produce what is necessary and not what can be sold – in tomorrow's world all nations will have to work on that same basis.

This, of course, can only happen when colonialism and imperialism have disappeared from the face of the earth. And we know that there are needs to be filled in this world, that there will always be a need for whatever we produce, and that someone will always produce the things that we need. Therefore, the advantages from our agricultural development; therefore, our thrust towards mass application of technology in the gigantic development of our plans for different branches of production, so that our production may both fill our needs and meet demands abroad. We know that all we produce will always be useful to someone else and that other countries can do likewise, produce things that are useful to us. But, beginning with the domestic market, we will produce everything we need, as much milk as we need, and the day that we have more than enough milk we will not begin to throw it away. What have many capitalist countries been doing in the last decades? There is a surplus of coffee, they burn coffee; they have a surplus of other products and they burn them and throw them away, and the restrictions ... We do not suffer from these ills. If we have a surplus of milk one day we will ask ourselves what the average consumption is and we will either lower the price or we will give the milk away free ...

There is frequently abundance, but egoism remains. There can be abundance without communism; communism will be abundance without egoism. But communism is not achieved through abundance alone but through education, through genuinely socialist consciousness, genuinely communist consciousness. Egoism is so absurd and blind that at times it does not content itself with what it needs, but wants to appropriate even what it does not need. In capitalism man appropriated much more than he needed simply to exploit others. The people of tomorrow in our society will live very differently from that period in which man lived in the midst of egoism, in which a few men appropriated almost everything to exploit the vast majority of the people.

We are doing both things. The important thing about the work you have completed is that you have worked on both aspects; you have been forging your own revolutionary consciousness, you have been forging your socialist and communist consciousness. And at the same time that you have been educating yourselves for communism, you have been helping to create the material base that along with education and consciousness will allow us to live according to truly communist norms, that is, according to truly fraternal norms, truly human norms, in which each man and woman will see others as his brothers and sisters, and no one will see others as enemies; no one will be seen as a rival. And that is precisely the strength that socialism and communism gives to people; it is the strength of brothers as contrasted with the weakness of those who are divided, those who hate each other.

Here we have seen that strength in a practical way: we have seen what can be done through human collectivity; we have seen what you have been able to accomplish in three months, a small army of young people working here enthusiastically, because you did not see work as a punishment, but rather as an ennobling activity, one that inspires man, that can fill him with happiness. That is work when it is not slave work; that is work when man is not exploited. Before, the concept of work was associated with the concept of suffering, because work meant suffering for exploited people. Work will never again be an ordeal but rather the most enjoyable, noblest, most creative activity of mankind.

You will see what I am talking about when you return here, those of you who do not go elsewhere, if you come back here next year, when you really see how these lands have been enriched, when you really see the fruits of your work. Because the work you have left here will increase; it will produce more and more fruits.

The plants that you have sown here will remain in the earth; your example will remain with our youth; and the heartening response of the new revolutionary generation will remain with our revolution.

Patria o Muerte! Venceremos! [OVATION]

IV. The Revolution Continues

CHAPTER 1

The Revolutionary Offensive: 'We Did Not Make a Revolution to Establish the Right to Trade.'*

In March 1968, Castro proclaimed a new revolutionary offensive in Cuba. With this offensive, as he announces in this speech, the Cuban government plans to nationalize the burgeoning retail-trade business which included 55,600 small private businesses and accounted for approximately one third of retail-trade sales. This series of nationalizations meant that in less than a decade over ninety per cent of the Cuban economy was taken over from private ownership; only in agriculture does a significant share of production still remain in the private sector. After the second and last Agrarian Reform, in 1963, thirty per cent of the farms in Cuba – no larger than 168 acres – were left in private hands.

The purpose of the offensive transcended economics. The small but profitable private sector remained a privileged part of the socialist economy. As Raúl Castro said on May Day, 1968: 'To say that the small merchants lived better because they were in-fluenced by material incentives is true. And for that very reason, we reject material incentives. We don't want a small-merchant mentality for our people!' They lived better by dealing in the black market, or by buying cheap and selling dear – not by contributing to the development of the society. He referred to the criticism of the Eastern European press: 'Some have said that we are idealists, romantics, and adventurers, that we are violating the laws of economics, that we have decided to reach our goals by substituting enthusiasm for economic principles.'

---

* Delivered on 13 March 1968, 'Year of the Heroic Guerrilla', on the eleventh Anniversary of the attack on the Presidential Palace, at at the University of Havana.

In fact, of course, Fidel's answer is eminently 'realistic' in the sense that it is grounded in Cuba's practical experience; his answer is also a general affirmation of the great potentialities of man for creative, peaceful development. The Cubans have in the past overcome great obstacles, as Fidel often points out – overthrowing Batista, defeating the US mercenaries at the Bay of Pigs, and withstanding the US blockade and initiating the many measures towards improving the quality of life in the community. These examples of goals attained through collective efforts point to the real possibilities of overcoming the moral as well as the technological obstacles to realizing a communist society.

In this speech Fidel explains the reasons for the nationalization of the retail trade. He also goes through a long, detailed explanation of the economic situation of Cuba. The speech is reprinted in full for it shows another side of what it means to be a revolutionary people, that is, an informed people, one able and willing to sit through long discussions on the details of problems confronting the community. People learn from participation and observation; participation means knowledge of the details. Fidel, in this speech, criticizes the Cuban on this score: 'We are still a people characterized by great enthusiasm and decision at decisive moments, a people capable of any heroism at any moment, but a people that still lacks the virtue of daily heroism, a people that still lacks the virtue of tenacity, the demonstration of this courage and heroism not only in the dramatic moments but on each and every day.'

The wealth of detail shows the calm didacticism that characterizes his long speeches. It condemns the lingering institutions and ideas of privilege that remain in socialist Cuba – the retail trade, the disparities between country and city – and it stresses that the revolutionary people of Cuba must depend only on themselves. (In his ninth anniversary speech in January 1968, Fidel announced a cutback in petroleum because of reduced shipments from the Soviet Union. In this speech he discusses the microfraction – old line communists who conspired with members of the Soviet embassy – and Cuba's refusal to send a delegation to the party congress in Budapest.) The call for self-reliance in the face of Soviet coolness and for a new revolutionary offensive *demonstrate the Fidelista response to challenge – intensification of the struggle.*

This speech contains an analysis of the differences between industrialized countries and the Third World. Together with his speech to the UN, in 1960, it provides an excellent primer on economic development and economic backwardness, and shows the terrible journey ahead of the poor countries in their struggle for development.

Comrades of the Central Committee; Comrade students; Comrade Party members, members of the Committees for the Defence of the Revolution, leaders of the Women's Federation, of the unions, and all workers gathered here this evening.

It appears that this area is not large enough to hold the representatives of our revolutionary forces gathered here tonight.

I want to begin by telling you that this evening's speech is going to be boring, and it is going to be boring because we are faced with the need to enumerate a series of data and figures in order to demonstrate what we mean. It will be necessary for all of you on your part to pay close attention, because when statistics and figures are involved it is always necessary to pay close attention if we don't want to be bored or not understand.

We know that there are several questions in the air; we know that many persons have been waiting for a public occasion such as this one to hear our opinions concerning these questions. It is true that, in the early days of the Revolution, public opinion in the capital, which has always had the characteristic – and I say this in all frankness – of being somewhat inconsistent, required our appearing on television with a certain frequency in order to explain every kind of problem, major or insignificant. We still recall the times when, if a Pardo Llada left the country, it was necessary to appear on television to explain why a Pardo Llada had left; if a traitor such as Díaz Lanz resigned or deserted, it was necessary to appear on television to explain the significance of such desertions; if one day, after presenting us with a beautiful fish specimen, a Señor Miguel Quevedo departed on his yacht from Varadero for Miami, it was necessary to appear on television to explain that matter, that scandal. We still recall that on that occasion, while still convalescing from pneumonia, we had to leave our bed and appear on television to explain that incident. Why? Because of this certain inconsistency that characterized public opinion, above all in the capital, which had its periods of optimism and pessimism, of enthusiasm and discouragement.

On some occasions, with the appearance of the first problems of the Revolution, this fact was much in evidence. Later the political awareness of the population of the capital became firmer and more stable. It is no longer necessary to explain something every week or every day, but it has become apparent to us that public opinion is requiring some explanations concerning certain questions.

A series of things has occurred. And, in connection with this matter of explanations, we wish to state certain facts – with the aim of better clarifying matters for the people. The style of this Revolution has always been to explain problems to the masses. This Revolution has been characterized by the explanation of the greatest possible number of problems. And I say 'the greatest possible' because, unfortunately, not all problems can be dealt with publicly. We are a constituted State, and, as a constituted State, we logically have to observe certain norms; and, in the complex and difficult world in which we live, each and every problem cannot always be discussed publicly. Because of lack of confidence in the people? No, never! It is simply because there are questions of a diplomatic nature, questions having to do with relations between states, and so on, and questions that could be prejudicial if they were known by the enemy.

We count on our people to have faith in their leaders

Certainly, we don't go to the extremes here that are gone to in the United States, for example, where, it has been stated, certain documents related to the assassination of Kennedy will not be made public – if I remember correctly – until the years 2050 or 2060. However, logically, not all questions can be dealt with every day, nor can all matters be made public. And this is not – I repeat – nor will it ever be, for lack of faith in the people. But, at the same time, we count on our people to have faith in their leaders and their Revolutionary government. And that they let the revolutionary leadership be aware, always, in the difficult and arduous tasks and responsibilities it must assume, of that confidence and that support.

Some of the questions, such as that of the microfraction, have been amply publicized, at least as amply as was possible. On that occasion we spoke for many hours, clarifying a number of questions, and that discourse was not published. And it wasn't published for the very reasons we have explained. We had been considering the possibility of publishing part of it, but we preferred to publish all of it or none, so as not to offer partial explanations. Nonetheless, we trust that 150 years won't have to pass before anyone has an opportunity to read some of these documents.

But if it is true that some of the microfraction's political manifestations and the phenomenon of microfractionalism could have been more amply publicized – and this aspect was fully analysed in the Central Committee meeting – it must be made clear that, as a political force – I repeat, political force – the microfraction had no significance whatsoever. As a political intention and as a tendency within the revolutionary movement, a frankly reformist, reactionary, and conservative current, its actions were of a very serious nature, although we fully realized that many tendencies of this kind are circulating in the atmosphere of our times. But, after all, we consider the microfraction a question that has been solved.

The revolutionary courts were not as severe as some would have wished but, in the final analysis, unnecessary severity has never been a characteristic of this Revolution. However, in our opinion, there are questions which are more urgent, more timely, and of greater interest and importance. Obviously, tonight I am not going to deal fundamentally with problems of an international character with reference to our international affairs. At the moment there is very little to say, and all of you, for example, know perfectly well the decision of our Central Committee not to send a delegation to the meeting of the Communist Parties that was held in Budapest. And for the moment this is also not a fundamental question. That is, the analysis of this matter is not, at the moment, of primary importance.

There are questions of a national character, questions related to our present situation and to the development of the Revolution which, in our opinion, are much more vital. Concretely, we want to refer to the circumstances of protest – yes, of protest – of a certain discontent, confusion, and dissatisfaction related to the matter of availability of consumer goods and, fundamentally, to several concrete measures, such as the suspension during these months of the milk quota for the adult population of Havana. Some persons were apparently dissatisfied with the explanation that appeared in the press, and if some people were dissatisfied, then possibly the well-intentioned people who were dissatisfied were right. A brief note explained the basic reason for the measure. It did not mention all the factors, nor was it an exhaustive explanation. At the same time, a certain number of rumours have been circulating in the capital of the Republic in recent weeks . . .

Rumours, of course, are an old phenomenon, and even the absurdity of certain rumours is also old.

But, of course, at the same time – as I was saying – false rumours were spread to the effect that eggs were going to be rationed, and lines formed at the markets where they are sold in order to buy eggs, in some cases in excessive amounts. Rumours were also spread that bread was going to be rationed. And, side by side with these questions related to food supplies, a line formed – we have been told – at 'The Wedding Palace' because someone, or some persons, said that marriages were going to be prohibited until who knows what age.

That reminded us of that story about the case of extraordinary State Powers that, complete with copies of the law and all – an apocryphal law, of course – was circulated (several years ago) by counter-revolutionary elements. The matter of the State Powers is so ridiculous that, if we were to ask Comrade Llanusa to give us an idea of the efforts made by the Ministry of Education to make room for all those who request scholarships, for all those who request school dining rooms and day nurseries, we would get some idea of the real material impossibility of some of those absurd ideas. And, as far as we can see, it would appear that humanity has obeyed that old commandment, said to be divine, to go forth and multiply. And really we don't know by what means or ways people here could be kept apart by passing a law – it would be ridiculous. But, of course, it may be that some opportunist took advantage of the rumour in order to hasten his marriage. [LAUGHTER] I just heard someone comment: 'He's making a good speech.' Perhaps he was one of those who was worried about that problem of the rumour. [LAUGHTER]

In reality, we asked ourselves what the reasons might be for that certain uneasiness, that certain uncertainty that was evident, and, naturally, we found explanations. In part, they have a real basis in real difficulties, and in part they may be related to such circumstances, for example, as the international relations of our party and government. It is possible that the need to ration gasoline, and the circumstances surrounding the Central Committee meeting in which the pseudo-revolutionary current, the microfractional elements, were severely judged, have been factors that contributed to creating a certain state of disquiet and uncertainty. And, as I said, all this together with real difficulties.

One day an oil well came in, and it is possible that it would not even have been given publicity had it not been for the circumstance that the well is situated no less than a few metres from the Vía Blanca Highway and practically in the centre of the town of Guanabo.

We said that perhaps we wouldn't even have published it, because really we are opposed to creating illusions, we are opposed to creating exaggerated optimism about anything. And, logically, first we wanted to know the potential of the well to really evaluate it, and naturally to avoid a situation in which, because of the well, everybody would say, 'Well, that takes care of the fuel problem!' – as if drilling a well were as simple as digging a trench or digging a well for water. And, of course, a brief, clear-cut account was published, in which it was explained that it was necessary, first of all, to evaluate the well.

However, the news of the well spread like wildfire throughout Havana, and, of course, it was well grounded – grounded in oil. Tremendous optimism! Excessive optimism can, to a certain extent, be related to excessive uncertainty or concern. And we are of the opinion that the revolutionary's spirit must always be serene in all circumstances; in the face of adversity, in the face of difficulties and in the face of success. And a revolution, in any case, is of necessity a process full of emotions of all kinds, efforts of all kinds, and struggles of all kinds. This is why there is ample time to experience every single emotion under the sun.

But we were saying that such a tremendous excess of optimism could be related to a certain situation of uncertainty. If you are sure of what you are doing, an oil well is good news; but, in any case, you have to be prepared to solve problems with the well or without it, with oil or without it. [APPLAUSE]

We don't make the most effective use of the news media

Another thing that these events showed us was that information was somewhat deficient, that we don't know how to make the most effective use of the news media at our disposal and that we don't even know how to make the best use of the tremendous organizations that the Revolution has at hand. It is a known fact that, through the Party, the Committees for Defence of the Revolution, the Women's Federation, the unions and the youth organizations, the Revolution can, in a matter of hours, rally the whole nation, it can mobilize the whole country, it can take the starch out of any rumour, it can cut the ground out from under all the rumour mongers and all the spreaders of pessimism and defeatism.

Let us say that we are at fault when we don't keep up an adequate flow of information to the revolutionary ranks because we don't make the most effective use of the communications media and organization channels at our disposal. But, at the same time, certain ideological weaknesses can still be observed in the masses of our people; a certain defect of political education is to be observed, a certain lack of political education, in the meaning that we really give to political education today.

There must be a better understanding of contemporary world problems, greater familiarity with the tremendous problems facing mankind today, greater knowledge, of course, of the problems of economic structures and, above all, of the problems that a country such as ours must solve, and in what conditions.

For ignorance leads to thinking that everything is easy, to the over-simplification of problems and to thinking that everything, no matter how complicated, has a solution right around the corner – a fast, easy, and immediate solution. There is a greater tendency to speak without sufficient grounds, to analyse things facilely and superficially than to analyse in depth. We have always been a little prone to produce a great many 'street-corner philosophers'. And this is a tendency that has hung on from the past, as if the Revolution hadn't taught us enough about the profundity of these processes.

And it must be said that a certain factor has contributed to that lack of sufficient political instruction, and that factor has not been so much the use as the abuse of the manuals of Marxism-Leninism. It must be said that many revolutionary militants went through the schools known as Revolutionary Instruction Schools – which did, in fact, have the aim of giving revolutionary instruction – and philosophic questions were studied, the elements, the fundamentals of Marxism.

Naturally, all this is as useful as it is necessary and convenient; but there's something the Revolution itself has taught us – because, after all, the Revolution is the greatest teacher of revolutionaries – and that is the enormous gap that sometimes exists between general concepts and practice, between philosophy and reality. And, above all, it has taught us how far the manuals have gradually become outdated, have become something of an anachronism, since, in many instances, they don't say one word about the problems the masses should understand. Often the manuals are nothing but a series of abstract generalities, vague and devoid of content, so that, just when you think you have a truly developed revolutionary, you find that what you have is a militant who does not understand many of the most serious problems of the contemporary world.

We must also say that the manuals contain a large number of clichés and stereotyped phrases and, what is more, some falsehoods – although it is not our intention to go into an analysis of manuals here.

This is a factor which, unquestionably, has been instrumental in that weakness of formation, of instruction, from which our people are still suffering. And we believe that a more thorough understanding of these problems would be most helpful ...

Of course there isn't much literature in the field of Marxism dealing with such problems. And, naturally, it would be a good thing for all who somehow are able to do something about it, for those who somehow may be able to supply information on the subject, to think on what questions and in what way we should proceed to give our people an increasingly more profound revolutionary training.

There is, in addition, another factor; a series of questions as to how communism is to be constructed. A series of questions which are discussed in academies – and which are either applied or not applied to reality – which, by themselves, become thorny problems, because, with the mere disclosure of viewpoints, many of them turn into political problems of international scope. It has come to a point where a certain international hypersensitivity has developed about these problems, since some countries apply the ideals while others do not. And, when one of the countries does not apply them and says why it does not, there are those who feel deeply offended and tend to look upon the country which does not apply the ideas as the black sheep of the family because it does not follow the beaten path, even if the path leads nowhere.

Most certainly, all these factors have become so many obstacles to the people's best formation. Of course that is not all. Real difficulties do exist. We revolutionaries must never deny the existence of difficulties. To do that would be equivalent to hiding one's head in the sand. Moreover, revolutionaries must never shirk their responsibilities.

If it were said that all of us, or the vast majority of us, were utter ignoramuses at the time of the triumph of the Revolution, it would be the simple truth. It would also be true to say that a good many of us were conscious of our own ignorance. We always think back to the 8 January when we expressed a feeling we had experienced before – that is, when we had arrived in the capital we had the same feeling we had experienced on 2 December, at the time of the 'Granma' landing. Perhaps it was not exactly the same sensation but rather the realization we later had that day that there was still a great deal to be learned in the sphere of guerrilla fighting, in the sphere of warfare. And, having had that experience once, the second time it did not take us by surprise. So we realized that we were faced by a similar situation and that there would be a great deal for us to learn in the coming years.

We believe that an awareness of those truths, each revolutionary's awareness of his own limitations and ignorance, is invaluable; a man who is not aware of his own ignorance will never learn, never make any progress.

We have also known cases of revolutionaries who not only were ignoramuses but also thought themselves the possessors of great knowledge. And not only did they think they knew a great deal, but they also managed, on occasion, to make some of us believe they knew something.

Now we can say that all of us have learned something in the course of this process, though once again we must say that we still have much to learn. No revolutionary should ever be ashamed to recognize his limitations, inasmuch as the life of every revolutionary should be a continuous learning process. And I say this because we maintain that no revolutionary should ever shirk any responsibility, no revolutionary should ever try to conceal difficulties; a revolutionary should never hold back from facing any responsibility or any difficulty.

I said that those difficulties do exist. And how much of the responsibilities must we bear? This can only be ascertained in the long run. What matters is our conviction; what matters is the conviction of each of us that, at every moment and under every circumstance, we have done the maximum possible, we have tried to do our very best.

How much could greater experience on the part of all revolutionary leaders have contributed? No one can say. But one thing is certain; the real and objective circumstances in which a people in our position must face the future are objective difficulties, real difficulties, and difficult to overcome. In other words, objectively speaking, even if we had today's experience nine years ago – if we exclude matters of detail, if we exclude our having believed in some lies – without doubt we would have done just as we did.

The Revolution has passed through various periods, through various circumstances, has experienced special moments; and we could say that, regarding each decisive matter, regarding each fundamental decision, if we had to go through such circumstances again, even with today's experience, I believe that our decisions would stand unchanged.

And at certain moments perhaps the Revolution did not curb in time the creation of certain tendencies among the masses. One of those tendencies led to something of an attitude of complacency: the idea that we were defended, the idea we would never have a problem. Because when, on one or two occasions, the famous intercontinental missiles were mentioned, everyone here began to speak of intercontinental missiles the next day, and to count on them as if he had them in his pocket. At meetings in farm districts or anywhere else, everywhere, speakers referred to the famous missiles. And I recall that this theoretical use and abuse of the alleged missiles always caused us a certain amount of concern. In my opinion, this 'we are defended; let's cross our arms' attitude led to a certain sit-back-and-take-it-easy mentality when the only correct, the only intelligent, the only truly revolutionary attitude was always to depend on ourselves, always to rely on our own strength and never cease to do everything possible, in case one day we should find ourselves faced with the need to confront a direct aggression by the imperialist enemies; to rely first on ourselves and only on ourselves, and always be ready to place a high price on our lives without waiting for anyone to come and defend us.

A certain attitude of complacency was created in the economic field

A certain attitude of complacency was created in the economic field also, in the use and abuse of the idea that, in the event of any problem, help would be immediately forthcoming to solve it. This created an attitude of complacency in the sense that it could lead the people to forget that we ourselves would always have to make the fundamental effort, the decisive effort, to act decisively – that our first duty as a country with an underdeveloped economy was to exert ourselves to the maximum, to spur development of that economy to the maximum, and not to view the path of the Revolution as an easy path, one with all problems solved. It would have been far preferable from the beginning to develop in ourselves the awareness that while foreign aid and resources obtained from abroad might be important in these difficult times in which our people are undertaking the hard path of economic development, what would always be decisive would be our determination, our conviction that with foreign resources or even without any foreign resources, we were forging our will to make this country march forward.

We state with certainty that that would have been the people's best revolutionary education. And, of course, such revolutionary thinking is not for weaklings, the fainthearted, the irresolute, the inconstant, pessimists, or sowers of defeatism.

And we must say that our masses have still not rid themselves sufficiently of these very real factors, of these subjective factors, which hang on to a certain degree.

We are still a people characterized by great enthusiasm and decision at decisive moments, a people capable of giving up life itself at any hour, on any day, capable of any heroism at any moment, but a people that still lacks the virtue of daily heroism, a people that still lacks the virtue of tenacity, the demonstration of this courage and heroism not only in the dramatic moments but on each and every day. That is, there is a certain tenacity and perseverance still lacking in that heroism.

We must also say that truly bourgeois institutions, ideas, ties, and privileges still exist among our people. Concerning this, we cannot escape our guilt and our responsibility. We have always sought to do things in the best possible way; we have always sought to deepen the Revolution day by day; but there is no doubt whatsoever that certain institutions have lasted much longer than they should have, that certain privileges have lasted much longer than they should have. And these privileges and institutions feed those currents we are talking about, and they keep those weaknesses alive among the people.

In the light of these facts, these circumstances, these background factors, and this certain uneasiness and heeding of rumours, I wish to go into certain things tonight. For your information, allow me to point out some of the real problems and explain what they consist of.

I am going to speak concretely of a problem that gave rise to a certain state of misunderstanding or inconformity – that is, the problem of the milk. This will serve as a concrete illustration of other, more important questions that we must analyse. I am going to give you some data on milk production in recent years – what the increase has been, what the present situation is.

In 1962, 219,414,000 litres of fresh milk were purchased by the state procurement agency; 217,151,900 in 1963 – I am going to give round figures – 225 million in 1964; 231 million in 1965; 329 million in 1966; 324 million in 1967.

Apart from the production of fresh milk, the purchase by the state procurement agency of which increased (production is, naturally, greater than purchases) – by somewhat more than 100 million litres per year – apart from that, condensed milk was imported as follows: 4,663 tons in 1959; 6,683 in 1960; 6,719 in 1961; 12,698 in 1962; 16,643 in 1963; 21,637 in 1964; 22,197 in 1965; 16,455 in 1966; and 19,692 in 1967, and the acquisition of 18,000 tons is planned for 1968.

Fresh Milk		Condensed Milk Imports	
Year	Litres	Year	Tons
1962	219,414,000	1959	4,663
1963	217,151,900	1960	6,683
1964	225,000,000	1961	6,719
1965	231,000,000	1962	12,698
1966	329,000,000	1963	16,643
1967	324,000,000	1964	21,637
		1965	22,197
		1966	16,455
		1967	19,692
		1968	18,000 (Planned)

Irrespective of the importation of condensed milk, we also imported powdered milk to be processed back into milk – as follows: skim milk, 27 tons in 1959; 1,826 in 1960; 1,494 in 1961; 5,561 in 1962; 10,857 in 1963; 11,346 in 1964; 17,045 in 1965; 16,248 in

1966; and 18,837 in 1967, and 16,405 tons are planned for 1968. The 18,837 tons purchased last year cost 5,977,000 pesos in foreign exchange – that is, in convertible currency. An outlay of 5,642,000 pesos is planned for this year.

Powdered Skim Milk Imports

Year	Tons
1959	27
1960	1,826
1961	1,494
1962	5,561
1963	10,857
1964	11,346
1965	17,045
1966	16,248
1967	18,837
1968	16,405 (Planned)

Additional imports of whole powdered milk were also made in countries with which we trade on a clearing basis, as follows: 232 tons in 1959; 117 in 1960; 3,209 in 1961; 405 in 1962; 19 in 1963; 711 in 1964; 3,675 in 1965; 1,561 in 1966; and 2,156 in 1967, while in 1968 we have been able to obtain 2,000 tons.

Powdered Whole Milk Imports

Year	Tons
1959	232
1960	117
1961	3,209
1962	405
1963	19
1964	711
1965	3,675
1966	1,561
1967	2,156
1968	2,000

Last year, we obtained 5,547 tons of dehydrated cream – that is, powdered milk – to produce another type of milk, and this year we have obtained 3,000. Imports of milk-containing cereals were 1,467 tons in 1967, while 3,000 tons have been obtained this year.

In other words, during the last few years there has been an increase in milk imports as well as in the national production of fresh milk.

The production of evaporated milk – that is, the part of the fresh milk which has been made into evaporated milk – was as follows: 317,415 cases in 1957; 355,000 in 1958; 129,000 in 1959; 214,000 in 1960; 314,000 in 1961; 360,000 in 1962; 267,000 in 1963; 223,000 in 1964; 640,000 in 1965; 713,000 in 1966; and 715,000 in 1967. That is, it went up from 129,000 in 1959 to 715,000 in 1967.

Evaporated Milk Production

Year	Cases
1957	317,415
1958	355,000
1959	129,000
1960	214,000
1961	314,000
1962	360,000
1963	267,000
1964	223,000
1965	640,000
1966	713,000
1967	715,000

And, in the same way, the production of condensed milk increased from 1,726,880 in 1959 to 2,705,524. This has been more or less the pace maintained in milk production.

However, in the current year a decrease became noticeable in the output and, therefore, in the procurement of milk. For example, the daily procurement in three provinces of the interior and in Havana Province was as follows: the daily amount purchased in Las Villas for the month of January 1967 was 131,000 litres. This year it was 122,000. In Camagüey, 159,700 in January 1967 and 135,400 in 1968; in Oriente, 180,200 in January 1967 and 133,700 in January 1968, while the daily rate went from 190,000 litres in February 1967 to 138,700 in February 1968. That is, the daily procurement for those two months registered a considerable decrease.

Drop in Production
and Procurement of Fresh Milk

Province	Litres daily	
	January 1967	January 1968
Las Villas	131,000	122,000
Camagüey	159,700	135,400
Oriente	180,200	133,700
Havana	184,000	173,800

Litres Daily – Havana

January 1967	184,000
January 1968	173,800
February 1967	190,000
February 1968	138,700

On the other hand, even though the amount in tons of powdered milk obtained with convertible currency remains practically the same, there has been a decrease of about 4,000 tons in the amount obtained from countries where we trade on a clearing basis. And this posed the need either to spend several million dollars in the acquisition of more powdered milk or else to adopt the measure that was finally taken; to suspend the quota of milk that was being supplied to the adult population of Havana. The only other choice would have been to reduce the milk quota in the provinces and cities in the interior of the country, that already have a milk consumption level lower than that of Havana.

We have explained how the milk distribution per province has been carried out during these two months. As you have heard, Las Villas, Camagüey and Oriente provinces had already registered a considerable decrease in fresh milk production. Nevertheless, in January of last year 119,000 litres of milk were distributed daily in Las Villas. This year the amount distributed was 130,000 litres.

In Camagüey, 106,000 litres were distributed in January of 1967 and 127,000 in 1968. The same thing happened in February. In February of 1967 the daily distribution in Las Villas was 111,000. In February of this year, 113,000. In Camagüey 98,000 in February 1967 and 113,000 in 1968. In Oriente, 154,000 litres per day in February 1967 and 185,000 in 1968.

Milk Distribution for Two Months

Province	Litres Daily	
	January 1967	January 1968
Las Villas	119,000	130,000
Camagüey	106,000	127,000
Oriente	155,900	182,000
	February 1967	February 1968
Las Villas	111,000	113,000
Camagüey	98,000	113,000
Oriente	154,000	185,000

It has been necessary for the first time to send powdered milk for reconstitution to provinces such as Camagüey and Oriente, which never before received powdered milk. Otherwise the levels of consumption in those provinces would have been notably lowered.

What, in general, is the national consumption of milk? It is not exactly the same in all provinces. Some regions have a more established dairy tradition and higher milk production, and consumption itself has traditionally been higher in some regions than in others. But what, in general, is the level of consumption in various parts of the country? For the year 1967, in Guane, Pinar del Río, for children under 6 years old, one litre daily – in all cases, the children in the age groups referred to receive one litre daily. In Artemisa, under 6 years old; Guanajay, under 6; Costa Norte, under 6; San Cristóbal, under 6 and 7 to 13. Children in these age groups, and also people over 65, received one litre of milk daily in 1967.

In metropolitan Havana, under 7, one litre, and, in addition, each family unit composed of five persons over 7 years of age received one litre daily. This distribution of one litre daily for every family unit of five persons over the age of 7 did not exist in practically any other part of the country.

In Matanzas the distribution was one litre for each child under 7 years old; in Jovellanos, under 7; in Colón, under 7; in Cárdenas, under 7; in Jagüey, under 7; and in Unión de Reyes, under 7.

In Las Villas Province the figures vary. In Santa Clara, from January to May, one litre, under 4; from May to December, one litre, under 6, and half a litre, 7 to 13. May to December is, of course, the rainy season. In Cienfuegos, from January to May, one litre, under 4; from May to December, under 6, and half a litre, 7 to 13. Thus in various provincial cities larger amounts of milk were distributed in the rainy season than in the dry season.

In Camagüey the distribution was similar, although almost all children from 7 to 13 received half a litre. This year those under 6 have this quantity. In Oriente the distribution was quite different; one litre in Santiago de Cuba, under 3; in Bayamo, under 7; in Guantanamo, under 4; in Palmo Soriano, under 4; in Manzanillo, under 5; in Holguín, under 2; in Mayari, under 2; in Banes, under 2; in Baracoa, under 2; and in Victoria de las Tunas, under 6. And this year, in almost all regions, children under 2 received one litre.

Last year's rainfall picture

In order not to cut the milk that the adult population of Havana was receiving, it would have been necessary to take it from infants under two years of age in many parts of the province of Oriente. Now for other factors. We have indicated the problems of the drop in national production and some drops in imports. Now what was last year's rainfall picture compared with that of the year before? There is one province, Pinar del Río, where the rainfall wasn't bad: 1,558 millimetres in 1966 and 1,349 in 1967. Havana: 1,651 in 1966 and 1,242 in 1967. A difference of about 400

Milk Consumption by Age and Region (1967)

	Ages	Litres Daily	Months
Guane	under 6	1	
Pinar del Río	under 6	1	
Artemisa	under 6	1	
Guanajay	under 6	1	
Costa Norte	under 6	1	
San Cristóbal	under 6	1	
	7–13	1	
	over 65	1	
Metropolitan Havana family unit of 5 persons	under 7	1	
	over 7	1	
Matanzas	under 7	1	
Jovellanos	under 7	1	
Colón	under 7	1	
Cárdenas	under 7	1	
Jagüey Grande	under 7	1	
Unión de Reyes	under 7	1	
Santa Clara	under 4	1	Jan.–May
	under 6	1	May–Dec.
	7–13	½	May–Dec.
Cienfuegos	under 4	1	Jan.–May
	under 6	1	May–Dec.
	7–13	½	May–Dec.
Santiago de Cuba	under 3	1	
Bayamo	under 7	1	
Guantanamo	under 4	1	
Palma Soriano	under 4	1	
Manzanillo	under 5	1	
Holguín	under 2	1	
Mayari	under 2	1	
Banes	under 2	1	
Baracoa	under 2	1	
Victoria de las Tunas	under 6	1	

millimetres. Matanzas: 1,702 in 1966 and 1,338 in 1967. However, rainfall was not bad in these three provinces, but it did start to rain very late; here in Havana Province, for instance, it hardly started to rain until June.

In Las Villas, 1,587 millimetres of rain fell in 1966; it was 1,042 in 1967. A difference of over 500 millimetres.

In Camagüey, rainfall was 1,468 millimetres in 1966; it was 960 millimetres in 1967.

In Oriente, 1,324 millimetres in 1966 and 837 millimetres in 1967.

Rainfall in Millimetres

	1966	1967
Pinar del Río	1,558	1,349
Havana	1,651	1,242
Matanzas	1,702	1,338
Las Villas	1,587	1,042
Camagüey	1,468	960
Oriente	1,324	837

These figures are from data on the sugar mills of the Sugar Ministry. We also have the much more extensive data of the Hydraulic Institute.

Even so, perhaps the total figures, although they reflect a considerable decrease in the rainfall in three provinces: Las Villas, Camagüey and Oriente, do not really reflect the extent of the drought, because it is not only the amount of rainfall that is important, but also when it falls and how it is spaced. We remember that in Las Villas and Camagüey at the beginning of June more than 10 inches fell in 24 hours, and, afterwards, more than two months passed with practically no rain. And we remember the province of Oriente in July, around the 26 July, and this year we have hardly let a day go by without looking at the rainfall picture and feeling genuinely disheartened to see that, in the province of Oriente, practically no rain fell in the spring or fall.

Thus, for example, to get an idea of the importance of rain, for the period from May to October, in the two driest years since the triumph of the Revolution previous to this year – that is, in 1962 and 1965 – from May to October 1962, a dry year, rainfall was 718 millimetres, and in 1965, another dry year, in the same months, it was 753 millimetres. However, this year – that is, 1967, the year that has just gone by – between May and October it rained 582 millimetres. In other words, in the decisive months of spring and autumn, precipitation was the lowest recorded in the province. It was really a dry year. We cannot blame the weather, just as we cannot exonerate the weather. We are merely commenting on reality.

I have read you the statistics on rain. Now we can add some other very interesting data : the prices for sugar in the areas of convertible foreign exchange, in the last few years.

In 1963, the price reached an average of 8·48 cents a pound. In 1964, the average price was 5·86 cents a pound. In 1965, 2·12 cents. In 1966, 1·86. And in 1967, 1·99. In 1968 it is still below 2 cents a pound. And it is well known that we must use convertible currency to purchase a part of the raw materials and essential products that we cannot acquire in the countries with which we

Price of Sugar	
	Cents per lb.
1963	8·48
1964	5·86
1965	2·12
1966	1·86
1967	1·99
1952	4·28
1953	3·52
1954	3·37
1955	3·35
1956	3·58
1957	5·27
1958	3·71
1959	3·08
1960	3·25
1961	2·91
1962	2·96

trade on a clearing basis. And sugar prices are the lowest they have been in the last 30 years. If we look at the prices between 1952 and 1961 we see they were 4·28, 3·52, 3·37, 3·35, 3·58, 5·27, 3·71, 3·08, 3·25, 2·91, 2·96, 8·48 and 5·86, then dropping to 2·12, 1·86, and 1·99.

Possibly few people have an idea of the tremendous effort, the hard work which has been put forth to keep the nation's economy on the go – despite those incredible prices – and not only that: considerable effort at development has been made. How many have thought for a moment or have pondered at all about these prices, about the consequences these prices would have had in any period of this country's history? It is not simply a matter of the reduction or the suspension of the distribution of milk for adults, but one of assuring each child up to the age of 7 his daily litre of milk, just as when the price of sugar – with which we obtain foreign exchange, with which we have imported considerable amounts of milk for reconstitution – was 8·48 cents a pound; as was done in 1965, as was done throughout 1966, and as was done in 1967, and we will maintain that litre of milk in 1968. How many, how many have asked themselves this question? How many have analysed it, how many have pondered over it?

Our population has been growing at a considerable rate

Of course, our population has been growing at a considerable rate; and, naturally, this country does not have food backlogs; it has been living from hand to mouth. Moreover, this country has had to make, year by year, important purchases of equipment and machinery for its development, and each year it has to faithfully meet these obligations. This country has been confronting that task with sugar prices that have stayed below two cents a pound in areas where we have to obtain an important part of our resources to pay for our imports.

Under such circumstances, one year of a bad drought such as this is enough.

And if many have not had the opportunity during the year,

perhaps, to think about this even once, those at the head of the economic organizations and those who head the Government have, day after day, hour after hour, been concerned about these questions and have been trying to find solutions to these problems.

In the past year enormous efforts have gone into the fertilization of sugar cane, from which we expect considerable returns. The country has also been making a considerable effort in the field of livestock development; those who are connected with that work, those who keep up to date on it, and those who occasionally hear a speech or read a newspaper and are interested in such things must know – and 'know perfectly well – all that has been done in that sector. And it can be said nowhere have there been more intense, serious, and promising efforts in that sector than the efforts being made in Cuba. Suffice it to say that since the triumph of the Revolution more than 10,000 pure-bred stud bulls have been imported; suffice it to say that, whereas at the triumph of the Revolution there was not one artificial insemination expert in this country, now we have more than 3,000.

The *latifundistas* did not leave us thousands of stud bulls, or thousands of technicians who knew anything about artificial insemination; the cattle they left were typical of an extensive type of cattle raising. The immense majority were zebu, which is not generally a milk producer, and when it does give milk it gives only a miserable litre, or litre and a half. And thousands, tens of thousands of men have been struggling during these years with these foul-tempered, angry animals; and the increases in milk production have been derived principally from zebu cows. For cows don't reproduce in twenty-four hours, nor do calves mature in another twenty-four hours, or begin to produce in another twenty-four.

And at this time our country has hundreds of thousands of calves and heifers that are the product of crossing the zebu cows with the dairy-type bulls, but we must wait, we must wait until they can begin to produce. And that process, to a certain extent, can be accelerated, as we have been doing till now, having these heifers inseminated at the earliest possible age.

Of course, time has passed since this work began, since we discovered what artificial insemination was and the need for artificial insemination, since we trained the first artificial insemination expert in this country. We later trained dozens more and began inseminating the first cows. We sent some veterinarians abroad, to Europe, to learn modern techniques. We set up laboratories and built artificial insemination centres and one by one imported more than 10,000 stud bulls. That has not been done in any other country the size of ours, or even in larger countries with many more resources; it's more than improbable that any of them have matched us. And I am sure in these years all the countries of Latin America together have not imported even half the number of stud bulls that Cuba has imported in these years.

But between the time that the country makes an investment of 100,000 dollars to acquire one of the best specimens we have ever had to begin the upgrading of our livestock of the future, and the time when the first offspring of that bull begins to produce milk in the best of cases, at least fifty months go by. And not fifty months, if we refer to the results that should come from the use of the offspring of that bull. When a stud is acquired for that high price, it is with the idea of using thousands of its offspring to upgrade the nation's livestock; but, in any case, the time that it takes is considerable.

Such a process cannot be hastened. It is a natural process that inevitably involves a waiting period, for the *latifundistas* did not make plans for us. The exploiters of this nation, the imperialists and their allies, were not concerned with creating conditions for this people to one day have a litre of milk, or more than a litre of milk, available not only for each child but for every person in the nation.

The Vietnamese are giving something more for us and for the world

Some elements, undoubtedly counter-revolutionary ... for such circumstances, such difficulties are seized upon by the enemy with an organized, directed campaign – directed from abroad. And among some of the sad absurdities going around was the rumour that we were sending milk to Vietnam. The Vietnamese have never asked us for milk, but, if the Vietnamese should ask for milk, our fitting response, our most basic duty, would be to send it to them! A part or half or, if necessary, all of it. Because the Vietnamese are giving something more for us and are giving something more for the world! [PROLONGED APPLAUSE] They are offering and shedding their blood for us, and they are shedding it for all the peoples of the world!

It seems to me that only the basest persons, who want to destroy that beautiful sentiment of solidarity developed by our people, that internationalist conscience, would be interested in spreading such malicious rumours, in the interest of the imperialists, of those who are causing the bloodshed of a nation by the ton. And there the case is not of 7- to 15-year-olds without milk or of adults without milk, but of children destroyed by bombs, children burned alive with napalm.

While we are working, while we here, with difficulties of varying degrees, confront problems of development, the civilian population and the combatants in North and South Vietnam, those heroic people, see their work of many years destroyed, see tens of thousands of their best sons and daughters die on the battlefield.

And the day we haven't sufficient honour, dignity and self-respect to react and fight, confront and crush the scoundrels who sow such discord, that day there won't be any point in calling ourselves revolutionaries! [APPLAUSE]

Who would call himself a revolutionary, and what would the word 'revolutionary' mean, if the concept of being a revolutionary could be whittled down so miserably?

And such elements exist. Propaganda, intended to weaken us, is made and directed by the imperialist enemy. Because the efforts like those our country is today making, tremendous efforts to secure today's bread and above all tomorrow's bread, have been made by no one else, unless we consider the efforts that the imperialists have made to hinder us, place difficulties in our path and create all types of problems in order to crush this Revolution by hunger. The imperialists' hopes lie in these weak, soft, cowardly elements. Their allies, their conscious or unconscious allies. That is their hope.

Of course, there are those who for quite a while now have been anxiously awaiting the opportunity to go there to receive miserable crumbs of bread from the hands of those imperialist murderers who blockade our country – that disgraceful bread which they receive for renouncing their homeland; and they renounce their country, not at a time of national infamy, but in the most glorious hour of her history. [APPLAUSE] It is logical for the imperialists to try to cover up and hide the truth of how this country has carried out a tenacious policy. They have been relentless, they have used all their political and economic influence to hinder the development of this country to such a degree that, except for Vietnam and Korea, no country has been more isolated in its trade relations with the rest of the world, as a result of imperialist manoeuvring, than has Cuba.

And often it is not just the availability of foreign exchange; sometimes we have the foreign currency and there is no market where we can buy, or we must buy at very high prices. The imperialists have done all within their own power to create difficulties, with one strategy in mind: to defeat this people by hunger; with one hope: that placed in the softies, the weaklings, the cowards, and the traitors.

It is interesting to see, for example, how it is right here in the capital where these attitudes reach their greatest intensity – that region of the country that has historically, and even after the Revolution, enjoyed a higher standard of living. Even now, after nine years of Revolution with a policy of attending to the needs of the interior of the nation, even today Havana Province, with 27 per cent of the country's population, accounts for 38 per cent of the wages, 35 per cent of the consumer goods and 49 per cent of the commercial services.

And in 1967 the total amount of wages paid out to the population of Havana Province amounted to 1,094 million pesos. Moreover, other sources of income in Havana, added to wages, bring the total up to 1,433·8 million in income for the province of Havana.

Now, the expenditures. In consumer goods 847·7 million pesos were spent by the population; in hotel and restaurant services, 254·5 million; and in other fields, 321 million. Not only were there high incomes, but expenditures in this province were similarly high.

And in the medical services, despite the hospitals built in the interior, magnificent hospitals, the capital enjoys the benefits of many things that the countryside still does not have. You can, at times, walk dozens of kilometres and not find a road – or could not find a road, for now it is becoming possible to find roads, and plenty of them. But you don't find electric lights, and there are those who have never seen them and don't know exactly what they are, unless they've been to a city; and this is true of many other things ... sports facilities ... and, in many cases, houses. There is not enough housing, but many families have had the opportunity to have a good home for a tiny amount of money – in fact, by now, gratis for the vast majority. And so on for sports facilities and sports and cultural events. In short, the population of the capital enjoys a much better situation than the rest of the country; and it must be said that, without any doubt, the rest of the country has been putting forth much greater efforts during these years.

We recall the battalions of workers and students mobilized from Havana

Naturally, this is not to blame the population of Havana, because the population of Havana is joining in work *en masse* and with incredible enthusiasm. The people of Havana are fundamentally above the currents that still remain in people whose ideology is against the Revolution ... We recall the battalions of workers and students from Havana that were mobilized at each difficult moment by the tens of thousands, fighting bandits in the Escambray, or marching forward to engage the mercenaries who invaded our country at Girón; mobilized at each difficult moment, such as the October Crisis; mobilized on other occasions. We also recall the tens of thousands of workers who cut cane for entire months in isolated and sparsely populated regions of the province of Camagüey: and we recall that militant, revolutionary section, evidently in the majority, from the people of Havana.

But it is necessary to state this in order for revolutionaries to be informed, in order for revolutionaries to know what to stand on, in order for revolutionaries to be knowledgeable, to raise their guard, to keep from becoming confused, to refuse to remain silent when some miserable provocateur speaks up.

Because of such things, lines formed where they sell eggs, in front of poultry stores, and people bought up 20 or 30 pesos worth of eggs. We nearly had to ration them. Because if people tried to buy up all the available eggs in a few days, we would have had to ration them. And of course those who react that way are the ones who create even more difficulties in food supplies.

How have production and purchases of eggs by state procurement agencies increased? In 1962, 174 million; 1963, 190 million; 1964, 297 million; 1965, 911 million; 1966, 1,011 million; 1967, 1,173 million; 1968, approximately 1,200 million. Without doubt, there are more laying hens now than ever before. It is also true that the weather is not the most propitious now. This year there were late cold snaps; as you know, the weather has been strange this year. But production will at least equal that of last year. And, of course, if the laying hens don't go on strike ... [LAUGHTER] We're pretty sure if they won't object to fulfilling the plans. And if a hen says, 'I'm not going to lay this egg, because I know a counter-revolutionary is going to eat it,' this hen may be quite right. [LAUGHTER] Because there are many of those waiting for 'their time' who eat more eggs than anyone else while they're waiting for their flight out of Cuba.

Production and Procurement of Eggs

Year	Units
1962	174,000,000
1963	190,000,000
1964	297,000,000
1965	911,000,000
1966	1,011,000,000
1967	1,173,000,000
1968	1,200,000,000 (Estimated)

Naturally no one can know to what level consumption will climb here. Our plan was for 60 million eggs a month and now production is 100 million, and still these problems crop up.

Reserves are accumulated during one period of the year, for the hens also have their 'season', laying more in some periods than in others.

And this year, without doubt, the weather conditions were adverse. The rains were late in the west, considerably affecting the production of ground provisions in Oriente, Camagüey, and Las Villas. Crops were affected during the spring and autumn, practically the whole year. Milk and even bean production were affected . . .

This year's situation is not at all bountiful, but we will have more or less the same amount of cooking fat as last year; this is also true of rice. Not during this year, but by the end of the year, we will begin to reap the fruits of the effort that is being made – a considerable effort – in upping rice production. Beef production will be more or less the same; we will have 10,000 tons of beans less this year – that means 82,400 instead of 93,100 – and the same holds true : we can only find a solution by using foreign exchange, which is needed for more important things; above all, to meet the nation's obligations. We will have 27,000 tons more of wheat flour than last year. We will have 6,000 tons more of fish and seafood than last year. It is not a bountiful situation, as we must consider the population increase. But we expect that the weather will not be as poor this year.

It still has not rained in the provinces of Las Villas, Camagüey, and Oriente. Perhaps you have read this in the newspaper, but one must be careful, because the rain maps come in three colours – the maps from the Meteorological Institute – red when it rains a lot, blue for moderate rain and green for little rain. But the newspapers do not carry coloured maps, and you can see a shaded area where three millimetres fell and believe that a lot of rain fell. Unfortunately, the newspapers are going to have to invent some symbols, as they can't use colours, symbols to indicate when rainfall is heavy and when it is light, so that the people . . . We feel that everyone should know what the situation concerning the rain is so that he can be better informed about those problems. And still no rain.

However, there are frequent rainfalls in the west at this time; the weather is good, and we believe that the general conditions are more humid. We have hopes that this year's rainfall will be better.

These droughts have given rise to considerable speculation about the sugar crop. It is certain that the drought has affected the size of the sugar crop. In Oriente Province the drought has caused a drop that is the equivalent of practically a million tons of sugar. Had this been a normal year, national production would have hit approximately 8 million tons for this year's crop. But that does not mean that this is a disastrous sugar harvest. We have already produced 2,476,306 tons, having milled 1,916.5 million *arrobas*. [1 *arroba* equals 25 lb.] We still have 2,217 million yet to grind. And so, despite a bad drought, we have every certainty of surpassing 5.5 million tons of sugar.

We still have more than half the cane to grind, and this is precisely the moment when the sugar yields are highest.

But how much longer will the country have to depend on whether or not it rains? Can we enjoy a secure economy, assured production, so long as such conditions have not been overcome?

In what direction should we head the nation's efforts at this time? Our greatest efforts are being directed towards the construction of water conservation projects. It is more evident each day, more beyond doubt, that if we hope for assured agricultural production the first contingency we must guard against is drought.

A perennial crop, such as sugar cane, can be reduced thirty or forty per cent by drought. An annual crop will be killed off. You can plant something like corn or beans, and you'll lose the crop. You can plant eddoes[1] out of season – in June – and they won't produce; if you don't plant them in March, or April at the latest, you don't get an eddoe crop; and if you plant them and it doesn't rain, the eddoes won't grow either.

The areas of irrigated land in Cuba were insignificant in number. Unrealistic optimists and the 'coffee klatsch geniuses' think that constructing dams is like flying kites. But to construct a dam ...! Ask Faustino Pérez, Minister of the Hydraulic Institute; ask those who have worked in the Hydraulic Institute how many things are needed for a medium-sized dam.

---

1. Tropical plant with an edible root similar to the taro of Polynesia.

From establishing the place where the reservoir will be, to making the necessary geological studies, studying the soil, drawing up the blueprints ... If it were not for the work of several years, for the intensive work and studies, we would not at this moment be able to work on these water conservation projects with such momentum, and the equipment projects with such momentum, and the equipment would now be standing idle. However, this year, earth-moving equipment, meaning the capacity to move an additional 60 million cubic metres of earth a year, is being put to work on these projects. An intense, accelerated and large-scale programme is now being pushed ahead with the maximum use of available resources.

A sugar harvest of 10 million tons –
more than an economic goal

And what do we propose? We propose, in the first place, to make sure of the sugar cane crop. The question of a sugar harvest of 10 million tons has become something more than an economic goal; it is something that has been converted into a point of honour for this Revolution; it has become a yardstick by which to judge the capability of the Revolution. Our enemies have bet that we won't reach it; the microfractionists took glee in and predicted the failure of the Revolution – that is, the failure of the revolutionary line within the Revolution – with the idea that we would not reach the 10-million-ton mark, and would then have to draw in our horns, be more calm, more docile, more submissive – in short, cease being revolutionaries. And of course revolutionaries will cease to be, before ceasing to be revolutionaries! [APPLAUSE]

In other words, we understand how the 10-million-ton goal has become a yardstick by which to judge the Revolution; and, if a yardstick is put up to the Revolution, there is no doubt about the Revolution's meeting the mark.

We have to prepare ourselves, even to produce such a sugar-cane crop, even in a year as poor as this, as bad as this. At this moment the country is making considerable efforts in increasing the area of new planted cane. We will surpass the figure of 357,000 more hectares planted to sugar cane this year, and we hope to plant 286,000 additional hectares of irrigated land to cane within the next eighteen months, as well as to drain considerable tracts of land in cane-producing areas.

And this, naturally, does not mean giving up our other goals. This year, throughout the length and breadth of the country, a colossal effort is being made along various lines – not just cane, but sugar cane is the principal one – and the amount of equipment and number of men – and above all the mettle of these men – permit us to say that we are sure of success.

Those who read, those who are informed, must know that thousands of men have been working intensively for months, day and night, throughout the island. Those who leave the main highways, even to visit some friend or relative, can see that the farm equipment in this country does not stop day or night; and Havana workers can very often see the tractor lights as they work late into the night and even into the early morning hours. There seem to be many tractors working in the Green Belt, but the ratio with respect to the country as a whole is 1 to 170 or 180.

A news bulletin entitled *Noti-Cordón* [*Green Belt News*] is now being published. It is of such interest that it will be followed by another one called *Más Allá del Cordón* [*Beyond the Green Belt*]. To tell the truth, *Noti-Cordón* is the first paper I read when I get up in the morning. We must also inform our people as to what is going on beyond the Green Belt, because some people ask whether or not we are going to plant eddoes or plantains in some of the clay soil in the area. As I remember, we discussed this problem on the occasion of the inauguration of the town called Valle Grande. At that time we gave a comprehensive explanation of what was being done and why, what these projects consisted of and what was being done in other parts of the country. Some ask, 'Why is so much coffee being planted?' If all this coffee had been planted over a twenty-year period, nobody would have thought of it as an excessive amount. But if it's done in one year it does seem that way. That is because never before was planting done or a project carried out as quickly as the Havana Green Belt Plan is being carried out, with the mass participation and enthusiastic co-operation of the capital's workers.

But suffice it to say that Oriente Province, where approximately one million hundredweight of coffee is grown, has already produced this year – as a result of the great effort being put forth and despite unfavourable weather conditions – approximately 900,000 hundredweight of coffee. We should point out that these 900,000 hundredweight of coffee are produced on small farms scattered over an area of 20,000 square kilometres, while here the Havana Green Belt area will produce – as a secondary crop, planted between rows of citrus fruit trees – practically as much coffee as Oriente Province had been producing, and this is an area of only 200 square kilometres.

We estimate that the number of vehicles needed to haul the coffee from the Green Belt will be approximately 100 times less than that needed to bring in the present crop from Oriente Province, coming from farms which are dispersed all over the mountains, not counting the problems involved in transporting the necessary fertilizer, the labour force, and the product itself. The problem consists not only of harvesting the coffee over an area of 20,000 square kilometres but also of shipping it another thousand miles to be consumed here in the capital.

Now the capital will, at least, plant and produce its own coffee, and this promises to be in the near future. It should even be able to export a small amount of coffee . . .

The Oriente coffee farms will not be neglected by any means. Coffee will continue to be picked in and exported from Oriente Province. We do not think that we will have an excess of coffee, but, if we do, so much the better; if we could only begin to have problems of too much rather than too little! We are trying to rationalize our efforts, taking into consideration a series of factors such as requirements, consumption, available markets, trade possibilities, and economic plans.

A microfractional jabberer was saying, 'Look how they're planting there, and they're not planting citrus fruit trees, they're going to plant mangoes.' It's one of the many cases of malintentioned ignoramuses; he probably never read a page on citrus fruit production in his life and doesn't know where the devil to plant a citrus fruit tree so that it won't be killed by blight, so that the tree won't rot. And the fact is that there are 5,360 hectares set aside specifically for citrus fruit trees in the Havana Green Belt on red clay, magnificent land.

And all that effort makes it possible to plan, organize, and rationalize agriculture well throughout the country. The country is making a really great effort right now, and not on just one front but on a number of fronts; and not only in the water conservation projects but also in road and highway construction.

The figures on the area of land that is going to be worked for the first time this year are unparalleled in the history of this country and in the history of the Revolution itself. It will take a little time, but everything does, and we must know how to wait.

At a time when many of us only carried the idea of revolution in our heads, we were locked up, isolated in prison cells, but it never occurred to us to think that it was impossible to bring the Revolution about. Some have had more experience than others with adversity and difficulty. Those who have not learned from such experience, logically, become disheartened; others have learned – and it is of primary importance that our people and all revolutionaries learn – that nothing can subdue or deter the will of a people.

We have spoken about those factors which originally gave rise to the analysis of these problems. There's still some material left, but don't be alarmed ...

Recently, while going through some papers, someone found a study – on the matters we are talking about – made by none other than the Catholic University Association in 1956. I believe that *Bohemia* magazine is planning to do an article based on this material. If you have a little patience, I'm going to read you some of the things – some of you will not remember them, because you are too young, but perhaps others will recall the things referred to. There is a survey that states:

The inquiry had three principal aims: to make, for the first time in Cuba, a detailed, accurate, statistical study of the living conditions of agricultural workers, which may serve as a firm base for analysing economic and social problems and finding solutions to them; to give our members in the cities an opportunity to become aware of the reality of our countryside and learn its difficulties. And, last but not least, to be able to affirm, with certain knowledge and proof ready at hand, that the Cuban peasants find themselves in the no-man's-land between abandon and helplessness, thanks to national egoism, and that our nation cannot aspire to true progress as long as it does not give proper attention to our countryside.

The city of Havana is enjoying an epoch of extraordinary prosperity, while the countryside, and especially the agricultural workers, must live under almost unbelievable conditions of stagnation, misery, and hopelessness.

At the end of our meetings held during the last few months, Dr José Ignacio Lasaga made a statement that we shall never forget: 'In all my trips through Europe, America, and Africa, I have seldom encountered peasants who lived under more miserable conditions than the Cuban agricultural worker.'

The report states that 350 thousand agricultural workers, with 2·1 million dependents, had a total annual income of 190 million pesos. 'That is, in spite of constituting 34 per cent of the population, they have only 10 per cent of the national income.'

The survey states that everyone should feel a sense of guilt about all this, etc.; that Cuba is still young as a Republic; that as 'a small nation, it is subject to the economic orientations of the great powers'. Read 'imperialism' – very delicately put so as not to antagonize the Yankees.

Our beloved homeland continues to suffer greatly from the evils of absentee landlordism, under which wealth is produced in the countryside but enjoyed in Havana.

The Cuban agricultural worker, betrayed by the government and forgotten by the leaders of all the national sectors, remains amazingly honest, moral, and human, hoping in sadness but with dignity that those who are better prepared and more endowed will come to open the way for him and teach him how to go forward towards development and progress. God willing, this study of the economic situation of the Cuban agricultural worker will serve as a light to show the present injustices, as information for a careful analysis of their causes, and as a basis for their just and prompt rectification.

It seems that God was willing!

They state that they made a well-organized, methodical investigation of the peasant's diet and how he lived. Of course, I'm not going to read the whole thing, but ... Just a minute, while I look for ... 'Only 4 per cent of those interviewed mentioned meat as a regular part of their diet. Fish is reported by less than 1 per cent; 2·12 per cent of the agricultural workers eat eggs, and only 11·22 per cent drink milk. Bread, the universal food par excellence, symbol of human food, is only consumed by 3·36 per cent of our agricultural working population.'

Here you have the levels of consumption of two and a half million people, those who planted, cut, cleaned, and sustained our sugar cane.

'The index of tubercular infection.' With reference to the index of tubercular infection: 'Presumably 14 per cent of the peasants interviewed are suffering or have suffered from tuberculosis.' Thirteen per cent had suffered from typhoid fever. Thirty-six per cent had parasites – or, rather, 36 per cent were aware that they had parasites.

They continue with an explanation of the problem of medical attention.

The most glaring fact is the following: 80·76 per cent declared that they had received medical attention only from 'paid' doctors – that is, private physicians who charged for their services. Only 8 per cent had received free medical attention from the State, and this is a very significant fact. We should keep in mind, however, that we are talking of the man who works on the land in the interior of the country.

The employer or union provides medical attention for 4 per cent of the agricultural workers, and an equal proportion, 4 per cent, receives the professional help of private dispensaries.

Medicines. In order to study this chapter, each investigator first inquired if there were any medicines in the house at that moment and then asked that those on hand be shown to him. In each case, the kind of medicament was noted and, in the case of standard pharmaceutical products, the laboratory that had prepared it. The most important information thus obtained was the following: medicines were on hand in 70·49 per cent of the houses at the time of the interviews; of these 46·67 were of a general formula type – what we commonly call prescription medicines – and the rest consisted of products commonly known as patent medicines that are prepared in laboratories and distributed, already packaged, to pharmacies.

Of these patent medicines, 74·77 per cent come from reputable laboratories – that is, from accredited firms.

The other 25 per cent came from disreputable sources commonly known in Cuba as 'goat labs'. These laboratories operate in the following way: they prepare a series of almost completely useless products that cost very little to produce and are sold through unethical doctors who agree to prescribe the products in exchange for half the profit. As the product is sold at a high price, such illicit transactions constitute an important source of income for the doctors, to such an extent that frequent instances exist – especially in the interior of the Republic – of doctors who charge nothing at all for consultations, living exclusively from the profits they receive from their arrangements with the 'goat labs'.

One fourth of the medicines recommended to peasants by their doctors are quack medicines, and useless.

This report does not come from a 'red' or subversive organization, but from an organization that decided to make an investigation and recorded incredible conditions under which a great part of our people lived.

There are still many people among the masses who are unaware of one of the most worrisome and serious of contemporary problems: the problem of underdevelopment – this word that is heard so often. What does underdevelopment consist of? What is the significance of the underdeveloped world? How can this be explained clearly and precisely?

The world is divided into developed countries and countries termed 'underdeveloped'. The euphemism of calling them 'developing' countries is also used; in the argot of international organizations they are called developing countries. And we would like to call attention to some data that may help our masses to situate the problem of Cuba within the context of the present world situation ...

Many of the developed countries embarked on their development more than a hundred years ago. They developed slowly and, in many cases, with the aid of the resources of their colonies, which were plundered mercilessly, and with resources amassed from the sweat of their masses, who were exploited to an incredible degree. Written testimony exists; there are the chapters written by Marx and Engels concerning the plight of the working class in England; workers who laboured fifteen or sixteen hours a day, children under ten years of age who worked full time under the worst material conditions. In other words, the resources which enabled those countries to accumulate investment capital and on which they based their development were extracted from the workers.

Industry was mainly developed in Europe, the United States, and Canada, in such a way that nowadays these countries of developed economies have an extraordinary head start in relation to the underdeveloped world, which they exploited yesterday and which they exploit today in many ways, either directly, via new institutions, or indirectly.

But let's take a look at the figures on the gross product of the developed countries, what their production was in 1960 and what it is expected to be in 1975. The United States, with a population of 180 million inhabitants had a gross national product of 446,100 million dollars – we'll say pesos. This was a gross national product of the US economy in 1960, and it should reach $865,400 million for a population of 235 million in 1975. Western Europe had a gross product of $394,659 million in 1960 for a population of 353 million; it is estimated that this figure will reach $750,748 million in 1974 for a population of 402 million inhabitants. Japan, in 1960, had a gross national product of $55,604 million for a population of 93 million inhabitants, and it is estimated that this figure

Gross National Products of Developed Countries

	1960 (in pesos and inhabitants)	1975 (in pesos and inhabitants)
USA	446,100 million (180 million in- habitants)	865,400 million (235 million in- habitants)
Western European countries	394,659 million (353 million)	750,748 million (402 million)
Japan	55,604 million (93 million)	138,350 million (106 million)
Canada	31,530 million (17 million)	63,527 million (23 million)

will rise to $138,350 million for a population of 106 million inhabitants in 1975. Canada had a gross national product of $31,530 million for a population of 17 million; it is estimated that this figure will rise to $63,527 million for a population of 23 million in 1975.

These are the major developed capitalist countries of the world. We should also include the Republic of South Africa and Australia.

So that all these countries – the United States, the Western European countries, Japan, and Canada – had a total gross national product of 927,893 million pesos in 1960. It is estimated that this figure will rise to 1,818,025 million pesos in 1975. That is almost 2 billion – the Spanish billion, at least in my time, was a million millions; I believe the US billion is a thousand millions; here I'm talking about Spanish billions.

So. What was Latin America's gross product in 1960? It was 61,750 million pesos for a population of 204 million inhabitants. That is, $61,750 million in all of Latin America as opposed to $446,100 million in the United States. According to optimistic estimates, which, it appears, will not be borne out, in 1975 Latin America will have a gross product of $117,800 million for a population of 299 million inhabitants.

Africa: a gross product in 1960 of $21,720 million for a population of 240 million. For 1975, an estimated gross product of $40,500 million for a population of 338 million.

The Middle East: a gross product in 1960 of $7,300 million for a population of 51 million inhabitants. For 1975, an estimated gross product of $13,700 million for 76 million inhabitants.

Asia, excluding China, a gross product in 1960 of $68,750 million for a population of 797 million. For 1975, an estimated gross product of $129,300 million for a population of 1,140 million.

In 1960 all of the countries of the underdeveloped world together produced a total of $159,520 million for a population of 1,294 million. That is, all the underdeveloped world together produced a third of what the United States produced and less than half of what Western Europe produced. And it is estimated that this will reach $301,000 million in 1975. That is, in 1975 the entire underdeveloped world's gross product will be very much lower than the US gross product for 1960.

Gross Product of the Third World

	1960	1975
Latin America	61,750 million	17,800 million
	(204 million)	(299 million)
Africa	21,720 million	40,500 million
	(240 million)	(338 million)
The Middle East	7,300 million	13,700 million
	(51 million)	(76 million)
Asia (excluding China)	68,750 million	129,300 million
	(797 million)	(1,140 million)

The entire underdeveloped world, now with 1,294 million inhabitants, will reach 1,853 million by 1975. So that today the developed world produces, or rather produced in 1960, twelve times as much per capita as the underdeveloped world, and in 1975 this per capita production will be fourteen times as great.

While the developed world will increase its production by almost a billion, its population will only increase by some 122 million. That is, 122 million new inhabitants, but $890 thousand million increase in production. Meanwhile, the underdeveloped countries' population will increase by some 559 million, but their total production will increase by only $142 thousand million.

So that from 1960 to 1975, in developed countries, production will increase by $7,300 a year for every additional inhabitant, while in the underdeveloped world the increase for each new inhabitant will be just $250 a year. That is, for each new birth in developed countries production will increase 29 times as much as it will increase for each new birth in the underdeveloped world.

Translated into available income, this means the following: the per capita available income in the USA in 1960 was $1,762; in 1975 it will be $2,564, an increase of $802.

Canada, 1960, $1,296; in 1975, $1,981, an increase of $685. France, 1960, $1,078; in 1975, $1,838, an increase of $760. Britain, 1960, $1,087; in 1975, $1,620, an increase of $533. Italy, 1960, $960; in 1975, $1,733, an increase of $773. Japan, 1960, $393; in 1975, $860, an increase of $467.

Per Capita Incomes

	1960	1975	Increment
USA	1,762	2,564	802
Canada	1,296	1,981	685
France	1,078	1,838	760
England	1,087	1,620	533
Italy	960	1,733	773
Japan	393	860	467

To take the underdeveloped countries, as a whole, in 1960. (This does not mean that they all have the same available yearly income. This is only an average; you add the available income in this, that, and the other country and you divide it by the total amount.) As a whole, the underdeveloped world's available per capita income in 1960 ranged from $70 to $85, while in 1975 it will range from $90 to $110.

Therefore, the available per capita income will increase as follows: USA, by $802; Canada, by $685; France, by $760; Britain, by $533; Italy, by $773; and Japan, by $467; the underdeveloped countries will increase their available income by approximately $20 to $30. So that if in 1960 the average increase or rather, the per capita available income in the USA, for example, was 22 times as much as that of the underdeveloped countries, in 1975 it will be 25 times as much.

Prices paid for the products of the underdeveloped world are ever lower, while the articles manufactured in the developed world are sold at ever higher prices

The imbalance – that is, the deficit in the balance of payments, between the underdeveloped nations and the developed capitalist countries in world trade – was $4,640 million in 1960, and it will come to $10,500 million in 1970 and $18,900 million in 1975.

To this incredible situation of poverty, we must add the syphoning-off of profits from investments. That is, the amount syphoned off by consortiums and monopolies must first be subtracted from the profits that would have accrued to the underdeveloped countries. And there's still an even more subtle – although quite evident – method of exploitation: the fact that the developed world imposes its own conditions upon the underdeveloped world: the prices paid for the products of the underdeveloped world are ever lower, while the articles manufactured in the developed world are sold at ever higher prices. It is estimated that tea, for example, will drop some 6 per cent in price by 1975; wool, 6 per cent; cotton, 6 per cent; cacao, 9 per cent; skins and hides, 9 per cent; jute fibre, 14 per cent; rubber, 32 per cent.

This is the situation. Does it have any solution? Is there a way out? How was this situation created? Can any underdeveloped country today repeat the history of those countries when they began their industrialization? If not, why not? What factors constitute the major obstacles? One factor is population increase.

Let's see just how the population of the world is increasing. In 1967 the world's population increased by 70 million persons. It will reach a total of 3,500 million in 1968. In 1968 there will be 118 million births and 49 million deaths.

At this rate of population increase, by the year 2000 the world's population will reach 7,000 million. And for many of you, especially the students, the year 2000 is not so far off.

Earlier FAO[2] estimates had set the figure at 6,000 million, but at the present rate of increase the world's population will reach 7,000 million by the end of this century.

And what is the situation in Latin America? Let us look at what the United States Demographic Office states in information received on 10 March.

The Demographic Office today predicted that within 32 years the population of Latin America will increase by 157 per cent, the highest rate of increase in the world.

The present population of this region, some 268 million, will increase to 690 million by the end of the century.

In contrast, the US agency states that the population of North America and the Soviet Union will increase by 42 per cent and that of Europe by just 25 per cent.

That is, Europe – whose population of 353 million produced some $400,000 million in 1960 – will increase its population by 25

---

2. United Nations Food and Agricultural Organization.

per cent in 32 years. In contrast, Latin America, whose population of 204 million produced a total of $61,750 million in 1960 – that is, less than one sixth as much as Europe – will have a population of 690 million in 32 years.

The US Demographic Office warns that, with the exception of Argentina, Chile and Uruguay, Latin America is in only a slightly better position than Africa, the region with the highest infant mortality and illiteracy rates and the lowest per capita income and life expectancy in the world.

The most rapidly increasing rates of population growth in the world are those of El Salvador, 3·7 per cent; the Dominican Republic, 3·6 per cent; and Venezuela, 3·6 per cent.

At the same time, this agency observes that the area from Mexico to Panama is the part of the world with the highest rate of population growth, where the population will double in 20 years if the present rate of growth continues.

The report goes on: 'Almost invariably, the countries having the greatest population increases are those in which the great number of cases of needy and unprotected children creates serious social and economic problems.'

The report goes on to say that a 'shocking aspect' of the present demographic situation is the growing gap between the rates of food production and human reproduction.

'Every day there are more than 190,000 new mouths to feed,' the research group asserts. 'Yet, of the thousand million additional calories needed to provide this human mass with even a starvation diet, less than one third is being produced.'

This is affirmed by the Demographic Office of an imperialist country, the most imperialist of all imperialists.

And constantly, almost daily, news dispatches come in concerning this tremendous problem of the increase in world population with which the increase in food production does not keep pace.

New Delhi, India, March 12, *Reuters*: The mass sterilization drive which has been put into effect to date in India will prevent the birth of 10 million children in the next ten years, it was stated today in Parliament.

The Minister of Family Planning, Sripati Chandrasehar, told the

Council of States (Upper Chamber) that a total of 3,500,000 persons have been subjected to sterilization operations to date.

Surgical operations are voluntary in India, whose population of 515 million is increasing, according to recent official statistics, by 13 million every year.

In November, following a virtual storm of questions brought up in Parliament, a plan for the compulsory sterilization of parents who already have three children was thrown out.

Chandrasehar also said today that the Indian Government plans to introduce legislation this year which will raise the legal age for marriage from 15 to 18.

Perhaps one of our 'rumourmongers' read this dispatch and got his wires crossed.[3]

But, in reality, this is something that will require ever greater attention, since it truly constitutes one of the most serious problems of today's world. And let us see how this is related to the problems of development.

You all can see what the imperialists propose: formulas for birth control, including sterilization and practically forced sterilization. In other words, their solution for this situation is sterilization of the human race.

Not long ago, the US Secretary of State declared in alarm that, if science and technology fail to find a solution to this problem, the world will find itself exposed to a thermonuclear explosion. These people are so frightened by these unsolved realities that they are beginning to see thermonuclear bombs exploding everywhere. And presumably this other bomb that is now in the process of gestation is indeed going to continue to develop, and it cannot be subjected to agreements or controls of any kind. Now, then, how and why does this phenomenon –together with other factors – have such a tremendous influence on the development of the underdeveloped world?

The countries that began the Industrial Revolution in the last century were – among others – England, France, Belgium, Germany and Italy.

What was the rate of population growth in England when that

---

3. A humorous reference to the rumours in Havana that the Revolutionary government planned laws to discourage marriage.

country began its industrial development. It was 0·6 per cent a year. At that time, various plagues, illnesses and epidemics still provided a kind of natural balance. Plagues appeared and wiped out large parts of the population. Modern developments, modern-type medicines which have practically eradicated many of those epidemics, were then nonexistent.

So, the rate of population growth in England was 0·6 per cent; in France, 0·4 per cent; in Belgium, 0·7 per cent; in Germany, 0·8 per cent; and in Italy, 0·8 per cent.

With a 0·7 per cent increase the population could grow 40 per cent in 50 years. That is, on the basis of a 0·7 per cent growth, the population could increase 40 per cent over 50 years.

During the first 60 to 100 years of their development these countries achieved only a one per cent increase in gross product per inhabitant per year. That is, when they had a four times greater available income, per capita, than that of a person in an underdeveloped country today. In other words, once they had reached a level four times higher than that of any under-developed country today, they raised, or a rise occurred – since this was not the product of specific planning but rather what resulted from the prevailing reality – of 12 per cent in the amount of gross product invested in furthering their economic development.

Now that is the story of how development began, what the population increase was, what per cent of the gross product they invested, what percentage of growth they got and how much they grew in a period of 60 to 100 years.

If on the other hand a country's population grows at a rate of 2·2 per cent, in 50 years, it will be tripled. So whereas the developed countries' population in the beginning of their development increased by 40 per cent in 50 years – or could have increased by 40 per cent – the countries that are now under-developed, any underdeveloped country that increases its population by 2·2 per cent, will triple its entire population in 50 years and will need to invest no less than 12 per cent of the gross product to compensate for the population increase.

This means that, while the countries that we were talking about compensated for the population growth by investing six per cent and increased production by one per cent annually, an under-developed country with a 2·2 per cent population growth at present needs to invest double that, just to compensate for the population increase, without augmenting its annual per capita production.

If, because of that enormous population growth, such a country wants to increase its gross product per inhabitant by one per cent annually, it must invest no less than 16 per cent of its gross product. Thus, a country with a 2·2 per cent rate of growth, investing 16 per cent of its gross product, will compensate for the population increase, and its production will grow by one per cent annually. Thus, in 80 years, it would only double its income, and that income is today 10 times less per capita than Europe's and 20 times less than that of the United States.

That means that a country whose population grows by 2·2 per cent, by investing 16 per cent of its gross product, will increase its annual production by one per cent and in 80 years will double its present income, which is one twentieth of the per capita income in the United States.

In order to increase the per capita gross product by 2 per cent, a country whose population grows by 2·2 per cent should invest 20 per cent of its national gross product.

None of those developed countries reached an investment of 20 per cent until its income was already five or six times as high as the present income of the underdeveloped world.

Now, then, in the case of Latin America, as we see it, the population growth rate is not 2·2 per cent. So where does that 2·2 per cent come from? It was taken by the United Nations as an average population increase in the underdeveloped world. But it does not reflect the real situation; the growth is greater than that.

Thus, Latin America, with a 3·2 per cent population growth rate, would need to invest 25 per cent of its national gross product in order to achieve a 2 per cent annual per capita increase in its gross product. It would need to invest 25 per cent of its national gross product, which it doesn't invest, nor can it invest, nor under the present political conditions will it ever be able to invest.

Even with an incomparably higher per capita income, no currently developed country ever invested such amounts.

Now let's look at another problem related to this population increase. Don't get scared : we're not promoting family planning or birth control. Those are the measures that the imperialists are proposing for the underdeveloped world. The only measures that we believe will solve the problem are different. In countries with a 2·2 per cent population growth and a low average life expectancy – that is, where there is a high birthrate and the people die younger – more than 30 per cent of the population is under 10 years of age and cannot participate in production. That is, another factor related to this enormous annual increase is that more than 30 per cent of the population is under 10 years of age, while in the developed countries the percentage of children under 10 years of age fluctuates between 15 and 18 per cent of the population. This means that the rich countries, that have more, much more income available, have much less population under 10 years of age – about half of the same population category as the poor country with a very low per capita income. The percentage of the population under 10 years of age in an underdeveloped country is double that of a developed country.

In the developed country per capita food production increases nearly 2 per cent a year, the slow increase of their population notwithstanding; with all their technology, the developed countries achieve an increase of 2 per cent, more or less.

In Latin America as a whole – when I say as a whole I mean the average, because some have more, others less – with a population growth of over 3 per cent, the per capita food production in 1961 was 2 per cent lower than what it had been prior to the Second World War.

The United Nations Yearbook for 1967 states : 'Both in Africa and in Latin America, where there has not been any increase in food production since 1965, food production decreased in 1966. This loss of level cannot be easily made up, because it would require an increase of 7 per cent in 1967 in order to equal the 1964 level per person.'

In this desperate race against time, a year when the population increases 3 per cent, when there is a production stagnation, or a decrease, the effort needed to reach the previous level is almost impossible to make. That is, this conduces to a phenomenon of progressively decreasing per capita food production. The problems of the development of food production are very serious, very serious. Above all, when much of the best land nearest to the cities is already used for agriculture, the problems posed by the requirements of transportation, roads, technology, irrigation, and fertilization are very serious. You can increase production incredibly, above all when you begin with a very poor technology, but the difficult part is the effort necessary to reach the application of higher levels of technology.

What factors facilitated development in the times of those early developing countries which today are obstructing it? We have already spoken of the population, of the increase of population, of the percentage of the population under 10 years of age. One factor is modern technology, which involves an investment comparably higher than in that earlier period. You understand that, in the period of the horse-drawn carriage, in the period of the first textile machines, in the period of the first machinery with low technological requirements, low cost, low levels of investment, men who had practical experience would invent certain machinery. The necessary investment per active worker – that is, investment in machinery necessary to keep a worker active – was equivalent to a worker's salary for 5 to 8 months in that period. The necessary financial investment was the same as that earned by a worker in 5 to 8 months.

Today, in order to construct an industrial plant with modern technology in an underdeveloped country, it is necessary to invest in machinery the equivalent of a worker's salary for 350 months – that is, for 30 years. Therefore, take any example, any of the cement factories, or, if you wish, the nitrogenous fertilizer plant in Cienfuegos, that will cost more than 40,000,000 dollars in foreign exchange alone, and in all, more than 60,000,000, and will employ fewer than a thousand workers. Naturally, this fertilizer cannot be produced in any other way than with a really modern industrial plant; otherwise, it means wasting fuel, wasting all sorts of things. That production of nitrogen, if it is to be economical, must be carried on with very modern machinery, and that factory will cost the country some $60,000,000, more than $60,000 per worker to be employed there. That is, the complexity of modern technology demands an enormous investment – that is, 60 times as great as that needed when the Industrial Revolution began in those industrialized countries.

Another question: almost all the rudimentary machines with which the Industrial Revolution began could be produced in the country, so that England and France imported approximately 1·5 per cent of the machinery they used. They imported only 1·5 per cent.

The underdeveloped countries, given the technical complexity of modern machinery, have to import no less than 90 per cent of the machinery they need – it is obvious that there is a difference between manufacturing a carriage and manufacturing a locomotive.

Today, when an underdeveloped country needs an industrial plant, it must import machines at a high cost.

That is, the first machines with which the Industrial Revolution began were constructed within the country. Today, when an underdeveloped country needs an industrial plant, it must import machines at a high cost because those machines are necessarily and unavoidably costly, and the equipment costs the country 60 times more than it used to cost per worker employed. And not only that: that same technical complexity demands skilled workers and specialists who must be trained over a long period of time, in costly training programmes.

Naturally, these are not the only problems, not at all. But I am pointing out some facts that serve as examples to explain the present phenomenon, the unavoidable difficulties that the countries of the underdeveloped world face.

There is another question that has to be taken into account, and it is that many underdeveloped countries have sectors of the population devoted to many unproductive activities, such as bureaucratic and commercial activities, so that a very high percentage of the population and the resources are invested in these activities.

This is speaking about the objective problems, the objective difficulties. Now, then, the subjective ones: the social system, political régime, feudal exploitation of the land, strong-arm oligarchial governments imposed by imperialism or neocolonialism, control of the economy by imperialist monopolies, sacking of natural resources, even sacking of technical resources. And one of the most serious problems is illiteracy. In 1950, 90 per cent of the countries of the underdeveloped world had an illiteracy rate of over 50 per cent, more than 50 per cent.

Of course an understanding of these things can make us more clearly aware of the monstrous crimes the imperialists are committing the world over, the monstrous crime implicit in imperialism's policy of repression of the revolutionary movement, a policy which unleashes aggression and war and manufactures all kinds of puppet régimes. For what purpose? So as to keep the world in this situation. And why? To satisfy the interests of the financial oligarchies in those countries.

Because, once a country has become industrialized, its standard of living largely depends, or will depend, on the productivity of the labour force and the type of equipment used in industry, which will permit it to achieve a high per capita production. And, of course, even if all privileges and the exploitation of man have not been eliminated, the standard of living of a worker in a developed capitalist country is different from that of a farmer or worker in an underdeveloped capitalist country.

The United States not only possesses up-to-date technical equipment and a high rate of productivity, it not only is able to extract natural resources, cheat and exploit a large part of the world through its monopolies, through unequal terms of exchange, but in addition it drains technical personnel from the underdeveloped world.

As an example, we can cite that, of the 43,000 engineers who emigrated to the United States between 1949 and 1961, 60 per cent came from underdeveloped countries. Underdeveloped countries! Remember the statistics cited: increasing population, the amount of gross product, the incredible current difficulties of an underdeveloped nation. And, to make matters worse, of the 43,000 engineers who emigrated to the United States in a period of 12 or 13 years, 60 per cent were from underdeveloped countries. Of the 11,206 emigrants from Argentina who entered the United States between 1951 and 1963, 50 per cent were qualified engineers. Half of the 11,206 Argentine emigrants were qualified engineers.

Of course, in such countries, where there has been no revolution, those who are permitted to go to the United States are selected from personnel who will benefit the US financially. It is not the same here, where they have taken the *lumpen* elements, the bourgeoisie, the *latifundistas*, the thugs, all types of persons. Here they have not had a chance to make much of selection. They permit a limited number from Latin America and give preference to highly qualified technical personnel.

In 1950, the number of engineers and scientists who emigrated to the United States from all over the world was 1,500. By 1967 the rate at which engineers and scientists emigrated to the US was 6,000 a year. So the United States, with its enormous economic resources, drains the world – especially the underdeveloped world – of scientific and technical brains.

And this is a situation which is resented not only in the underdeveloped world. Europe, too, in spite of its standard of living and development, despite its advanced technology, is beginning to resent this trend, because it is beginning to fall behind the United States. Because the United States drains technicians and buys out any European enterprises it can. They even invest a mere 10 per cent of the value of an enterprise. For they do not invest just US money in Europe, but controlling the most advanced methods of technology, they raise the capital in Europe itself for their investments.

And we have observed that this has been occurring quite frequently. That they buy up an Italian factory here, a Spanish factory there, or a French or British plant, or that of any other country. And, at times, as in the matter of the rice-harvesting combines, this can virtually cause a social problem. When we attempted to purchase a certain type of rice combine in Europe, we discussed this purchase with a Belgian firm, and it turned out to be an impossibility. Even though the workers were idle, they would not sell us any equipment. The workers favoured the sale, but it was impossible because a US company held stock in that plant. And when a US company holds stock in a European firm, the one who gives orders concerning that plant is not the government of that country, but the US Department of State or the Department of Commerce, the US government. And Europe resents the fact that the United States is taking over its industry, infiltrating, draining off each nation's best technicians and carrying out a policy of penetration which threatens to leave Europe far behind the United States.

We have been observing, or trying to observe, attempting to gain an overall picture of such matters, which are not discussed in any manual, just as they do not deal with a number of very important matters, such as the problem of unequal terms of exchange, by which the developed world contributes to, or in one way or another takes part in, the plunder of the underdeveloped countries.

A concrete example is Cuba, a country which began its economic development after the Revolution. The average rate at which the population of Cuba has been increasing during the past five years is 2·3 per cent annually. This rate is three or four times as great as the population growth of the industrial countries when they began to industrialize.

In 1953, 36·3 per cent of the population was under 15 years of age. In 1967 the percentage of those under 15 reached 37·9 per cent. In 1953, 6·9 per cent of the population was over 60. In 1967, because of the increased life expectancy, 7·2 per cent of the population was over 60. Perhaps these increases seem small, from 36·3 to 37·9 per cent and from 6·9 to 7·2 per cent.

But let us look at how this affects the percentage of the population that is active. Taking 15 and 60 as the age limits for active work, the change in the age structure represents some 226,000 fewer persons engaged in active work in 1967 than if the age structure had been the same as it was in 1953. That is, if we had the same age structure we had in 1953 – 36·3 per cent under 15 and 6·9 per cent over 60 – we would now have 226,000 more persons between the ages of 15 and 60. The increased birthrate, on the one hand, and, on the other, greater life expectancy, means that there are over 200,000 fewer people in the active work age group.

By 1970, according to present estimates, the population will reach a total of 8,349,000 – that is, that will be the number of inhabitants in 1970. There will be 1,214,000 persons under five years of age; 1,125,000 from 5 to 9; 916,000 from 10 to 14. In all, there will be 3,255,000 persons under 15 – that is, 39 per cent of the total population of Cuba. Think how production will need to be increased, milk production, food production, the production of everything, for a population whose youth sector is increasing.

Estimated Population for 1970

Total	8,349,000
Under 5	1,214,000
From 5 to 9	1,125,000
From 10 to 14	916,000
Under 15	3,255,000

With an annual rate of population growth of 2·3 per cent and with almost 40 per cent of the population made up of persons under 15 years of age, the effort that our people must make is considerable. Just to offset the population increase alone, no less than 12 per cent of the available gross national product must be invested to compensate for such growth. And to assure a one per cent rate of production growth, and double our income in 80 years, we must use no less than 16 per cent of the gross national product. And to develop the economy at a rate of no less than five per cent of the gross per capita product annually, 30 per cent of the available gross national product must be invested. And this effort must be primarily made by half the population, excluding children and persons over 60.

We have many more possibilities in agriculture, because this is a natural resource that is available to us.

Naturally these are only some of the indexes. What is the picture in general in world terms with regard to the investments that must be made? This does not mean that it all occurs in an absolutely exact mathematical way. Everything depends on what fields are selected for investment. We have many more possibilities in agriculture, because this is a natural resource that is available to us; it's a matter of climate. Moreover, the same level of technology is not required for the development of agriculture as is needed for a steel industry, for example, nor does it require the same level of investment. Clearly, some fields require greater or lesser investments than others. But I merely wish to give you an idea, and this is the only way to explain how a country develops, what obstacles are involved, the significance of population growth and its influence on development – an idea of the size of investments that must be made. Investing in developing necessarily implies not consuming everything we might consume. A good example for us: our foreign exchange. If we spend it all on consumer goods and nothing on a single machine, irrigation equipment, or machinery to build drainage systems or water conservation projects, the sure result is all too clear. We would eat today, but it is certain that we wouldn't be able to eat next year, and as time went on, there would be less and less food. Steadily less! With a growing population and greater and greater dependency on climatic factors, on imponderables of every kind. The picture is clear.

So, then: how have our investments increased during these years? In 1962 State investments were $607.6 million; in 1963, $716.8 million; in 1964, $794.9 million; in 1965, $827.1 million; in 1966, $909.8 million; in 1967, $979 million; and in 1968 State investments are expected to reach 1,240 million pesos. In 1967, including State capital investments and other accumulations, such as the increase in our reserve of cattle – cattle spared from slaughter so as to build up our herds – the increase in our cattle population, and the increase in inventories, the nation was able to devote 27.1 per cent of the available gross national product to investments. This is including national resources and those capable of being obtained abroad, as well.

In other words, with foreign credit we can buy bulldozers or powdered milk, one or the other. 'Credit' means that payments must be made later on. And those who have had occasion to stroll along Havana's Malecón Drive know how much equipment is coming into this country. Moreover, this is not the most important factor. What is the work yield of equipment arriving in Cuba today that is put to use by organized brigades, with military discipline and optimum maintenance? It is incomparably greater than at any other time.

State Investments (*in millions of pesos*)

Year	Amount
1962	607·6
1963	716·8
1964	794·9
1965	827·1
1966	909·8
1967	979·0
1968	1,240·0 (Estimated)

In 1968 we will be able to invest approximately 31 per cent of the available gross national product. We believe that no other underdeveloped country today is making anything even remotely – not even remotely! – like this kind of effort. It doesn't matter that we cannot yet see the results, because the investments being made in Nuevitas (Camagüey), for example, are for long-term construction projects. Finally, this year, the first of the cement factories will begin operating, the Siguanea cement plant. Construction work on the Cienfuegos fertilizer plant and that at Nuevitas has begun. There have been investments such as that of the El Mate Dam, under construction for four years, whose wall was completed in August. It has not yet provided us with a single drop of water, but our investment is there in the 250-million-cubic-meter reservoir, which we expect will accumulate a good amount of water this year for irrigating an extensive area.

We have been making great efforts. The nation has made enormous investments in education, in universities, in educational programmes. It does not matter if the fruits of these sustained efforts, which began from practically zero with the literacy campaign, cannot yet be seen. We must point out that no value has been assigned to voluntary work in these investment figures – that is, all voluntary work done is in addition to the figures already cited. All those hundreds of thousands of people who have been mobilized at one moment or another to fill bags for coffee seedlings, to plant, those who are working from one end of the island to the other in similar mobilizations, all the efforts they make, and all the trees they plant, is in addition to this 31 per cent of the gross national product invested in economic development. And our people will some day see the results of this effort with profound satisfaction and will be extremely proud of what they are doing now. It is true that we are working for the future, but not only are we working for future generations but also, in a certain measure, this generation will have the opportunity of seeing the results of today's work. There is no doubt about this.

In general, what is the present state of education? We have a total enrolment of 2,193,741, including children, youngsters and adults. Of these, approximately 250,000 are in boarding schools and 150,000 in semi-boarding schools.

Incidentally, there is one item that does not precisely belong in this part of my report, but it would be lamentable to leave it out completely, since it is related to the problem of food supply already referred to.

For example, in 1965, educational social services provided meals for 156,300 persons; in 1968, for 389,300. This includes boarding and semi-boarding schools.

Public health and welfare provided meals for 62,300 persons in 1965 and 108,500 in 1968.

Recreation and sports: 900 persons in 1965 and 16,800 in 1968.

Our fishing fleet and boat crews increased from 6,300 to 9,400. Personnel for boarding schools increased from 30,600 to 50,500.

Sugar-cane harvests and other mobilizations: 228,000 persons in 1965 and 397,000 in 1968.

Workers' dining rooms provided meals for 130,400 persons in 1965 and 544,000 in 1968.

Thus, in addition to the food distributed through the rationing system, the number of persons served meals daily outside their homes has increased from 626,300 in 1965 to 1,529,000 as of today, an increase of almost one million persons. The total number of persons being provided meals in the field of education alone – if I remember correctly – equals approximately 80 per cent of the population of the province of Matanzas. But the total of 1,529,000 people equals approximately three times the population

Food Distribution (number of persons)

	1965	1968
Education	156,300	389,300
Public Health and welfare	62,300	108,500
Recreation and sports	900	16,800
Fishing fleet and crews	6,300	9,400
Personnel for boarding schools	30,600	50,500
Sugar-cane harvests and other mobilizations	228,000	397,000
Workers' dining rooms	130,400	544,000

of the province of Matanzas. And the increase in the number of meals served outside the home has been from 626,300 to 1,529,000 since 1965.

Whenever and wherever a mobilization is made, meals must be served. And this does not include our armed forces or police personnel.

So, in referring to the present state of education, I remembered this information.

Primary school: total enrolment, 1,391,478; secondary school, total enrolment, 177,087, including 160,308 in junior high schools and 16,779 in senior high schools; technical and professional schools 45,612, including schools and institutes of industrial technology, the school of fishing etc.; primary teachers' training schools, 18,121; universities, 34,532; adult education, including worker-farmer and women's improvement courses, 405,612; and other schools, 7,092.

Workers' technological institutes, 46,595; agricultural and livestock training schools for young people, 28,832; construction-shop schools, 10,663; the Military Technological Institute, 1,626; Ministry of Public Health schools, 6,060; the School of Higher Physical Education and Sports, 2,462; and day nurseries, 36,622.

The present number of primary school pupils, 1,391,478, will increase to 1,443,000 in 1969, and by 1974–5 will total 1,636,698. This implies an enormous need for teachers because, in spite of the great number of teachers being trained at Minas del Frio and Topes de Collantes and in courses for popular teachers (volunteer, temporary teachers), the number is not sufficient.

There is still a certain failure to send children to school. For example, of the school age group between 6 and 12, there are still between 50,000 and 100,000 children who do not attend school, which represents the beginning of a national mortgage for the future: from 50,000 to 100,000 children who are not in school.

The number of students at the intermediate level today totals

Education

	Students
Primary school total	1,391,478
Secondary school (high school) total	177,087
Junior high	160,308
Pre-university (senior high)	16,779
Technical and professional training	45,612
Primary schoolteachers' training	18,121
Universities	34,532
Adult education	405,612
Others	7,092
Workers' technological institutes	46,595
Agricultural and stockraising schools for young people	28,832
Construction workshop schools	10,663
Military Technological Institute	1,626
Ministry of Public Health	6,060
School of Higher Physical Education and Sports	2,462
Day nurseries	36,622

240,820. This total by now is quite impressive. And it will reach 260,000 in 1970 and some 530,000 in 1974 or 1975.

This does not include the programmes of guided studies or workers' institutes, since, in the measure that our higher schools of education begin to receive their students directly from the primary schools and the national education system, these programmes will become less and less important.

This is the situation in education, in which an enormous effort has been made, and yet the effort is still not great enough. The Ministry of Education is shortly going to offer more than 40,000 additional scholarships in various fields, and efforts are being made to guide young people into fields in which they are most needed. They are needed in a number of specializations and in an increasingly greater number of fields of study. And the problem of teachers is especially important.

In order to satisfy all these needs, television will have to be used. The increasing number of intermediate-level and pre-university students cannot be taught unless a technical aid such as television is utilized. Because, in any event, we are not going to have enough teachers, and it will be impossible to train enough teachers for this great mass of students, which is growing at such a rapid pace.

Ours will be one of the first countries to introduce television as a major instrument of education.

We are making the first experiments in television and we believe that ours will be one of the first countries to introduce television as a major instrument of education. We have two powerful broadcasting stations, and yet education has been relegated to a channel that barely covers the country.

Any future investment in television must be made in educational television, and in the future we must establish technological institutes and real universities, since the future will demand, as a vital need for the solution of contemporary world problems, uninterrupted, practically lifelong, study. And any country that does not take heed of this will stagnate, will be left behind the rest of the world. We must employ television to the greatest degree as an instrument of education and to back up our enormous educational movement, taking into account our dire shortage of teachers.

We were saying that our people are making a tremendous effort. Nevertheless, we do not believe that this is the generation that has had to make the greatest effort. Other generations of Cubans, such as the generation whose heroic, historical effort we commemorate this year with the first centennial of the beginning of this country's struggle for independence. . .

Perhaps we still do not fully and clearly understand how much we owe to that generation, which pointed out the way of struggle and took up arms at a time when there were also those who sought autonomy, reform, and even annexation. It seems that even at that time, discussions were being held as to ways and means, and there were blatherskites of every type who avoided facing the challenge of history. And that generation fought for 10 years and for 30 years and never even got to witness the independence of its country.

And the generation of the first years of the Republic, a generation that saw its country's status as a nation humiliated by the Platt Amendment, which gave Yankee forces the constitutional right to intervene – even though those forces have little need of constitutional clauses to perpetrate their crimes. Not even those generations got to see many of the things which our people now enjoy.

We have spoken of economic development, and our country has, in the past few years, made considerable social progress; illiteracy has been virtually eradicated; every young person has the opportunity to study; every young person, every citizen, in fact, has the opportunity to work; there are social opportunities, opportunities to participate in sports, opportunities for decent housing, opportunities to enjoy good health. An endless number of opportunities exist which the generations of Cubans that preceded this one did not know or never had the chance to enjoy.

This generation is making a great effort and should be ready to make a still greater effort should circumstances so demand.

But when we speak of this generation of Cubans, to whom are we referring? To all Cubans without exception? No! That would be false, it would be untrue. It is a part of the people, though a considerable part, that bears the main weight in the heroic battle for the country's development. It is not all the people.

I was saying we have been too benevolent, even too generous, because in our society, while hundreds of thousands – even millions – of workers pitch in wherever they are needed, cutting cane, working in the Green Belt or anywhere else, all over the country, a considerable number of people do not participate in the slightest in this effort. And, in a certain sense, we have been calling upon the masses to work not only for themselves but also for those who do not work, for the loafers, for the parasites, for the privileged, and for a certain kind of exploiter that still remains in our country.

If any reproach can be cast upon this Revolution it certainly will not be that it has been extremist, but rather that it has not been radical enough. And we should not lose the opportunity, nor let an hour or a moment go by, to make this Revolution ever more radical. We must complete the job of making our people fully revolutionary.

Today there is still a small segment of the population living off the work of others, living considerably better than the rest, sitting idly by and looking on while others do the work. Lazy persons, in perfect physical condition, who set up some kind of vending stand, any kind of small business, in order to make 50 pesos a day, violating the law, violating health regulations, violating everything, while they watch the trucks go by filled with women on their way to work in Havana's Green Belt, to pick tomatoes in Guines or somewhere else. [APPLAUSE]

Many people may ask themselves what kind of a revolution this is, that permits such parasites to exist after nine years of revolution, and they would be right in asking. I believe that it is time that we make it our business to put an end to every parasitic activity that is still going on in the Revolution. [APPLAUSE]

We see incredible things, things whose full significance becomes clear only after profound analysis. For example, right here in Havana, in the capital of the Republic, there are still 955 privately owned bars, making money right and left, consuming supplies. And, in fact, the fewer bars that remain, whether privately or publicly owned, the better off we will be. [APPLAUSE]

Nobody here is against gaiety; nobody here is against the people relaxing and enjoying themselves. But the problem is that our people are now facing much more important, much more vital tasks. I was speaking of the effort our people must make. These are years of hard work! Until we realize this clearly, on the basis of the facts we have been talking about, we cannot say we have fully and correctly adopted the correct line of the Revolution!

Nine hundred and fifty-five bars! For various reasons, I'm not going to read you the reports on these bars, but I have here many investigations made of these bars; who the owners are, what they purchase and where they purchase, how much they sell, what their profits are, what goes on there, who meets there, and what they talk about. And they can't even imagine ... We have their names, everything. But, as always, since we do not wish to make things unnecessarily difficult for anyone – and since everyone has a family – I'm not going to read reports or mention names. Suffice it to make a general review.

Following the orientation of the Party, an order was issued to carry out a series of investigations and statistical studies of the material collected by various Comrades, so as to obtain more concrete knowledge of the problem and seek solutions in keeping with the social and economic character of our Revolution.

Study made by Communist Party of Cuban Militants, gathering information from the Districts of Plaza de la Revolución, Centro-Habana, Guanabacoa, Boyeros, Marianao and 10 de Octubre.

For this study, the Party militants carried out every kind of investigation with the cooperation of the members of the Citizens' Vigilance Front of the Committees for the Defence of the Revolution. This study – as a result of the methods utilized – cannot be considered a true statistical sample, giving a faithful picture of the universe, but there is no doubt that its contents will be useful in understanding the magnitude of the problem and thus serve as a guide for future actions. For their political importance, we enclose the cases investigated by the militants.

Results of the investigation, types of sales, Chart No. 1. It can be seen by the chart that leading sales are in alcoholic beverages. The Comrades doing this work learned that for more than four months these businesses had not been supplied alcoholic beverages by the State. The district showing the highest percentage is Centro-Habana, with 100 per cent.

Sales and profit: 16 per cent have a daily take of up to 50 pesos (10, 25, 30); 43 per cent have a daily take from 50 to 99 pesos; and 41 per cent register 100 pesos or more a day – some of them going over the 200-peso mark. This is in gross sales.

Profits: 55 per cent register a daily profit of up to 25 pesos; 13 per cent, from 25 to 49 pesos; and 32 per cent register over 50 pesos – 50, 100, 150, and even 300 pesos ...

Revolutionary attitude, morals, social service, and other entries:

Revolutionary attitude: 72 per cent maintain an attitude contrary to our revolutionary process.

Customers: 66 per cent of the customers are anti-social elements.

Public service: none of these establishments provide any worthwhile service for the population; the percentage is 78 – that is, 78 per cent provide no service whatever.

Other businesses: 28 per cent of the bar owners also have other businesses.

Source of supply: 66 per cent of the bars under investigation were shown to be making illegal purchase; the source of supply of seven bars was not specified.

Summary: results of studies made in privately owned bars:

Illegal purchases of alcoholic beverages, non-revolutionary attitude on the part of both owners and employees, anti-social clientele, bad service to the public.

Recommendations: bars must be either taken over by the State or closed down. [APPLAUSE] After being taken over, the bars should not be continued as such. A study of the zone's needs must be made. Many of these establishments are located in buildings that were once living quarters which can be returned to their original use. Most of the bars have good refrigeration equipment which can be usefully employed in workers' dining-rooms or other State establishments.

The following concerns a general investigation of privately owned businesses in Havana.

'Results of the Party's investigations:

'Legality: of the 6,452 privately owned businesses studied in metropolitan Havana, 1,819 lack legal authorization to operate. This figure represents 28·2 per cent of the businesses.' In other words, almost one third of the businesses were illegal.

The districts of Boyeros and Plaza de la Revolución registered the highest percentage of illegality; Boyeros, 41 per cent, and Plaza de la Revolución, 38 per cent. The lowest percentage is that of Centro-Habana, with 20 per cent of the private businesses lacking licences.

The 60 investigations carried out by the Municipal Administration show a lower percentage of illegality; only 10 per cent.

Sanitary conditions: almost one half of the businesses did not have good sanitary conditions – that is, they were classified as fair to poor. Of the 6,102 businesses investigated, we find 2,471 with fair sanitary conditions and 567 with poor sanitary conditions. The businesses investigated in the 10 de Octubre District showed the most terrible sanitary conditions; 61·9 per cent of them – almost two thirds – had fair or poor sanitary conditions. One third of the businesses investigated in Plaza de la Revolución and Guanabacoa showed condition classified as not up to par.

Departure from the country: another one of the items investigated deals with those who plan to leave the country; 499 individuals of the 8,508 investigated have requested permission to leave the country.

The highest percentages of requests for permission to leave the country correspond to the districts of Guanabacoa, Marianao and San José, the lowest percentage being that of Centro-Habana.

The data gathered on hot dog stands and similar vending stands showed that a great number of people who intend to leave the country are engaged in this type of business, which not only yields high profits but permits them to be in constant contact with *lumpen* and other anti-social and counter-revolutionary elements.

Physical condition of owners; approximately two thirds of the total number of owners of private businesses seemed to be in good health, with percentages ranging from 59·6 in the 10 de Octubre District to 77·8 in the Guanabacoa District.

Of the 6,176 cases reported, 3,914 seemed to be in good physical condition.

The physical condition of 8·8 per cent of the proprietors was classified as poor, while 3·3 per cent were incapacitated.

There were 24·6 per cent classified as in fair physical condition – that is, almost 90 per cent are classified as good or fair.

Other characteristics: the investigation included the number of owners working directly in their businesses. Metropolitan Havana registered 87·6 per cent – that is, 12·4 per cent of the owners merely take in the profits and do not themselves work in their businesses.

The investigation showed that 14·9 per cent of the owners have other sources of income in addition to the business under investigation. Boyeros District showed the highest percentage, with 22·4 per cent of the owners having other sources of income.

The study of 60 investigations made by the Municipal Administration shows that 80 per cent of the owners live entirely off their businesses. That owners of private businesses are exploiters becomes clear when we examine data on the utilization of employees, which is the case in 31·1 per cent – almost one third – of the businesses investigated. The highest percentage is in Centro-Habana, where 40 per cent of the owners have employees, whom they exploit. Boyeros District registers a lower percentage. A survey was made as to whether or not the owners' family groups had other sources of income. This was so in 27·9 per cent of the cases. Guanabacoa District showed the lowest percentage (18), while Boyeros showed the highest (35·2).

Political integration: the Municipal Administrations in the various towns in Havana Province, as well as the Municipal Administration of metropolitan Havana, investigated this aspect in 2,056 owners of private businesses and, specifically, owners of vending stands, with most dissimilar results.

The greatest percentage of those not integrated into the Revolution was among owners of hot dog stands; of 41 individuals who answered this item, 39, or 95·1 per cent, were counter-revolutionary.

The percentage of non-integrated individuals in towns in Havana Province was 77·7 with a peak 80·7 per cent of the proprietors in the San José District not integrated into any mass political organization.

The moral and social conduct that goes together with a revolutionary attitude was taken into consideration in the survey of the proprietors of stands.

In the survey carried out by the Municipal Administration the percentage of unintegrated proprietors diminished.

The moral and social conduct that goes together with a revolutionary attitude was taken into consideration in the survey of the proprietors of stands, where, of the 18 individuals who answered this point, all 18 were anti-social amoral elements.

In Table No. 9 the time that the proprietors have been working in their businesses is analysed: 10·2 per cent of the proprietors in towns in Havana Province have been in business less than a year, and 36 per cent less than 8 years – that is, they went into business after the triumph of the Revolution.

The lowest percentage is found at Mayabeque, 35·7. In the survey carried out by the Municipal Administration of Metropolitan Havana, the percentage is 51·7.

Specific survey of the fried-food-stand owners: in this project a group of proprietors of stands and individuals who sell various kinds of fried food was studied in a special way. The most-sold product is the omelet, generally an omelet sandwich. Of the 50 stands investigated, 43 sell omelets; this is due to the availability of eggs.

The sale of croquettes and fried fish is in second place, followed by meat fritters. Stuffed potatoes, fritters, and sardines are sold to a lesser extent.

Other studies include stands where shrimps, fish, squid, hamburgers, sugar-cane juice, cigarettes and matches, milk shakes, candy, coffee, and soft drinks are sold.

The work carried out in these cases by a group of militants is of extraordinary interest. These studies show plainly the political importance of seeing to the solution of problems that are created by this mercantile infrastructure, which appears in those cases where State organizations do not give adequate service to the public. *Lumpen* elements find adequate room to make money and live in a vice-ridden atmosphere, exploiting the rest of the people. We add ten cases that clearly show this problem.

Gross sales and profits: the gross cash receipts of the stand owners reach unexpected proportions. Twenty per cent of the stands have a gross sale of more than 100 pesos daily; 35.5 per cent have a daily sale of 50 to 99 pesos; and 44.5 per cent have sales of less than 50 pesos daily.

In Centro-Habana all the stands investigated have sales of more than 50 pesos.

The profit made runs parallel with these sales. Twenty per cent of the proprietors make more than 50 pesos daily, and 53.3 per cent of the stand owners make more than 25 pesos a day.

This profit is explained by the great differences existing between the cost of production and the sales price, as well as by the volume of sales. As an example, we quote the case of a fried-food stand in the Calzada de Luyano that makes more than 200 sales a day. Croquettes: cost of production, 8 cents; sales price, 20 cents; 150 per cent profit. Fritters, cost of production, 8 cents; sales price, 20 cents; 150 per cent profit. Fried fish: 10 cents; sales price, 35 cents; 250 per cent profit. Omelets: 11 cents; sales price, 30 cents; 173 per cent profit.

Average daily sales were $66.40 and profits $43.57, with a cost of $22.83.

Characteristics of exploitation: 46 per cent of the proprietors do not employ any help, 44 per cent do, and in some cases the owner himself does not work but only comes by to pick up the money from sales. Forty per cent lease their stands but have employees.

Finally, 10 per cent run their businesses on a partnership basis, sometimes with relatives.

Regarding the origin of the merchandise, 20 per cent of the owners, according to the study, obtain their raw materials legally through quotas set by the Ministry of Domestic Trade or their family quotas.

Another group, 18 per cent, gets its supplies illegally, in ways ranging from buying raw materials on the black market to stealing lard from bakeries or engaging in illegal traffic in cooking oil from grocery stores – even State-owned grocery stores. Others get their supplies from the countryside, buying the products at premium prices. Most stand owners use both legal and illegal channels to obtain their merchandise.

Table No. 15 shows that 18 per cent of the proprietors have other businesses, jobs or incomes in addition to what they get from the fried-food stands. The kind of proprietor who will enter any kind of sales transaction is commonplace. Some are employed in State-owned work centres, while others receive some kind of pension or retirement benefits.

Summary and conclusions: we present the results of investigations carried out by the Municipal and Provincial Administrations and the Party regarding private businesses. The following characteristics are found: the lack of legality of the businesses, the reigning bad sanitary conditions. The proprietors' low degree of integration into the Revolution, the anti-social way of life, the dirty business transactions, robbery, and bribery in obtaining their supplies.

San José has the largest number of proprietors who are not integrated, the largest percentage of proprietors who engage in counter-revolutionary activities and the largest number of stands established since the triumph of the Revolution.

Recommendations: the absolute prohibition by the Ministry of the Interior, the Ministry of Public Health and Local Government of the opening of new establishments of this type. There should be a gradual suppression of this type of business, guaranteeing the people, through Local Power and the Institute of the Tourist Industry, the availability of similar food stuffs of better quality under more sanitary conditions.

For this we propose three consecutive stages ...

They proposed many stages; we can skip some of them.

Are we going to construct socialism, or are we going to construct vending stands? [LAUGHTER] It is not even a question of their economic bearing, in spite of the evident effect all those businesses have.

Is there any stand over there ..? Are you going to turn it in?

'Through private grocery stores, the private sector sells 77 million pesos' worth of goods, out of a total of 248,961,703.'

Truly, they have made a study of the entire country. We spoke of this problem on the 26 July: we saw how this type of business was increasing, how it was growing year after year, how the amount of income and profits was increasing, the number of people who were abandoning some kind of productive work to go into this kind of business, and the sanitary problems. For there is even a public health study here on the health problem that all this means; a study has been made. The problem of children, how they took children out of school, the corruption, the bribery, all kinds of illegal activities.

Gentlemen, we did not make a Revolution here to establish the right to trade! Such a revolution took place in 1789 – that was the era of the bourgeois revolution – just about everybody has read about it – it was the revolution of the merchants, of the bourgeois. When will they finally understand that this is a revolution of socialists, that is a revolution of communists? [AP-PLAUSE] When will they finally understand that nobody shed his blood here fighting against the tyranny, against mercenaries, against bandits, in order to establish the right for somebody to make two hundred pesos selling rum, or fifty pesos selling fried eggs or omelets, while the girls who work at State enterprises earn the modest salaries, the modest incomes that the present development of our country's economy allows? Who gave them that right?

Warnings mean nothing, reality means nothing to them. They are squeezing out the last drop. While privilege lasts, they will cling to privilege up to the last minute – and the last minute is near at hand, the last minute is near at hand! Clearly and definitely we must say that we propose to eliminate all manifestations of private trade, clearly and definitely. We will give work to those who can work, and, as for those who can't work, we will give them what they need, because we don't deny a living to anyone. How many tens of thousands of persons has the Revolution helped, every time it has been asked to do so, and it helps them not as a concession but as a duty of the Revolution. It has been stated that today nobody has reason to be needy, nobody! Everybody has the right to help and to work, and if we can't provide jobs, we give aid. We hope to continue providing more and more jobs for everybody; in the long run we'll have more than enough jobs, and only through work will we win the battle of underdevelopment.

A whole plague of businessmen remains ... We recall how the *Diario de la Marina*, which was the press organ of capitalism, spoke up and threatened that any measure whatsoever that harmed the 'sacred freedom of trade' discouraged business and constituted a brake on the development of trade.

Who is going to make us believe such a thing in this country, where all the measures that could have been taken against capitalism were adopted, and where capitalism still tries to make a comeback anywhere it can?

True, this has been partly the fault, naturally, of our unwary, naïve and careless revolutionary comrades and some who are not comrades; some of the latter work in grocery and other stores, where they do outrageous things, stealing and selling on the black market. This shows the need for increased vigilance. All kinds of contracts were entered into. Orders were given, to the tune of 100,000 or 200,000 pesos, to manufacture this, that, or the other thing. The Ministry of Light Industry was created in order to get to the bottom of all these problems and to look for possibilities of solving all these needs, because many of these businesses sprang up because of needs, from sandals to a gadget for something or other; from a scrap of this, that, or the other, they made something or other. One day in Las Villas they discovered an individual who farmed out work to 300 women with scraps of some raw material or other he got here or there, from which they were making rope, hammocks, this or that.

Whoever says that capitalism is easily deterred is a liar; capitalism has to be dug out by the roots; parasitism has to be dug out by the roots; the exploitation of man has to be dug out by the roots. [APPLAUSE]

Anyway, it must be said very clearly – and it goes without saying that the Revolution is not out to make enemies for the fun of it, but neither is it afraid of making enemies when necessary – it must be said that private trade, self-employment, private industry, or anything like it will not have any future in this country. Because whoever is self-employed can then pay the hospital and the school, can pay everything and pay dear! [APPLAUSE] It is very comfortable: let others pay the school, pay the hospital for me, for my family – if medical care costs 5,000 pesos, the expenses are taken care of, everything is taken care of, and he pays nothing. This, too, is a way of living off the work of others and of exploiting others.

We cannot encourage or even permit selfish attitudes among men if we don't want man to be guided by the instinct of selfishness.

Capitalism was a pyramid of exploitation, a pyramid where those on top exploited those below them, who in turn exploited those below them, etc. ... And often it spread even among the workers, for there were workers who had salaries five times as great as the ones who had cut sugar cane. There were workers who could buy used cars from the United States, who had salaries of 300 to 400 pesos a month, perhaps working in a US-run bank or for one of the monopolies. And the one who cut sugar cane and sustained the economy was the one who really paid for that car, the gas and everything, and he didn't have enough to eat. Capitalism, by principle, establishes this ladder of exploitation, and it is clear that capitalism has to be pulled out by the roots. We cannot encourage or even permit selfish attitudes among men if we don't want man to be guided by the instinct of selfishness, of individuality; by the wolf, the beast instinct; man as the enemy of man, the exploiter of man, the setter of snares for other men.

The concept of socialism and communism, the concept of a higher society, implies a man devoid of those feelings; a man who has overcome such instincts at any cost; placing, above everything, his sense of solidarity and brotherhood among men.

And this brings to mind the famous topic of incentives. For a long time they were theoretically discussed, and it appeared to be a question of method, but, in our opinion, it is a much more profound question. And we don't feel that the communist man can be developed by encouraging man's ambition, man's individualism, man's individual desires. If we are going to fail because we believe in man's ability, in his ability to improve, then we will fail, but we will never renounce our faith in mankind! [APPLAUSE]

We have known many cases of men acting from a sense of honour, giving something more than their work; offering up their blood, giving their lives, driven by profoundly moral factors.

And, of course, I do not intend to make an exhaustive analysis of this matter, but suffice it to say that this is not only a matter of principle for us, but an objective and real matter. Can an underdeveloped country afford to do anything else? Could it be that when we saw the figures we did not clearly understand the profound abyss, the misery from which a country that colonialism and imperialism had left backward in all fields, technically, economically, in all senses, has to rise? Isn't it plain that this country must invest its last cent, that it cannot invest in anything superfluous? Are we going to encourage the people by offering them money with which they could buy nothing? Can we stop investing to close the enormous gap between us and other countries in order to buy trinkets and superfluous paraphernalia so that the purchasing power of the peso is greater and so that a man earning a peso and buying that trinket thinks he has everything?

We have been seeing the effects here of money, how, while it is the instrument that gives man access to wealth, it permits him to enjoy everything whether or not he works. Just look at how some raked in 300 pesos – or 150 or 100 – owning bars, exploiting people, just for money, money and the power of money ... Unfortunately, we cannot eliminate money at this stage as an instrument of distribution, but we must cut off at least unlimited access to and any privilege connected with money. At present we still cannot eliminate money, but, some day, if we are to reach communism, we will do so. [APPLAUSE]

There are thousands of people here, tens of thousands, who do not use money ... scholarship students. Of course, money is still a means of obtaining many things: going to the movies, going here and there, for lots and lots of things. There are not enough things, and money serves as a means of distribution, but it is a bitter instrument, a transitory instrument, the elimination of which we should set as a goal. [APPLAUSE]

I know perfectly well what saying some of these things will cost, and how some out-dated academicians devoid of revolutionary sensitivity, some great-grandchildren of revolutionaries, will call us idealists, will say that we propose idealistic, unfeasible things; and there might even be some microfractional elements around who will chalk it up to petty bourgeois idealism. These ideas might be petty bourgeois, but not the fact that there are private grocers and owners of bars who make 300 pesos; that is not petty bourgeois, or anything like it! The rule of money, the corruption it causes, the instrument standing between man and the goods he creates!

And we are working, are creating wealth; and we are witnessing the incorporation of hundreds of thousands of people into work, and we see how work engenders enthusiasm and enthusiasm work, and work brings forth wealth, armfuls of it. And the Marxism that we believe we understand is that of Karl Marx; we could be mistaken, we cannot say we are infallible sages who are never mistaken, but at least the type of communism we have believed in is that communism we are proclaiming here. [PROLONGED APPLAUSE] And, basing ourselves on our understanding of Karl Marx and his most profound ideas, we must and will struggle for and further that true, fraternal, humane, generous communism – because no other kind of communism would be worth struggling for. What sense would it make?

And, furthermore, material incentives here? Who can offer more material incentives than imperialism? With its developed economy, with its technically equipped industry, it can offer more than any other, and, indeed, does. And many of those who pack their bags and leave with I don't know what excuse are simply fleeing from the realities of their country, are fleeing from today's work to go there as parasites in a way, to earn more and have more things that a country with a standard of living, as we said, with income standards twenty times as great, on the average, as those of an underdeveloped country can offer. Well, they are not twenty times as great as Cuba's, but they are six or seven times as great.

We are beginning to narrow that gap with the efforts we are making. But, really, many use the pretext of the Revolution, people who have no ideals, who have no spirit of struggle, who are incapable of having intense feelings about anything, on behalf of anything. And they emigrate. Then the imperialist country uses the advantage of that standard of living as a lure whenever possible – with technicians, *lumpen* elements, and all kinds of people – anyone. They take anyone. Some day they'll learn!

And there are some who are beginning to bring things from there, because yesterday some brought in an airliner, and it appears that it was brought it by three of those Cubans who left, got bored, grabbed the plane and brought it here. And the crew wandered about there talking nonsense and making mysterious comments about some characters ... And the truth of the matter is that we charged them [for airport facilities] and let them go. But we must remind them that they have a good number of our boats and aircraft in the United States that have not been returned and which they should return, because there is no real reason why we should bother to return anything to them under the circumstances. [APPLAUSE] They even have one of our helicopters. They have received assassins who have murdered members of the crews of our vessels, and they have them there. True, they only serve as scrap, but it is a matter of principle. They had better start taking measures, the Swiss Embassy and all the rest, to load those old wrecks on a ship and bring them back here, because now they can't blame us for the planes being here. They started this 'game'; they encouraged, taught, and for a long time, harassed this country. They encouraged it with: 'Bring a plane.' We have not encouraged it, but are now quietly seated here watching them reap the fruits of their shamelessness and piracy of all kinds. [APPLAUSE] They encouraged all sorts of crimes, and now they are beginning to suffer the absolutely spontaneous consequences. They rejoiced and enjoyed making trouble for this country, and now they are suffering the consequences; now there is practically an air route set up by those who bring planes for reasons of all sorts, even just for the fun of it.

But, of course, with its standard of living arising from a developed economy whose income is incomparably higher than that of any underdeveloped country, imperialism can offer material incentives of many types, and, in the face of this, what are we to do? What is the duty of the Revolution if not to strengthen its determination, to exalt all types of moral values among the people? Feelings of internationalist solidarity, justice, equality, love of country, love for the people, for the struggle; the satisfaction of having a giant task, a historic task, to carry out, and accomplishing it, facing up to it, overcoming obstacles. That is the kind of people we have to create. Anything else is ridiculous. And the results of having gone too far along that road are already beginning to be observed elsewhere.

We will continue along our road; we will build our Revolution, and we will do so fundamentally through our own efforts. Great is the task that faces us! A people that is not willing to make the effort has no right even to utter the word 'independence', no right even to utter the word 'sovereignty'! Let us struggle bravely, among other reasons, to minimize our dependence on everything from abroad. Let us fight as hard as possible, because we have known the bitterness of having to depend to a considerable extent on what we can get from abroad and have seen how this can be turned into a weapon, how, at the very least, there is a temptation to use it against our country. Let us fight for the greatest independence possible, whatever the price!

Of course, that offended the 'principles' of the microfraction; that was a crime: dignity was a crime, honour was a crime, the Revolution was a crime!

The country is exerting itself; it has made an effort in regard to fuel, to gasoline; considerable savings have been made, making it possible to allocate a part of that fuel for the big job of agriculture. The situation is not easy: our tractors, working day and night, are facing a tight situation, with regard to fuel, to oil, but we are taking the fullest advantage of what we have and are working at top speed. That means that our tractors will not be paralysed, that our plans will not go unfulfilled. And, since even all of the equipment we have is still not enough, oxen, draft animals, are being used on a mass scale, and we must train the oxen and learn to drive them now in order to do what the tractors are doing, and if one day we have more serious problems with fuel, then, with oxen, we will do a part of what the tractors are doing. [APPLAUSE]

In the country, in our subsoil, there is oil. Our problem today is to drill wells. And, of course, drilling is not easy. But suffice it to say that, of Cuba's total area of 111,000 square kilometres, 56,000 show possibilities of yielding oil; the existence of oil has been proved in many regions of the country. We have to drill and drill more deeply, and there is even high-grade oil at various sites at greater depths. Our basic effort must be directed towards drilling.

Of the oil wells in Guanabo, one has kept up a daily production of 90 tons, and the other being drilled 125 metres away has also begun to yield oil, and has at least twice the pressure the first well in Guanabo had. There is fuel in this country. Our problem is to drill for it, and much of our effort is being directed towards this end. In agriculture, water projects; in fuel, oil wells.

Naturally, our refineries are producing at almost full capacity. And all three plants working at full capacity indicates the future need for new refineries, because, logically, when the plants are working at full capacity, any repair work, any problem, even any sabotage ... We must double, triple our vigilance over our refineries and raise the revolutionary conscientiousness of our workers, because the CIA has always done its utmost to strike at us in that area, and any sabotage of the refineries could constitute a blow to the country at this time.

Of course, at any rate, we will always have to import some type of fuel, since not all the oil can be converted into gasoline, gas oil, or whatever one might want. Rather, nature establishes certain proportions, and, of course, what is increasing for us is our need for gas oil.

Now in gasoline, a part of that fuel saved is being converted as far as possible into gas oil, because a small part ... I mean, in the refineries, within certain limits, the production of gas oil can be increased at the expense of gasoline. Thus, from the gasoline saved, a part of it is going for gas oil and fuel oil. But, in addition, the first steps are already being taken for the mining of asphaltite, which will begin producing at a rate of half a million tons annually; and studies are being made on the possibilities of using asphaltite in the production of cement and electricity and in the sugar mills – that is, drawing on national resources as much as possible. Plans are also under way to use the gas from the Guanabo wells to run some industrial plants.

Thus, the press of necessity, without a doubt, will lead us to accelerated exploitation, the exploration and most rapid exploitation of our natural resources. Our vast nickel deposits are well known. Logically, we will need to make new investments in nickel, the price of which is going up. But some day we must produce steel, as well; fuel and steel, technical development, the training of technicians on a mass scale – for us this is an essential matter. Often you find a machine paralysed for want of steel parts, for want of angle bars, for want of a series of things. The need for steel is everywhere. We can produce steel, chrome, and nickel, and, above all, we can produce nickel and with its by-product – iron – develop our steel industry.

These investments cannot be made at present because what we need are not large investments that take many years to begin producing but rather those which immediately produce the maximum possible yield; a small dam or a large dam or what have you, but those that immediately begin to contribute to the production of goods, of use values, of food products. Efforts are now being made in all areas which can contribute to strengthening the general situation immediately, and in certain lines, such as fertilizers and cement, things which have an immediate bearing on development. Investment in the steel industry will have to be much greater, and this should be done between 1970 and 1975. Until 1970 our greatest efforts will be concentrated on agricultural development, and all the other fields in which work has heretofore been concentrated. The fishing industry will continue to be developed, as will transportation and the building industry. And this year will be a year of intensive work in water conservation projects, in road building, and in the general preparation of new lands, one of establishing the conditions which will safeguard us from all contingencies: droughts, plagues ... And then we have the problem of hurricanes, but we plan to provide all fruit plantations with strong, resistant windbreaks. So that, if there is a hurricane, it may destroy the year's crop of some item or other in some parts of the country; but not the plantations themselves. And this problem has received special attention. All these matters are being studied by research teams at the University.

The rector of the University was telling me that today we have a real university. That, in matters of research and other work, great efforts are being made, and that our University is devoting much attention to all the nation's economic problems, as pressing issues.

We can say that our work, until 1970, is clearly outlined, and,

from 1970 on, great emphasis must be placed on industrial investments of another kind. However, our agricultural development,
our dairy industry, will oblige us to construct a good number of
plants for producing powdered milk and cheese. The development
of farming, of citrus fruit production, will oblige us to set up
related industries. And it is the same for coffee and many other
things. We have great tasks ahead of us in the coming years, but
we have the deepest conviction that in the not-too-distant future
we will begin to reap the first fruits. And we anticipate that some
of the difficulties which lie ahead will not be like this year's
difficulties. However, we must always be willing to face any kind
of trouble. The important thing is our attitude. If things improve,
so much the better. And if things turn out twice as well, that will
be even better. But we must be prepared for better or for worse.

This means that we should not be discouraged. We should not
let anyone come along and try to demoralize a revolutionary,
without hitting back, without replying, without acting. This is
our duty, the duty of all of us, all militant revolutionaries and all
our mass organizations.

Everything should teach us more, each event should strengthen
the Revolution, each new experience. And we realize that this is a
time for undertaking a thorough, powerful, revolutionary offensive. [APPLAUSE]

Let us increase the seriousness, the spirit of work, the revolutionary conscientiousness, and the combativity of the masses, so
as not to give the enemy hope. Because some of the counter-
revolutionary rabble, and the imperialists, too, have felt encouraged because we hold our own opinions, because our country
has its own personality and its own position on international
political issues, fully developed and absolutely independent views.

But we must tell all of them – these members of microfractions
and counter-revolutionaries, who, when all is said and done, are
tied by the same umbilical cord – not to be encouraged by anything or anyone; they must not forget that this Revolution was
kept alive by a handful of men – six, seven, a dozen – and that
the banner of this Revolution is now held aloft by the best,
the noblest, the bravest and the most militant of our people.
[APPLAUSE] And they will know how to be worthy of this

hundred-year tradition of struggle, which began with the fight for independence, the independence which was begun by that generation and completed by our own generation. And they will know how to defend it with their last breath, with their last drop of blood. Because when we say *Patria o Muerte* we mean *Patria o Muerte, Venceremos!* [OVATION]

CHAPTER 2

'Creating Wealth with Political Awareness, not Creating Political Awareness with Money or Wealth.'*

In this speech Fidel explains how Cuba intends to proceed towards communism. The role of moral incentives, the abolition of money, the drive towards egalitarianism and the equalization of income, are explained as part of the vision of the future and, at the same time, elements in reforms that the Revolutionary government has already put into practice. Basic social services – education, health, housing, sports – are already provided in a communist manner. The intention is to continue that process. Money becomes increasingly irrelevant as more goods become free, and to the extent that money remains, incomes will be equalized throughout the society. This process will continue in accordance with the development of the economy – increasingly, those on the lower rungs of the ladder will be given more until everyone has the same income.

Guests;
Citizens of Las Villas;
Workers:
... Does our country, by chance, resemble at all the country we had fifteen years ago? [SHOUTS OF 'NO!'] You say no, but many of you are only seventeen years old – those who are here in the front row – or sixteen, and I have no doubt that some of you among the members of the Centennial Column are fifteen, and perhaps some of you were not born yet on the 26 July 1953. Then why do you say there is a great difference? [SHOUTS OF 'WE HAVE READ ABOUT IT!'] Oh, because you have read it! And

---

* Delivered on the 26 July 1968, 'Year of the Heroic Guerrilla', at Santa Clara.

to have read it and to have experienced it, is it the same thing? Possibly your parents know it better because they experienced it.

Anyway, it is not always necessary to have experienced a thing in order to know it. But those of you who were old enough to register anything will surely remember many things about which at the time you, young people, did not have the slightest inkling, and above all, you will recall what our country was like, what our people were like, a humble man or woman of the people, what a worker represented, what a student represented and who were students.

Of course, things existed in the past that we have not experienced, either. But sometimes, touring the countryside in many places – in Matanzas Province, for example – we have come upon dark and sinister ruins where the slaves who did the work during the last century lived in chains. Those ruins give us an idea of the extent to which man was capable of exploiting and enslaving man, of the extent to which man – in his selfishness, in his privileges and in his class interests – was capable of inhuman acts and was capable of treating his fellow men like beasts and sometimes worse than beasts . . .

When slavery disappeared – and it began to disappear precisely on that historic day of 10 October when those who initiated the armed struggle decreed the freedom of the slaves, slaves who made up a very important part of our army of liberation and struggled for our independence for thirty years – that form of slavery was replaced by another which was not based on the form of slavery in which a man was enchained, but nevertheless constituted a form of virtual slavery with invisible chains, which at times were worse than those worn by the early slaves.

And we still have left in our country many, many vestiges of that past, of that shameful past, of that past of injustices, of that past of abuses, of that past of exploitation, of that past of crime from which we inherited so much ignorance, from which we inherited so much poverty, so much misery, which left us an underdeveloped and poor country, which left us – as the comrade who spoke here in the name of the students recalled – a million illiterates, which left us an inheritance of 700,000 unemployed; those painful days in which men had to stand in endless lines to get a ten-day job, or to work twenty days or a month; those times in which, in order to find a common labourer's job in road construction, a worker had to have piles of references, he had to bring a letter from a political boss, a ward boss, and he had to pledge part of the money he was going to earn in order to have a right to work there, to make a living. What a difference between those times and these, in which all the people, intensively at work, find that their hands are not sufficient, that the hands of men and women, of young and old, of students, are not enough for the huge tasks we have to carry out, and that we need machines, we need airplanes, we need chemistry, in order to carry out the tasks that will permit our country to eradicate poverty and complete the triumph of the rebellion.

We must say with profound satisfaction that few things can give us – all of us who have gone through this process – more satisfaction than that statement, that declaration containing the thought of our students, containing the thought of our youth: this revolutionary process; the students had much to do with our revolutionary process.

And the fact that the students in our country, all the students in the centres of learning – in the technological institutes, in the junior high schools, in the high schools and the universities – have discussed and approved these points and have given a magnificent expression to this statement indicates that this Revolution has already begun to reap the fruit, the most lasting fruit, which is the fruit developing from the conscience of the people, from the conscience of our youth.

Because the Revolution ... the great task of the Revolution is basically the task of forming the new man of whom we spoke here, the new man of whom Che spoke, the man of a truly revolutionary conscience, the man of a truly socialist conscience, the man of a truly communist conscience. [APPLAUSE]

And when we reach the point where our young people are capable of such deep thought, when our young people are capable of expressing themselves correctly on all these questions, when our young people are capable of such profound meditation and analysis, and when they reach these conclusions and in these conclusions categorically express the conscience of young people who really want to live in a communist society, it is then that we can be completely sure of the fact that the effort in favour of liberation which began one hundred years ago and which marked a milestone fifteen years ago, on that morning of 26 July 1953, when many young men like them gave their lives for the future of their country, gave their lives for the Revolution.

No person or thing on earth can make this revolutionary process retreat!

And we can certainly say, with complete assurance, that there is no person or thing on earth that can make this revolutionary process retreat! [APPLAUSE] There will be nothing and no one that can hold back this revolutionary process! Because its strength stems not just from the number of men and women who defend it, from the mass of people who support it, from the formidable weapons which we have to fight with in a war, but basically from the degree to which it has taken root in the people's conscience, from the very high degree to which it has become the conscience of the people. And when a whole people takes up a cause, an idea, there is no force in the world capable of destroying it. [APPLAUSE]

It is not the attitude of a nation of fanatics, it is not the attitude of a people accustomed to blindly taking orders, of people who do things because they are told to, because they are ordered to, or because it is demanded of them. This is the attitude of people who really do things because they understand them, because they grasp them, because they want to do them.

And this morning our youth have expressed the essence, the core of Cuban revolutionary thought. There have been many revolutions throughout history, but the socialist revolutions are the most profound.

Every people, every nation, has its way of making its revolution; every people, every nation, has its way of interpreting revolutionary ideas. We do not pretend to be the most perfect revolutionaries. We do not pretend to be the most perfect interpreters of Marxist-Leninist ideas, but we do have our way of interpreting these ideas; we have our way of interpreting socialism, our way of interpreting Marxism-Leninism, our way of interpreting communism.

No human society has yet reached communism. The ways along which a superior form of society is reached are very difficult. A communist society means that man will have reached the highest degree of social awareness ever achieved; a communist society means that the human being will have been able to achieve the degree of understanding and brotherhood which man has sometimes achieved within the close circuit of his family. To live in a communist society is to live in a real society of brothers; to live in a communist society is to live without selfishness, to live among the people and with the people; as if every one of our fellow citizens were really our brother.

Man comes from capitalism full of selfishness; man is educated under capitalism amidst the most vicious selfishness, as an enemy of other men, as a wolf to other men.

The students here expressed the idea that communism and socialism will be built simultaneously, and that idea and the expression of the idea have led to the situation where Cuban revolutionaries have been described as wishful thinkers; have led some people to say that these are petty bourgeois ideas; have led some people to say that this is an erroneous interpretation of Marxist-Leninist ideas, that it is not possible to build communism if socialism is not achieved first and that in order to build socialism, it is necessary to develop the material base of socialism. We do not deny this last point.

In the very essence of Marxist thought, socialist society and communist society must be based on a thorough mastery of technology, on the complete development of the productive forces, so that man may be able to create material goods in such quantities that everyone may be able to satisfy his needs.

It is unquestionable that the Middle Ages society, with its minimal development of the productive forces, could not have aspired to live under communism; it is very clear that the old society, with even more backward and poor productive forces, could have aspired even less to live under communism; and communism arises as a possibility of man's control; a full command of nature, a full command of the processes of material-goods production . . .

The day will come when it will not be necessary to pay fare to travel from one place to another. We have another interesting example in the case of bus fares. There was a conductor on every bus in this country; thousands of men were devoted to collecting fares. A system was set up, a system that could only be set up by a revolution, in which each passenger, fully aware of his obligation, deposits his own fare. The country recovered for its productive force thousands of workers who, like the box-office attendants at sports events, had been utilized only for making change, giving out tickets and engaging in other such activities.

Logically there are still many cases and will be for many years, for a long time – in which it will not be possible to dispense with money, but it will have a different meaning: that of a simple instrument of distribution. For a long time our country will have a different meaning: that of a simple instrument of distribution. For a long time our country will have to use this symbol that is money; money as a means of distribution, money as a measure of the amount of products or specified services that are to be received. But our Revolution's aspiration – and certainly it is not utopian – is to do more than merely change the role of money. Because the role of money in a capitalist society is that of an instrument of exploitation, an instrument for exploiting the work of others, an instrument for accumulating wealth. Naturally, money does not have nor can it have that meaning in our country. Since even the smallest street vendors' stands disappeared and private businesses were ended with the revolutionary offensive, money cannot be utilized as a means of individual enrichment by someone who sets up a street stand and buys twenty pesos' worth of bread and other things in the stores or on the black market, to sell fifty, sixty or seventy pesos' worth of merchandise. Certainly, when the Revolution suppressed private enterprise, it took an extraordinary step forward. There is now no one who can earn thirty times as much as a hard-working worker does. There is now no one who can earn, without sweating his shirt, thirty times as much as the one who sweats his shirt. Why must money still exist to such a great extent? Why are there still so many prices that are high? Many times some people ask: 'Why is this so high?' 'Why is this service so high?' Let's say a restaurant. This question has been asked many times; this problem has been raised many times. If everybody earned the same amount, then a given price could be set and everyone would have the same chance to go to a restaurant; everyone would have the same chance to acquire many things. The fact is that in our country there are many inequalities of income, some of them quite considerable. Many people have an income which is much greater than that of others. There are some people who ask: 'Why aren't wages equalized?' And we say it can't be done, because if the Revolution took this measure it would not achieve its objectives. The Revolution cannot equalize incomes overnight. The Revolution's aspiration is to arrive at equal incomes starting from the bottom up, not from the top down. It would be incorrect for the Revolution to do it the other way.

There are many people who are accustomed to a certain income, to certain activities, and, if the Revolution sought to equalize incomes from the top down, we are sure the Revolution would run into many obstacles. By what method will the Revolution achieve equality of income? By increasing production and by gradually increasing the incomes of those who earn less, of those who receive less money . . .

A few days ago we said that the first thing the Revolution will do is to increase the old-age pensions and survivors' benefits until they reach the level of today's lowest wages. Likewise, once these levels are reached and our economy grows, the wages of those who earn less will be gradually increased. Thus, the Revolution will establish equality in incomes gradually, from the bottom up, keeping pace with the progress of our production.

That is, the Revolution aspires – as one of the steps towards communism – to equalize incomes, from the bottom up, for all workers, regardless of the type of work they do. This means this principle will surely be given a name by 'learned', 'experienced' economists – who will claim this goes against Marxist-Leninist principles and against the laws of economics. The question is 'which' economics: capitalist economics or social economics, the truly Marxist-Leninist economics or a mercantilist economics.

To these economists, an assertion of this type sounds like sheer heresy, and they say that the Revolution is headed for defeat. But it so happens that in this field there are two special branches. One is the branch of the 'pure' economist, be he capitalist or socialist. In short, just a plain economist. But there is another science, a deeper science which is a truly revolutionary science. It is the science of revolutionary awareness; it is the science of faith in mankind; it is the science of confidence in human beings.

If we agreed that man is an incorrigible individual, that man can only make progress through egoism, through selfishness; if we agreed that man is incapable of learning; if we agreed that man is incapable of developing his conscience – then we would have to say that the 'brainy' economists were right, that the Revolution would be headed for defeat and that it would be fighting the laws of economics.

But the actual fact is that the history of this Revolution has furnished us with many examples, repeated examples of the fact that those who were in error were those who did not believe in man, that those who made the mistakes and failed were those who had no confidence in the peoples, who had no confidence in man's ability to attain and develop a revolutionary awareness.

In the past, those of us who proclaimed the revolutionary struggle, who proclaimed the need for a revolution, were told the same thing; that we were mistaken, that we were a bunch of dreamers and that we would fail.

This was what the politicians, the 'savants' of politics, the 'professors' of politics, the 'brains' of politics, the leaders of the traditional, bourgeois parties, had to say. They did not believe in the people; they underestimated the people. They thought the people incapable of accomplishing anything. They thought of the people as an ignorant herd to be manipulated at their will. Those of you who are here today – especially those who are here as guests – and can take a good look at this enormous congregation of people which is the living expression of our Revolution's power, should not forget that only fifteen years ago we were a small group of youngsters whom many considered dreamers, who had been told they would fail because it was impossible to make a revolution in a country only ninety miles from the United States, that it was impossible to make a revolution in a country of illiterate, ignorant people. And yet, what is it that we see today? What has been the result of the effort begun fifteen years ago by a small group of youngsters at that stage of our revolutionary history? How much has been accomplished by this people? How much has this unarmed people accomplished? How much has this people that they called ignorant, that they underestimated, that they considered lacking in every virtue, accomplished?

This was an unarmed people faced by an army equipped by the Yankee imperialists. This army was 50,000 strong, counting soldiers and police. They had all the weapons, while the people did not have any weapons. And yet, this people, the people the 'savants' of politics scorned, this uneducated people, this people of illiterates, this people without weapons, took up the struggle, continued the struggle, defeated that army and disarmed that army, and it is this people that today has an army, a true army of the people, because it is the people in arms, and this army is ten, twenty times more powerful than that other army! [APPLAUSE] ...

And those of us who at that time spoke of this possibility were called failures, dreamers, and wishful thinkers. But that is not all. The people they scorned, that people of illiterates, made a profound Revolution, a deep Revolution never before made by any country in America. And it made it right under the very nose of Yankee imperialism, the most powerful, most aggressive exponent of world reaction!

The imperialists, who also underestimated the peoples, were used to defeating revolutionaries; they were used to buying off revolutionary leaders with a few miserable dollars; they were used to crushing revolutions through the use of counter-revolutionary gangs or through invasions, using mercenary troops.

So what happened? What can we say today? That this people that only fifteen years ago had no weapons, this people of illiterates, has waged one of the greatest revolutionary and political battles of modern times by uniting, developing its revolutionary awareness and building up its forces. And it has successfully resisted ten years of aggressions, ten years of economic blockade. And all the tricks, obstacles, manoeuvres, and resources of the imperialists have been unable to force this people into submission, to weaken this people, to crush the Revolution !

It is true that we were a people of one million illiterates, that we had few engineers, few doctors, and few technicians. In their effort to make us fail, the imperialists did their best to leave us without doctors, without engineers, and without technicians. They were not satisfied with having forced our people to remain ignorant; they tried to take away many of the few who had an opportunity to attend our universities – and in many cases succeeded.

The imperialists have used every weapon against our country to keep our people from making any headway, to make our people fail, to make our economy fail. And what have they achieved? All their weapons and their resources have failed against our people.

And all the 'experts', all the political brains, all those who thought this Revolution was impossible, what must they be thinking now? What do they have to say now? It must be very hard for them to accept that all of this is possible !

But, while these victorious struggles carried forward by our people were hard and difficult, the struggles they are carrying forward today, the struggle to win the battle against underdevelopment, this fight in the midst of the blockade, is – if possible – even harder and more difficult. The struggle to arrive at a higher form of social relationship is among the most difficult of struggles, one of the most difficult courses that any people can take.

And the certitude that we felt yesterday is the same that we feel – stronger than ever – today, when we assert that this people, that with its awareness, revolutionary spirit and firmness, has been able to win such difficult battles, will also win, and is already winning the battle of the economy and will also win the battle to attain a higher form of society. [APPLAUSE]

We have set forth some ideas, a few ideas, in order to describe many of the things that our Revolution is doing today that are practically communist. I also explained that today it is materially impossible to do everything in a communist way . . .

The basic social services: education, health, housing, sports, all those services that contribute to the development of the people in all spheres – the Revolution provides them today in a communist manner; but most material goods are still not distributed in a communist way; there are still many inequalities. And one of the first battles in the march towards communism is to move progressively upward – I repeat, lessening income inequalities, moving towards income egalitarianism, towards income egalitarianism! This still does not mean communist distribution, but it will be a big step in the direction of that form of communist distribution.

We made this explanation thinking of the words of the students, how they said that the problem of payment is no longer discussed among the students. At first the students acted as teachers; they taught classes, and they received some payment; and the students progressively have been acquiring awareness, above all because many of them were scholarship students who received everything, and it made no sense that they who had received everything free, all that they needed to develop, should demand payment for giving a little of their efforts and knowledge to others. They have said that material incentives do not matter to them, that what does matter is the awareness of their duty, and that their behaviour is not motivated, nor will it be motivated, by money; their acts are motivated not by material incentives, but by their conscience and their sense of duty. Does this mean that they give up what they need? No, of course not. Give up food, clothing, all that they need? No! What they are giving up is the method, the procedure based on material incentives. With this they express their confidence in the future, their confidence in the possibility of a communist society, their confidence in a society where all work for all and all receive what they need. They said that they were not going to work by the clock, but that their work day would be dictated by their conscience. They stated very well that our country must emerge from underdevelopment; they expressed the idea that our people have to work very hard in these years – as much as they possibly can, give or take a few hours. Some day – and that day will not be far off – at a surprisingly rapid pace, with the aid of technology, with the aid of machines, with the aid of chemistry, many of the hard jobs done by our people today will become unnecessary. In the not-to-distant future no one will have to cut cane with a machete, no one will have to weed a field with a hoe; no one will have to do those hard jobs that we have to do today, while we don't have those machines, while we don't have that technology to win the battle of underdevelopment. Our students expressed here ideas of high moral worth by giving voice to those opinions, to those thoughts, by unfurling those banners: the idea that each person work according to his conscience; and that work is not an individual tool with which to earn one's living but is rather the tool of the whole of society, not the resources of an individual. An individual alone can do nothing, an individual alone is very little, but an individual integrated into the strength of society is everything!

They expressed the opinion that the Revolution will not use the tool of material incentives as the instrument for raising productivity, for raising the level of accomplishment. Of course this does not mean that in our society all citizens – not by any means – have reached these levels of conscience; there are many who have achieved this, but there are many who still have not done so.

What this means is that they express the conviction that every day the awareness of our people will become more developed in the direction of communist mentality and attitudes.

Many workers have given up overtime pay; the extraordinary thing here is that workers who don't have very high incomes have given up overtime pay. That is really a sacrifice for many of our workers. Now, what must be done? What must we do in keeping with this? Ah, workers give up their overtime pay; we are going to raise the pensions of all who receive low pensions, those who have worked all their lives and are now old. [APPLAUSE] Many workers have given up overtime pay? Fine! Then we have to take a step in keeping with this. For example, what step? When the worker becomes ill he does not get his full pay, and that is contrary to the development of conscience; when a person gets sick, you can assume he needs his income more than ever . . .

However, what happened? Old concepts, old opinions from other times prevailed. In our opinion, the fairest thing, in all the work centres where the workers have had that attitude, when one of those workers gets sick, no matter for how long a time, is for him to receive one hundred per cent of his pay. [PROLONGED APPLAUSE]

Unfortunately, in one way or another, many workers have labour accidents, accidents which sometimes cost their lives or cause partial disability or incapacity to do the work they were doing, and at such a moment, at that bitter moment, in all those work centres which have attained the high level of political awareness that is represented by the revolutionary workday and renunciation of extra pay for extra hours, the workers should receive, in case of accident or disability, the complete amount of the wages they had been earning. [APPLAUSE] And the benefits should also be extended, in case of death, to their dependents.

This example shows us that without the development of political awareness we cannot act as communists. If the old, selfish concept is maintained – the more I work, the more I earn – then, when such a man gets sick, society has to pay him less; when that man is disabled, society has to give him less; when that man retires, society has to give him less. And on the basis of these concepts, of these incentives, man depends exclusively on himself, and society can do very little for him. A collective sense, a communist conscience, is not instilled.

In the same way, we believe that now that a review of pensions and increases in pensions is to be undertaken, those workers in these vanguard work centres who have that awareness should, at the time of their retirement, also receive one hundred per cent of the wages they were earning. [APPLAUSE]

Could anything be considered more just, more humane? And from where do the necessary resources come? From the communist spirit of our workers. Those resources spring from that communist spirit. And here we find a contradiction : money plays, and for a long time will still play, an important role in distribution. We mentioned the services that are already provided free of charge. Money will have less and less significance when nobody pays rent any longer – and the majority of our people already do not pay rent – when all children are granted scholarships or are in day nurseries or in day boarding schools. Families have begun to realize that many of the payments they had to make before now no longer exist; they are beginning to find that the money they cherished before, because it meant the health of their child, the bread of their child, the medicine of their child, the recreation of their child, the education of their child, is losing its meaning. They worshipped that money because it was the instrument that made all of those things possible.

Money continues to be used for other things, but for these things it is becoming increasingly unnecessary. To enjoy oneself, to take a trip, to drink a beer, for any of those things, all right; and people value these, but they value more the health of their child, the roof over the head of their child. In other words, all the essential things, the things they value most and for which they sacrificed recreation, beer, and all the rest, are no longer obtained with money.

Money will have less and less meaning. But it still plays an important role; the majority of the individual needs of the workers are still satisfied through money, and, as long as money plays that role, it is fair that those work centres which have proved their political awareness, those work centres that gave up extra pay for extra hours, that adopted the revolutionary work day, should receive from the community, from society, those things and those resources they were receiving in payment for their work, when they get sick, or have an accident, or retire.

And these examples we have given, which you all understand perfectly well, are sufficiently clear and illustrative of the meaning of a communist spirit ...

And we should not use money or wealth to create political awareness. To offer a man more to do more than his duty is to buy his conscience with money. To give a man participation in more collective wealth because he does his duty and produces more and creates more for society is to turn political awareness into wealth.

As we said before, communism, certainly, cannot be established if we do not create abundant wealth. But the way to do this, in our opinion, is not by creating political awareness with money or with wealth, but by creating wealth with political awareness, and more and more collective wealth with more collective political awareness. [APPLAUSE]

The road is not easy. The task is difficult, and many will

criticize us. They will call us petty bourgeois, idealists; they will say we are dreamers; they will say we are bound to fail. And yet, facts will speak for us, realities will speak for us, and our people will speak and act for us, because we know our people have the capacity to comprehend these roads and to follow these roads.

In the same way, some day we will have to receive the same. Why? Some will ask: will a cane cutter earn as much as an engineer? Yes. Does that mean that an engineer will receive less? No. But some day a cane cutter – and I say cane cutter symbolically, because in the future we won't have any cane cutters – let us say, the driver of a harvest combine or a truck, will earn as much as an engineer today.

And why? The thing is clear, very logical. The Revolution has thousands of young students in the universities. The Revolution has thousands of young people studying abroad, dedicated to studying, to becoming engineers, chemists, specializing in different fields. Who pays for their expenses? The people.

If the Revolution needs to send many young people to study in Europe and others in universities, all right; we ask them to study, and they do it in a disciplined way, but that doesn't mean they are privileged. It is important to the Revolution that they study, that they prepare themselves. But at the same time that thousands of our young people study abroad, thousands of others have to go into the fields to plant cane, to weed cane, to do very hard work. Within a few years there will be much more wealth in our country. The former will have finished three, five years of studies and will have become technicians, engineers; and the latter will have been working those years in the fields, and they will not become engineers, but they will develop our economy, they will be building the future of our country [APPLAUSE]

Under what concept and in what way would it be just for us to tell these young people after a few years, in a more prosperous country, in a country with much more wealth, you are earning one fourth of an engineer's wages? Would it be just, would it be basically just, that those whom the country called on not to go to the university but to work to win the battle of the economy, to make the effort which at this time we cannot make with chemistry or with the machines which we do not have, but must make with our hands, with our sweat – would it be just, whenever the nation is able to enjoy the riches which they are creating now, for us to treat them as fourth- or fifth-class citizens, entitled to receive from society an insignificant part of what in the future will be received by those who are in the universities, those who are studying abroad? . . .

No ! Not at all. Communist conscience means that in the future the wealth that we create through everybody's effort should be equally shared by all. That is communism, that is communist conscience ! [APPLAUSE] And there will not be a single honest citizen, there will not be a single head of a family, there will not be a single person in this country with human sensitivity who will not be able to understand how just this concept is which our people defend, which our Revolution proclaims and which our students have made their watchword.

And it is encouraging that it is precisely our students, our future engineers, our future doctors, our future professors, our future technicians, who put these things forward, the first ones to proclaim these things. Logically, it is because of this that we have to feel optimistic, that we have to feel enthusiastic, that we have to have faith in the bright future of our country. Classes will disappear in our country, and once classes have disappeared the struggle between the Revolution and the counter-revolution will disappear. Because, in the future, who will remember those who dared to defend the past? Who will forgive those who one day shed the workers' and farmers' blood to defend that past; who will defend that imperialist system; who will forgive that imperialist system, which shed the blood of our youth, of our workers, and of our farmers to stop the just march towards the future, to uphold that repugnant, immoral, selfish, shameful past which our youth will not even be able to imagine?

And that is why I do believe that these young people who were here in the front row – who were three, or two, or one year old, or babies, or unborn at the time of the attack on the Moncada – are capable, through reasoning, sensitivity, education, and awareness, to have an idea about that past, even though they did not live through it, and to reach this high level they have attained. Because that is sacrifice, real sacrifice; that is heroism, real heroism! There is the heroism of the battle at the moment or danger, of the young man who generously gives his life, and there is the heroism of the revolutionary, creative work of the young man who offers his sweat, his hands, his time, who is capable of going over there to wage that battle for the future of the country. [APPLAUSE]

Fortunately, we understand what we are doing; we understand what we want, how we want it and why we want it. And that is why, as the conscience of the people develops, the march of the Revolution will be more victorious. We will have a lot of things to do in this country. A lot! We could say that a good part of them are still to be done; tens of thousands of kilometres of roads, hundreds of dams, and, in the next ten years, thousands of buildings, thousands of shops, thousands of schools, hundreds of large factories, factories for everything.

A few days ago we were speaking of the accelerated growth in our rice production, of the fact that, by 1971, we will not need to import rice. But more mills than we now have will be needed to process all the rice the nation is going to produce in 1970; more installations and plants than we now have will be needed to process all the coffee the country is going to produce in 1970 and many more pasteurizing and bottling plants than we now have will be needed to process the milk which will be produced in 1970, just as our sugar industry has had to be considerably enlarged throughout these years to make it possible to reach ten million tons of sugar. This increase in the capacity of our sugar industry by 1970 will be equal to that of ninety sugar mills of the average size in Matanzas Province. Ninety sugar mills! That is, there are sugar mills which are practically being rebuilt, and there are sugar mills which are more than doubling their capacity.

Our people will have to work very hard in the next few years, and our resources will have to be given over to this purpose ...

And this is true in every field ... In this same province the Siguaney cement plant is being completed – let us hope that we have enough fuel to put it into full production. An excellent industrial plant has been built – the machine-building plant of Santa Clara. The INPUD [home appliances] factory has been built. But, unfortunately, it is operating far below capacity, due to a shortage of raw materials. A very up-to-date fertilizer plant is under construction in Cienfuegos, a plant which will have an annual production of almost half a million tons of fertilizer. A huge bulk-sugar shipping terminal is being built which will save the labour of thousands of workers – that overwhelming, exhausting labour of the stevedore, who must load 250- or 325-pound sacks – because in the future that work will be done by cranes and other equipment. So, our country must make great efforts.

Irrigation works must be developed in this province. In this province alone, fifty dams must be built, fifty dams so as to make use of all the water in this province, so that our agriculture will have supplies of no less than three thousand million cubic metres of water for irrigation.

Those of you who live in Las Villas Province know what droughts are. Last year there was a very severe drought. This year not a drop of rain fell during the first months of the year. When it began to rain, it rained a great deal – actually, too much. For this is one of the provinces which has had the greatest amount of rainfall since the month of May. There are periods of heavy rain, and then five or six months without irrigation, without water, with the disastrous results which all this means for agriculture.

Thus, we are developing irrigation works throughout the country. And for some weeks the equipment needed for these projects has been arriving in this province so that all the farmland in this province will be irrigated.

You can well imagine what this means for the nation's economy, what it means for the productivity, what it represents in the way of agricultural yields, how we will be able to plant the year round and not have to wait for rain in order to plant everything in a month, when the weeds are also coming up, and all those problems which you know about.

I only want to stress that the years that lie ahead will be years of great effort, of tremendous work.

But our country is winning the battle against underdevelopment. Our country, faced with the criminal imperialist blockade, with all the damage it has caused, with the burden of the additional hundreds of millions of pesos it has forced us to spend to acquire goods on various markets, transport such goods greater distances, make purchases under difficult conditions – all of which has cost this country hundreds of millions of pesos – in spite of all this, the country is winning the battle against underdevelopment; this country is winning the battle of the economy; and, what is more important, this country is winning the battle of revolutionary conscience. What a magnificently just homage, what a magnificently just homage to the one who best symbolizes these ideas, the strongest defender of man's conscience as an instrument of development in the Revolution, that comrade, who one day, through his audacity, courage, and intelligence, won the battle of Santa Clara, the eternally beloved Comrade Ernesto Guevara! [APPLAUSE]

And this 26 July, on which our students make these watchwords their own, on which our people make these watchwords their own, with true pride, and filled with confidence in the future, we can say: Che, we dedicate this fifteenth anniversary of our Revolution to you!

Patria o Muerte! Venceremos! [OVATION]

Selected Readings

Pre-Revolutionary Society

Foreign Policy Association, Report of the Commission on Cuban Affairs, *Problems of the New Cuba*, New York, 1935. (Ruling class analysis of Cuba after the abortive revolution in 1932–3.)

Lowry Nelson, *Rural Cuba*, University of Minnesota Press, Minneapolis, 1950. (A comprehensive survey of life in the Cuban countryside *circa* 1945.)

United States Department of Commerce, *Investment in Cuba: Basic Information for U.S. Businessmen*, Government Printing Office, Washington, DC, 1956.

The Cuban Revolution

Edward Boorstein, *The Economic Transformation of Cuba: A First Hand Account*, Monthly Review Press, New York, 1968. (An insider's story of the reforms and economic policy of the revolution through 1963.)

Warren Miller, *Ninety Miles from Home*, Boston, 1961. (The diary of a talented North American writer during his stay in Cuba from 1960 to 1961. Embellished with news clippings and poems.)

José Yglesias, *In the Fist of the Revolution*, Allen Lane The Penguin Press, 1968. (An account of life in a small town in Cuba.)

James O'Connor, *The Origins of Socialism in Cuba*, Cornell University Press, Ithaca, 1969. (An analysis of the old Cuba and the revolution that transformed it.)

Lee Lockwood, *Castro's Cuba, Cuba's Fidel*, Vintage, New York, 1969. (Photographs and the transcript of a five-day interview with Fidel in 1965.)

Granma, English edition, Weekly Review, Havana. (This is the single best source for information on Cuba. It is the English edition of a

weekly summary of the official party newspaper. It carries all of
Fidel's speeches as well as those of other Cuban leaders.)

Cuba and the United States

Robert F. Smith, *The United States and Cuba: Business and Dip-
lomacy, 1917–1960*, College and University Press, New Haven, 1960.
(A careful study of the influence of US business on US-Cuban relations.)

Maurice Zeitlin and Robert Scheer, *Cuba: Tragedy in our Hemisphere*, Grove Press, New York, 1963. (The best study on the reaction
of the US government and press to the Cuban Revolution. It contains appendices analysing US press coverage and the State Department White Paper justifying the Bay of Pigs. Covers the period up to
the invasion in April 1961.)

More about Penguins and Pelicans

Penguinews, which appears every month, contains details of all the new books issued by Penguins as they are published. From time to time it is supplemented by *Penguins in Print*, which is a complete list of all available books published by Penguins. (There are well over three thousand of these.)

A specimen copy of *Penguinews* will be sent to you free on request, and you can become a subscriber for the price of the postage. For a year's issues (including the complete lists) please send 30p if you live in the United Kingdom, or 60p if you live elsewhere. Just write to Dept EP, Penguin Books Ltd, Harmondsworth, Middlesex, enclosing a cheque or postal order, and your name will be added to the mailing list.

Note: *Penguinews* and *Penguins in Print* are not available in the U.S.A. or Canada

Political Leaders of the Twentieth Century

Each of these political biographies examines one great contemporary statesman – the formation of his political outlook and his route to power and subsequent methods of exercising it.

Some titles in this series

Lenin*

David Shub

David Shub was born and educated in Russia and exiled to Siberia for his part in the 1905 revolution. He escaped to the U.S.A. but kept up his contact with the leaders of the revolution, many of whom he knew personally. His biography of Lenin is both readable and scholarly.

Stalin*

Isaac Deutscher

An appraisal of a revolutionary despot which aroused a storm of controversy on publication in 1949. This edition contains a chapter on Stalin's last years but none of the information released since his death has caused the author to revise his views on Stalin.

Also available

Ho Chi Minh * *Jean Lacouture*
Mao Tse-tung *Stuart Schram*
Political Leaders of Latin America *Richard Bourne*
Macmillan * *Anthony Sampson*
Verwoerd *Alexander Hepple*
Hitler *Alan Bullock*

* Not for sale in the U.S.A.

The Pelican Latin American Library

This series aims to dispel current ignorance of the internal concerns and external relations of the countries of South America and their many peoples.

The Twenty Latin Americas

Marcel Niedergang

In this work Marcel Niedergang, the well-known journalist on *Le Monde* and acknowledged expert on Latin American affairs surveys twenty independent Latin American republics from the geographical, social, economic and political points of view.

Capitalism and Underdevelopment in Latin America*

Andre Gunder Frank

'It is capitalism, both world and national, which produced underdevelopment in the past and which still generates underdevelopment in the present.' This study includes historical essays on Chile and Brazil, a discussion of the 'Indian Problem' in its relation to capitalist policy and an analysis of foreign investment in Latin America.

For the Liberation of Brazil

Carlos Marighela

A collection of writings by the man who, more than any other, shifted guerrilla opposition to Brazil's fascist regime into the towns. Practical and non-doctrinal, Marighela's papers which were instantly banned when they appeared in France, can be read as a handbook for Latin American fighters and demonstrate how the struggle has developed since the death of Che Guevara.

* Not for sale in the U.S.A.

The Pelican Latin American Library

Guatemala – Another Vietnam?*

Thomas and Marjorie Melville

Through ignorance and a monstrous lack of understanding the United States is creating the conditions for peasant war throughout Latin America. In this book two missionaries, whose ministry was terminated when they backed the cause of the landless Indian peasantry in Guatemala, describe the way in which the U.S. government engineered the now notorious coup which brought an oppressive right-wing junta to power in place of the liberal government of President Arbenz.

Zapata and the Mexican Revolution†

John Womack Jr

The definitive study of the legendary Mexican guerrilla hero, leader of a forgotten rural peasantry against the opportunist politicians of Mexico City, from 1910 until his assassination in 1919.

Cambão – The Yoke

Francisco Julião

Julião, a lawyer from the North East of Brazil, has devoted his career to fighting corruption. His book tells the story of the Peasant League which he organized in 1955, and which was suppressed in 1964; it is the story too of the peasants themselves.

Also available

Brazil: The People and the Power   *Miguel Arraes*
Servants of God or Masters of Men? The Story of a Capuchin
    Mission in Amazonia   *Victor Bonilla*
Guerrilla Warfare *   *Che Guevara*
Revolution in the Revolution? †   *Régis Debray*
The Shadow: Latin America Faces the Seventies   *Sven Lindqvist*

* Not for sale in the U.S.A.
† Not for sale in the U.S.A. or Canada

Political Leaders of the Twentieth Century

Castro

Herbert L. Matthews

Castro – 'the extraordinary young man who transformed his country, shook up a hemisphere, and brought the world to the brink of a nuclear war' – began his revolution in two years of hard fighting, with a handful of men, in the Cuban mountains. There Herbert Matthews first found him, and from there he reported to America that the world would have to reckon with Fidel Castro. Now, some twelve years later, Castro has shown his strength, and Matthews, who has retained contact with him, goes a long way towards explaining, in this percipient biography, the astute blend of charisma and communism which converted an unruly law student into a modern *caudillo*.

'Mr Matthews has seized and isolated the spirit of the Cuban leader and his revolution' – *New Statesman*.